W9-AMY-542

Study Guide

Introduction to

LOGIC

EIGHTH EDITION

THIS BOOK IS THE PROPERTY OF THE
LAKE LAND COLLEGE BOOKSTORE
MATTOON, ILLINOIS
A $5 LATE FEE WILL BE CHARGED IF NOT
RETURNED BY EACH SEMESTER DEADLINE.

Irving M. Copi

University of Hawaii

Carl Cohen

University of Michigan

Prepared by

Richard W. Miller

University of Missouri-Rolla

Macmillan Publishing Company

NEW YORK

Collier Macmillan Publishers

LONDON

Copyright © 1990 by Macmillan Publishing Company,
a division of Macmillan, Inc.

Printed in the United States of America

All rights reserved. No part of this book may be reproduced or
transmitted in any form or by any means, electronic or mechanical,
including photocopying, recording, or any information storage and
retrieval system, without permission in writing from the Publisher.

Macmillan Publishing Company
866 Third Avenue, New York, New York 10022

Collier Macmillan Canada, Inc.

Printing: 2 3 4 5 6 7   Year: 0 1 2 3 4 5 6

ISBN   0-02-381311-3

ACKNOWLEDGMENTS

I would like to thank Professor Irving Copi for his helpful comments about the earlier editions of this *Study Guide* and for an advance copy of new sections of his 8th edition. I also appreciate the patience of Ms. Helen McInnis of Macmillan Publishing Co., Inc. as this edition was prepared.

Early versions of some of the material in this work were prepared under the auspices of the University of Missouri Center for Independent Study Through Correspondence and with the aid of its Coordinator of Curriculum, C. Alex Phillips. I am grateful for the opportunity that they gave me to fit get my ideas on paper. I also appreciate the comments that I have received, both from teachers and from students who used the earlier edition of this *Study Guide* and from the generation of students who have had many of the examples and expressions tried out on them.

Sufficient thanks, also, cannot be given to my children, Mark and Morna, whose acceptance of the impact of book revision on family life, especially of both Dad's priority access to the computer and the need to have stereo volumes minimized, was mature beyond their years.

Much as I owe to these, and others too numerous to identify, for what appears here, all errors and infelicities are my responsibility alone.

My greatest debt, however, is to my wife, Margaret, who taught me that writing is more than using words to put ideas on paper. A quarter of a century of living with a philosophy teacher surely qualifies anyone for sainthood. With love, thanks and respect I dedicate this book to her.

TABLE OF CONTENTS

Part One: Language

Part Two: Deduction

Part Three: Induction

How To Use This Book

This *Study Guide* is designed to help you in your study of logic, especially in the use of *Introduction to Logic*, 8th **edition** by Irving Copi and Carl Cohen. Whether you use the *Study Guide* as a supplement to lectures in a logic course or as you study the material on your own, think of the material here as a means of getting another view of the ideas in the primary volume. In most cases Copi and Cohen's explanations of material will be substantially more detailed than the discussion here. This book is supposed to supplement the *Introduction to Logic*, 8th *edition* (hereafter *ITL*). It is therefore wise for you to read sections of *ITL* before you read similar parts of this book. Since, however, the two volumes do work well together, you should have no great problem reading the *Study Guide* first. After studying the material in both books, you are not likely to have any great difficulty with the many exercises in *ITL*. Sometimes you may be surprised to find that Copi and Cohen's explanations and mine (and, if you have one, your classroom teacher's) may approach material from slightly different perspectives. This is not necessarily a sign of great disagreement, but is more likely a display either of different teaching styles or of the diversity of philosophic perspective. You may find such diversity quite helpful to you; if one of us doesn't explain a point in a way that seems clear to you, it is likely that another one will.

Please notice that about one exercise in five in *ITL* is marked with a star, indicating that there is a solution to it in the back of the book. About another one-fifth of the exercises are discussed here, frequently, but not always, in more detail than in *ITL*. The difference in explanations lies in the fact that the solutions here are used to clarify specific terminology, show step-by-step how answers are obtained and suggest other material that may be helpful to you. Copi and Cohen's solutions are intended to give you answers, their *how-to*'s are in the text. In the *Study Guide* the solutions are intended to supplement, expand on and clarify what is said in *ITL*.

One last suggestion: many students find that the easiest way to approach logic is as a game, with rules, strategies and all the sort of properties you'd expect from any other mental game. If you don't let yourself become too impressed with logic as a highbrow activity, it is much more likely that you will enjoy your learning. Have fun--it's great to play.

R.W.M.

Part One:
Language

Chapter One
Introduction

1.1 What is Logic?

Part of the reason that such multiple approaches to logic are possible is that logic is both a skill and an art. It is a skill in that anyone who is willing to devote a bit of effort to its study ought to be able to operate in it comfortably. It is an art insofar as there are some people for whom it seems to "just come naturally." If you are one of the former, then your study should help you acquire logical skills; if you are one of the fortunate latter group, the work should fairly fly past. In either event logic can be more than just a learning experience. If you think of logic as a sort of sophisticated game of solitaire or as a great puzzle, you should find the working of the problems more interesting.

There is some wise advice that you ought to hear before beginning this, or any other work in logic. It comes from the celebrated Englishman C. L. Dodgson, from the Introduction to his book **Symbolic Logic**. (By the way, Dodgson was better known by the pseudonym under which he wrote *Alice in Wonderland*: Lewis Carroll.)

The Learner, who wishes to try the question *fairly* whether this little book does, or does not, supply the materials for a most interesting mental recreation, is *earnestly* advised to adopt the following Rules:--

(1)   Begin at the *beginning* and do not allow yourself to gratify a mere idle curiosity by dipping into the book, here there. This would very likely lead to your throwing it aside, with the remark "This is *much* too hard for me!", and thus losing the chance of adding a very *large* item to your stock of mental delights. This rule (of not *dipping* is very *desirable* with *other* kinds of books--such as novels, for instance, where you may easily spoil much of the enjoyment, you would otherwise get from the story, by dipping into it further on, so that what the author meant to be a pleasant surprise comes to you as a matter of course. Some people, I know, make a practice of looking into Vol. III first, just to see how the story ends: and perhaps it *is* as well just to know that all ends *happily* the much-persecuted lovers *do* marry after all, that he is proved to be quite innocent of the murder, that the wicked cousin is completely foiled in his plot and gets the punishment he deserves, and that the rich uncle in India (*Qu.* Why in *India Ans.* Because, somehow, uncles never *can* get rich anywhere else) dies at exactly the right moment--before taking the trouble to read Vol. 1. This, I say, is *just* permissible with a *novel* where Vol. III has a *meaning* even for those who have not read the earlier part of the story; but, with a *scientific* book, it is sheer insanity: you will find the latter part *hopelessly* unintelligible, if you read it before reaching it in regular course.

(2)   Don't begin any fresh Chapter, or Section, until you are certain that you *thoroughly* understand the whole book *up to that point*, and that you have worked, correctly, most if not all of the examples which have been set. So long as you are conscious that all the land you have passed through is absolutely *conquered*, and that you are leaving no unsolved difficulties *behind* you, which will be sure to turn up later on, your triumphal progress will be easy and delightful. Otherwise, you will find your state of puzzlement get worse and worse as you proceed, till you give up the whole thing in utter disgust. [Of course, if Copi and Cohen have promised to more fully explain a

concept later in the book, you ought not to be disturbed at not fully understanding it before that later explanation is given.]

(3)   When you come to any passage you don't understand, *read it again* [and] if you fail, even after *three* readings, very likely your brain is getting a little tired. In that case, put the book away, and take to other occupations, and the next day, when you come to it fresh, you will very likely find that it is *quite* easy.

(4)   If possible, find some genial friend, who will read the book along with you, and will talk over the difficulties with you. *Talking* is a wonderful smoother-over of difficulties. When I come upon anything--in Logic or in any other hard subject--that entirely puzzles me, I find it a capital plan to talk it over *aloud*, even when I am all alone. One can explain things so *clearly* to one's self! And then, you know, one is so *patient* with one's self: one *never* gets irritated at one's own stupidity!

If, dear Reader, you will faithfully observe these Rules, and so give my little book a really *fair* trial, I promise you, most confidently, that you will find Symbolic Logic to be one of the most, if not *the* most, fascinating of mental recreations!

If you follow this advice, you will have no trouble in your study of logic. Now you are ready to begin. Just a few more words from Carroll:

Once master the machinery of ... Logic, and you have a mental occupation always at hand, of absorbing interest, and one that will be of real *use* to you in *any* subject you may take up. It will give you a clearness of thought--the ability to *see your way* through a puzzle--the habit of arranging your ideas in an orderly and get-at-able form-- and, more valuable than all, the power to detect *fallacies* and to tear to pieces the flimsy illogical arguments, which you will so continually encounter in books, in newspapers, in speeches, and even in sermons, and which so easily delude those who have never taken the trouble to master this fascinating Art. *Try it*! That is all I ask of you!

As suggested earlier, you should begin by studying *Introduction to Logic, 8th* edition (hereafter, for brevity, referred to as *ITL*). In particular, now, you should begin with sections 1.1 and 1.2. After reading the first two sections in *ITL* you should understand that the task of logic is to evaluate arguments.

The 19th-century American logician Charles S. Peirce (pronounced "purse") once claimed that the whole business of logic was to toss arguments into two piles: good ones and bad ones. In general that does summarize what this book is designed to do. It points out, too, that the fundamental element in logic is the *argument*. No matter what else a logician may study, it is done so as to be better able to analyze arguments.

1.2 Premises and Conclusions

An *argument* is always composed of at least one premiss and exactly one conclusion. The premisses provide (or are claimed to provide) support, evidence, justification, etc., for the conclusion. It is the logician's business to determine just how good that support is.

As Copi and Cohen suggest, one of the great difficulties in sorting out premisses and conclusions is the fact that their being identified as either premiss or as conclusion is always relative to some context. And, curiously enough, his example of the analogous employer/employee relativity can be extended to show the property of circularity, which arguments, too, sometimes possess: If your gardener happens to be a stockholder in the company for which you work, then, at least in an indirect or partial sense, not only is he your employee, but he is also your employer.

A second significant problem in your sorting out is that on some occasions premisses and/or the conclusion may go unstated. Particularly in contexts where some of the evidence needed for support of the conclusion is part of the generally accepted knowledge of both the arguer and the "arguee" this will occur. And conclusions that the arguer takes to follow obviously often will go unstated. It's important, therefore, as you analyze an argument that you look for such omitted premisses and conclusions.

When there are problems available to work, you should always attempt them. It is only through such "hands-on" experience that you come to know whether or not you really did understand the information that you have so carefully studied. As Copi and Cohen tell you at the beginning of 1.2's exercises, they have provided answers to roughly 20% of the exercises (and has starred them). In this study guide roughly another 20% are solved--usually the ones following the starred ones.

Two words of caution in working logic problems: first, in deciding that you do understand, don't be lulled to sleep by working only the first few problems (usually the easiest); try the later, tougher ones too. And, second, try to work the problem **before** you look at the answer; most magic tricks, too, seem obvious **once you know the solution**. Try 1.2's exercises and then go on to check your work with the following answers. Please note that in some cases the solutions here involve paraphrases of the original text. Also be aware that, given the different backgrounds that each of us brings to analyzing such problems, different interpretations of the materials may result in different answers to the same problem.

(2)   *Premisses*: [1]   Western, Chinese and Indian astrologies have long traditions.
           [2]   If one of them is right, the others are wrong.
       Conclusion: The long tradition of western astrology does not prove it right.

Note that first premiss is set off by the premiss-indicator "because." The statement that occurs first looks like a premiss but is not a premiss at all, it's the conclusion. It is not at all uncommon for arguments to have such a form.

(6)   *Premiss*:   The advanced technologies applied in supercomputers tend to quickly permeate the entire computer industry.
       Conclusion: The nation that leads in supercomputer development tends to have the jump on other countries in producing more powerful--and more lucrative--lower-level computers.

Here you find the conclusion identified by the conclusion-indicator "so."

(11)   *Premiss*:   There are no mental diseases.
        Conclusion: There can be no treatment for mental diseases.

Here the premiss is very clearly flagged by the "since."

(16)   *Premisses*: [1]   Pain is subjective.
            [2]   Animals cannot talk.
        Conclusion: It is difficult to gauge the pain of animals.

Here the premisses are flagged by the word "because."

(21)   *Premisses*: [1]   Everybody thinks himself abundantly provided with common sense.
            [2]   No one wants more common sense than he presently has.
        Conclusion: Good sense is the most equally distributed thing in the world.

The premisses are marked by the premiss-indicator "for."

(26)   *Premiss*:   The investigation of supernatural phenomena lies outside the realm of science.
            Conclusion: Science can't prove or disprove the God's existence.
Here the rather common conclusion-indicator "therefore" makes the structure clear.

1.3 Diagrams for Single Arguments

In the study of logic, as in many areas of life, we must "walk before we can run." The reason for this is simple: if one masters a set of skills in its least complicated occurrences, then, when it needs to be applied in a complex situation, the skills come naturally and without much effort. This is exactly the idea underlying the ordinary teaching of life-saving and first aid skills (as, for example by the Red Cross, Boy Scouts or Girl Scouts). It is also the reason for fire drills in schools, businesses and homes. If you repeat an action or behavior pattern **consciously** many times in varied simple (or non-stressful) situations, then it is far more likely that, when you encounter a complex (or stressful) occasion on which the earlier-practiced skills are needed, the skill will come to you **unconsciously**. It is for this sort of reason that Copi and Cohen have you begin your analysis of arguments by representing the "flow" of premiss(es) to conclusion in single arguments.

The procedure is quite straight-forward: you draw arrows downward from a premiss to the conclusion which it supports. In the event that you have a group of premisses which provide support only in combination and not individually for some conclusion, then you join them with a "curly brace" and draw the arrow from the brace to the conclusion. To focus your attention on the flow of the argument instead of the ideas it involves, Copi and Cohen suggest that each separate proposition be numbered sequentially and that in the diagram the enclosed numbers replace the appropriate propositions. In cases like exercise 21 of 1.2, where a proposition is not stated, the "understood" character of that proposition is represented by having the enclosure broken, or dotted.

With these tools in hand you should try the problems following 1.4 (pages 22-25), then check them with his answers and these:

(2) ① Even if heroin is identical to morphine in terms of how it affects patients, it has the advantage of being easier to inject. ② Heroin is 50 times as soluble as morphine ③ when you have a wasted person who has very little muscle mass and very little fat, an injection is extremely painful. ④ 5 cc's of morphine is a tablespoon ⑤ the equivalent dose of heroin is so small that it can be given to anyone.

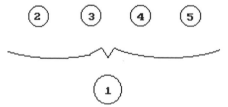

In this case there is no premiss-indicator or conclusion-indicator, but the argument seems to infer that heroin, despite its socially unpopular reputation, has significant medical value.

(6) ① By making drugs a criminal matter, we have made the problem worse. ② If we de criminalize [drugs], at least we would only have a massive public health problem, a massive corruption problem and a massive foreign-policy problem.

The argument, without indicators but still pretty clear-cut, does leave the reader uncertain about whether Ms. Bennett is serious or being ironic.

(11) ①To say I believe in spanking children implies that spankings are in some way essential to their proper upbringing. ② I do not hold that opinion; ③ therefore, I do not believe in spankings.

The conclusion-indicator "therefore" clearly marks the conclusion. But, since neither premiss, if taken alone, would provide sensible support for the conclusion, they must jointly imply it.

(16) ① Furthermore, if you look at the history of the death penalty in this country, you'll find that its application has been arbitrary, capricious and discriminatory. ② ... The poor and minorities tend to be overrepresented on death row. ③ Blacks who kill whites are overrepresented in relation to blacks who kill blacks. ... ④People who can afford expensive lawyers can beat the system when it comes to the death penalty as well as other kinds of punishment.

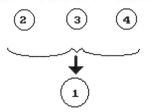

Again the first statement is the generalization for which each of the following ones provides evidence. Note that the sentence "That tells us something about the way the system works" is not treated as a premiss. In a significant sense it serves a role like a premiss-indicator. It is telling the reader that the information just given should be considered to be but one of many similar cases.

(21) ① There are more people learning English as a second language than speak it as their first. ② It is therefore discourteous to address a foreigner in his own language ③ since it deprives him of the opportunity to improve his English.

Neither of these premisses would provide adequate (or even reasonable) support for the conclusion. The two of them, taken together, do, however, plausibly argue for it.

Having mastered this material, you should to go on to study 1.4.

1.4   Recognizing Arguments

Before you can analyze an argument, you must be able to recognize it. In the ordinary daily discourse this is no mean feat. The key to identifying a group of propositions as an argument is whether or not they can be divided into a set of premises which are asserted and a conclusion which is asserted to follow from them. Often you find clues in the language: "since," "because," and the like are *premisses-flags*; *thus* and *therefore* are marks of the conclusion. These are not, unfortunately, infallible guides. They can all be correctly used in non-argumentative ways. They do, however, provide a point where you can begin looking for an argument.

Most commonly confused with arguments are conditional statements. They indicate an "if - then" sort of relationship, usually between propositions, but assert nothing beyond the conditional relationship. In the following examples, the "a" line is an argument; the "b" line is not:

> 1a. Since racism is un-American, the federal government cannot tolerate bias in hiring.
> 1b. If racism is un-American, then the federal government could not tolerate bias in hiring.
>
> 2a. Logic is easy; therefore, you should do well.
> 2b. Logic is part of intelligent thought; therefore, take it.
>
> 3a. Since college is good training for life, college graduates should live good lives.
> 3b. Since attending college, John has had seven different jobs.

Number 1a asserts that racism **is** un-American and that from the evidence we may correctly infer that the federal government cannot tolerate hiring bias; 2a asserts that logic is easy and asserts that, on that basis, it is justifiable to infer that you will do well; 3a infers that college graduates can be expected to live good lives from the assertion that college is good training for life. By contrast, 1b says that *if* racism is thus, *then* the government, etc., but clearly admits even the possibility that racism might not be un-American; 2b is directive, telling you what to do, but this imperative does not follow in any clear sense from logic's nature; 3b describes a time sequence, not an inference. From these you can see that there are no simple ways to tell whether a passage is or is not an argument; you simply have to think about each case individually.

One of the most difficult elements in analyzing arguments is deciding how much to "add to" the argument as stated. How can you know whether the added material was really intended? The answer surely is not clear cut. However, the basis for decision, usually, is analogous to the judicial "innocent until proven guilty" principle: unless there's good evidence to the contrary, assume that the arguer is being as reasonable as possible.

The sort of thing that gets omitted from an argument is so-called "common knowledge." That's the sort of information that your teachers told you did not have to be footnoted, "since anyone with a reasonable education would have known it." The difficulty is that there is no standard as to what should count as a reasonable education or as common knowledge. Some things are obvious. For example, look at the following argument.

> Horses are mammals.
> [Mammals bear their young alive.]
> Therefore horses bear their young alive.

People who have had enough science to know some biology would be insulted if told that the assumed premiss, "[Mammals bear their young alive.]," had to be stated for them. On the other hand, a child who had no knowledge of the essential properties of mammals would find it indispensable for evaluating the argument. It is all, as Copi and Cohen say, a matter of understanding the context in which the argument is proposed.

At the end of 1.4, Copi and Cohen say that there is a significant difference between an argument and an explanation. It is well to notice that followers of one rather clearly defined philosophic view of explanation, the so-called deductive-nomological model, would claim that anything that serves as a satisfactory explanation after-the-fact of an occurrence would also serve well before-the-fact of an occurrence as a prediction of it (or argument that it will occur).

It also is a defensible, although not self-evident, position that any explanation does in fact constitute an argument. In the case of the explanation by Dyson what one might argue is that you are not dealing with an argument, but the conclusion of one. The missing premisses of the argument would deal with people's disinclination to get excited about technological issues, while being quite easily stirred up about human ones. Copi and Cohen are correct when they indicate that the "because" in Dyson's statement is not a standard premiss-indicator. In this regard, their description of the importance of knowing what the writer (or utterer) intended the passage to do is particularly significant. The issue which causes the difficulty in this area, that is, whether or not explanations are arguments, is not one that you should expect to see resolved in an introductory logic text. It is one on which there is significant, reasoned difference among professional philosophers who have devoted substantial portions of their lives to studying. You will encounter further discussion of explanation in chapter 14, and, if you are particularly interested in the topic, you might wish to look at R.B. Braithwaite's *Scientific Explanation*, Ernest Nagel's *The Structure of Science*, Pap's *An Introduction to the Philosophy of Science*, or any of the standard philosophy of science texts.

To test your ability to sort out arguments and non-arguments, you should work your way through the exercises after 1.4 (pages 30-33), checking your results with *ITL* and these:

(2)   ① Because their best physicists were not zealous for weapons, ② because they made uncorrected mistakes, ③ because Hitler was Hitler, and ④because men like Speer had more urgent production priorities, ⑤ the Germans never really tried to make an atomic bomb.

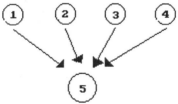

This appears to offer several reasons for the Nazi government not putting effort into the development of an atomic bomb and, if that were all that was being done, would not be an argument. When, however, you "unpack" what is asserted and think about the relationships claimed--the "because" clauses--it is evident that an argument was intended. Note that each of the premisses would, by itself, provide support for the conclusion.

(6)   This explains the law and the rationale for it, but offers no argument.

(11)   ① ... the number of strategic warheads on each side far exceeds the number of significant nonmilitary targets, so ② the majority of the weapons must be aimed at military targets if they are aimed at anything at all.

This argument is simple in structure, but the simplicity masks the complexity of the issue it argues. [It is, of course, possible that weapons are aimed at insignificant nonmilitary targets or that more than are needed for total annihilation are aimed at those nonmilitary targets.]

(16)   This explains why the Russians use unusual orbits for their communications and early-warning satellites, but argues nothing as it stands. It could, of course, be converted into an argument by inserting issues relating to the pragmatic purposes of such devices.

(21)   This simply explains how it is that learning about cures informs us about the causes of what they cure.

Now that you have achieved enough skill to recognize a simple argument and then diagram it, you are ready to study 1.5 in *ITL* in order to learn how to sort out the component arguments from passages in which the arguments are intertwined.

1.5   Passages Containing Several Arguments

Multiple-argument passages are basically of three types. Simplest are those where two (or more) separate arguments are mixed together, rather like playing cards which are shuffled. All that is necessary in analyzing these is to "unshuffle" them, much as you would sort a shuffled deck of cards according to number or suit.

Only slightly more complex are sequential arguments. These function much like dominoes that fall in order: the first's falling leads to the second's also falling, but the second results in the third, and so on. In a sequential argument, a conclusion is supported by one (or more) premiss(es) but in turn serves as premiss for a further conclusion. In such cases it is often easiest to identify the ultimate conclusion, then its premisses, then theirs (if any) and so on.

Most complicated are arguments which involve overlapping premisses, where the same proposition serves as support for more than one conclusion. In such cases, it usually is easiest to sort out the several conclusions, then identify what serves as premiss for each of them without regard for its previous use as premiss for something else.

If you look carefully at the examples that Copi and Cohen present, you will see that they are continually increasing the level of complexity and interconnection among premisses and conclusions. Of course, if you wished to seek some sort of ultimate complexity, you could mix three approaches together, but even then the sorting out could be done by applying the identification techniques one-by-one. First you would untwist those arguments whose elements had just been shuffled. Then, within each of those you would lay out sequences. Finally, within all of these you would note the elements which are shared. In such a case, as you will find so often in the study of logic, the key to success is patiently handling difficulties one step at a time.

Now that you understand how arguments that are interconnected can be sorted out and diagramed, work the exercises following 1.5 (pages 40-45) and check your results here and in *ITL*.

(2)   ① The Creative is heaven, ② therefore it is called the father. ③ The Receptive is the earth, ④ therefore it is called the mother.

This, clearly, is a pair of extraordinarily simple arguments with their conclusions set off by the conclusion-indicator "therefore."

(11)   ① When drug dealers kill in the course of their business, they often kill other drug dealers.... If ② the bill [allowing the death penalty for drug dealers who kill in the course of their business] works as it is supposed to, drug dealers will be deterred from killing other drug dealers. ③With less of a threat of death from other drug dealers, we can expect more people to engage in drug dealing and the peddling of drugs to rise. [④If the bill passes we can expect more people to engage in drug dealing and ⑤If the bill passes we can expect the peddling of drugs to rise.]

There is good reason to claim that this is just a single argument based on two "if...then...." statements and with another assumed one as its conclusion. In any event statement ①is just background information, not part of the premises. If, instead, you break the unstated conclusion into its elements, it could be seen as shown above.

(16) ① Hunting was a valuable adaptation to the environment since ② meat could supply more calories and protein than a vegetarian diet. ③ Peking man was evidently able to compete successfully with large carnivores as a hunter. ④ An abundance of fossil bones of mammals of various sizes found in the cave indicates that ⑤ Peking man not only hunted small game but also ⑥was capable of killing large animals.

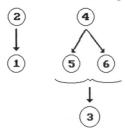

A reasonable case can be made for claiming that statements ⑤and ⑥should be considered as one, since they both are derived from the same premiss and they function together to yield the conclusion ③ It might also be claimed that the initial argument, from ②to ① is really an explanation used to put the later "real" argument in context.

1.6   Deduction and Induction

Philosophers traditionally classify arguments either as *deductive* or as *inductive*. You will find *ITL* divided into three parts: Language, Deduction, and Induction. The difference between a deductive and an inductive argument is, in a significant way, the difference in the sort of claim made for the argument. If the arguer alleges that the premises are **conclusive** evidence for the conclusion, then the argument is deductive; if the assertion is that they support the conclusion but don't guarantee it, then the argument is inductive.

Deductive arguments may be further classified as being *valid* or *invalid*. Clearly any deductive is one or the other. There are three alternative ways to define a valid argument.

An argument $[P_1, P_2, P_3, \ldots, P_n$ therefore $C]$ is *valid* if and only if

(A)   If all the premises $[P_1, P_2, P_3, \ldots, P_n]$ of an argument are **all** true, then the conclusion $[C]$ is also true, **or**

(B)   If the conclusion $[C]$ of an argument is false, then at least one of the premisses $[P_1, P_2, P_3, \ldots, P_n]$ is false. is also false, **or**

(C)   It is not possible for all the premises $[P_1, P_2, P_3, \ldots, P_n]$ of an argument to be true and the conclusion $[C]$ to be false.

It doesn't take a great deal of analysis to see that, in effect, these are simply alternate ways of looking at the same set of conditions. It also follows, then, that any argument that is not valid must have some possibility of having all the premisses $[P_1, P_2, P_3, \ldots, P_n]$ true yet still have the conclusion $[C]$ be false.

Inductive arguments, on the other hand, are not capable of being valid. [In the formal deductive sense, all inductive arguments are invalid, since they never have conclusions guaranteed by the premises. To consider this, however, as any kind of criticism is foolish. You wouldn't, for example, criticize a symphony for not being purple enough. Similarly, when validity is a property that an inductive argument could never have, you're not supposed to complain because the argument lacks that property.]

Through the years there have been many attempts to clarify the distinction between deductive and inductive arguments. The American philosopher Charles S. Peirce, for example, argued that there are three forms of inference: deduction, induction and *abduction* (sometimes *hypothesis*).[1] He sometimes showed the differences among them using the elements of a simple argument. First consider three statements:

> ***Rule***:   All the balls in this bag are green.
> ***Case***:   All the balls in that box came from this bag.
> ***Result***:   All the balls in that box are green.

Their "names" are references to their function in a normal deductive argument. But, if you consider the possible arguments that can be formed from these three statements, you will find there are three, not two. These arguments would be

Rule	Result	Rule
Case	Case	Result
———	———	———
∴ Result	∴ Rule	∴ Case
Deduction	*Induction*	*Abduction (Hypothesis)*

This set of distinctions divides the non-deductive arguments in a way that Peirce believed was instructive. The separation of hypothesis as a distinct form, Peirce thought, paid attention to the significance that this sort of "educated guessing" has in science. But, whether you categorize into two or three types of arguments, the most crucial element in beginning your analysis of any specific argument is determining what sort of claim is being made. If the arguer maintains that the conclusion follows necessarily from the given premises, then the argument must meet the standards of validity in order to be considered acceptable. If no such claim is made then the argument only has to meet the less-demanding requirement of reasonability.

----

1.   See his **Collected Papers**, volume 5, paragraph 145 and surrounding. This is from the fifth of his "Lectures on Pragmatism from 1903.

1.7   Truth and Validity

One of the hardest things to accept on the battlefields of argument is the distinction between *truth* and *validity*. The assertion that an argument is valid (remember only deductive ones can be valid) is surely a claim that the argument is a good one. It seems intuitive to most people that the good arguments must be true. What they don't realize is that, at least in the world of the logician, an argument cannot be true at all. Truth is a property of statements while validity is a property of arguments. This means, also, that statements, assumptions, and the like cannot be valid either.

In the world in general, we determine whether a proposition (an idea which will later be explained in detail, but for now think of it as a statement) is true by comparing what it claims with the way the world is. As was explained in the last section, we determine whether an argument is valid by looking to see if there is any way for its premises to be true and its conclusion false. This view of truth and validity identifies some strange-seeming arguments to be considered valid. How would you react to this argument?

> If China has never produced any tea, then the Roman Empire currently rules all of central Asia.
> China has, in fact, never produced any tea.
> Therefore it is certain that the Roman Empire currently rules all of central Asia.

This argument has several curious elements in it. The second premiss and conclusion are clearly false. The first premiss is strange. What, for example, has China's tea production to do with the Roman Empire? It would also be a legitimate question to ask how one could ever determine the truth of such an odd claim. But, as you will learn in chapter 8, this *is* a valid argument. If the premisses **could** somehow be proven to be true, then the conclusion would **have to be** true, too.

Other arguments can seem equally peculiar. Consider your reaction to this one.

> If you mistakenly fed him a massive serving of poisonous berries, then William Shatner (Captain Kirk of the original *Star Trek*) is dead.
> You didn't mistakenly feed him a massive serving of poisonous berries.
> Therefore (at least as of the writing of this book) Mr. Shatner is alive.

The conclusion and both premisses are true, but the argument itself is invalid. The fact that the argument is bad does not tell us anything about the truth of these particular statements, nor does the truth of the statements entail anything about the argument. The following argument, of the same form, has true premisses but still a false conclusion.

> If you went to Ford's Theater and fired the assassin's bullet into his head then Abraham Lincoln is dead.
> You didn't go to Ford's Theater and fired the assassin's bullet into his head.
> Therefore Abraham Lincoln is alive and well.

This argument with the same structure but a different result (called a *counter-example*) shows that the initial contention was in error.

One of the primary reasons for determining whether or not a deductive argument is valid is to save mental energy. If, tomorrow, you had to attend a meeting twenty or thirty miles away, how would you get there? It would usually look foolish for you to set out walking to get there. Most of us, given the opportunity, would drive or take some public transportation, arrive early enough to relax and then proceed with full energy. By analogy, if you are going to invest energy and effort in trying to determine what was true and what was not, doesn't it make more sense to devote that labor to information that would yield further data? Why waste time checking the truthfulness of premisses that don't support the conclusion anyway?

1.8 Problem Solving

All of us spend most of our lives solving problems. One of the simplest ones is figuring out what we did with the car keys the night before. A reasonable way to solve the problem is to think "when was the last time I specifically recall having had the keys and what did I do immediately thereafter?" More complex problems range up to finding a means to achieve world peace (which, to my knowledge, is yet to be solved). There is one element, however, that virtually all successful problem solutions have in common: the organized application of whatever background information is available. In many cases there is a general approach that is usually both helpful and fairly simple to apply. Sherlock Holmes frequently told Dr. Watson that the best way to solve a problem was to lay out all the alternatives, then proceed to eliminate all those that cannot be the case. When only one remains, no matter how unlikely it seems, it is the solution. That dictum is the guide for solving almost all the problems in this section. In some cases the best approach is to lay out a grid which includes all possible combinations of properties in the problem. Exercise number 4 in *ITL* shows how this can be done.

Person\Job	Cash	Clerk	Mgr	Asst Mgr	Steno	Teller
Miss Ambrose						
Mr. Black						
Mrs. Coffee						
Miss Earnshaw						
Mr. Kelly						
Mr. White						

If you label all of the information given in the problem (for ease of reference), you can sequentially eliminate all but one space in each column and row, thus deciding who holds each job. Below is one possible eliminative sequence.

a. The asst. mgr. is the manager's grandson.
b. The cashier is the steno's son-in-law.
c. Mr. Black is a bachelor.
d. Mr. White is 22 years old.
e. Miss Ambrose is the teller's step-sister.
f. Mr. Kelly is the manager's neighbor.
1. Since the asst. mgr. is male, he is not A, C, or E (from a).
2. Since the mgr. has a grandson, s/he (he or she) is married, and thus is not A or E (a).
3. The cashier is male (b), and thus not A, C, or E.
4. The steno has a son-in-law (b), and thus is not A or E.
5. Given (c) and (1) and (2) we know that B is not the mgr. or steno.
6. Given the ages of the children of the mgr, and steno. (a & b), and W's age (d), W is not mgr. or steno.
7. A is not the teller (e).
8. Since the only job left for A is clerk, she is clerk and no one else can be.
9. Since only the teller's job is left for E, she is the teller and no one else is.
10. K is not the mgr. (f).
11. C is the only one left who can be mgr., so she and no one else is.
12. K is the only one left who can be the steno., so he is and no one else can be.
13. The cashier is married (he's a son-in-law, b), and since B is a bachelor (c), B can't be the cashier.
14. By elimination W must be the cashier and B the asst. mgr.

In the second form of the grid (below) you can see what it looks like with all of the steps (above) filled in. The reason for using the numbers rather than just crossing out squares is that, should you make an error and find one column or row completely eliminated or someone with two jobs, you would be unable to check back to see why you had performed each elimination without some sort of specific referencing method. With the numbers as a reference tool you can look at any specific job/person intersection and determine how it was that you decided either to eliminate that option or to assert it. You will also see that the statements *given in the problem* are referenced alphabetically (*a-f*) to distinguish them from *inferred information* referenced (*1-14*).

Person \ Job	Cash	Clerk	Mgr	Asst Mgr	Steno	Teller
Miss Ambrose	3	XXXX	2	1	4	7
Mr. Black	13	8	5	XXXX	5	9
Mrs. Coffee	3	8	XXX	1	11	9
Miss Earnshaw	3	8	2	1	4	XXXX
Mr. Kelly	12	8	10	12	XXXX	9
Mr. White	XXXX	8	6	14	6	9

Please notice that there is a slight difference in the way this grid and the one in *ITL*. Copi and Cohen suggest that you place "N" and "Y" in the intersections of the grid as you solve or eliminate. The grid you have just looked at replaces the "N" with the letter or number of the elimination sequence on which you based the elimination, and it replaces the "Y" with "XXXX." If you don't make a mistake, Copi and Cohen's approach and mine are, for all practical purposes, the same. If you should find, however, that you have some person or job completely eliminated (or forced into two roles), the approach I suggest will let you check specific eliminations to find your mistake. If you have used "N" and "Y" then you'll have to scrap your effort and start from scratch. Your choice of approach should be guided by your own propensity for mistakes.

Exercise number 2 in the same set may also be solved by a process of elimination, but a different approach may prove more effective. If we lay out all possible hat color combinations for the three prisoners, we get the following:

	Blind	One Eye	Two Eyes
Case 1	White	White	White
Case 2	White	White	Red
Case 3	White	Red	White
Case 4	White	Red	Red
Case 5	Red	White	White
Case 6	Red	White	Red
Case 7	Red	Red	White

Note that there is no Red/Red/Red case, for there are only two red hats.

After hearing both companions admit that they could not tell the color of their hats, the blind prisoner infers his hat color. You should always, however, look for "cleverness of inference" and sets of hidden assumptions. Such cleverness is required for problem 2's inference step three. The likely process is, again, elimination.

1. Had the two-eyed prisoner seen two red hats, he would have known that, there being no more red hats, he wore white. Since he did not know this, case 7 must be eliminated.

2. Had the one-eyed prisoner seen red hats on both of his companions, he would have known his hat was white. Since he did not know this, case 6 must be eliminated.

3. The tricky piece of reasoning is that the one-eyed prisoner can infer that there are two possible cases here he would see a red hat on the blind man and a white one on the two-eyed man: cases 5 and 7. The one-eyed man would eliminate case 7, as in step 1. Thus, if the one-eyed man saw the blind/red, two-eyed/white combination (knowing case 7 could not be), then he would have inferred that case 5 obtained. Since the one-eyed man did not reason in this way, the blind man can infer that case 5 can be eliminated.

4. When the blind man reasons that cases 5, 6, and 7 are to be eliminated, he can "see" that the remaining possibilities **all** require that he be wearing a *white hat*. In this example, you can see that, despite the apparent difference in approach, the underlying technique is still a process of elimination.

A third sort of approach can be applied to a problem like exercise 7. In this case it is easiest to lay out the men and their statements (in an abbreviated form), then eliminate where possible.

Otto:	1.	Otto in Chicago during murder.
	2.	Otto innocent.
	3.	Kid guilty.
	4.	Otto & Mickey are pals.
Curly:	1.	Curly innocent.
	2.	Curly never owned a gun.
	3.	Kid knows Curly.
	4.	Curly was in Detroit on March 17.
Slim:	1.	Curly owned a gun.
	2.	Murder was on St. Pat's Day.
	3.	Otto in Chicago during murder.
	4.	One of 5 is guilty.
Mickey:	1.	Mickey innocent.
	2.	Kid was never in Pontiac.
	3.	Mickey never saw Otto before.
	4.	Curly was in Detroit on March 17.
Kid:	1.	Kid innocent.
	2.	Kid was never in Pontiac.
	3.	Kid does not know Curly.
	4.	Otto lied when he said Kid guilty.

The key datum to keep in mind is that each man made three true and one false statement. A possible reasoning sequence is:

1. Since K-1 and K-4 (the Kid's 1st and 4th statements--note that, for brevity, the initial and statement number will be used for references) amount to the same statement and only one statement can be false, it must be true that the Kid IS innocent.

2. Since the Kid is innocent, O-3 must be false and O-1, O-2 and O-4 must be true.

3. S-2 and S-4 are part of the premises of the problem, so must be true. S-3 is the same as O-1, a known true statement, so must be true. Thus S-1 must be Slim's false statement.

4.   Since M-3 is the denial of O-4, a known true statement, M-3 must be false and M-1, M-2, and M-4 must be true.

5.   Since K-2 is the same as M-2, a known true statement, and step 1 says K-1 and K-4 are true, then K-3 must be the Kid's false statement.

6.   Since S-1 is the denial of C-2 and S-1 is false, C-2 must be true. Since K-3 is the denial of C-3 and K-3 is false, C-3 must be true. Since M-4 is true and the same as C-4, C-4 must be true. With C-2, C-3, and C-4 true, C-1 must be Curly's false statement. If it is false that Curly is innocent, Curly must be the guilty party.

One of the most satisfying things about working such problems is that they are, in a sense, self-checking. In general, if you get an answer that you can retrace to your conclusion, you are likely correct. With these hints about ways to approach various types of such "Exercises in Reasoning" in hand, you should be ready to tackle them on your own. You have seen exercises 2, 4, and 7 above; solutions to 1, 5, and 10 are in the back of *ITL*; and solutions to a problem from earlier editions (#6 in them) and 12 of this edition are below.

(12)   This problem looks hard, but solves directly using the grid approach. Begin by laying out the information given. Again, as in problem 4 (page 12, above), notice that the evidence stated explicitly is referenced with letters and that information inferred is identified with numbers.

a.   The 3 VP is the pampered grandson of the Pres, but is disliked by Mrs. Brown and ATell.

b.   The ATell and 2 S shared equally in their father's estate.

c.   The 2 VP and the ATell wear the same style of hats.

d.   Mr. Grant told Miss Hill to send him a steno at once.

e.   The Pres's nearest neighbors are Mrs. Kane, Mr. Grant, and Mr. Long.

f.   The 1 VP and the Cash live at the exclusive Bachelor's Club.

g.   The Jan, a miser, has occupied the same garret room since boyhood.

h.   Mr. Adams and the 2 S are leaders in the social life of the younger unmarried set.

i.   The 2 VP and the Book were once engaged to be married to each other.

j.   The fashionable Tell is the son-in-law of the 1 S.

k.   Mr. Jones regularly gives Mr. Evans his discarded clothing to wear, without the elderly Book knowing about the gift.

l.   There are 6 men and 5 women. by a, f, g, and j, we know that 1-VP, #-VP, Cash, T and J are men. Thus, from this and c we know that 2VP and ATell are women.

m.   Since 2-VP is a woman (l), from i Book must be a man.

n.   Since Book is the 6th man (l&M), Pres, l-S and 2-S must be women.

o.   The only person left to be Pres is Mrs. Ford.

p.   The only person left to be 2-S is Miss Dale.

q.   Since ATell and 2-S are sisters (b) and Miss Dale is 2-S, ATell must be married (or they share a name). This means, be elimination, that ATell is Mrs. Kane.

r.   The only person left to be l-S is Mrs. Brown.

s.   The only person left to be 2-V is Miss Hill.

t.   Since Mr. Grant gives Miss Hill orders (d), he must be her superior, thus must be l-VP.

u.   Since Grant is among the Pres's nearest neighbors (e) and he and the Cash live at the Bachelor's Club, then Long (another near neighbor) must be Cash.

v.   The only job left for Adam is 3-VP.

w.   The only job left for Jones is Tell.

x.   The only job left for Evans is Jan.

y.   The only job left for Camp is Book.

Persn Job	Mr. Adam	Mrs. Brown	Mr. Camp	Miss Dale	Mr. Evans	Mrs. Ford	Mr. Grant	Miss Hill	Mr. Jones	Mrs. Kane	Mr. Long
Pres	a/g	a	n	a	n	XXX	e	a	n	e	e
1 VP	t	f	t	f	t	f	XXX	f	t	f	t
2 VP	l	r	l	p	l	o	l	XXX	l	q	l
3 VP	XXX	a	v	a	v	a	t	a	v	a	u
Cash	u	f	u	f	u	f	t	f	u	f	XXX
Tell	h/j	j	w	j	w	j	t	j	XXX	j	u
ATell	l	a	l	p	l	o	l	q	l	XXX	l
Book	h/k	m	XXX	m	k	m	t	m	k	m	y
1 S	n	XXX	n	p	n	o	d	d	n	q	n
2 S	g	h	n	XXX	n	o	d	d	n	h	n
Jan	g/h	f	x	f	XXX	f	d	f	k/g	f	u

One more solution to a problem from earlier editions (#6 in them) might be helpful to you also. There are two general approaches to it--as a sketch of the actual physical layout of the problem or as a traditional elimination grid.

Ms. Adams, Ms. Baker, Ms, Catt, Ms. Dodge, Ms. Ennis, and Ms. Fisk all went shopping one morning at the Emporium. Each woman went direstly to the floor carrying the article that she wanted to buy, and each woman bought only one article. The purchases were a book, a dress, a hanfbag, a necktie, a hat, and a lamp.

All the women except Ms. Adams entered the elevator on the main floor. Two men also entered the elevator. Two women, Ms. Catt and the one who bought the necktie, got off at the second floor. Dresses were sold on the third floor. The two men got off on the third floor. The woman who bought the lamp got off at the fifth floor, leaving Ms. Fisk all alone to get off at the sixth floor.

The next day Ms. Baker, who received the handbag as a gift from one of the women who got off at the second floor, met her husband returning the necktie that one of the other women had given him. If books are sold on the main floor, and Ms. Ennis was the sixth person to get out of the elevator, what did each of the women buy?

Sketch solution:

	6	
	5	
	4	
	3	
	2	
	Main	

The store's "floor plan"

a. Adams stayed on 1st floor, all others got on elevator.
b. 2 men got on the elevator, too.
c. Catt and the tie-buyer got off on 2.
d. Dresses are on 3.
e. The men got off on 4.
f. The lamp-buyer got off on 5.   GIVEN
g. Fisk was left alone on 6.
h. Baker got the bag as a surprise from a 2nd floor person.
i. Baker's husband got the tie, but not from Baker.
j. Books are on 1.
k. Ennis got out 6th.

Fisk (g)	6	**Handbag (3)**	1 wmn off
Ennis (k)	5	Lamps (f)	1 wmn off
	4		2 men off
Baker (1)	3	Dresses (d)	1 wmn off
Catt (c), **Dodge (2)**	2	Hat (1), Tie (c)	2 wmn off
Adams (a)	Main	Books(j)	7 get on

1. Since Baker didn't buy the tie (c), she cannot have been on 2, so must have been on 3.
2. Since then only person left is Dodge, she must have been on 2.
3. Since the only purchase left is the bag, Fisk must have gotten it on 6.

Elimination Grid Solution:

a. Adams stayed on 1st floor, all others got on elevator.
b. 2 men got on the elevator, too.
c. Catt and the tie-buyer got off on 2.
d. Dresses are on 3.
e. The men got off on 4.
f. The lamp-buyer got off on 5.   GIVEN
g. Fisk was left alone on 6.
h. Baker got the bag as a surprise from a 2nd floor person.
i. Baker's husband got the tie, but not from Baker.
j. Books are on 1.
k. Ennis got out 6th.

Number off elevator:

l.   5 women and 2 men got on (a,b)   0
     Carr and tie-buyer off on 2 (c)   2
     Dress-buyer off on 3 (d)   3
     Men off on 4 (e)   5
     Lamp-buyer off on 5 (f)   6 ∴ Ennis (k,l)
m. Books are on 1 (j)
     Ties and bags are on 2 (c,h)
     Dresses are on 3 (d)
     Lamps are on 5 (f)
     Since Fisk was on 6, the only thing left for her is the hat.
n. Since the only item left in Baker's column is the dress, it must be hers.
o. Since the only item left in Dodge's column is the tie, it must be hers.

Item/Pers	Adams	Baker	Catt	Dodge	Ennis	Fisk	FLOOR
Book	XXX	a/j	a/j	a/j	a/j	a/j	1 (j)
Dress	a/d	XXX	h/c	n	f/c	d/g	3 (d)
Handbag	a/j	h	XXX	h/c	h/c	h/c	2 (h)
Hat	a/j	m	h/c	m	f/l	XXX	6 (m)
Lamp	a/f	f/l	h/c	f/l	XXX	f/l	5 (f)
Necktie	a/c	8	c	XXX	f/l	m	2 (c)
floor	1 (a)	3(D/n)	2(c)	2(c/o)	5(f/l)	6 (g)	

Since, between *ITL* and this book, so many of the Exercises in Reasoning have been worked, a few more of that type of problem are included below.

1.   Abe, Boz and Cal are the best students in their class, ranking first, second and third (not necessarily in that order). Their favorite fruits are apricots, bananas and cantaloupes (again not necessarily in that order). Only bananas are yellow; only apricots are fuzzy; and only cantaloupes are rich in vitamin C (at least among the three). The top ranked student likes only fruit rich in vitamin C. Abe was ranked above Cal but below the cantaloupe lover. Cal gave away the apricots on his salad because he hated them. Identify the class rank and favorite fruit of each person.

2.   Williams, Xavier, Yates and Zeldon have 1, 2, 3, and 4 children. Their hobbies are archery, bowling, chess and darts. Xavier's children play one-on-one with some of Zeldon's. The bowler asked Yates to be the godfather of his only child. Zeldon feared a scratch from one of Yates' or Xavier's hobby devices. The chess player had two more children than Yates. Xavier took his children to the archer for lessons. How many children and what hobby did each man have?

3.   Four long-time friends, Alice, Ben, Carol and Dan, have decided to go into business together. A major factor in their decision was their realization that their skills--accountant, baker, calligrapher and deliverer--complemented each other beautifully. They had each gone to college, in Alabama, Baltimore (Maryland), California, and Denver (Colorado). Determine the skill and college of each of the four friends.
    a.   No one went to a school whose initial matched his/her name initial.
    b.   No one had a skill whose initial matched his/her name initial.
    c.   No one had a skill whose initial matched his/her school initial.
    d.   Neither Alice nor the Denver graduate could cook anything well.
    e.   The accountant used to date the Baltimore grad's wife.

4.   Jacobs has recently completed a study of European nobility. He judges that the key kings were Karl I, Charles II, Carlos III and Karol IV, absolute rulers of German, England, Spain and Poland. One was a hemophiliac, one a diabetic, one an alcoholic and the fourth addicted to morphine. Karl I and the German played whist, but the Spaniard and the alcoholic didn't. The hemophiliac and the Pole formed an alliance against Karol IV. The Englishman, the diabetic and Karl I shared a grandfather. The diabetic, the German and Karol IV were noted horsemen. Charles II married the Spaniard's daughter. Identify each king with his country and ailment.

5.   Adams, Brown and Clark have for pets a dog, an elk and a fox. The men's hobbies are golf, hockey (on ice) and ice-fishing. Clark never has anything to do with ice, even in his drinks. Adams and the dog owner watched the hockey player as he received his league's Most Valuable Player award. The hockey player then rode the bus back to town with the elk owner. Determine the pet and hobby of each man.

6.   Six friends, Al, Beth, Chet, Dawn, Ed, and Fran decided to rent a house together while going to college. To make things easier on themselves they agree to divide responsibilities. The basic chores, they decided, were 1: washing and drying clothes, 2: food shopping, 3: cooking, 4: kitchen cleaning, 5: house cleaning, and 6: yard work. Discover the chores of all the friends.
   a.   Al had allergies that wouldn't let him work with either pollens or house dust.
   b.   Beth had sensitive skin that wouldn't let her handle chemicals (like detergents, many cooking materials, or fertilizers).
   c.   Chet tutored the people who did the cleaning and washing in calculus.
   d.   Dawn's twin sister had dated Al, the cook and the kitchen cleaner.
   e.   Fran was so fair that she got sunburns from 100-watt bulbs; thus she couldn't take an outside job.

7.   Three children (Phil, Quint, and Ray) had their letters to Santa were read on local radio. They asked for gifts of a sled, a truck amd a ukelele (Hawaiian musical instrument) and trips to Vienna (Austria), Warsaw (Poland) and Xanadu (mythological). Determine which gift and trip each boy asked for.
   a.   Phil and the uke-wisher neever had fantasies.
   b.   The sled-wanter thought that the Warsaw-seeker and Ray were both selfish.
   c.   Quint and the truck-wanter hated Austria and all it stood for.
   d.   Ray though music was "sissy."

8.   Five students at a major midwestern technical university were accused of having cheated on a final examination. An investigation by the Dean indicated that only one of them was guilty. A graduate student in the Psychology Department offered to run a lie detector test on the accused students. Each of the students made four statements each of which an independent student monitor recorded on cards. The grad student recorded each student's response (without having listened to the questions) on a continuous printout. The test results clearly showed that each of the accused students had made three true and one false statement. Unfortunately, as she was handing the evidence to the Dean, the psychologist dropped the stack of cards, effectively randomizing them. Each card had had a code indicating whose response it was, but nothing to show what the order the responses were made. Determine who cheated.

Jane: I have never cheated in my life. I studied for the test with Ken. I'm making a 3.6 GPA and thus don't need to cheat. Nita is the one who cheated.

Ken: I've been tempted to cheat, but never did it. I studied hard, but alone for the exam. Marty is the one who cheated. This is the easiest course any of us has ever taken.

Lisa: Nita lied when she said I cheated. I saw Jane studying for the test with Ken. Marty used to date Jane. I'm ashamed to admit that I had cheated before, but I didn't this time.

Marty: This is the easiest course any of us has ever taken. Ken is the one who cheated. I've never done anything socially with Jane. Nita borrowed my notes.

Nita: My religion forbids me to cheat, so I haven't. One of us did cheat. Lisa is the guilty one. Jane has a 3.6 GPA.

CHAPTER ONE SUMMARY

I.   The business of logic is the analysis and appraisal of **arguments**.

II.   The "things" of which arguments are formed are **propositions**.

A. Propositions are the sorts of things that are true and false.

B. Propositions are independent of the language they appear in.

C. Propositions are usually expressed by sentences.

III.   There are two roles for propositions in arguments.

A. *Premiss*--

1.   Premisses are asserted as evidence or support for a conclusion.

2.   Every argument must have at least one premiss.

B. *Conclusion*--

1.   Conclusions are derived from, supported by or inferred from premisses.

2.   Every argument has exactly one conclusion.

IV.   One or more arguments may occur within a given passage, but none has to.

V.   Arguments differ from non-arguments that resemble them because arguments not only assert the relationship between premisses and conclusion but also assert the truth of both premisses and conclusion.

VI.   Arguments, whether simple or complex, may be diagramed with arrows showing the "flow" of information (or support) from premisses (or groups thereof) to a conclusion.

VII.   Most "problems" in reasoning can be solved, or at least simplified, by using an evident (usually mechanical) means of laying out what you do and do not know.

Chapter Two
The Uses of Language

2.1 Three Basic Functions of Language
2.2 Discourse Serving Multiple Functions
2.3 The Forms of Discourse

You may recall that, in the early days of your learning English, you were taught that sentences were declarative, exclamatory, imperative, and interrogative. The first three of these seem, roughly, to correspond to Copi and Cohen's classifications of informative, expressive, and directive, but there is obviously nothing like a question included. This is because he is concerned essentially with the sort of sentences that are used to convey information of some sort. If you think that a sentence could be pigeon-holed very neatly, you would probably be over-simplifying. In general, the sentences that Copi and Cohen want to consider are ones that have informative, expressive, and directive elements all at the same time.

Since the analysis of the Burns passage ("O my Luve's like a red, red rose . . .") is in the section in which they are differentiating the functions, you might have the impression that it is solely expressive. While the directive element of this passage seems to be negligible, Burns surely means metaphorically to inform the reader of the beauty and delicacy of his love. What Copi and Cohen have done is to show you as "chemically pure specimens" of simple function as are likely to be found in ordinary usage. But, as they point out at the beginning of 2.2, even these seem to serve multiple functions. Natural language, having evolved over centuries of use, seems to have grown too sophisticated for "real" simple functions to occur.

An added difficulty in the understanding of what people say or write is the context. Under ordinary circumstances, your saying to a man and a woman "You are married" would be some sort informative statement. Since, you would assume, they already know that they are wed, your statement probably means something like "I am aware that you are married to each other." There is, however, a circumstance in which that statement is quite different: if you are a minister, priest, justice of the peace, or otherwise-designated person with the legal power to perform marriage ceremonies, then your statement *may be* what Copi and Cohen call a *performative utterance*. Basically such verbal "actions" *do by saying*. Other performative utterances include saying "I promise....", I intend...." and so forth.

Please note that the issue is not as clear-cut as it may seem. Let's assume that John and Jane intend to wed: they have done all the appropriate things (including license, blood tests, invitations, etc.). Frank is a duly ordained minister whom they have asked to perform their ceremony. They stand before him as he asks them the traditional questions and they each respond "I do" accordingly. This would seem to be as unambiguous a case of performative utterance as one could hope for. However, consider the possibility that all three -- John, Jane and Frank -- are all members of a local little theater group and are, by coincidence, cast in a play as groom, bride and minister, respectively. In such a case the lack of *intent* during the performance of the play, is more important than the fact of their impending matrimony. The recital of the right words, under this odd circumstance, is **not** a performative utterance.

As Copi and Cohen point out, there is a similar kind of utterance called a *ceremonial utterance*. When you go to a religious service and listen to the sermon you will, possibly, hear what sound like statements about how you ought to behave and what you ought to believe. But most of those there already long ago accepted (at least on an intellectual level) those beliefs. Their presence (and possible-but-not-necessary listening) are part of a ceremony. If, in such a circumstance, the preacher asks "*Do you believe?*", the congregation's enthusiastic "We do!" is less a conveyer of information than a bonding together, a ceremonial action that makes a whole of the separate individuals.

One of the greatest problems you will encounter in your attempts to "sort out" what you hear and read will be the use of what appears to be one kind of discourse but really is another. A few examples might make this a little clearer.

1. A young man and an attractive young woman are talking when a very large football player comes up and says to him, "That's my girlfriend."

2. A teacher, disgusted by a student's poor performance on a test, comes into class, gives the student the graded exam and says, "What kind of idiot are you?"

3. A mother says to her teen-aged son, "Would you like to take the trash out?"

In case 1 prudence would suggest that they young man make his farewells rapidly, for what looks like a simple declarative sentence, an information-conveyer, is surely a directive (possibly with a veiled threat thrown in for good measure).

In case 2, if the student were to reply, "Type Six, subgroup Alpha-3, sir," the teacher would probably be the most surprised one in the room. Although the teacher's utterance sounded like a question, undoubtedly including the appropriate rising inflection at the end, it was actually either a "cute" way for the teacher to **assert** that the student was an idiot or an unpleasant way of expressing feelings of anger and frustration.

Case 3 actually happened to me. Without thinking, I foolishly responded, "No, I wouldn't" and got a verbal blast that I can recall after a thirty-year interval. Had I thought for a moment I would have realized that my mother's apparent question was, in fact, her way of politely giving an order.

What if you encountered a case similar to # 1, but with a couple of critical differences? Suppose, instead that you are sitting at a college commencement ceremony and as, they are announcing the award of a major graduate fellowship to one of the female graduates, the young man sitting next to you says, "That's my girlfriend." The utterance was identical, but the intent surely wasn't. In the altered situation you have surely encountered an expression of happiness and pride, with only the minor informative element and probably no directive properties at all.

There simply is no currently-known way to mechanically determine the function of a sentence. In fact that difficulty has been one of the sources of great embarrassment to workers in the field of so-called Artificial Intelligence. Twenty or so years ago AI researchers were routinely predicting that a "Natural Language Parser" [that is, an AI program that could "understand" language as it is commonly spoken] was to be available *Real Soon Now*. Despite the phenomenal hardware and software revolution of the past decade, there is still no functional, general natural language parser (nor does one appear to be on the near horizon). What it takes to sort out language is a sensitivity to meanings, shadings, distortions and context that come from long years of using it. You have to listen or read carefully and then ask yourself "*What did she/he mean to say?*" As practice it may be instructive to examine a few of the exercises after 2.3.

I. (2)   This clearly has the information function of telling the reader that criminal rehabilitation is an area in which we have no definitive knowledge. Also, this statement almost surely expresses frustration at our inability to deal effectively with problems of rehabilitative techniques, to pleas for understanding for unrehabilitated former convicts, or, perhaps, to reprimand those who have criticized judges' decisions.

(6)   This is an argument for the conclusion that pleasure is often sought only by seeking something else. As such it is primarily informative, telling you the conclusion and evidence for it. There are, however, significant directive and expressive elements in it. The tone is rather condescending, indicating some scorn for persons who did not understand the importance of indirectly seeking pleasure. And, probably, Blanshard is encouraging the reader to focus more upon the activities which give him or her pleasure, thereby increasing the likelihood that she or he will experience pleasure.

(11)   Machiavelli in informing you that bearing arms results in your being respected, expresses scorn for the unarmed, and (probably) directs or at least suggests that you bear arms.

(16)   Shaw is informing you that patriotism is the cause of the unrest in the world, indicating his disgust for it and suggesting that it ought to be eliminated.

(21)   Butler is explaining that the pleasure derived from the satisfaction of an appetite or passion is a by-product of the appropriateness of the thing that does the satisfying to the need to be satisfied. He seems to be expressing a pleasure at that harmony (probably as a manifestation of Divine Harmony). And it is likely that he wished that his parishioners would thus seek appropriate means to satisfy their appetites.

II. (2)   Will is asserting that the government has foolishly included ice in its category of "food products." He would probably like you both to oppose such a classification and to be wary of the government as an authority. He has a good, but caustic, sense of humor and an eye for the ridiculous, and is not bound by authority.

(6)   Spinoza is asserting that he has tried to understand human action, despite the times when it seemed humorous, lamentable or detestable. He would very likely wish that others follow his lead, and accept the sincerity and accuracy of his analysis of human action. The passage would indicate that Spinoza was earnest, objective and, probably, rather humorless.

(11)   Cecil is asserting that the primary cause of current social unrest is the middle class, that this is not what we would have expected, and that we are unduly proud of the middle class. He would like to redirect social antipathy from the lower to the middle class. (In fact, in an appropriate context, this could almost be taken as an incitement to revolution.)

        This probably provides evidence that Cecil is a member of neither the middle class nor the lower class, thus letting him take such an "objective" stance. It may also indicate that he has had some rather unpleasant dealings with representatives of the middle class.

(16)   The assertion is that keeping your mouth shut is a good way to appear to be wise. The goal is to persuade people that they will be better off listen-

ing more and talking less. The author is a bit sarcastic, impatient with those who talk too much, and quite sure of himself.

(21)   Mill's assertion is that if your material needs are met and you are still not happy, then the cause is probably that you are too self-centered. His goal is to get the reader to think more of the wants, needs and aspirations of others, to become outward-directed. One would infer from this that Mill was socially conscious and aware of the emptiness of a self-centered life.

2.4 Emotive Words
2.5 Kinds of Agreement and Disagreement

The entire subject of emotional language and its impact could be (and has been) the topic for a very extensive work. Essentially, the point Copi and Cohen wish to make is that most words have some emotional associations, ones which incline us to favor or oppose, frequently without our being aware of that effect. One TV critic, belittling the mentalities of television executives, pointed out that shows about dogs, babies, doctors, and Abraham Lincoln always do well and suggested that most networks would jump at the chance to produce a series about Lincoln's doctor's baby's dog. The positive associations with those four subjects is surely not, as the supposed executives would hope, additive. As a matter of fact, it is quite likely that each would tend to offset or dilute the effect of the others. Copi and Cohen mentioned the more positive associations we have with a can of tuna fish than one of horse mackerel. A similar, very conscious, alteration of name was made within the last few years. New Zealand had long grown a fruit with a fuzzy brown coat, with roughly the size and shape of a duck egg and with a bright green interior. It had, for many years, been called a Chinese gooseberry. [I assume the name came in part from the similarity in color of the flesh of these fruit and that of standard gooseberries.] The fruit is tangy but sweet, rich in vitamin C and attractive when peeled and sliced, but the name "turned people off." Some bright marketing person recognized that difficulty, then noticed that there was a (very) modest similarity between the appearance of the coat of the fruit and the appearance of New Zealand's national bird. And thus started the sale of the now-fashionable and popular Kiwi fruit.

The emotional meaning of a word can have quite subtle effects on our values and ideas, too. One of the great battles of the movement for women's rights (a movement called by its supporters "Women's Liberation)" has centered on the so-called "generic" use of masculine pronouns. Advocates of Women's Lib have argued, with some justification, that the use of "he" and "his" in documents, for example, about human rights or social order subconsciously educates us to think of these as issues relating more to men than to women.

I became aware of a similar sort of "verbal discrimination" when, as a teenager, I sought to annoy my younger sister. While taking Latin I learned that the Latin word for lefthanded is "sinister" ("dexter" means righthanded). Since she is lefthanded, for an unreasonably long time I delighted in referring to her as my "sinister sister." But the negative impact of "sinister" is not only terminological unpleasantness. A person who uses both hands effectively is said to be ambidextrous (having two right hands) while someone who is clumsy is said to have two left feet. If you were to tell someone that, for a fat person, they didn't sweat much, you would be offering a "lefthanded compliment." And, in medieval heraldry, a diagonal ribbon across a coat of arms was a sign that the bearer was the son of the man whose arms were there--the bar dexter (right-handed ribbon) was carried by the legitimate son, the bar sinister (lefthanded ribbon) by the bastard son. There is little question but that we were conditioned by our vocabulary to regard lefthandedness unfavorably. Words have power beyond their "objective" meanings.

The purpose of the presentation of Russell's "conjugations of irregular verbs" is to familiarize you with the ways in which a single person, object, or event may be described so that the reader has a positive, negative, or neutral response. The emotional attitude we have toward something affects the way we choose to describe it. Thus it is possible for two people to observe the same occurrence but describe it in what seem to be radically different terms (as a result of their opposed attitudes toward that occurrence). One of the "traditionally" positive words in the English language is 'mother.' This is based on mothers' expected behaviors. (Watch a rerun of *Leave it to Beaver* or *Ozzie and Harriet* to see these stereotypes in action.) If a person were, instead of the commonplace sort of mother, to have one who was an alcoholic, abusive harridan, that person would not react emotionally to the word 'mother' in the usual way.

There are times when we claim that we wish that our language could not express emotional attitudes. It would appear that that would free us from the "loaded" appeals, for example, of advertising. But, unless we (like such a language) were totally without emotions, it would be quite likely that the emotion would creep in through the way in which we **saw** what happened. That is to say, our emotional attitudes can strongly affect the way in which we see the world. For example, assume that you and I both have known Jane for many years. We both know that she is strong, decisive, impatient, very self-confident and that she served a tour of duty in Vietnam as a paramedic. Let us further assume that my experiences with her have been uniformly positive--she has been a good friend, a staunch defender, and once in my presence saved a heart attack victim's life. But finally let's assume that your experiences with her have not been good--she has butted in when she did not understand the circumstances, has seemed conceited, and once in your presence almost killed a man when she tried to use the Heimlich maneuver on him when she thought he was choking but wasn't. Your attitude toward her is that she is boorish, conceited and prone to rash and irresponsible actions; mine is that she is realistic, self-assured and heroic. If both of us were to come into a room and were to see her cutting at the throat of a man who was lying on the floor, our "unemotional" descriptions of her actions would probably be quite different: you would likely say she was cutting his throat, while I would probably say she was performing surgery. Neither is a terribly emotional loaded description, but mine conveys information which approves of Jane's action while yours does not. And, if pressed, I would claim that I saw her trying to save his life while you would assert that you saw her trying to end his life. For this reason it is important to realize that even the most sincere effort to be "objective" (including the most neutral of languages) may fail.

It is clear that there are two ways in which persons can agree and disagree--with regard to the "facts" and with regard to their feelings about what they take to be the facts. Thus, there are four combinations of complete disagreement. If you put in a sort of chart form you'd have:

I	Agree in Belief (Fact) Agree in Attitude	*III*	Disagree in Belief Agree in Attitude	
II	Agree in Belief Disagree in Attitude	*IV*	Disagree in Belief Disagree in Attitude	

All four cases are relatively common. If you and your next-door neighbor each see a third neighbor's dog in your shared garden, digging holes, and each judge the third to be irresponsible in allowing his dog such freedom, then you agree in belief (the "fact" that the dog was allowed loose and damaged the garden) and in attitude (the "wrongness" of it being allowed).

If you and the neighbor both see the third neighbor's two-year-old son toddling nude across the back yard, you might think it "cute" and the neighbor think it "immoral." Here the two of you agree in belief (that the child was outside unclad) but disagree in attitude (yours being positive, your neighbor's negative).

If you see the third neighbor as a political opportunist, who has been picketing a local factory with a pollution problem only (you judge) because she believes it will get her elected mayor, and your neighbor sees her as a dangerous-but-sincere fanatic who overlooks certain economic realities, then you both will probably oppose her election. Here you disagree in your beliefs (you that she is a fake, he that she is sincere) but you both agree in the attitude that she is an undesirable political option.

Of course you are used to encountering the fourth case. If you and your younger brother each have Mrs. Jones for an advanced biology class, you may think that she is the most inventive, instructive teacher you have ever had while he sees her as very strange and totally incapable of following the text. Here you disagree in belief (you that she is a responsible teacher, he that she is not) and in attitude (you like her, he does not).

Ultimately, the reason you want to be able to sort out such differences in attitude and belief is so that, in trying to communicate with another person, you can discover where and how (if at all) you differ. If you disagree in belief, you may have the chance to change another's mind by presenting additional information. But the sad truth is that, if you differ in attitude (especially attitude only), it is most likely that no amount of information or argument will resolve your differences.

You now are well-prepared to analyze the exercises following 2.5. The key is to try to decide whether the two statements could reasonably be made by different persons in describing the same situation. If so, then there is agreement in belief; if not, then there is disagreement in belief. Similarly, try to decide whether both statements are positive or both negative. For example, if both refer to a person, could both speakers be used as character witnesses (pro and con) together in a court trial? If the same side would subpoena both, then there probably is agreement in attitude; if not, then not.

(2)   Clearly Rice and Lombardi differ about the importance of winning (disagreement in belief). Again, here, there is some fuzziness about the attitude. Obviously, if their attitude toward winning is the issue, they disagree. But, if at stake is each man's attitude toward his own (or the other man's) position, then Rice has a positive attitude toward concern for playing as best you could and Lombardi has a positive attitude toward winning. Without a resolution of which of these "targets" of attitude you are discussing, you can't decide whether they agree or disagree in attitude. [One sportsman suggested that an attitude like that of Tevye (in Fiddler on the Roof) would be a good compromise, that is, losing is no sin but it's no great honor either.]

(6)   Here Jimmy the Greek and Ecclesiastes differ in both their beliefs and attitudes. Actually Snyder (the Greek's real name) would accept the possibility that *on rare occasions* the swift and strong might lose. He just thinks that there is good historical evidence that such an occurrence is quite unlikely. Given the Biblical tone, one ought to suspect that the prophet is pleased by the "fact" of his statement. Similarly it seems that Snyder is not unhappy with what he perceives the likelihood to be.

(11)   Washington and Russell seem to disagree about the status of agriculture, but there is genuine reason for doubt. If you look carefully at what each says you will see that they are not actually addressing the same issue. Washington is discussing the importance of agriculture to a society; Russell is discussing the effect of working in an agricultural society upon the people themselves. It is possible that something can be of great social value and yet be awful for the person who has to do it. If you interpret Washington's statement as an endorsement of the agricultural life, then they would disagree in belief. On the other hand, it is fairly clear that Washington's attitude to-

ward the patriotic service rendered by the agriculturist is positive, while Russell's toward the conditions people live under in an agricultural society are negative.

(16)   In distinction to problem 11, this one is fairly obvious. Stobaeus sees agriculture as futile and dull, while Jefferson sees it as rewarding and delightful. They disagree completely. [Case IV]

2.6 Emotionally Neutral Language

One great difficulty we are likely to encounter in our attempts to avoid emotional distractions, whether in what we read and hear or what we write and say, is our difference in background. If I had been raised in and had accepted a very conservative religion and you had been raised in and had accepted atheism, it is likely that terms to which you relate negatively (such as "divine," "prayer," "devout") are ones to which I relate quite positively. Similarly, if you have studied medieval history and I have not, use of the phrase "yoke of serfdom" (such as in *The Communist Manifesto*) will probably strike you as quite emotionally loaded while it will be not only unemotional but probably meaningless to me. In general, the best we can hope for is to try to be sensitive to the sort of emotional impact our choice of words have.

The other significant problem in our trying to "neutralize" our language is the difficulty we have in separating the emotion of the language from the emotional elements of the situation *per se*. Quite evidently the language is emotional if I say that Herb split Hank's head open in the best tradition of the mad axe-murderers. If I re-write the idea unemotionally (as best I can) I might get something like: Herb vertically bifurcated Hank's cranium in the manner usual to those who are unable to understand why they ought to behave in certain acceptable ways when they bring about the non-vital state in others by means of an implement usually reserved for the felling of trees. This "talks around" the event sufficiently to seem to accomplish the goals of preserving the factual content and deleting the emotional. But, once you wade through the mass of words, seeing what the sentence says, you have an intense emotional reaction (like "Good Heavens, he's talking about an axe-murderer"). It seems fair, here, to claim that the language was neutral; it was the situation that wasn't. You have to be very careful not to confuse the two.

It is possible to get so wrapped up in the business of avoiding emotion that you lose touch with what was intended. This is particularly true when you try to replace emotional terms one at a time. One student, in de-emotionalizing a very hostile letter about a leading politician, confronted the writer's use of the reference 'dirty S.O.B." Rather than recognize this as a basically emotional term with little information content, he "translated" it as 'individual who needs a bath and whose mother is registered with the American Kennel Club.' That is the literal meaning of the words, but has nothing at all to do with the probable intent of the writer. [This treatment of metaphorical language as if it were intended literally is often identified as the fallacy of *Hypostatization*.]

CHAPTER TWO SUMMARY

I.   For our purposes language has three primary functions:

      A.   Language is informative; it conveys information.

      B.   Language is expressive; it conveys emotional reactions and intensities.

      C.   Language is directive; it conveys orders, suggestions and instructions.

II.   In most cases language performs all three functions at the same time.

III.   In some cases the apparent linguistic form, e.g., a question, is not a reliable indicator of the primary function being performed, as in a rhetorical question.

IV.   Some words and phrases are particularly evocative of emotion.

V.   There are different ways to agree or disagree.

      A.   You may agree or not in belief, that is, concerning the "facts" involved in a situation.

      B.   You may agree or not in attitude, that is your emotional reaction to what you perceive to be the "facts."

VI.   Emotionally neutral language tries to eliminate the expressive element from discourse as far as possible.

      A.   Perception of a word or words as emotional may be a function of experience, making it hard to tell whether or not a given locution will be emotional to a given person.

      B.   A situation may itself be so emotionally charged that any description of it, no matter how bland and roundabout, will appear emotional.

Chapter Three
Fallacies

3.1 What Is a Fallacy
3.2 Fallacies of Relevance

You will find that the explanations of the logical fallacies are quite straightforward and clear. This commentary will indicate a few additional characteristics of some fallacies, characteristics that may make it a bit easier for you to distinguish between related fallacies. In real life, of course, it becomes slightly less important to be able to apply the correct "label" to a fallacious argument; what is important is that you be able to identify an argument as fallacious and that you be able to put your finger on what it is about that argument that makes it problematic. What is critical is that you be able to see how it is that the so-called fallacies tend to persuade you.

Argument from Ignorance (*Ad ignorantiam*) arguments derive some sort of assertion from a lack of evidence of any sort. One person might argue that the lack of hard physical evidence of a reliable sort for the existence of flying saucers is proof of their nonexistence. A second could as easily argue that any species advanced enough to build such vehicles would be skilled enough to hide all such traces of their visits, and thus the combination of many "sightings" but no hard data (like a wrecked saucer with the squashed remains of little green people) is justification for asserting their existence. And, of course, the point is that we really ought to say that we just don't know, that the data so far is insufficient to draw any reasonable conclusions.

It has often been claimed that 99-44/100% of all we know is a product of our accepting what-someone-else-tells-us-is-the-case as if it is the case. In that way each of us does not have to rediscover gravity, the spherical shape of the earth and that hot things burn. As a matter of fact, what you are learning in this course you are accepting, as it were, on faith--the faith that neither Copi, Cohen, nor any other logician would deliberately misinform you about logic. That faith, hopefully, is not misplaced. If, however, this study guide were to have a section telling you which political party to join, what religion to follow, or where to seek employment, and you were to do what it said, then you would have accepted an **Appeal to Inappropriate Authority**--an *ad verecundiam* argument. Authorities ought only to be consulted and/or accepted when they *are genuine authorities*. Joe Namath's expertise on the football field in no way makes him an authority on popcorn poppers, french fryers, hamburger cookers, or pantyhose. In each case, his endorsement of the product is merely playing upon the supposed warm associations the viewing audience has with him as a person.

Many of us have had a smile from obvious **complex questions** like "Have you stopped beating your wife?" (Although, when you think of it, there is nothing at all funny about wife-beating), but have never thought about the serious implications of such questions. Most of us, if asked apart from the context of a course in which we were on guard, would reply that we believe that a person's "taking the Fifth Amendment" (refusing to answer from fear of self-incrimination) really is an admission of guilt, that you could not incriminate yourself unless you had something to incriminate, that is, unless you were guilty. During the "witch-hunt" period of the investigations of the House UnAmerican Activities Committee, however, the questioning frequently was:

Just give a simple "yes" or "no" for an answer, we don't want any speeches. Did you really believe that you could hide your communist affiliations from the government forever?

If you say "yes" then you have admitted such affiliations, but if you answer "no" you have still admitted them. If you are not allowed to give the answer that you have no communist affiliations, then (assuming that you do not have them) your only option is to "take the Fifth."

Being an **attack against the man**, *Ad hominem* arguments direct one's attention to the person who has asserted something rather than whatever it is that he or she has asserted. The attack on the person sometimes takes the form of abuse or criticism of that person's character. When William O. Douglas was a Justice of the Supreme Court, some elements of the populace would argue that his opinions ought to be discounted because he was a "dirty old man." Their evidence was his marriage to a woman almost 50 years his junior, his fathering a child by her, and his authoring an essay on the evils of censorship, even censorship of pornography, which was published in a magazine whose editor was convicted of distributing pornography--that very magazine--through the mails). While this evidence might be used as a way to call into question his objectivity on an obscenity issue--at least the last item might--it appears in no way relevant to his competence and objectivity in ruling, for example, on the constitutionality of a newly-imposed poll tax in Montana. And, of course, even if one granted the assumption that he was a dirty old man, that still does not show that any decision in particular is wrong.

A second sort of *ad hominem*, for example, involves an attack on people because they are in some sort of special circumstances. If you reject an argument for the defeat of hand-gun registration legislation because the arguer is a member of the N.R.A., you are not focusing on the argument but on the arguer. Certainly it would be expected that such a person is predisposed against registration of firearms, but that in no way proves that the **argument** offered in defense of the position is in any way objectionable.

The fallacies of **accident** and **converse accident** (or hasty generalization) deal with what might be called a class-member relationship. Since classes are usually identified by some set of properties that its members have in common, it is natural to expect that, once you know what those properties are for a certain class and know that an individual is a member of that class, that individual will possess all of those properties. Similarly it is normal to expect that some prominent feature of an individual will be shared by the other individuals with which it shares class-membership. Usually these inferences are fine. The only problem is that you have to check to make sure that there are not special circumstances that affect the situation. Thus, while it is true that Americans can say what they want to say when they want to say it (as a Constitutional Right), there really needs to be the qualifier "usually" added. For example, you may not lie under oath in a court of law without incurring the risk of being found to be a perjurer. To apply the freedom of speech generalization to the special circumstance of being under oath in a court would be to commit a fallacy of accident.

When you place a chunk of zinc in a beaker of sulfuric acid, the colorless gas that bubbles off is hydrogen. Doing this experiment once would incline anyone familiar with scientific processes to make the following generalization: when I put this zinc in that acid I got hydrogen; thus, when anyone puts any zinc in any sulfuric acid they get hydrogen. Given the way one piece of zinc tends to be pretty much like any other and the way all sulfuric acids tend to be pretty much alike, the generalization is reasonable. If you had hired a philosopher as a bodyguard and he had failed to protect you from an assault, then you might generalize that all philosophers make incompetent bodyguards. (You might even go so far as to infer that all philosophers are incompetent at whatever they try to do). But you have had no reason to infer that that individual was in any way representative of philosophers, taken as a group. People, generally, tend to be far more individual than lumps of zinc. Without some evidence that the sample from which you are generalizing is truly representative of its class, and that the property that you are inferring is generally true of members of that class, you have no reason to infer that the particular property is a property that is somehow related to being in that class. You might find some characteristic of philosophers that made them incompetent bodyguards, thereby supporting the inference. Had you noted that the individual had a mole on his left hand but not his being a philosopher, you might have drawn the analogous conclusion that all people with moles on their left hands are incompetent bodyguards. However, it seems unlikely that you will be able to find any relevant connection between moles and incompetence. The key, in both the case of accident and that of converse accident, is that of relevance: fallacies of accident ignore relevant circumstances which exempt a member of a class from a generalization that usually holds for such members; a hasty generalization does not establish the relevance of a property to the class of which an individual is a member before inferring that all members of that class share that property.

Arguments about causation are quite difficult to handle. Later (in Chapter 13) you will study one of the major attempts to discover causal relationship. Here, however, you will note that many arguments which claim to uncover causes fail to do so. Most obvious are *post hoc ergo propter hoc* (meaning "after this therefore because of this and commonly called *post hoc*) arguments. They are the basis of most superstition. If you happen to notice that you did better than you had expected to do on your last three exams and that you were wearing your red-and-green-striped socks each time, it is no long step to thinking of them as your "lucky" socks. The problem is that, the way we usually think of causes, causes must precede effects, but the mere fact that one event happens before another is not enough to show that the first caused the second. It was *post hoc* reasoning that led the rooster to believe that he had to crow every morning to make the sun rise.

Another common causal fallacy, which Copi and Cohen do not discuss in detail, is that of confusing conditions and causes. Oxygen (or something which serves as an oxidizer), a combustible material, and heat, all taken together, might be seen as the "cause" of fire. If two of the three were already present, we might be led to say that the introduction of the third "caused" the fire. But, being more critical, we would probably prefer to say that each of the three is a *necessary condition* for a fire, that the three together provide *sufficient conditions* for a fire.

Circular arguments (begging the question or *petitio principii*) come in all shapes and sizes. Simplest are arguments like: "Aspirin relieves pain since it is an analgesic." Of course, to say that something is an analgesic is just to say that it relieves pain. More complex arguments might resemble:

A. The Bible is the Revealed Word of God.
B. *How do you know?*
A. Jesus said so.
B. *How do you know what Jesus said is true?*
A. He is the Son of God.
B. *How do you know that?*
A. The Bible says so.
B. *How do you know that what it says is true?*
A. Because it is the Revealed Word of God.

The circularity is obvious. Unfortunately, these are not the only forms that such arguments may take. Entire books have been written to argue an idea, only to have that idea be one that must be assumed to make the argument understandable. There is no question but that if you assume some datum, say X, as an element in your argument, then you will have no trouble showing how it is that X follows from your assumption--it is a very unusual logical system in which X does not follow from X. Thus, while the proof of X from premiss X is easy, it is neither particularly valuable or interesting, and it surely does nothing to *establish* X's independent truth.

One extraordinarily clever use of an **Appeal to Emotion**, an *ad populum*, occurred in 1962 at Colorado State University. The student council, in the attempt to overcome what they saw as the "apathy" of the student body, invited George Lincoln Rockwell to speak. Rockwell, the founder of the American Nazi Party, had been frequently featured in the media as a result of his vocal opposition to the then-growing civil rights movement. Over 1000 students had come to hear him. He entered the hall wearing a conservative suit, white shirt, and narrow tie, rather than the Nazi uniform that had been expected. He stepped to the microphone and said something like

> Good morning. I imagine some of you are disappointed, having come to watch the monkey in the funny suit scream, shout, and offer to hit an old woman with a club to entertain you. Well, if you think for a minute, you will realize that that is the sort of thing that I have to do to get any sort of news coverage. And I have to have such coverage so that people will know that National Socialism is an option for patriotic Americans. But I don't have to resort to that sort of thing with you. You are all intelligent, fair-minded people. I can present my ideas and you will give them a hearing, then discuss them in a mature, rational fashion.

At that point he already had the entire audience, if not on his side, at least no longer hostile to him. He had appealed to their prejudices about themselves: what college student would fail to recognize the intelligence of a man who saw that he or she was intelligent, fair-minded, mature, and rational? He had skillfully used their emotions to "argue" that his position was one that deserved their serious attention.

In our society, where each of us is taught from earliest childhood that we are responsible for the welfare of others, the **Appeal to Pity** or *Ad misericordiam* fallacy is quite common. It is the basis of most of the advertising of such worthwhile organizations as C.A.R.E., the U.S.O., Save the Children, and so forth. The mere facts that people abroad are hungry, that young servicemen away from home are lonely, or that many children need some sort of minimal aid to become functional adults do not entail your sending money to these causes. The entailment is a product of a whole series of additional premises about social responsibility and being one's brother's keeper. In this case, as in all fallacious arguments, the conclusion may be altogether an objectionable one; the problem, logically, is that it does not follow from the premises that are given.

The fallacies of relevance generally create the impression of leading straightforwardly from premises to conclusion. Their problem is that, when you carefully look at the relationship, the premises do not really provide *evidence* that supports the conclusion. The *Ad baculum* (or appeal to force) gives a "practical" reason for doing whatever is specified in the conclusion--the threat of physical, emotional, or financial violence for non-acceptance. If I tell you that you ought not block a doorway and the reason is that you are creating a fire-escape hazard, then I have given evidence justifying the assertion that you ought to move; if I tell you that you ought to move because if you don't move I will tear your arm off and beat you with it, then I am threatening, not reasoning. In a sense, the first argument might be rewritten as follows:

Premiss 1   (Explicit)   If one stands in a doorway, one is creating a fire hazard.

Premiss 2   (Explicit)   You are standing in a doorway.

Conclusion 1 (Intermediate)   You are creating a fire hazard.

Premiss 3   (Implicit)   If you create a fire hazard, you are endangering others.

Conclusion 2 (Intermediate)   You are endangering others.

Premiss 4 (Implicit) If you are a moral person you do not wish to endanger others.

Premiss 5 (Implicit) You are a moral person.

Conclusion 3 (Intermediate) You do not wish to endanger others.

Premiss 6 (Implicit) If you are doing something that results in your endangering others when you do not wish to, then you ought not to be doing it.

Conclusion 4 (Explicit) You ought not be standing in that doorway.

Notice how much "unpacking" the argument underwent, making explicit the assumed premisses and the intermediate conclusions. In contrast, the *ad baculum* argument would become something like this:

Premiss 1 (Explicit) You are standing in the doorway.

Premiss 2 (Explicit) If I do not want you to be in the doorway then if you are in the doorway then I will forcibly remove you. (Assumes the threat actually made is meant to be metaphoric.)

Premiss 3 (Implicit) I do not want you to be in the doorway.

Conclusion 1 (Intermediate) If you are in the doorway then I will forcibly remove you from it.

Conclusion 2 (Intermediate) I will forcibly remove you from the doorway.

Premiss 4 (Implicit) If you do not like to be forcibly removed, then you must not stand in the doorway.

Premiss 5 (Implicit) You do not like to be forcibly removed.

Conclusion 3 (Intermediate?) You must not stand in the doorway.

Premiss 6 (Implicit) If you are doing something that results in your being forcibly removed when you do not wish to be forcibly removed, then you ought not to be doing it.

Conclusion 4 (Explicit) You ought not to be standing in the doorway.

Notice that the second argument has been unpacked in as similar a manner to the first as seems possible, but the argument thus generated just doesn't follow in the same way. In a sense, the real conclusion of the argument may be found in the "Intermediate?" conclusion 3. But that conclusion is solely the result of *implicit* premisses 4 and 5. It seems to be a questionable way to reason when what are explicitly stated as premisses and what is explicitly stated as a conclusion are only incidental to what we claim the argument "really means."

In a sense, the use of an **Irrelevant Conclusion**, the *ignoratio elenchi* fallacy is a catch-all. It, and the related *non sequitur*, which Copi and Cohen include as a subcategory of the *ignoratio elenchi*, could probably be used to describe any fallacy of relevance. In general, however, it is best to classify a fallacy as one of the more specific forms (if possible) so that you more precisely indicate what is wrong with the argument. Ignoratio elenchi arguments are frequently used, as a sort of misdirection approach, when one does not have adequate support for a position in which one deeply believes. The very heated debate over the Equal Rights Amendment during the mid-70s generated a wealth of such arguments. Proponents of the amendment would frequently claim that the ERA had nothing to do with the drafting of women (that being a charge frequently leveled against the ERA). They would point to the text of the amendment, showing that it made no mention of the draft. The problem is that from the fact that the amendment does not specifically mention the draft it does not follow that it has no implications regarding the amendment. As a matter of fact, the provisions of the amendment are such that if Congress reinstated the draft then women could not be exempted from it simply because they are women. The term *non sequitur* means "it does not follow." Thus this argument is a "textbook" example of a *non sequitur* fallacy. The information may be relevant to the conclusion, but the conclusion simply does not follow from the premisses as they are presented.

Opponents of the ERA made equally fallacious arguments. One common one was that if the federal government forced all children to spend their formative years in state day-care centers, then the core of family life would be destroyed. The conclusion drawn from this would be that the ERA ought to be defeated. Few would doubt the undesirability of *compulsory* state-run nurseries for all children, but that is irrelevant to the issue of support for or rejection of the ERA. At least it would be necessary for an opponent of ERA to show that it would entail such state action.

All of the arguments that are classed as fallacies of relevance share a common characteristic: they mislead by misdirection. In that way they resemble the "patter" of a stage magician: by calling attention to the fact that there is "nothing up his sleeves" he gets you to focus on his sleeves and ignore his pockets. In either event you have been misled: in the case of the magician you are watching the wrong thing; in the case of the argument you are thinking about the wrong issues. And, even when you are aware of the potential for misdirection, it is easy to err anyway. For the next 30 seconds don't think about monkeys! See? Once you were told *not* to do it, you couldn't avoid it. Even if you haven't thought of monkeys for months, you are now. Once the misdirection is offered, most of us "bite."

You should now be able to recognize the common fallacies of relevance and should be able to explain briefly why any argument which you judge to be fallacious is so. Please be careful of two pitfalls of such explanations. To repeat a definition of a fallacy as explanation does not show why that particular argument is a case of that particular fallacy. Also, to repeat the argument as explanation does not explain: it actually constitutes a claim that the fallaciousnes of the argument is self-evident. But, of course, had it been so obvious that the argument was bad, its author, we hope, would not have used it.

I (2) *Ignoratio elenchi* (irrelevant conclusion). The fact that the sage's timing is good says nothing about where his emotions are located.

(6) *Petitio Principii* (Begging the question). One might have thought that this was an appeal to authority, but one would hope that the head of the Bullfight Association would be properly knowledgeable relative to bullfighting. Instead, note that the pre miss "...a bullfighter is and should be a man" amounts to the same thing as the conclu sion "women shouldn't fight bulls...."

(11) *Ad Baculum* (Appeal to force). In a normal society the only "unfortunate conse quences" of allowing a newspaper subscription to lapse would be ignorance of the news which only it carried and overlooking of any advertisements it might have car ried. In this case there is the not-too-subtly-veiled suggestion that some unspecified, but terrible repercussions might occur after cancellation.

(16) False Cause. Evidently, according to the joke, Fernandez took membership in the Republican Party as a causal condition for wealth. All that had probably been in tended was the assertion that, in the mind of the person who spoke with him, the policies of that party tended to be allied with the interests of the rich.

(21) This case would be funny if it didn't demonstrate so effective a method of misleading people. The attorney here is trying to "impeach" the witness that is, to convince the

jury that the doctor on the stand is neither a competent physician nor a reliable witness on medical (and perhaps other) matters. If the jury had taken a long look at the questioning they surely would have realized that *any* doctor who has been in practice for a substantial length of time is going to have had some patients die. In such cases the crucial inquiry should be whether the patients had had a reasonable expectation of survival before seeing the doctor.

II (2)   *Petitio Principii* (Begging the question). The ultimate evidence given for believing that the men of old were offspring of the gods is the last sentence: "How can we doubt the word of the children of the Gods?" But that assumes that they are what you were trying to prove they were.

(6)   *Petitio Principii.* The one man's getting three pearls is justified immediately by his being the leader, but that depends upon his getting the three pearls. Thus, you conclude where you began.

(11)   Although this argument has the appearance of being an appeal to ignorance -- we can't prove the resurrection by reason so it must come from faith -- this is more likely a case of complex question. Even if there is no actual question, there is the same sort of two-level assumption occurring. Scotus has assumed that the resurrection *is certain*. Whether your religious beliefs agree or not, the argument he has offered here certainly allows the possibility that the reason that argument has been unable to prove the resurrection is certain is because it isn't. If you feel uncomfortable calling an argument which doesn't ask a question a complex question, then the obvious alternative is to point out that proof by faith does not follow from the lack of reasoned proof. That would make the argument an *ignoratio elenchi* or *non sequitur*.

(16)   *Ad Hominem* (abusive, gently). Santayana says nothing about the content of Nietzsche's philosophy. Nietzsche's health, age, interests (and shoe size) are all irrelevant to the discussion of the **correctness** of his ideas.

(21)   There are at least two possible ways to read this argument. One might interpret Anytus's pointing out the ease with which one person could harm another in Athens as a way of threatening Socrates with moral censure (perhaps even his own). That would make this a sort of appeal to (moral) force. Alternatively it would reasonable to respond "So what?" If the "harm" done men is warranted, then there is serious question as to why one ought not do the harm. Again we have a *non sequitur* or *ignoratio elenchi*.

3.3 Fallacies of Ambiguity

The second group of fallacies arises not so much through a conscious (or unconscious) desire to misdirect, but through the "slipperiness" of the language. The problems they cause result from words and phrases with multiple meanings being treated as if they each had but one meaning, or from the use of vague or imprecise terms being used as if they were not so. Often this sort of fallacy is more pronounced in the words of children or those who are not native speakers of the language.

One of the most common of this sort of fallacy is **equivocation**. In the early 1960s people in Colorado were shocked when, in the defense arguments of a divorce suit where the wife charged her husband with beating her with a whip from a willow tree, the attorney for the husband read to the court an 1898 law making it a misdemeanor for a man "to beat his wife with a willow whip any bigger around than the base of his smallest finger." The whip the man had used was in evidence, was measured and found to be smaller than the base of his smallest finger. Conclusion -- the divorce was denied. (She immediately re-sued on different grounds and won.) The point is that this case raised a hue and cry about the need to have laws periodically reexamined and to repeal those that were causing problems. One small town newspaper editor (who favored space exploration, but evidently understood little science) offered "Einstein's Laws" as an immediate candidate for repeal. He argued that "since Einstein's Laws prevent us from developing a faster-than-light space drive, we can't get to the stars. And since we want to get there, we ought to repeal them as soon as we can." His problem was an unintentional equivocation: he didn't realize that the laws we can repeal are those that men choose to put into effect, and that laws like Einstein's are observed physical regularities that will be there whether or not we acknowledge them.

One possibility always exists in an equivocal situation, that there really is a good argument there. consider the argument

What happens almost every day is a probable event.
Improbable events happen almost every day.
Therefore, improbable events are probable events.

You can think of this as an equivocation. The phrase "improbable event" has a meaning shift. In the second premiss, it means that some member or another of the class of things which are improbable occurs almost every day. In the conclusion it means that each specific event happens almost every day. If you preserved the meaning of the premiss in the conclusion, you'd read the conclusion as something like "it is very probable that some improbable event or other will occur." And that, given the premiss, is quite a reasonable conclusion.

Amphibolies are usually the result of sloppy grammar. When English teachers point out problems of reference, agreement or dangling phrases, they are generally identifying amphibolies. A want-ad appeared several years ago saying, "For sale, a piano by a woman with carved legs." Don't you wonder, as many readers did, why she ever had her legs carved? Phrases can also be amphibolous when they involve a series of ideas in which strict parallelism has not been maintained. Television advertisements have recently been appearing, asking for volunteers "to work in care of the aged, rehabilitation of drug offenders, and child abuse." Caring for the aged and rehabilitating persons with drug problems are certainly worthwhile activities, but isn't it questionable whether one wants people to volunteer to abuse children? Had the third classification of volunteers been listed as "counselors for child abusers" or as "foster parents for abused children" not only would the original request have been more rhetorically correct, but the amphiboly would not have occurred.

A few minutes watching the public service advertisements on television of reading them in magazines would surely show you the National Safety Council's running slogan

Safe Driving Is No Accident.

At first glance this seems to make the obvious statement that safe driving will result in your not having accidents. But the message that the Council really wants to convey is that safe driving is the effect of serious work, that you can't drive safely by chance, that it is the result of conscious choice and effort.

The sloppiness need not be grammatical; it may result from the physical display of the words. On one midwestern college campus there recently was an enthusiastic campaign begun to encourage conservation. Students covered the campus with signs encouraging everything from recycling to showering with a friend to save water. Posters appeared on bulletin boards across campus. The message of the posters was unobjectionable, but the formatting done by their computerized poster-maker made them amphibolous. The posters read:

```
┌─────────────────┐
│                 │
│     SAVE        │
│                 │
│     CANS        │
│                 │
│     AND         │
│                 │
│     WASTE       │
│                 │
│     PAPER       │
│                 │
└─────────────────┘
```

If you saw the text on a line SAVE CANS AND WASTE PAPER it would seem unambiguous that you were being asked to save both the cans and the paper. On the sign there is at least the possibility that you could misread the "waste" as a verb. This would result in understanding its message as exhorting you to save the cans but to waste the paper. It's unlikely that this misinterpretation would occur to a reasonable user of the language, but one should be conscious of this sort of possibility.

The fallacy of **accent** has its most common occurrences in relation to the language as we speak it. Oral communication is very fragile because it is so dependent upon the tone, inflection and stress of the voice. This makes it particularly hard to transfer the full import of what someone says into a written record. That was the basis of Richard Nixon's attorney's arguments when they tried to prevent public access to the so-called White House Tapes. Their contention was that, in a written transcript, one could not identify irony, sarcasm, and the like. Thus, a statement like "I can solve the financial problems of New York City except for one minor problem: how to keep the nuclear fallout from drifting into New Jersey" could be said in the attempt (rather tastelessly) to describe humorously how completely frustrating NYC's problems are, In its literal written form, however, it sounds like the ravings of a madman.

A teacher could speak with three logic students, using the same words to each, but communicate quite different messages:
   A) You're not expected to learn much of a *factual* nature in a logic course.
      [This suggests that *facts* are not the primary material of a logic course.]
   B) You're not expected to learn much of a factual nature in a *logic* course.
      [This suggests that *logic* courses are different than other disciplines.]
   C) *You're* not expected to learn much of a factual nature in a logic course.
      [This suggests that the teacher has low expectations for the student addressed.]

A consciously misleading case of accent occurred in the advertisement of a movie. A major newspaper (let's call it the *Daily Planet*) had reviewed the film saying: "Except for wooden acting, incompetent direction, an infantile plot, raucous music, and unimaginative camera work, the movie is great." Obviously, the critic was not pleased with the show. The movie company, however, included part of the review in their ads, saying "'...The movie is **great**,' says the *Daily Planet*." Those words, in that order, had as a matter of fact occurred in the review; so the movie company could not be accused of fabricating the quotation, only of quoting out of context. (Incidentally, the newspaper sued and the film maker had to run corrective ads everywhere the original had appeared.)

A fallacious inference called **special pleading** is sometimes considered separately and sometimes as a form of accent. Like quotation out of context it involves the omission of relevant evidence. Probably the most famous case of this sort of reasoning came in France's famous Dreyfus case. Alfred Dreyfus, highest ranking Jewish officer in the French Army, was accused of treason -- selling information to the then-enemy Germans. He was convicted (despite protestations of innocence), stripped of his rank and pay, and sentenced to Devil's Island. Later, with the support of essayist Emile Zola, his defenders proved that the Army had known (after his arrest but before the trial) that he was blameless. They had chosen to conceal their evidence on the ground that public knowledge that they had accused an innocent man would have undermined confidence in the Army.

The fallacies of **composition** and **division** often cause students difficulties because there seems to be so much similarity between them and the fallacies of accident and hasty generalization. Roughly, the difference between them is that accident/converse accident deal with the relationship between classes or sets and their members while composition/division concern part/whole relationships. If we were to sample randomly ten of the thousands of members in the American Philosophical Association, find them to be impoverished, and then to infer that all members of the Association were poor, we would be hastily generalizing. Instead, if we were to make a rather larger sampling, find the same results, and then to infer that the Association is itself financially hard-pressed, we would be committing a composition (although the conclusion would happen to be true). Even if several of your favorite dishes happen to be sauerkraut, sardines, lime sherbet, pizza, and corn flakes, it is unlikely that a sardine pizza, topped with a layer of sauerkraut, a scoop of lime sherbet, and a sprinkling of corn flakes, would be high on your list of gourmet delights. Tasty as you may find each of the parts, the whole would probably spoil any appetite; the inference is a composition. Similarly, misapplication of statistics can be fallacious. It is the case that every fifth child born in the world today is Chinese. If, however, you anticipate gloating over your racially prejudiced neighbor's distress when his expected fifth child is born, figuring that, as a fifth, it will be Chinese, then you are due for a disappointment. One child out of five, on the whole, will be Chinese, that is, 1/5 of the total number of babies born will be Chinese, but no matter how many children a black Congolese couple or a white Danish couple give birth to, they'll never get a Chinese child. The statistic doesn't transmit down from the whole (of the human race) to the part (represented by any one couple).

As Copi and Cohen suggest, people often confuse the fallacies of composition and division with those of accident and converse accident. One way to keep them clearly separated is to think of the composition/ division pair as dealing with a part/whole relationship while the accident/converse accident pair deals with a class/member relationship. You might check the financial background of half a dozen members of a sorority, find that their families were all in the $100,000-a-year-and-up group, and infer that all members of the sisterhood were financially well-based. That is probably a converse accident, inferring the all members of the class have the same property as the sample. Instead one might check all the members of the sorority, find they all *were* from such a financial group and then infer that the sorority itself was financially sound. That would be a composition, inferring that the whole (the house) shared the parts' (members) property (when, in fact, the institution's financial standing is dependent more upon how reliably its bills are paid thanupon the reserve wealth of its members).

You are now prepared to identify and analyze the fallacies of ambiguity. The same cautions, about repeating the argument and about stating a definition, apply here as they did in the fallacies of relevance.

I   (2)   Composition. It may well be that every "thing" in the Universe had to be as it is for the Universe to exist. In that event, relative to the existence of the Universe, every part of it is essential. But there may also be infinitely many possible Universes and the one that we happen to have may have been arrived at purely by chance.

(6) Composition. It would be possible that the individual "happinesses" stood in direct opposition to each other and to the general good. For example, if eating-all-you-wanted-whenever-you-wanted-to were the individual happiness for each member of humanity, then the attempt of all to be happy would outstrip food supplied and make us all miserable.

II (2) Composition. Part of the difficulty here comes from Pascal's use of the word "affinity." Today we tend to use it to mean something like "attraction" as in "he had an affinity for trouble." Pascal's uses here, however, are more like "kin ship." And, as our knowledge of tadpoles and frogs or caterpillars and butterflies indicates, resemblance in one area does not require resemblance in others.

(6) Accent. Emphasis here is put upon the necessity of paying more to get people to do dirty or dangerous work. However, the conclusion is stated in terms of what **ought** to be. If you had had free choice of all the fallacies, you might quite reasonably have argued that this was an ignoratio elenchi.

(11) This is a reasonable argument. If *understanding* is the crucial difference between man and the beasts, it is of importance, for example, in arguments about abortion and mercy killing. Thus, it ought to be worth our efforts to try to understand *understanding*.

Perhaps the single most important thing to remember in all this analysis of informal fallacies is that there is **not** a necessary relationship between truth and fallaciousness. The fact that an argument does **not** mean that its conclusion is false, All that you prove about the conclusion of a fallacious argument is that the information offered as premises for its support is insufficient to support it. Don't forget that if you were to infer that a statement was false because it was the conclusion of a fallacious argument, you would be guilty of an *ad ignorantiam* fallacy yourself.

If you can find a copy of Max Shulman's book *The Many Loves of Dobie Gillis*, you will find it both profitable and fun to read the chapter entitled "Love is a Fallacy." In it you will have a humorous review of several of the fallacies and will see the pitfalls in the unthinking application of what you have learned in this chapter. In particular you will see how Dobie, who supposes himself to be a proficient logician, lapses into fallacious reasoning when pressed emotionally. You might want to pause a moment yourself before you condemn someone for the fallaciousness of their reasoning, remembering Dobie.

3.4 Avoiding Fallacies

The only thing left for you to do is to try to work exercises where you don't already know whether they are fallacies of relevance or of ambiguity. The problems following 3.4 are of that sort. Try them and check your results here and in *ITL*. Remember that in **analyzing** an argument it is not your business to **argue** with it. You may disagree with its premises, but should give the author/speaker the benefit of the doubt. If you want to claim an argument is fallacious, you want to be able to say "This one wouldn't work even if its premises were true."

(2) False Cause. Without any information about the real estate markets, appropriateness of asking price and other relevant conditions it is hard to identify any causal relationship between the configuration of the stars and planets and the sale of Stine's property. The time sequence is interesting, but, without information about the causal mechanism modern science remains agnostic.

(6) *Petitio Principii* (Begging the question). Premiss (justice can be achieved only by ... order) is basically the conclusion (justice finds order indispensable).

(11) False Cause (or perhaps ignoratio elenchi or non sequitur). As it stands the argument seems to suggest the fact that men marry younger women cause men not to marry until they are out of their teens. A reasonable question is, since there are eight teenage years, what is the causal mechanism? Looking at the argument in another light it may be that there are good reasons for the conclusion, they're just left out here -- men's traditional responsibility for financial support of the family, social prohibitions against "child marriage," and the like.

(16) Division (or non sequitur or even a sort of "value-by-association"). Begin by granting that religion is crucially important and that mysticism touches all religion. The important question is what sort of contact that is. One might also argue that greed also touches religion with alarming regularity, or that loud voices are often associated with religion, too. These do not prove that greed and loud voices are pivotal elements in human history. If mysticism is a part of religion, then may be a minor and/or atypical element.

(21) Composition. Broad is treating the general happiness as if it were somehow additive, the sum of the individual happinesses. Since happiness is such an imprecise clarification of this problem), there is little possibility that one could quantify the "average total happiness" of all the individuals, let alone sum them. It is also likely that individual is significantly a product of some general social happiness. You could also see this as an equivocation on the phrase "total happiness of the community." In the argument for unlimited reproduction (which Broad opposes) the phrase means something like *the summation of the individual happinesses*, while in his assertion that such social growth is bad he is reading the phrase in the sense of general, communal, corporate happiness.

SUMMARY CHAPTER THREE

I.   There are fallacious reasoning patterns which tend to distract us from the parts of arguments that ought to be most significant.

   A. Appeal to Ignorance (*Argumentum Ad Ignorantiam*) tries to draw conclusions without evidence.

   B. Appeal to Inappropriate Authority (*Argumentum Ad Verecundiam*) tries to use as authority those who are not authorities **in this area**.

   C. Complex question derives its conclusion by smuggling the real issue in as a presupposition of an, apparently, innocent question.

   D. *Argumentum Ad Hominen* (abusive) distracts by attacking the opponent rather than his/her argument.

   E. *Argumentum Ad Hominen* (circumstantial) points to special circumstances surrounding an arguer to shift attention to her/him instead of her/his argument.

   F. Accident applies general principles in cases where special circumstances render them inapplicable.

   G. Converse Accident seeks a general conclusion from evidence which is not known to be representative.

   H. False cause sees causal links where, at best, there are only simultaneous or sequential occurrences.

   I. Begging the question (or *Petitio Principii*) assumes the conclusion as a premiss.

   J. *Argumentum Ad Misericordiam* distracts you from the argument to someone's sad plight.

   K. *Argumentum Ad Baculum* substitutes overt or covert threats for reasons.

   L. *Ignoratio Elenchi* infers a conclusion from evidence which is logically irrelevant.

II.   Improperly used grammar and reference can result in misunderstanding (or mis-leading) inferences.

 A. Equivocation occurs when words or phrases are treated as if they meant the same thing when, in fact, they do not.

 B. Amphibolous arguments occur when the grammar is used in a sufficiently loose or incorrect manner to result in multiple or erroneous interpretations of what is said.

 C. If the intent of an argument or a statement is altered by shifting the emphasis within it, then a fallacy of accent has occurred.

 D. Composition results from inferring that some whole (or composite) has the same properties as do its elements.

 E. Division results from inferring that the individual elements of a composite whole have the same properties as the whole itself.

III.   The distinction drawn in identifying the various kinds of fallacious argument all have imprecise (or fuzzy) edges: depending upon how you read an argument, you may reasonably attribute several different fallacious characters to it.

Chapter Four
Definition

Most of us tend to think of definitions as the strings of words that we can look up in a dictionary that explain, clarify or describe how and when we ought to use some specific word. If you looked in a dictionary, you would likely find that there are several definitions of *definition*: the meaning or essence of a word or phrase, the degree of clarity of something, and the power of determining. Viewed in the last way, definition is an activity, something that people **do**. Possible synonyms of the word *definition* include meaning, clarification, denotation, explanation, and translation. In general, Copi and Cohen use the term in the first sense listed above.

4.1   Disputes, Verbal Disputes and Definitions

You should recall Copi and Cohen's discussion of agreement and disagreement in belief and attitude. In chapter one his analysis of actual and verbal disputes is a quite straightforward way of uniting that discussion with the question of ambiguity in definitions. They point out that, in this area, they are not discussing the obvious case of simple attitude-disagreement. Rather, they divide the question of possible verbal dispute into three realms: real differences, verbal differences, and real differences that appear to be only verbal. It may seem to you that there ought to be a fourth area, that is, verbal differences that appear to be real (to "round out" the combinations). The reason that it is not included is that such a group IS what is meant by merely verbal differences; they would not be significant unless they gave the impression of being real.

In the case that two people genuinely differ about the facts, whether those facts be things, words, or whatever, there is a real difference. If we disagree about who won last year's Super Bowl, or about the spelling of the word "premiss" (or, as some would have it, "premise"), or even the attitude of the person-in-the-street toward a full-blown free market economy, then our differences can be resolved by the appropriate research into the facts. In the first case, we'll go to an NFL record book (or some other appropriate reference tool); in the second, we would consult dictionaries, logicians and etymologists; in the last, we would need to see if such a survey had been done recently and if so consult it and if not do it ourselves. In any event, in each case our resolution would be made by checking out the facts. We might be left with a further difference in belief about the reliability of the consulted source, but, insofar as we could get "the facts," we would no longer disagree.

If our dispute were strictly verbal, then it would have to hinge upon the occurrence of some ambiguous term in the discussion. There is a puzzle often given astronomy students after they have, they believe, come to know the parts of our solar system. It asks: What planet is closest to Pluto (the outermost in the Solar System)? The answer is not, as we expect, Neptune (the next-outermost) but Mercury (the innermost). When the answer in explained, it seems that it is based upon the fact that Pluto's "year" is almost 250 of our Earth-years, Neptune's is almost 165 and Mercury's is 88 days. This means that, if you *average* the distance between the planets when they are closest and farthest from each other, then the average distance between Pluto and Neptune is about 4.5 billion miles while the average distance between Pluto and Mercury is about 3.6 billion miles. In this case the surprise occurred because the idea of being "closest to" was ambiguous. There is no real disagreement about the facts: clearly, when their orbits are properly aligned, the planet that *passes closest to Pluto* is Neptune (in fact Pluto's orbit swoops inside Neptune's on rare and brief occasions); while the planet *whose average distance to Pluto is smallest* is obviously Mercury.

The third sort of disagreement that Copi and Cohen describe involves a double problem: an apparently verbal disagreement and a genuine disagreement in fact or attitude. You may recall how some of the fallacies (*ad misericordiam*, for example) concealed the facts of an argument behind a mask of emotion. Well, the case of apparent verbal dispute does the same sort of thing. The difference here is that what might look like only a verbal problem is an indicator of a far more fundamental opposition. Think, for a minute, of the disputes you hear about **practical politics**. One person using the term will point to all the underhanded deals she has ever heard that politicians employ while another will discuss the "realities of cooperation" necessary to let the government function. To a casual eavesdropper it sounds as if their problem involves using the term 'practical politics' differently. But, if you get them to use it in a single fashion (whether it be the first's or the second's), it seems certain that they will still find themselves completely at odds. Whatever you choose to name the actions of trading votes and influence in the interest of advancing your own political agenda, the first person will believe that such actions are morally indefensible, while the other will accept them as unpleasant but acceptable. Their difference *appeared* to be one of definition but, in fact, was one of moral stance.

4.2   Kinds of Definition and the Resolution of Disputes

In many ways the simplest reason to use definition is to add to your vocabulary. There are many ways to make such additions, but not all are reliable. Persons who read a great deal tend to add to their vocabulary by reading unfamiliar words and figuring out from the context what the word must have meant. I recall having occasionally read of persons becoming *livid* with rage. Although I have never read a definition of "livid," I inferred, since all the people whom I had seen being enraged got red in the face, that "livid" must mean "red in the face." Imagine my surprise when I took the time to check a dictionary and found the definition was either "discolored, as by a bruise," or "ashen, pallid, as in livid with rage." Had I first checked the dictionary, I would have avoided years of misconception.

To further the discussion of definitions, Copi and Cohen introduce two "technical terms" of logic: *definiens* and *definiendum*. There is a mnemonic (memory device--like "I before E except after C") which defines: If you were "dumb" (meaning not very bright rather than mute), then you'd have to ask to have people define things for you frequently; thus, the definien**dum** is the thing to be defined. One statement of a definiendum and a definiens would be:

A *circle* [definiendum] is *a plane closed curve all of whose points are equidistant from the same point* [definiens].

Another device, which some logic teachers use, is the use of "=df" as a sign to indicate the occurrence of a definition. It is particularly useful in the case of what he calls a **stipulative definition**. Thus, if a situation came about in which I wished to introduce a new term (or specify some new use for an old term), I might use this symbol to show that I did not consider this definition to be an area for discussion, that I was asserting that this was how it was to be used. I might, for example, invent a machine that served a function similar to that of a helicopter, but did so by using bird-like wings. In essence I would have made a passenger-carrying humming-bird. Now, the word "helicopter" comes from two Greek words (*heliko* and *pteron*) meaning "spiral" and "wing." I might reason (as a matter of fact, several science-fiction authors actually have done so) that, since my machine's motion imitates a bird rather than a pinwheel, I ought to replace *heliko* with *ornitho-* (meaning "bird") thus calling the machine an ***ornithopter***. If I adopted the '=df' sign, then my stipulative definition would be

> Ornithopter =df A heavier-than-air flying machine capable of flight in any direction and of hovering by the use of wings which imitate in form and function those of a bird (particularly those of a hummingbird).

Once such a stipulative definition is made, ethics of the use of terminology ought to compel everyone to use the term in the way stipulated (or at least to acknowledge deviation from that use).

If you recall the example of equivocation from chapter 3 (p. 41 above) you should remember how definitions were used to clarify a misunderstanding. The core of the equivocal argument had been:

All laws which have undesirable social effects ought to be repealed.
Einstein's laws say we can't get to the stars and that has such effects.
Thus, Einstein's laws should be repealed.

The explanation of why this was considered to be a fallacy of equivocation involved defining the two senses of "law." The first meant "product of the legislative process" while the other meant "observed (or hypothesized) physical regularity."

A closely related function of definition is to reduce vagueness. In fact, some lists of synonyms will give "uncertain" both as a synonym of "vague" and of "ambiguous." Copi and Cohen, however, do not treat the latter terms as synonymous. Their position is that a term is ambiguous when it has two (or more) clear meanings which can, in the right circumstances, be confused. A term is vague insofar as it is fuzzy or indefinite in meaning. In the example of equivocation from chapter 3, the term "law" is, in *ITL*'s sense, ambiguous: it has two distinct, easily separable meanings. Similarly, the word "right" can be ambiguous: one use meaning "correct or appropriate" while another might be "that which is due one by law, tradition or nature."

When a word or phrase has multiple meanings, one which in an appropriate context could be confused, then definition has great value. If you carefully define terms as you use them, then you significantly reduce the chance of an equivocation occurring.

A type of definition that strongly resembles the stipulative one is **lexical definition**. It is the vocabulary-building form which is used to report (and sometimes clarify) a definition which has already been stipulated, either by common usage or by some authority. Copi and Cohen discuss such definitions as being true or false, but it might really be easier not to make them appear quite so clear-cut. Perhaps a preferable way to characterize such lexical definitions would be on a broadly divisible "good" to "bad" scale. That would mean that the definition "A chair is a thing for one person to sit upon" could be discussed as being clearerthan "A chair is something to sit on" but worse than "A chair is a (usually four-) legged artifact (usually) with a back and (usually) designed to have the feet of its single occupant reach the floor." Note that in this case the presence of the "(usually)'s" indicated that there is some variability in what we will accept as an example of a chair.

If you think of *the act of defining* as the source of definitions, then Copi and Cohen's discussion of the purposes of definition becomes an analysis of **why** we do what we do when we define. If you ask a surgeon **why** he cuts open people's bodies, he will answer by telling you the purpose of the surgery. If you ask a carpenter **why** she puts foam padding around a door, she will answer by telling you the purpose of weatherstripping. Similarly, if you ask someone **why** he/she is defining a word, he/she will tell you the purpose of the definition.

An old joke runs: "You ought to just sit down and read 20 pages of the dictionary every night; it has a wonderful vocabulary, although the plot is awfully thin." As a matter of fact, there are teachers who do recommend doing almost that. They suggest that you try consciously to add 10 (or 20 or some other magic number) new words to your vocabulary daily. Usually their technique is to have you note unfamiliar words that you encounter in ordinary communication, but, if you don't find the required number that way, you are usually told to thumb through a dictionary until you find enough new words to fill your quota. It's hard to tell whether this activity is worthwhile in any abstract sense, but it probably does make crossword puzzles easier.

In any event, the definiens in a lexical definition is a report of the generally-accepted meaning (or meanings) of the definiendum.

When the definiendum is vague, rather than ambiguous, you need to use a **precising definition**. It seems to lie somewhere between the stipulative and lexical types. It involves an already-accepted term as definiendum (like the lexical type), but it specifies more explicit detail than was understood by the earlier use of that term (somewhat like the stipulative type). The need to become more precise may result from changing factual circumstances, changing attitudes or mere curiosity.

But equivocal terms like *right* can also be vague. Social niceties suggest that it is sometimes **right** to lie (as to avoid needlessly hurting another's feelings), but persons of good will can (and do) debate endlessly about the correctness of applying this exemption from honesty. And, unless some authority is recognized as being capable of (or responsible for) defining the term *right*, we will have to struggle along with our intuitions about what is **right** and what is not.

The *that-which-is-due* sense of "right" is also vague. During and after the war in Vietnam the entire debate about the government's right to obtain and maintain records of the domestic political activity of citizens vs. the citizen's right to privacy and freedom from governmental meddling hinged upon the vagueness both of those rights and of the language in which we discuss them. What was finally required to clear up that vagueness was a series of Supreme Court decisions which spelled out the nature and extent of the rights both of the government, the states, organizations and of the individual. These decisions functioned as at least partial definitions of the terms "privacy," "public figures," "public responsibility" and "national interest." And, until another Court redefines those terms, they have the force of law.

Thus, in the case of vague terminology, definition may serve to eliminate the vagueness. One needs to recall, however, that for vagueness to be so eliminated there needs to be some authoritative structure that puts a seal of approval upon such clarifying definitions.

It seems likely that as long as we have had language we have had some word for death. If you look at any standard dictionary you will find a lexical definition much like: *the act of dying, termination, the cessation of life, the final stoppage of all vital functions*. And, for centuries, this surely seemed adequate. However, with the development of modern medical technology, we have come to see such as too vague. One can hook a drowning victim to a respirator and that person's chest will continue to rise and fall as long as the machine pumps. The function is just like pushing air into and out of a balloon. Traditionally, a person's chest rising and falling would be taken as a vital sign, but this seems inadequate in the case of respirator-use. And, of course, artificial hearts, kidneys, and the like make the "vital signs" test seem less and less definitive. The term "death" has become vague and is in need of precising definition in order that, for example, surgeons who wish to perform transplants will have some basis for deciding when someone is dead (so that a recently-deceased person can be used as a donor to the still-living). It is just this sort of case that has led both state and federal legislators to hold lengthy hearings (consulting doctors, lawyers, philosophers, theologians, and anyone else they can think of) to try to make the definition of death substantially more precise.

Another reason one would want to offer a definition is to clarify the exact limits of usage of a term relative to some theory. Terms in science are frequently derived from our ordinary usage of a term relative to some theory. Terms in science are frequently derived from our ordinary usage. However, frequently the "scientific" use of the term becomes far more precise than was that use it had had in ordinary usage. A good example of this is the term "valid" as used by logicians. In everyday language, one would use "valid" to mean "supportable, well-grounded, or cognent." As you recall, the logician is far more specific when defining the term (see the discussion of validity in Chapter 1 of *ITL* and this *Guide*). In this way, the logician restricts the usage of the term to the area in which it serves the most significant function for his purposes.

Theoretical definitions are part and parcel of the action of theorizing. Usually, when you offer a theoretical definition, you are trying to explain or expound a theory. Theories are developed generally as a means of explaining some set of occurrences which could not previously be well-explained. In the older, Ptolemaic, Earth-centered view of the Solar System, the Earth was defined as the immovable central object in the Universe. When the newer, Copernican, sun-centered view was theorized, a new theoretical definition of "Earth" was needed. Since part of the earlier definition had been Earth's immovability, without a definition that dropped that element, anyone who supported the Copernican view could rightly have been treated as being a candidate for a padded room: Only a madperson would talk of the motion around the sun of an immovable object (the Earth). The theoretical definition, then, will likely be no more satisfactory than the theory for which it is being introduced.

The fifth purpose which Copi and Cohen suggest for definition is to persuade or to alter someone's attitude. In many ways this use of definition resembles the ad populum fallacy. It usually involves playing upon the emotions of the reader or listener. For example, in the very emotional area of the discussion of abortion those who believe in the so-called "right-to-choice" might be found defining "abortion" quite differently than those who believe in the so-called "right-to-life." [As another matter of definition, it is interesting, also, to ponder the definitions of *life* and *choice* that each group accepts. Surely neither group would claim to be **anti-life** or **anti-choice** in general.] Respective definitions might look like:

> Abortion : The removal of parasitic tissue from the uterine wall of the human female.
>
> Abortion : The murder of an innocent child for the selfish convenience of his/her mother.

It would be a rare person who could accept the first definition as correct and still say they opposed abortion (for wouldn't that entail that it would be equally wrong to remove leeches, tapeworms, and harmful bacteria?). Similarly one would question the sanity of anyone who agreed with the second version and still claimed to favor abortion (for wouldn't that suggest that, if you had trouble finding a babysitter, then it would be ok to strangle your children instead?). Thus, you see, in some cases three-quarters of the battle is getting someone to accept your definition.

Persuasive definitions are just what their name implies--definitions whose purpose is more to bring others to accept your point of view than it is to inform. Using the definitions of "abortion," show how one might be persuaded by definition. After looking for examples of the five sorts of definitions, as assigned in part I (after 4.2 in *ITL*), try also the exercises in part II.

(2)   Here there is a genuine dispute between Daye and Knight. Daye's criterion for relevance is dealing with "eternally recurring problems," while Knight's is having something to "say about the pressing and immediate issues of our time." Since Knight's focus is upon what is unique to our time and Daye's is upon what is not unique to our time, they have a genuine dispute.

(6)   In this case Daye and Knight clearly have different attitudes toward Ann. There is used, however, an ambiguous use of the phrase "excellent student." By it Daye means a lively, interested, questioning student, while Knight means someone who completes assignments promptly.

(11)   This is a verbal dispute. Reasonable walking speed is between two and four miles per hour; that would put Helen's house between four and eight miles away by Daye's calculation. But one could drive four miles in ten minutes at 24 mph and eight at 48 mph, thus Knight's assertions are also reasonable. Once they have compared modes of travel, they can probably agree that Helen lives a-long-way-by-foot but not-too-long-by-car.

(16)   This is verbal in a way quite like the Pluto/Neptune/Mercury problem in the discussion above (p. 44). Daye's interpretation of the phrase "The average intelligence of college freshmen" is that, if one took the average intelligence of all col lege graduates and compared that with the average intelligence of all entering college freshmen, the graduate average would be higher than the freshman average. Knight's is that, if you compared the intelligence of each individual who graduated with *that same individual's* intelligence as a freshman, there would be no difference. What has occurred, in effect, is a fallacy of division.

4.3   Denotation (Extension) and Connotation (Intension)

There are two basic ways in which you can work out the meaning of a term: (1) list the things to which you would apply it (or the occasions on which you would use it), and (2) list the sort of things you could claim to know about an object (or occasion) to which the term was applied. Thus, if you listed *Chariots of the Gods*, *Secret Forces of the Pyramids*, *The Mystery of Atlantis*, and *Our Mysterious Spaceship Moon* as the things to which you wanted to apply a single term I would guess that the term you had in mind was something like "pseudoscientific books." If this were the term you were trying to clarify by your list, then what you did was list part of the **extension**, or **denotation**. The problem, of course, with using denotation as a method of defining is that the lists tend to be both too long and not unique. In the case suggested above, this surely is not a complete list of such books. In fact there have been times in the last few years that books of this sort seem to be being published faster than they can be listed. But it is also the case that the same four titles could have been used as samples of books first published in paperback, or even copyrighted titles for movies. Thus, you see, extensions or denotative definitions, although occasionally helpful, are usually not precise enough to make them reliable.

It would be easier, if you wanted to define what you meant by the term "pseudoscientific books," to list the characteristics you saw as common to such publications. You might include unsupported hypotheses, questionable interpretations of data, avoidance of the simplest explanations, the introduction of speculations which will later be treated as if they were proven facts, inconsistency with currently accepted scientific theory, and so on. Such a listing of the properties or characteristics of the things (or occasions) to which a term is applied is usually called the **intension**, or **connotation**, of the term. One of the most valuable assets of defining by intension is that when you encounter a new object or occasion you are in a good position to see if it "fits" the definition--if it has the properties on the connotative list then it does, if not then it doesn't. It is also convenient that, as you learn more and more about the things to which you apply your term, you can add to the list of properties which are part of the term's connotation. And, if you find that some groups of properties adequately separate off identifiable sub-groups of the original extension of your term, then you are able to identify the connotation of the new sub-groups in contrast to the original. An example of this kind of increasing specification might occur as you learned more and more about cooking. You might, early on, encounter the term "thickening." The first way you would probably be introduced to what a thickening is would be by being given examples of thickenings (like flour and cornstarch). This is, of course, extensional. In time, however, you would learn that there are many more things that serve this function. This ought to lead you to identify the intension of the term. Particularly if you are a novice cook, and adequate intensional definition will be "having the property of making a liquid more dense or viscous (i.e., thicker)." As you become more skilled, however, you learn that cornstarch and flour, when added to cheese liquids, tend to cause a grainy texture, but that potato starch does not. Further you may find that flour, corn- and potato starch, and other fairly common thickenings make the liquids into which they are stirred become rather cloudy, while arrowroot starch results in a clearer, more glistening liquid. However, you will also learn that arrowroot loses its thickening property if the liquid into which it is stirred is then boiled. With all this information you are in a position to identify the intensions of several kinds of thickening, all of which share the original intension, but which do not share simple intension suggested for "thickening" are part of the extension of the term. And, as the intension is increased, for example by adding "results in a clear liquid," the extension (in this case) decreases. This happens unless the addition to the intension is in a sense parallel to the already given intension. In the case, for example, of "clear" thickenings the further addition of "cannot be boiled without losing its thickening property" would, obviously, entail an increased intension, but, since arrowroot was already identified as the "clear" thickening, would not reduce the extension. You'd still be talking about arrowroot.

It is also important to remember that terms can have intensions without having extensions. Almost any schoolchild can give you a very detailed intensional description of Superman--faster than a speeding bullet, more powerful than a locomotive, able to leap high buildings at a single bound, vulnerable only to kryptonite in its various forms and magic, champion of truth, justice and the American Way, and so on. Unfortunately, except for orthopedists in hospital emergency rooms, children sometimes do not realize that being able to so fully characterize Superman does not mean that there is anyone who possesses those qualities. That is why numerous children each year break various assorted bones trying to fly like Superman. It makes perfect sense, at least to those of us familiar with the Superman myth, to discuss his assorted powers in detail, but expressing a desire to meet him (or, worse, claiming to have already done so) would suggest a need for intense psychiatric care.

You ought, now, to try the problems following 4.3 and to check your results of part I in *ITL* and here.

(2)   Beverage, alcoholic beverage, wine, white wine, fine white wine, champagne. Except for certain American versions, the name "Champagne" is restricted to the carbonated white wine that is naturally fermented and carbonated in the Champagne region of France. Each term in the list reduces the kinds of liquids which might be included by its predecessor in the list. Thus, "alcoholic beverage" eliminates milk which is a beverage, "wine" eliminates beer which is an alcoholic beverage, "white wine" eliminates claret which is a wine, fine white wine eliminates most restaurant house wines, and "champagne" eliminates even Savignon Blanc.

4.4   Extension, and Denotative Definition

As Copi and Cohen say, there is a fundamental connection between denotative definitions and the extensions of the terms define. A term's extension is the **complete list** of the items, cases and so forth to which you could correctly apply the term. That means that the denotative definition of a term is the statement of its extension. If you define denotatively, then you list everything to which the term applies.

This doesn't look as if there would be any significant problem, but there are a few quirks present. First, it is possible for two terms to have the same extention without "meaning" the same thing. Imagine for example, that Gene Roddenberry (the developer of *Star Trek*) had commisioned small statuettes in the form of the Enterprise, cast in silver, for all the members of the original cast of the show. Assume further that the mold was destroyed after the casting, so that those originally cast were the **only** ones made and that no one had disposed of her/his statuette. In such a case you could easily specify the extension of the term *original cast member of the origina Star Trek* -- William Shatner, Leonard Nimoy, George Takei, et al. -- and could also specify the extension of the term *owner of the classic casting of the Enterprise* by the same group of individuals. Because the situation was set up as it was, the extension of both terms must be exactly the same (at least for now), but there certainly seems no way that the two terms "mean" the same thing.

It is also the case that some terms have no extension at all. All you have to do is look at the entire beastiary of mythology to see that. The list of individuals who are centaurs, sphinxes, griffins and the like is short; in fact it is empty. That doesn't slow us down in talking about such beasts, even disputing whether representations in art are of, say, a hippogriff rather than a griffin. [Both have the forepart of an eagle: the former the hindpart of a horse and the latter the hindpart of a lion.] Thus it is evident that these terms have meaning, are capable of being defined, but still have no extension.

This means that attempts at denotative definition are always "partial." Since virtually everything we run into in the world can be seen as an example of many different classifications, these partial enumerations (which identify individual by individual) always seem to be subject to multiple interpretation (as in the *Star Trek* example just described. Sometimes this sort of confusion can be minimized by listing groups of things instead of individuals, as in denotatively defining the known universe by listing the known galaxies. Unless, however, each of those groups is easily denotatively defined, the problem has just been moved back a step. In the case of the supposed definition of the known universe, for all practical purposes, it is just as difficult to enumerate either the stars in the known galaxies.

Another attempt to denotatively define is called an **ostensive definition**. [The word 'ostensive' comes from the same root as 'ostentatious,'-- meaning showy, flamboyant or the like.] To define something ostensively is just to "point at" one or more appropriate uses of that term. Clearly this, as a kind of denotative definition, has the same problems as any such definition. In fact it has those and more. In H. Beam Piper's novella "Omnilingual" he has archeologists on Mars trying to figure out the language of the long-dead Martians. Their problem is not a lack of material, but too much of it -- they have discovered an entire library. Some amateurs in the group find captioned pictures and believe that they have found a Rosetta Stone [the object that led to the translation of Egyptian hieroglyphics] for Martian. Piper points out, however, that picture titles are not reliable for translation. His characters refer to a picture of a white-bearded man chopping wood and ask whether anyone would think to translate its title as "Napoleon III in exile." Or think about the famous painting known as "Whistler's Mother." Would you, upon seeing it, think of translating its title as "Study in Gray and Black?" [That is its correct name.]

The point that Copi and Cohen are making is that listing individuals (or groups) as a method of definition is not likely to be satisfactory. There must be more to defining than that. To make this need clearer, you should work the problems after 4.4.

70.290-04
0089

I (2)   Boxer: Muhammad Ali, Sugar Ray Leonard, Floyd Patterson.

(6)   Rose, Daisy, Iris.

II (2)   Former Olympic gold medal winner.

(6)   Girls' names not in wide use today.

4.5 Intension, and Connotative Definition

You may find the word **intension** a bit strange. If so it is probably because you are confusing it with its homonym (same sounding word) **intention**. **Intention** means, roughly, *purpose, goal*, or *end*; 'intension' means *the sum total of the properties shared by all and only things identified by a specific term*. For philosophers, the term **connotation** is usually used as if it were synonymous with **intension**. Some confusion may occur, however, because **connotation** is also used, sometimes, to mean *the total significance of a term*. In that usage, the term includes not only the intensional meaning but also the emotive associations. In fact there are times when the term 'connotation' is used to mean the emotional intent alone.

Even restricting 'connotation' to its strict sense (of all and only the shared characteristics of individuals identified by the term), Copi and Cohen point out that there are at least three ways in which you might understand the term: subjectively, objectively or conventionally.

The subjective connotation of a term is relative to some individual's understanding of it at some specific time. If I had been raised on a limited diet of John Wayne war and western movies, I might have come to believe that courage had as a part of its connotation **the confronting of physical danger**. As I grew up I might, say, read John F. Kennedy's *Profiles in Courage* and see examples of great courage where the danger faces was political, social, or the like. At that point my connotative associations with the word 'courage' would have changed. Obviously, if an individual's connotation of a term can change with time and circumstances, then it is likely that different people have different connotations.

In an attempt to avoid sliding into some sort of relativism of connotation, we might seek some objective connotation. That would include all of the properties *actually* shared by things to which the term was correctly applied. Unfortunately, that quickly is seen as one of those great-in-theory-but-impossible-in-practice ideas. We are not all-knowing, and there are many words we use quite satisfactorily without any idea of all of the actual attributes implied by the term. Early doctors, for example, were quite skilled at diagnosing many diseases. Their failure to know anything about bacteria, viruses and other disease-causes did not in any significant way prevent them from accurately identifying (and differentiating) substantial numbers of illnesses (or cures, for that matter). [For example, the term 'Limey' was applied to English sailors, and later all Englishmen, because their doctors correctly diagnosed scurvy -- caused by inadequate vitamin C in the diet -- and prescribed eating limes (which "kept" well) as a preventative. And the doctors did this long before medical science knew either of vitamins or of deficiency diseases at all.]

Well, if subjective connotation is too unreliable (being changeable) and objective connotation is too demanding (requiring omniscience), then what should we use? Copi and Cohen's solution is conventional connotation. All that it requires is that we have arrived at some agreement about the attributes implied by use of a term. Thus, if society agrees, for example, to use the term **turquoise** to refer to stones having a specific range of blue-green hues and a certain chemical composition, then stone, specific chemical composition, and determinate color-range make up the conventional connotation of the term 'turquoise.'

From a practical point of view, the arriving at a conventional connotation is what the act of defining is all about. But, how, you may wonder, do we do that *arriving at*? Several ways are possible. The simplest way to define is to offer a synonym. You may have noticed the many ads recently for pocket-calculator-sized electronic "dictionaries." When you "punch in" a word to be defined, most generally they offer a string of synonyms rather than the sort of definition you would find in a large dictionary. For example, when you look for a definition of *big*, you will get 'large or important.' [If you think back to the logical fallacy of *petitio principii*, you will realize that, in a sense, dictionaries and thesauruses resemble that fallacy: they are gigantic circular definitions.]

Another, perhaps more important, problem with using synonyms as a means of defining happens occurs when the term to be defined really doesn't have a precise synonym. This occurs frequently in areas where one wants precising or theoretical definitions. Synonyms that means something *similar to* the term in question **add to** the confusion rather than clarify.

Philosophers and scientists have introduced another kind of definition to try to clear up confusion -- the **operational definition**. The operational definition, for example, of 32° Fahrenheit (or 0° Celsius) might be *the reading one gets on a standard thermometer when it is placed in water that is at water's freezing point*. In such a case, the definition amounts to the substitution of an action to take for the term to be defined.

One question that many people consider, given the radical increase in the capacity of modern computers, is whether or not a computer can think. One reasonable response is to ask for a definition of the word 'think.' After examining the several synonyms for 'think,' one realizes that all those words have the same sort of ambiguity as 'think.' In such circumstances, an operational definition may serve well to clarify the original term. If you can specify what sort of behavior a being (or computer) has to exhibit in some well-understood circumstances, then you have, in effect, defined what it means to think.

There are, however, problems with ostensive definitions. We see this most frequently when we try to explain the meanings of words to children by pointing. Children, particularly, are inclined to take things quite literally. When a child asks, "What is the Moon?" and I reply "That is the Moon" and point skyward, she is just as likely to believe that my outstretched finger or the television antenna which she sees beyond it (from her perspective) is the "Moon" to which I referred.

In discussing connotative definition, Copi and Cohen first introduce the idea of definition by synonym. As they suggest, this is particularly useful for lexical, stipulatiive or (perhaps) persuasive definitions, but not for precising or theoretical ones. One of its commonest uses is in trying to develop vocabulary in a second language. In this case, rather than a lengthy denotative or connotative definition, all that most of us require is identification of the word in our native language that "means the same" as the foreign one.

Whether across languages or within them, however, this approach is not altogether reliable. Some words do not have exact synonyms (or, in some cases, any at all). The German words *essen* and *fressen* may both be rendered in English as *eat*. However, the former is used in German to refer to the eating done by people and the latter that is done by animals. Thus, to use them interchangeably (as a native English-speaker might do when venturing into German) could be a terrible social blunder. Similarly, in referring to an apple which was of ideal proportion but was 20% larger than the average apple, few would hestitate to call it a very big apple. In the case, however, of a woman who was ideally proportioned but stood six feet, six inches tall, most of us would feel some reluctance to call her a very big woman. The reticence would probably stem from the fact that the term "big" when applied particularly to women tends to carry an overtone of meaning overweight. And in a third case, where we encountered a man who stood over seven feet tall but was again ideally proportioned, we would again be reluctant to call him a very big man, but for different reasons. The phrase "big man" has become colloquial for a man of importance, regardless of his size physically. It is therefore clear that the use of synonyms as a method of defining is useful only as a first approximation of meaning and ought to be used with caution.

As Copi and Cohen suggest, the function and application of operational definitions is fit material for another book (or two or more). For a fuller understanding of operational definitions, you might find it interesting to search out a course in the philosophy of science.

But there are, unfortunately, cases where neither the statement of a synonym nor the laying out of an operational is satisfactory. If that happens, then one may move to what is called *definition per genus et differentiam*. This means of defining is by grouping things into classes, subclasses, and so on. This is usually referred to as species/genus classification. The third century Neoplatonic philosopher Porphyry is credited with originating the diagraming of such relationships and with noticing that they somewhat resemble trees, hence their commonly being called the Trees of Porphyry. An example of such a tree (with many branches missing) is below:

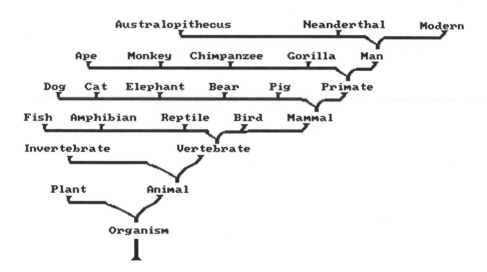

Of course, a term must have some complexity to its connotation or this approach will not work. "Organism" is the base of this tree, but could be a branch relative to inanimate matter. Those things that rest as ultimate bases, however, would not be definable by this technique because they could not be branches on any more general "tree." Such ultimate bases are so rare that we do not need to worry greatly about their occurring as limitations for this method.

Below are answers which you may wish to compare with your own after you have done the exercises following 4.5.

I (2) Buffoon: clown (although "buffoon" has a somewhat more negative connotation).

(6) Feast: banquet (although "feast" sometimes carries the additional connotation of celebrating some specific occasion, as in "a harvest feast").

(11) Kine: cattle (although "kine" is generally considered old-fashioned, romantic or Biblical).

(16)   Panacea: cure-all (although "panacea" frequently is taken to have the connotation of not being able to bring about what is claimed).

II (2)   Banquet -- 4. meal -- 5. very large

(6)   Foal   -- 2. horse -- 7. young

(11)   Girl   -- 8. woman -- 7. young

(16)   Mother -- 5. parent - 1. female Note here that you could have selected 8. woman from the first column, but then would have found nothing in the second column to characterize "son" fully.

(21)   Son   -- 1. offspring - 2. male Note that here, too, you could have selected a different first column term "man" but they would have had no choice in the second column to characterize "son" fully.

4.6   Rules for Definition by Genus and Difference

Language "works" as a way to communicate because, consciously or not, we all agree to use each work in the same way. In general we simply reject the approach of the caterpillar in *Alice in Wonderland* when he tells Alice that words mean whatever he wants them to mean at the moment. In defining terms, then, we have an obligation to include in the definition those characteristics which native speakers of the language would usually agree are the essential, important, or defining properties of things to which the definition is usually applied. Thus the first rule for definition by genus and difference is

> **Rule 1:**   *A definition of a term ought to include all the properties normally attributed to things to which that term is usually applied by persons familiar with the term.*

Note, please, that this formulation of the definition is not the one given in *ITL*. Since you are fully capable of reading the rule as it is stated there, it seems more useful to have an alternative way of stating it (and the other four, too) here.

There is an old joke about the man who gets onto a race track by mistake while trying to drive downtown. When his wife suggests that they pull off the track and try to find their way back to the road, he refuses, saying "How can you ask me to do that when I'm making such terrific time?" He fails to see that making great time but going nowhere is of questionable value. You should recall the Petitio Principii fallacy and all of the reasons that it was undesirable. For the same sorts of reasons, a definition which uses a synonym or another form of the term to be defined in the definiens will not take you far in understanding the definiendum.

> **Rule 2:**   *A definition of a term ought not include the term being defined (in any form) or any synonym or antonym of it.*

Since one of the primary purposes of defining terms is to in crease vocabulary, any definition which might reasonably result in misusing the term is obviously defective. Sometimes in the interest of simplicity or convenience we omit from definitions elements that ought to have been included. This can result either in the defini tion's admitting things to its extension that we would have wished to exclude or in omitting things that we would have wished to include. If you think back to Copi and Cohen's mentioning that a traditional species/genus definition of "man" is that man is a rational animal, then you will see a definition that is both too broad and too narrow. It is too broad because, if current research with dolphins, porpoises and whales proves that cetacians are thinking beings (which some researchers think likely) then such aquatic mammals must be men according to this definition. It may well be that we ought to treat them as people, but they don't seem to be men. It is too narrow because, if the natural offspring of a man and a woman--for whatever traumatic or genetic reason--is incapable of rational thought, then this definition would deny that that offspring is part of the class "man." Again, it may be well that we do not confer the same sorts of rights and responsibilities (voting, for example) on that individual, but that seems no reason to deny such an unfortunate's humanity. Caution, therefore, is necessary in formulating definitions.

Rule 3: *A definition of a term ought not exclude appropriate individuals from or include inappropriate individuals in the extension of that term.*

If you keep in mind the communication-purpose of most definitions, then you will see that it is important that the language employed in stating a definition ought to really communicate. If the words used in stating a definition are unclear to the reader or hearer, for whatever reason, then the effort expended in defining brought no benefit and may have done harm. If you are reading Hamlet's famous "To Be or Not To Be" soliloquy and encounter the term "fardels" in the question "Who would the fardels bear?" then you may seek a definition. If the one you encounter is "fardel: A sheaf of staves," then the definition may have proven worthless. Of course, if you knew that a sheaf was a bundle resembling the way grain in the fields used to be bundled and that a stave was a small strip or piece of wood, then you might have figured that a fardel was the large bundle of sticks that peasants used to gather and carry home at night to fuel their fires. Chances are you were baffled.

Similarly, the use of figurative, metaphoric, so-called poetic language is generally to be avoided in setting forth a definition. There is a delightful children's book called **Amelia Bedelia** by Peggy Parrish that every adult ought to read. It tells the story of a new maid who takes all of her instructions *very* literally: she dusts the furniture by spreading bath powder on it, she dresses the chicken by making little clothes for it, she changes the towels by cutting them into odd shapes, and so on. The humor, for adults, in the book results from our knowing what was intended by the mis-followed directions. In the case of a new (to us) term's being defined, however, the humor might not be so evident were we the ones to take metaphoric definition literally. Thus, the language of a definition ought to be as straightforward as possible.

Rule 4: *A definition of a term ought to be presented in clear, simple, understandable language.*

There is such variety in the universe that there are surely infinitely many things that any given thing is not, but only a few things that it is. If you owned a car painted the color of the sky at noon on a cloudless day in the Rocky Mountains, then there would be a very limited range of shades of blue in which your car's color would have to fall. The entire remainder of the spectrum of precision and in the interest of being able to finish the job, then, negative definitions ought to be avoided.

Rule 5: *A definition of a term ought to be presented positively whenever possible.*

The exercises at the end of Chapter 4 in *ITL* should provide you with good practice in developing and analyzing definitions. After you have worked them, you can check your answers in *ITL* and here.

II (2) This violates rule 3. It is too broad because it would allow, for instance, the conclusions drawn by a palm reader (if they happened to be correct) to be counted as knowledge. It is usually thought that knowledge must also involve some justification of the true opinion. [That might make this a breech or rule 1 also.]

(6) This violates rule 2. Since deceiving is an antonym for being honest, no real knowledge gain has occurred.

(11) This violates rules 1, 3, and 4. It omits the fact that wars must be waged by political units (countries or the like) and this makes it too broad. For it this social aspect is ignored, the compulsion of the weak by a bully would seem to count as a war. And the language is figurative, not conveying the usual violence and destruction image which we usually associate with wars.

(16) The primary problem here is the violation of rule 4, but there may be some broadness difficulty, too. Tolstoi (or Tolstoy) is not differentiating between art and the sciences or art and religion either. In the attempt to transmit his sense of awe at the endeavor of the artist, he has lapsed into poetry himself.

(21) Since Mao uses "analyzing" to define "analysis," he is violating rule 2.

III (2) This probably violates Rule 1. The traditional view of knowledge is that it, at least, includes "true belief." James' "folksy" definition ignores the fact that if one **knew** something to be false, that would entail a true belief that it was false. One could not, then, also believe (have faith) that it was true. [Unless, of course, you want to claim that James means to assert that faith is intrinsically self-contradictory.]

(6) Wilde is being metaphoric and, thus, violates rule 4. One who did not already know what a cynic was might well think that Wilde was describing a strange breed of economist.

(11) Keynes has made a very sharp turn to come back upon himself. One could have just as well said: "Slabulonics is the science which treats of the phenomena arising out of the slabulonic activities of men in society." In this case you must now find out what slabulonic activity is; in Keynes' case you need to know what economic activity is. [Slabulonic activity, incidentally, is what a teething child goes through--it's drooling.]

(16) For a philosopher writing an article in a series on the logic of science in **Popular Science Monthly**, Peirce is being very poetic. The figurative language is a clear violation of rule 4.

(21) So is a rock. The negative definition is clever but applies also to all inanimate matter. It's a clear violation of rule 5.

(26) There may be several minor problems with this, but most critical is the omission of the fact that female intuition is *supposed to be* based upon no real evidence at all. Greer is actually trying to overthrow the stereotypic view of women's reasoning process, however, and perhaps this ought to be treated as a sort of stipulative definition, or maybe a theoretical one.

SUMMARY CHAPTER FOUR

I.   Definitions have several purposes

    A. They increase vocabulary

    B. They eliminate ambiguity when terms have multiple meanings.

    C. They reduce vagueness when the application of a term is not clear.

    D. They show the place of a term within a theory.

    E. They influence attitudes.

II.   Some disputes are genuine and some are not.

    A. If a disagreement can be resolved by appealing to the facts, then it was genuine.

    B. If a disagreement can be reduced to agreement about the facts and difference about attitude toward them, then it is genuine.

    C. If a disagreement can be resolved by agreeing upon how the terms ought to be used, then it is verbal.

    D. If a disagreement about how terms ought to be used cannot be resolved, then there probably is a genuine disagreement.

III.   There are five types of definition which closely correlate with the purposes of definition.

    A. Stipulative definitions introduce new terms and state how they ought to be used.

    B. Lexical definitions state how a term is usually used.

    C. Precising definitions pinpoint how a term ought to be used, particularly within specific contexts.

    D. Theoretical definitions lay out the way in which terms are intended to be used within (usually) proposed theories.

    E. Persuasive definitions try to alter the hearer's (or listener's) point of view by altering the way key terms are understood.

IV.   There are two different kinds of meaning.

    A. Extensional meaning (or denotation) lists all the things to which a term may be correctly applied.

    B. Intensional meaning (or connotation) lists all the properties possessed by things to which a term may be correctly applied.

V.   There are several approaches to defining.

    A. Denotative definitions are usually impractical.

        1.   There is usually too little time to complete the list.

        2.   Lists of things to which one term applies are not precise enough to prevent another term from being correctly applied to them also.

    B. Ostensive definitions have the same flaws as denotative ones and are subject to ambiguous understanding too.

    C. Synonymous definitions are of variable value.

        1.   In learning a new language they are helpful.

        2.   In increasing vocabulary they are helpful.

        3.   For words without synonyms they are useless.

        4.   For words with imprecise synonyms they can be deceptive.

    D. Definition by species and genus lays out connotation nicely.

        1.   Terms which are ultimately basic cannot be defined this way.

        2.   There are five rules for defining by species and genus.

                a. Include essential elements in your definition.

                b. Don't define by using the defined term.

                c. Include and exclude all and only what you want to.

                d. Use clear, understandable language when defining.

                e. Say what things are, not what they are not.

Part Two:
Deduction

Chapter Five
Categorical Propositions

5.1   Categorical Propositions and Classes

The approach to logic developed by Aristotle was a product of his philosophical structure. He claimed that things fell into natural categories. For our purposes what he called a category we usually call a class. Whether one adopts the Aristotelian view, called realism, that such classes are natural or what philosophers call a nominalistic position that the limits of classes are just agreed upon conventionally, it is clear that a class is a clearly identifiable group of things, ideas, actions, or the like.

Given the convention that we will only examine the relationships of classes in pairs, then it turns out that there are only four ways in which two specific classes can relate to each other. Their relationship *as classes* will be extensional, that is, it will be one of inclusion or exclusion--either total or partial. If these possibilities were put in a grid form, like you used for the exercises in reasoning in chapter 1, the result would look like:

	Total	Partial
Inclusion	*All A is B*	*Some A is B*
Exclusion	*No A is B*	*Some A is not B*

Statements which relate classes (or categories) in the above ways are called **Categorical Propositions**. They are **Propositions**; that is, they are informational sentences which are either true or false, and they involve the relationship between two **Categories**. Traditionally, the property which was described above as total or partial relation has been referred to as the number (or universality and particularity) of the proposition; the property above identified as inclusion or exclusion has been called affirmation or negation. The classes identified in the grid above as "A" and "B" would traditionally have been "S" and "P," standing for the subject category and the predicate category respectively of the proposition. That grid, re-written in the more traditional format, would be:

	Universal	Particular
Affirmative	*All A is B*	*Some A is B*
Negative	*No A is B*	*Some A is not B*

Whatever S and P may be, the universal affirmative proposition asserts that anything you encounter which is included within class S will also be included within class P. The universal negative propositions asserts that anything that is within S will lie outside P (or, alternately, nothing is both in S and in P). The particular affirmative proposition claims that at least one thing in S is also in P. And the particular negative asserts that at least one thing within S is out-side P.

The intension of the terms used as A and P may become far more complex than the simple structure implies, but the nature of the assertions made in each of the categorical proposition-forms remains the same. If, for example, you encountered the complex-looking categorical proposition "All tall, dark, and handsome men are vain, shallow or boring," you might be tempted to pass it by as too complicated for you to analyze. But it's far simpler than it appears. Since it refers to *all* such men, you know that it is universal. Since it asserts that they *are* that way, you know that it is affirmative. Its form, then, is "All S is P." What are "S" and "P"? "S" is the class of all persons who are simultaneously tall, dark, handsome and male. "P" is the class of all persons who are vain or shallow or boring or any of the combinations of those characteristics. The proposition asserts that all of the members of the former class are also members of the latter one.

You should now work the problems following 5.1 (pages 164-65) and then check your answers in *ITL* and here.

(2)   S = Athletes who have ever accepted pay for participating in sports.

         P = Amateurs

     Form: Universal negative -- No S is P. The assertion is that, for an athlete, the properties of being paid to play and being an amateur are incompatible.

(6)   S = Paintings produced by artists who are universally recognized as masters.

         P = Works of genuine merit that either are or deserve to be preserved in museums and made available to the public.

     Form: Particular negative -- Some S is not P. The assertion that at least one work by a universally recognized master is excluded from those that should be hung in a museum, preserved, etc.

5.2   Quality, Quantity, and Distribution

The four sorts of proposition represented on the grids in section 5.1 (above) are traditionally identified as A, E, I and O propositions. Copi and Cohen explain the origin of these names at the beginning of section 5.2. In the long run, the key to identifying any categorical proposition as one of them is to categorize it as affirmative or negative and as universal or particular. Once that is done, you need to identify the proposition's subject and predicate. This being done, your understanding of any given categorical proposition should be satisfactory.

The property of being affirmative or negative we call the *Quality* of the proposition; the property of being universal or particular we call the *Quantity*. When you are speaking of all the members of a class, then the term used is said to be *Distributed*; when some members of the class are not being spoken of, the term is said to be *Undistributed*. Each of the four categorical proposition-forms has its own characteristic distribution pattern. If we were to add d to distributed classes and u to undistributed ones, and were to use "<" to represent the copula (the link between subject class and predicate class), then we wouldn't even need to indicate the quantity or quality. The pattern of distribution would tell us whether the proposition was affirmative or negative, universal or particular.

In propositions of the form "All S is P" your assertion says something about all S's but, at least possibly, only about some of the P's. For example, in the proposition "All Swans are Pretty," an assertion is made about *all* swans, but we have no reason to assume that we know anything about **all** pretty things. Our information is only about those pretty things that are also swans. The distribution pattern for an A proposition will always be $Sd < Pu$.

In propositions of the form "No S is P" there is an assertion about all S's (that they are not P's) **and** an assertion about all P's (that they are not S's). If no tasks asked of people are beyond the capability of humanity, then it is the case both that all tasks asked of people are excluded from the class of things beyond humanity's capability and that all things beyond humanity's capability are excluded from tasks which might be asked of humanity. The pattern of distribution in an E proposition will always be $Sd < Pd$.

In I propositions there is neither an assertion about all S's nor one about all P's. When some readers of this book are female, there is no universal knowledge either about the book's readership or about women. The pattern of distribution in a proposition asserting that some S is P is always $Su < Pu$.

An assertion that some S's are not P's tells us nothing about S's as a whole, but it does have information, albeit slight, about the whole of the class of P's. If some dogs are not friendly, then you know that if you had a complete list of things that are friendly there would be at least one dog that would not be on the list. O propositions' distribution patterns, then are always $Su < Pd$.

Note, then, the distribution patterns when they are inserted into the grids suggested above in 5.1.

	Universal	Particular
Affirmative	$Sd < Pu$	$Su < Pu$
Negative	$Sd < Pd$	$Su < Pd$

When you examine the grid, certain characteristics seem more obvious. You can look at these characteristics either from the point of view of the quantity or quality of the proposition:

1. Universal propositions have distributed subjects.
2. Particular propositions have undistributed subjects.
3. Affirmative propositions have undistributed predicates.
4. Negative propositions have distributed predicates.

or from the viewpoint of distribution:

1. Distributed subjects mean universal propositions.
2. Distributed predicates mean negative propositions.
3. Undistributed subjects mean particular propositions.
4. Undistributed predicates mean affirmative propositions.

or from the point of view of subject or predicate:

1. Subject distribution or the lack thereof determines number.
   a. Distribution means universality.
   b. Lack of distribution means particularity.
2. Predicate distribution or the lack thereof determines quality.
   a. Distribution means a negative proposition.
   b. Lack of distribution means affirmation.

If you use the information above or the diagram in *ITL* at the end of section 5.2, (page 168) the exercises following 5.2 should present no great challenge for you. You may wish to confirm your answers both here and in *ITL*.

(2)   The assertion is affirmative (that they *are* dupes) and universal (that *all* of them are dupes). Here, as an any A proposition, the subject is distributed and the predicate undistributed.

(6)   Sub-classes and conditions notwithstanding, this too is affirmative (that they ARE such people) and universal (that *all* of them will be so remembered). Here, too, the subject is distributed, the predicate undistributed.

5.3   The Traditional Square of Opposition

Copi and Cohen's very detailed discussion of the Square of Opposition may leave you a bit awed by the complexity of inferences that can be drawn from such a simple diagram. Perhaps a brief review will serve to simplify the complexity.

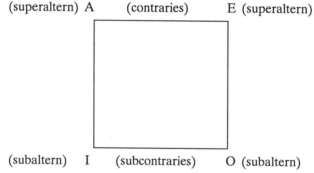

(superaltern) A   (contraries)   E (superaltern)

(subaltern) I   (subcontraries)   O (subaltern)

The contradictories (A and O, E and I) must have one of the pair true and the other false. The contraries (A and E) can both be false, but cannot both be true. The subcontraries (I and O) can both be true, but cannot both be false. If a superaltern (A or E) is true, then its subaltern (I or O, respectively) is true. And if a subaltern (I or O) is false, then its superaltern (A or E, respectively) is false.

From this review or from the list of immediate inferences at the end of section 5.3 of *ITL*, you should be able to work the exercises following 5.3. The answer to number 2 is below:

(2)   If *a* is true, then *b* is false (being *a*'s contradictory), *c* is true (being *a*'s subaltern) and *d* is false (being *a*'s contrary). If *a* is false, then *b* is true, and *c* and *d* are both undetermined.

5.4   Further Immediate Inferences

There are three forms of immediate inferences for categorical propositions other than those found on the *Square of Opposition*. To describe them easily, it is necessary to introduce the conception of a class and its complement. If you have studied geometry, then complementarity should already be familiar to you. Geometrically, the complement of an angle is another angle, the one which, when added to the original angle, would total 180°. Obviously, if angle B is the complement of angle A, then angle A is also the complement of angle B (Since if A + B = 180°, then B + A = 180°). In the case of complementary classes, they sum to totality (everything that is) instead of 180°. Thus, if class A is station wagons, then in class B will be anything that does not qualify as a station wagon. Class B will be non-station wagons.

Most reliable of these added immediate inferences is the one called *obversion*. If you take a categorical statement and change its quality, replace its predicate term with its complement, and leave the quantity and subject as they are, then you have obverted the original proposition. Explained in this form, the process sounds horribly complicated, but that impression is wrong. If you use S to represent the subject term of a categorical proposition and P to represent the predicate term, then any categorical proposition has the form:

quantifier *S* **copula** (qualifier) *P*

The qualifier is in parentheses because, in affirmative propositions, it is not stated.

You know that each class has a complement. Quality and quantity have similar related concepts, which might be called the quantifier-opposite and the qualifier-opposite. The quantifier-opposite of universality is particularity and *vice versa*. The qualifier-opposite of affirmative is negation and *vice versa*.

Based upon the general categorical form above, then the obverse of a categorical proposition has the form:

quantifier *S* **copula** *(qualifier-opposite)* *P-complement*

The nice thing about obversion is that it is valid as a means of inference: any categorical proposition ma validly obverted.

The simplest immediate inference is called **conversion**. Unfortunately it is not valid for all categorical forms. You arrive at the converse of a categorical proposition simply by exchanging the subject and predicate terms. Based upon the general categorical form above, the converse is

quantifier *S* **copula** (qualifier) *P*.

Conversion is entirely satisfactory for the contradictory pair E and I. Whenever no whales are fish or some horses are jumpers, we ought to feel perfectly confident that no fish are whales or some jumpers are horses. The other contradictory pair, A and O, do not fare so well in conversion. If we are sure that some scholars are not reliable, we remain utterly ignorant about the likelihood of finding any non-scholars among the reliable. Thus, nothing like conversion is possible, for an O proposition. The situation is not quite so dire for A propositions. When you know that all diamonds are crystals, you do have some knowledge about the membership of the class of crystals. What you do not have is universal knowledge. You know something about some crystals (that they are diamonds). From an A proposition, then, you may only validly convert by limitation, getting the form:

quantifier-opposite *P* **copula** (qualifier) *S*.

Of course, since you must have started with "All *S* is *P*" you must get "some *P* is *S*."

The third added form of immediate inference is called **contraposition**. In actuality it is just a combination of obversion and conversion. It is, however, easier to introduce contraposition as an immediate inference in its own right than it is to have to go through the process of obverting, then converting, then obverting again. Following the general categorical proposition-form, the contraposition is

quantifier *P*-complement **copula** (qualifier) *S*-complement

As you might infer, from the fact that contraposition involves an intermediate step of conversion, you are not free to contrapose any categorical proposition. If the pattern of obverting, converting, then obverting again is followed, you can see what can and what cannot be contraposed.

The original proposition validly obverts to the first derived proposition:

A.	All *S* is *P*	E.	No *S* is non-*P*
E.	No *S* is *P*	A.	All *S* is non-*P*
I.	Some *S* is *P*	O.	Some *S* in not non-*P*
O.	Some *S* is not *P*	I.	Some *S* in non-*P*

The first derived proposition converts to the second derived proposition:

E.	No *S* is non-*P*	E.	No non-*P* is *S* (valid)
A.	All *S* is non-*P*	I.	Some non-*P* is *S* (valid by limitation)
O.	Some *S* is not non-*P*		Will not convert validly
I.	Some *S* is non-*P*	I.	Some non-*P* is *S* (valid)

The second derived proposition validly obverts to contrapositive:

E.	No non-*P* is *S*	A.	All non-*P* is non-*S*
I.	Some non-*P* is *S*	O.	Some non-*P* is not non-*S*
	No valid conversion		Nothing to obvert
I.	Some non-*P* is *S*	O.	Some non-*P* is not non-*S*

Note that this shows the contradictory pair A and O have full contrapositives, that the E has a limited contrapositive (which happens to be the contrapositive of its subaltern), and that the I has no contrapositive.

For review, it is probably best to put all of the immediate inferences in chart form:

Valid Immediate Inferences
(other than from the Square of Opposition)

Proposition	Obverse	Converse	Contrapositive
A. All S is P	*No S is non-P*	*Some P is S*	*All non-P is non-S*
(when true) (when false)	(true) (false)	(true, limited) (indeterminate)	(true) (false
E. No S is P	*All S is non-P*	*No P is S*	*Some non-P is not non-S*
(when true) (when false)	(true) (false)	(true, limited) (false)	(true) (indeterminate)
I. Some S is P	*Some S is not non-P*	*Some P is S*	*None Valid*
(when true) (when false)	(true) (false)	(true) (false)	------ ------
O. Some S is not P	*Some S is non-P*	*None Valid*	*Some non-P is not non-S*
(when true) (when false)	(true) (false)	------ ------	(true) (false)

The answers to several of the problems following 5.4 are given below to be compared with your work.

I (2)   The converse is "All commissioned officers in the U.S. Army are graduates of West Point." It is not equivalent to the original. The converse by limitation is "Some commissioned officers in the U.S. Army are graduates of West Point" which is implied by the original, but still is not equivalent to the original.

II (2)   All organic compounds are non-metallic. Equivalent.

III (2)   Some non-officers are not non-soldiers. Equivalent.

IV (2)   This is the obverse of the assumed proposition. Since the obverse of any categorical proposition is equivalent to that proposition, this, too, is true.

(6)   This is the contrapositive of the original proposition. Since the contrapositive of any A or O proposition is equivalent to the original, this is true.

V (2)   This is the contrapositive of the subaltern of the original. Since the subaltern of a true E is a true O and the contrapositive of a true O is also true, then this proposition is true.

(6)   This is the converse of the contrary of the original proposition. Since the original is true, its contrary would have to be false. But the contrary of the original would be "All scientists are phil osophers" and would be false. But, when an A proposition is false, even its limited converse is indeterminate. However, since the originally assumed true proposition is "No scientists are philosophers," its obverse "All scientists are non-philosophers" must also be true. But the contrapositive of that true statement, "All philosophers are non-scientists," must also be true. If all philosophers are non-scientists, then it seems unlikely that they could also be scientists (as exercise 6 suggests). The only way to conceivably make exercise 6 anything but false is a by-product of the considerations to be discussed in 5.5 on Existential Import.

VI (2)   By obversion and conversion (both valid inferences) this statement may be transformed to "Some saints were nonmartyrs." Since it is quite possible (and happens to be true) that some saints could be martyrs while others were not, the truth of proposition 2 is indeterminate. Notice please that, although we may know on other grounds that the proposition is true, we are not permitted to claim to infer this from the original proposition.

(6)   By obversion and conversion this statement yields "All martyrs were saints." You surely can't infer such a universal proposition from only particular information. The proposition is indeterminate.

(11)   Essentially this claims that there were some people who were neither saints nor martyrs. This is consistent with the original proposition (that is, does not contradict it), but its truth is undetermined

(16)   This is the obverse of exercise 11. Thus it, too, is indeterminate.

(21)   The contrapositive of the original, "Some martyrs were saints," would be true. But it is also possible that some were not saints. We don't know from this evidence, so the given proposition is indeterminate.

(26)   The obverse of this would be "No saints were martyrs." This is the contradictory of the original proposition so must be false.

VII (2)   By conversion and obversion this would yield "All pirates are merchants." This does not contradict the original proposition nor does it follow from the original. Thus it is indeterminate.

(6)   This is the superaltern of the original proposition, thus is consistent with it but does not follow from it. It is thus indeterminate.

(11)   By obversion and conversion this asserts the sub-contrary. Since the subcontrary of a true proposition may be either true or false, this is indeterminate.

(16)   By obversion and conversion this is the same as exercise 6. Thus it, too, is indeterminate.

(21)   This asserts that some people are neither pirates nor merchants. This is consistent with the original but does not follow from it, thus is indeterminate.

(26)   By obversion this becomes "All merchants are pirates" which is the contradictory of the original proposition. It is therefore false.

5.5 Existential Import

The question of existential import is, basically, which (if any) categorical propositions imply the existence of the kind of things referred to in their subject terms. It certainly seems obvious that, if someone talked to you about some (or all) of his brothers being wealthy, you would feel deceived were you to learn that he was an only child. We usually think of a deception as the assertion of something false. Thus, it seems reasonable to infer that we do assume that assertion of a categorical proposition is also the assertion or the existence of the things to which its subject term refers.

There is a problem with this view. It seems unquestionable that the proposition "All unicorns have one horn" is true. But most people who would be certain that that is a true proposition would be equally certain that unicorns do not exist.

There are several possible solutions to this dilemma, none entirely satisfactory. The one that seems closest to "fitting" with the intuitions of most people is the one that Copi and Cohen have chosen to adopt. This interpretation, called the Boolean one, claims that A and E propositions do not assert existence while I and O propositions do. This means that the only immediate inference left for us are obversion and conversion (for E & I only -- contraposition by limitation is also eliminated). The only relationship which still holds from the traditional square of opposition is contradiction.

You should now work 5.5's exercises, then check your results.

II (2)   This is the conversion of (1) and is acceptable.

(3)   This is the obversion of (2) and is acceptable.

(4)   This is the subaltern of (3) and is no longer an acceptable inference. It commits the Existential Fallacy.

(5)   This is the conversion of (4) which, in itself, is fine, but since it is based upon (4) which committed the Existential Fallacy it also (at least indirectly) commits that fallacy relative to the original proposition (1).

5.6   Symbolism and Diagrams for Categorical Propositions

There are two means which Copi and Cohen offer for representing categorical propositions. One is in symbols, the other in diagrams. The systems are derived from the works of two
19th century British logicians: the symbolic from the work of George Boole, the diagrammatic
from the work of John Venn.

The Boolean system introduces zero (0) as a sign for an empty class. Thus, if a class
equals zero, it is an empty class; if it is unequal ($\neq$) to zero, it is a non-empty class. By juxtapos-
ing (writing together) two classes you symbolize the new class that is formed out of those things
that are in both of the juxtaposed classes. And you indicate the complement of a class by putting a bar ($-$) over the symbol for the class of which it is a complement. Given these new symbols, you can express all of the categorical propositions in Boolean form:

A.	All S is P	$\overline{S}P = 0$
E.	No S is P	$SP = 0$
I.	Some S is P	$SP \neq 0$
O.	Some S is not P	$S\overline{P} \neq 0$

From this, too, it is easy to see the contradictory relationships between A and O and between E and I.

Venn diagrams are very straightforward ways of representing class relationships. They
use circles to represent classes. There is, of course, no reason why other geometric figures could
not have been used except that the circle is easy to draw both singly and in combination. The
conventional reading of the areas within a Venn diagram is that any shaded area is empty, any
area with an "X" on it is non-empty, and any unmarked area is indeterminate. A convention
which Copi and Cohen do not introduce, but which seems useful, is to enclose the circle or circles in a square or rectangle. That puts at least visual bounds upon the classes which complement those represented by the circles. Circles occurring within the same box are usually drawn
with overlapping areas to represent possible common membership in those classes. Given these
diagrams and conventions for reading them, you can now express all of the categorical propositions in Venn diagrams:

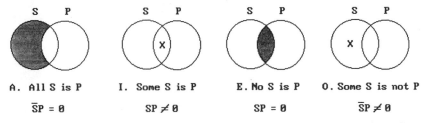

S P	S P	S P	S P
A. All S is P	I. Some S is P	E. No S is P	O. Some S is not P
$\overline{S}P = 0$	$SP \neq 0$	$SP = 0$	$\overline{S}P \neq 0$

Now that you have the basis for representing categorical propositions as either Boolean equations or by Venn diagrams, you are ready to work the problems at the end of chapter 5. Given
below are answers to some of the problems so that you can check your own results. Remember
that it really is important to try the exercises before you look at the solutions either here or in
ITL.

(2)   PM = 0

P = Peddlers

M = Millionaires

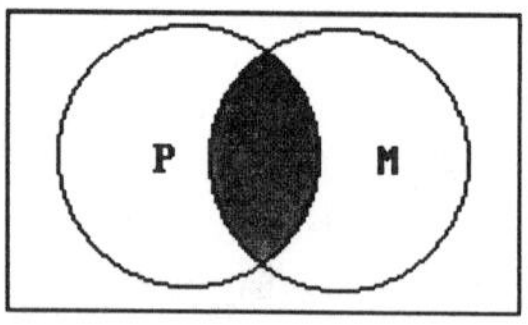

(6)   PS ≠ 0

P = Political leaders of
     high reputation
S = Scoundrels

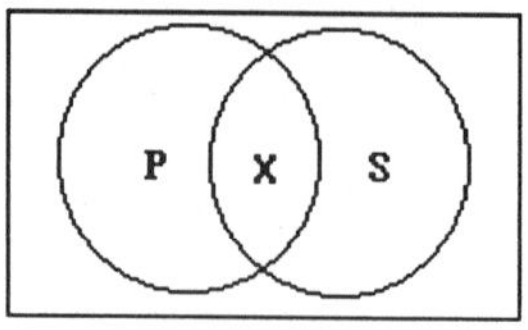

P   X   S

(11)   SM = 0

S = Student Activists

M = Middle-aged men &
    women striving ....

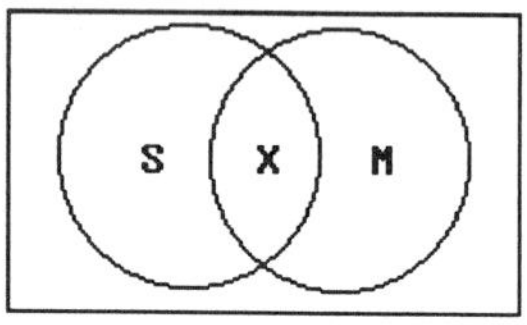

S   X   M

(16)   PS = 0

P = Passengers on the new
    large jet airplanes

S = Satisfied Customers

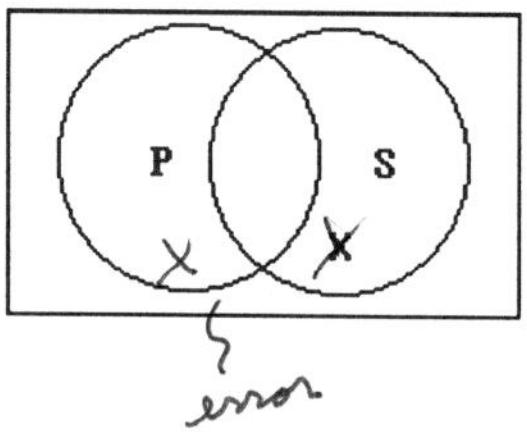

P   S

error

CHAPTER FIVE SUMMARY

I.   Categorical propositions assert a relationship between two categories (or classes).

   A. Universal affirmative (A) propositions assert that all of one class is included within another.

   B. Particular affirmative (I) propositions assert that at least one member of one class is a member of another.

   C. Universal negative (E) propositions assert that all of one class is excluded from another.

   D. Particular negative (O) propositions assert that at least one member of one class is excluded from another.

II.   Whether a proposition is affirmative or negative, universal or particular, may be determined by examining the distribution (or lack thereof) of the terms of the proposition.

   A. Universal propositions have distributed subject terms.

   B. Particular propositions have undistributed subject terms.

   C. Negative propositions have distributed predicate terms.

   D. Affirmative propositions have undistributed predicate terms.

III. The traditional square of opposition states relationships among the four propositional forms.

   A. A & E are contraries: they can be false together, but not true at the same time.

   B. I & O are subcontraries that can be true but not false together.

   C. A & O, E & I are contradictories, one of which must be true and the other false.

   D. A & E are the superimplicants of I & O, respectively. When the superimplicants are true, so must be the subimplicants.

   E. I & O are subimplicants of A & E, respectively. When the subimplicants are false, so must be the superimplicants.

IV.   Obversion occurs when the quality of a proposition is changed and the predicate term is replaced by its complement. It is a valid inference for all categorical propositional forms.

V.   Conversion occurs when the subject and predicate terms are exchanged.

   A. Conversion is valid for E and I propositions.

   B. Conversion is invalid for A and O propositions.

   C. Conversion by limitation allows valid inference from the A form "All *S* is *P*" to the I form "Some *P* is *S*."

VI.   Contraposition occurs when the complements of predicate and subject replace subject and predicate, respectively.

   A. Contraposition is valid for A and O propositions.

   B. Contraposition is invalid for E and I propositions.

   C. Contraposition by limitation allows valid inference from the E form "No *S* is *P*" to the O form "Some non-*P* are not non-*S*."

VII.   Existential import is the assumption that a proposition implies that there exist members of the proposition's subject class. The most useful assumption of existential import is that I & O propositions imply existence while A & E ones do not.

   A   This eliminates all square of opposition relationships except contradiction.

   B. This eliminates immediate inferences of conversion and contraposition by limitation.

VIII. Boolean equations state that classes do or do not equal the empty class (O).

   A. The juxtaposition of two class terms represents the class formed of things common to both classes.

   B. All four categorical propositions can be represented in Boolean form.

      1. All *S* is *P* (A)   SP = O

      2. Some *S* is *P* (I)   SP = O

      3. No *S* is *P* (E)   SP ≠ O

      4. Some *S* is not *P* (O)   SP ≠ O

IX.   Venn diagrams represent classes by circles, emptiness by shading and membership with an X. All four categorical propositions may be represented in Venn diagrams.

A. All S is P   I. Some S is P   E. No S is P   O. Some S is not P

$\overline{S}P = 0$ $SP \neq 0$ $SP = 0$ $\overline{S}P \neq 0$

6.1 Standard-Form Categorical Syllogisms

One of the most frequently-heard descriptions of a standard-form categorical syllogism is that it is an argument composed of three categorical statements (two premisses and a conclusion) which are in turn composed of a total of three categories, each of which occurs twice. Unfortunately that description serves better as a reminder for people who are already familiar with syllogisms than as an introduction to the idea. It is useful, however, as a starting point for understanding the structure.

The conclusion of a standard-form categorical syllogism is always a categorical proposition. The term which serves as subject for that proposition is said to be the subject term (or sometimes the minor term) of the argument in which it occurs. That subject (or minor) term will also occur in the second premiss (which is often called the minor premiss). Similarly the predicate term of the conclusion of the standard-form categorical syllogism is considered to be the predicate term (or major term) of the argument. That predicate (or major) term will also occur in the first (or major) premiss. The third term used in the syllogism, then, must be the term which **mediates** or comes in the middle of, the other two. It is called the middle term and will occur once in each premiss, but not in the conclusion. Thus, the standard-form categorical syllogism is composed of a major premiss containing the major (predicate) and middle terms, a minor premiss containing the minor (subject) and middle terms, and a conclusion whose subject is the minor term and whose predicate is the major term. Now you understand the original description: three categorical propositions, three terms each occurring twice.

Since what are considered to be the subject and predicate terms of the argument are identified relative to their function in the conclusion of such an argument, the conclusion always has its terms ordered as S-P. The premisses are not so limited. The middle term could be the subject or the predicate term in either of the premisses, **relative to that premiss**. That means that one can identify four different combinations of locations for the middle term in the premisses. [Of course, one could almost as easily refer to the locations of the major and minor terms in the premisses, but the fact that the middle term is found in both premisses makes the pattern easier to see when looking for the location of the middle term.] The relative locations of the middle term in a syllogism is called the figure of the syllogism and is easily displayed on a grid like the ones used in earlier chapters:

	Middle Term first in Major Premiss	Middle Term last in Major Premiss
Middle Term first in Minor Premiss	*M-P* *M-S*	*P-M* *M-S*
Middle Term last in Minor Premiss	*M-P* *S-M*	*P-M* *S-M*

When read with the conclusion form, these four possibilities constitute the four figures of the standard-form categorical syllogism:

I	*II*	*III*	*IV*
M - P	P - M	M - P	P - M
S - M	S - M	M - S	M - S
-----	-----	-----	-----
S - P	S - P	S - P	S - P

Within a given syllogism there are still many possible variations which result from differences in the forms of categorical propositions which occur as premisses and conclusion. The major premiss may be an A, an E, an I or an O proposition, and so may both the minor premiss and the conclusion. Thus, with both the premisses's forms being, say, A, the conclusion's form could be any of the four forms, yielding four possible arguments: AAA, AAI, AAE and AAO. The first letter always tells the form of the major premiss, the second the minor and the third the conclusion and the three together are called the mood of the syllogism.

To see how many possible syllogisms could be generated all you need to do is multiply out the combinations:

4 (major forms) x 4 (minor forms) x 4 (conclusion forms) = 64 (moods).

But you must recall that there are also four possible figures. That means that each of the 64 possible syllogistic moods could appear in each of the four moods, yielding 256 possible standard-form syllogisms.

The idea of having to deal with 256 different forms of argument may seem a bit overwhelming when you first encounter it, but there is hope. In the first place, in studying logic you want to learn to sort good from bad arguments. Since syllogisms are deductive arguments, the good/bad distinction for them will be a valid/invalid distinction. If the possible syllogisms were divided evenly between valid and invalid, then you'd only have to learn one of the halves -- anything that wasn't in the half you'd learned would have to be in the other. And if they are unevenly divided, then the prudent thing to do would be to learn the small "half." And it ought not take you much reflection to recognize that there are offered in the world many more bad arguments than good ones. That pattern is followed with syllogisms: most possible syllogistic forms are invalid.

You are now prepared to work the exercises following 6.1 and will probably want to check your results here and in *ITL*.

(2)   Some objects of worship are fir trees.
        All fir trees are evergreens.
        Thus some evergreens are objects of worship.
        IAI-4

(6)   No expensive and delicate mechanisms are suitable toys for children.
        All hi-fi sets are expensive and delicate mechanisms.
        Thus no hi-fi sets are suitable toys for children.
        EAE-1

6.2   The Formal Nature of Syllogistic Argument

You have now learned to look at syllogistic arguments in terms of the location of their major, minor and middle terms. You have also learned to look at the mood of a syllogism without concerning yourself with the specific content of the argument. Perhaps without realizing it, you have taken your first steps toward doing logic formally. (By "formally" I mean "according to its form.") In fact, the rest of the discussion of validity and invalidity both here and in *ITL* will be in terms of formal relationships.

The use of forms rather than the actual arguments has several benefits. Most obvious is the fact that looking at forms alone protects you from being swayed by the sort of emotional by-play that you studied in Part I. A second value of studying arguments formally is that you do not find yourself diverted from the analysis of the argument into the factual questions of the truth or falsity of the premises and conclusion. The greatest benefit, however, is likely to be the sharpening of your ability to argue from logical analogy. Two arguments are said to be logically analogous if their formal elements "line up" in the same way. In the case of two categorical syllogisms, they are logically analogous if their figures and moods are the same. As Copi and Cohen suggest, it is quite useful to be able to show an argument to be bad by being able to demonstrate its formal identity with another argument which is obviously bad.

There is a problem, however, with the use of logical analogy as a tool for proving arguments unsatisfactory. Clearly, if you can show that argument A is logically analogous to argument B, and you can prove that argument B is invalid, then argument A must also be invalid. But, if you cannot think of an invalid argument with a form matching the one you hope to refute, you do not have a proof that no such argument exists. That is, of course, a possibility, but it is also possible that such an analogy exists but that you are (or have been so far) unable to think of it. The fact that, no matter how hard we train, neither you nor I can run a sub-four-minute mile (or swim the English Channel, or lift a 200 kilo barbell, or whatever) certainly is no proof that that action cannot be performed by anyone. It is simply a biographical note about each of us as an individual.

The fact that disproof by logical analogy has limitations, however, ought not be taken as sufficient reason to ignore it as a reasoning technique. It is, as Copi and Cohen say, very useful in that way. You should now put it to use working the exercises following 6.2.

(2)   This is a valid argument with an EIO-1 form.

(6)   This is a valid argument with an AII-3 form.

6.3   Venn Diagram Technique for Testing Syllogisms

In the same way that a two-circle Venn diagram was used in chapter 5 to represent all the possible interrelations between two classes, a three-circle one can picture such relationships for three classes. The bare Venn Diagram for three classes looks like:

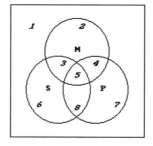

The areas in this diagram are numbered 1-8 and identify the eight possible combinations of occurrence and non-occurrence among three classes and their complements. If you find the diagram a bit confusing, the list below may help to clarify those relationships.

1. $\overline{\text{SMP}}$ 2. $\overline{\text{S}}\,\overline{\text{MP}}$

3. $\text{S}\overline{\text{M}}\text{P}$ 4. $\overline{\text{SM}}\text{P}$

5. SMP   6. $\text{SM}\overline{\text{P}}$

7. $\overline{\text{SM}}\text{P}$ 8. $\text{S}\overline{\text{M}}\text{P}$

In examining syllogisms you will not be given immediate relationships among three class-es. The major premiss tells you about the relationship between the predicate and the middle term; the minor about the subject and the middle term. The conclusion *claims* to follow from the premisses and to show the relationship between the subject and the predicate term. The problem, then, in applying a Venn Diagram to a standard-form categorical syllogism is to de-termine whether the information provided by the premisses is a satisfactory warrant for the con-clusion.

Copi and Cohen direct you to focus your attention on only two of the circles in the three-circle diagram at a time. That is easier for some people than for others, and is easier at some times than at others. An added suggestion, which some students find helpful, is to begin by rep-resenting each of the premisses and the conclusion separately on two-circle diagrams. Once that is done, it is rather easier to transfer the information about the premisses from the two- cir-cle diagrams to the three-circle one. When the premiss-transfer is completed, you check the argument to see whether the conclusion's two-circle version can be read from the three-circle diagram.

As an example, look at exercise 2 from the last set of exercises. It was described there as an EIO-1 argument. It's form, then is:

No M is P
Some S is M
Some S is not P

Its three propositions represented on two-circle Venn Diagrams are:

No M is P

Some S is M

Some S is not P

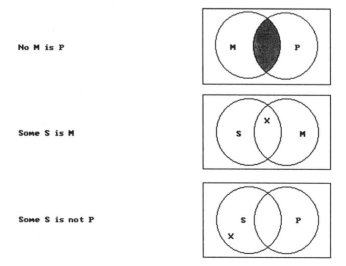

One rule of thumb in transferring information to three-or-more-circle Venn Diagrams is always to handle universal information first. That is, do your shading before you insert X's.   In this case you will need to first transfer the shading of the major premiss to the diagram.

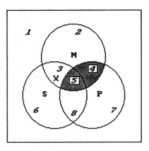

You should note that this shades both areas 4 and 5 since to deny that any M's are P's will include the denial for either S's or non-S's. You need next insert an X in the area shared by S and M (as shown above). But the third two-circle diagram required that there be an X inside the area of S but outside the area of P. When you look at the three-circle version above you see that there is an X in it and that that X is within S and outside P. That indicates that the conclusion of this particular argument-form **can** be read from the information provided by the premisses and that, therefore, the argument is valid. Incidentally, the fact that there is an additional area (area 2) that is also inside S and outside P is no problem. The minimal condition for the truth of the conclusion--that there be something in S and not in P--was met in one way, thus it need not be met in any other.

It is interesting to note that an EIO argument is going to be valid regardless of its figure. (Both E and I propositions are validly convertible, so neither the two-circle nor the three-circle representations above will change if the figure were to be changed). In contrast, the sixth exercise in that set, an AII, was valid in figure 3 (and will also be so in figure 1), but is invalid in figures 2 and 4. That is shown by the same technique as before:

All P is M

Some S is M   (or Some M is S)

Some S is P

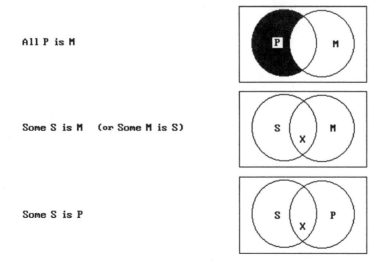

Transfer the universal major

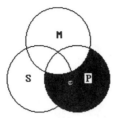

     Then you need to transfer the particular minor, but there is a difficulty with doing this. Note that in the diagram representing the minor premiss you have an X in the area shared by S and M. In the three circle diagram, however, there are two areas so shared. One (area 5) is not shared with P; one (area 6) is. Copi and Cohen's technique for representing such an ambiguous case (ambiguous because you don't have any knowledge whether the thing that is S and M is also P or not) is to place the X on the line between the two possible areas. So long as you are very careful in the placement of this X this will work quite satisfactorily. If you are, as many of us are, a little prone to inaccuracy when writing things down, there is a slight modification of Copi and Cohen's method which you may find helpful. If you place an X in **each** of the possible areas and join the two X's with a heavy line, you achieve the same result (showing the ambiguity of information) without such a need for precision in the placement of the X. In the AII-2 or -4 argument whose diagram was begun above, the diagram of both premisses on the three-circle form can be done by the "line" or "bridge" method:

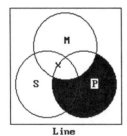

     Line   **Bridge**

To read the conclusion from either of these, you'd have to *know* that the things that were both S and M were also P. Since you don't know that, the conclusion doesn't follow and the argument-form is an invalid one.

     Being familiar with the techniques for testing the validity of categorical syllogisms as explained both here and in *ITL*, you should find the exercises following 6.3 quite straightforward.

I.   (2)

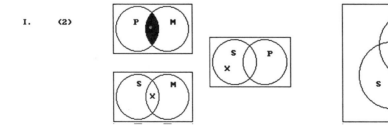
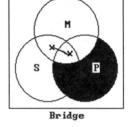

There is an X inside S but outside P; thus it's valid.

I. (6)

   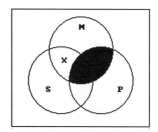

There is an X inside S but outside P; thus it's valid.

I. (11)

  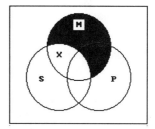

There is an X inside S but outside P; thus it's valid.

II (2)   Some philosophers are mathematicians.
            All scientists are mathematicians.
            Some scientists are philosophers.
                    IAI-2

  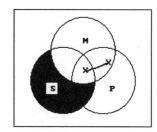

        Since the "bridge" between philosopher-mathematicians who are and who are not scientists does not specifically assert that there are philosopher-mathematician-scientists, the argument is invalid.

(6)   No pioneers were unsavory persons.
         All criminals are unsavory persons.
         No criminals were pioneers.
                 EAE-2

  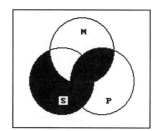

6.4   Rules and Fallacies

If you preferred evaluating categorical arguments without the aid of Venn Diagrams (or had you lived prior to Venn's work in the mid-19th century) you would have to approach the syllogism from the point of view of rules for its proper use. The way they are expressed here will be slightly different than their form in *ITL*, but the principle each is intended to state will remain the same.

RULE 1:   *Valid standard-form categorical syllogisms contain a major term, a minor term and a middle term. Each is used twice with no alteration in meaning in the argument.*

The original definition of a standard-form categorical syllogism (in 6.1) required that it have three and only three terms and that each be used twice and in specific locations. Thus, any argument with more (or fewer) terms than three will not be a standard-form categorical syllogism and lies outside the scope of what is discussed in chapter 6. Tradition says that arguments with four or more terms commit the Fallacy of Four Terms. There seems to be no traditional analysis of arguments with fewer than three terms, probably because they would be so obviously faulty they would almost never occur.

The area in which you have to guard most carefully against committing this error is in the case of an equivocation. An argument may include two occurrences of the same word or phrase (giving the impression of having the required two uses of a term) but in actuality be a four-term argument. If you look back at argument 12 following section 6.4 in *ITL*, you should see that it can be rewritten as an apparent standard-form categorical syllogism:

> All departures from law should be punished.
> All chance happenings are departures from law.
> All chance happenings should be punished.

This looks as if it were an AAA-1 syllogism, which is a valid form. The problem, as you surely saw when studying chapter 3, is that the phrase "departures from law" which is used as if it were the middle term is actually two different terms. In the major premise the phrase referred to violations of rules set down by legislative agencies; in the minor premise it referred to occurrences not in line with previously observed physical (or biological, social, etc.) regularities. If the argument were stated in terms of what the phrase means in each case, its four-term nature would be evident:

> All violations of social regulations ought to be punished.
> All chance happenings are scientifically unexpected occurrences.
> All chance happenings ought to be punished.

RULE 2:   *Valid standard-form categorical syllogisms include at least one distributed occurrence of the middle term.*

Traditionally any argument which violates this rule is said to have committed the Fallacy of the Undistributed Middle. Such a rule is necessary to insure that the interrelation of the two premises, through the mediation of the middle term, does not accidentally identify different individuals. If you recall the Venn Diagram analysis of the invalid AII-2 (and AII-4) argument form, (above) you will also recall that it involved the difficulty with diagraming "some S is M" when the class SM was divided in the diagram into SMP and SMP̄. That argument-form was invalid because you had no guarantee of the location of the known SM, in or out of P. In the case of the undistributed middle there is a similar lack of sufficient knowledge. If both occurrences of the middle term are undistributed, then in each premise you do not know whether your knowledge applies to all or only some of the individuals in the class named by the term. If both premisses actually refer only to part of that class, then it is possible that the individuals referred to in one premiss are wholly distinct from those to which the other premiss refers. But, if the middle term-possessing individuals in the two premisses are wholly separate, you have lost the point of interrelation between the premisses. Consider the argument

> All **M**essy people are **P**ests.
> All **S**lobs are **M**essy people.
> All **S**lobs are **P**ests.

You know that any individual who qualifies as a Slob will also be found within the class of Messy people. You do not know in which particular sub-class or sub-classes they will be, but you know that they're there somewhere. Similarly, you know that each and every Messy person, no matter which sub-class or sub-classes he or she is in, will be found somewhere within the group identified as Pests. In particular, you can be assured that the Slobs, wherever they were in the class of Messy people, will also be Pests, since no matter in what sub-class of Messy people they resided that sub-class (like all sub-classes of Messy people) is to be found within the class of Pests.

On the other hand, consider the argument:

> All **P**arts for a car are **M**anufactured.
> Some **M**anufactured things are not **S**eats of cars.
> Some **S**eats of cars are not **P**arts for cars.

Here you do not know anything about all manufactured things. What you do know is that there are four distinct sub-classes within that class: SMP, SMnon-P, non-SMP and non-SMnon-P. You do know that somewhere in the first two classes there is at least one thing. What this argument does not tell you, but you surely know independently, is that there are no individuals inside the class of Seats of cars that are outside the class Parts of cars. The first premiss provided you with information about some of the individuals in the classes SMP and non-SMP, namely that if there are any P's they are in one of these two classes. The second premiss provided you with information about the classes SMnon-P and non-SMnon-P, namely that there is at least one individual in at least one of them. The conclusion, however, wants to assert something about classes SMnon-P and Snon-Mnon-P, namely that there is at least one individual in at least one of them. Had you ever had information about all of the class M, you would hope that you might have made some inference about individuals in SMP, but you had no such knowledge so you could draw no such conclusion. The knowledge about Manufactured things, being only partial, didn't do anything to connect your knowledge about P's with that about S's.

RULE 3: Valid standard-form categorical syllogisms require that any term distributed in the conclusion must also have been distributed in the premiss in which it occurred.

Copi and Cohen and tradition subdivide the difficulties arising from ignoring this rule according to premiss-location of the term that "gets distributed" in the conclusion. Whether the "illicitness" was in the major or in the minor, however, the problem is the same. In effect both the Illicit Major and the Illicit Minor are guilty of fallacies of hasty generalization: in the premiss you have information about some of a class, but in the conclusion you make an assertion about all that class.

RULE 4: Valid standard-form categorical syllogisms have no more than one negative premiss.

The sort of difficulty that this rule is intended to avoid is most easily seen by using Venn Diagrams. There are only four possible premiss combinations involving two negative Premisses: EE, EO, OE, and OO. Typical Venn Diagrams of them are:

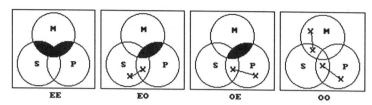

Of course, additional variations would come from varying the figure, but you should see a constant property of all four diagrams: nowhere is there unambiguous information about the relationship between individuals with regard to their being included in or excluded from S and P.

RULE 5: *Valid standard-form categorical syllogisms with a negative premiss (and there can be at most one -- see Rule 4) must also have a negative conclusion.*

Negative premisses deny, in part or in whole, that one class is within another. This results in your knowing where something *isn't* but not where it *is*. For the purpose of these arguments, then, you can't slide from isn't-information to is-information. If you were told (truly) that syzygy isn't a very common occurrence, you would probably feel quite reluctant to say that it IS an astronomical arrangement, a part of the body, a technical term from stamp-collecting, or anything else. You do know that either "occurrences of syzygy" or "common occurrences" is the middle term of any standard- form categorical syllogism in which the denial that syzygy is common was a premiss (since each such premiss must contain an instance of the middle term). But that leaves you in the dark about the inclusion relationships of the non-middle term in the statement.

RULE 6: *Valid standard-form categorical syllogisms do not draw particular conclusions without a particular premiss.*

The need for such a rule was basically outlined in chapter 5, in the discussion of existential import. Essentially, the problem is with drawing a particular conclusion, which thereby asserts some thing's existence. Deductive arguments which have information in their conclusions which was not, even in disguised form, in their premisses are suspect. With the exception of inferences like the rule of Addition (which will be discussed in chapter 9), new material in the conclusion of a deductive argument is a reliable sign of invalidity.

You ought now to feel prepared to work the exercises following 6.4.

I (2)   EAA-1 This violates Rule 5, thus commits the Fallacy of Drawing an Affirmative Conclusion from a Negative Premiss. Note that you can discover the fallacy here merely by looking at the argument's mood.

(6)   IAI-2 This does not obviously violate a rule, so you must examine the argument's internal structure. Since you know that the subject terms of universal categorical propositions are distributed, but that the subject terms of particular ones and the predicate terms of affirmative ones are undistributed, you can "map out" the distribution pattern of this argument:

$$P u\text{-}M u$$
$$S d\text{-}M u$$
$$\text{-------}$$
$$S u\text{-}P u.$$

Since the middle term is undistributed in both premisses, the argument violates Rule 2, committing the Fallacy of the Undistributed Middle.

(11)   EAO-1 As in exercise 2 the fallacy can be seen from the mood of the argument. Rule 6 forbids infer ring a particular conclusion from universal premisses. Any EAO argument will commit the Existential Fallacy.

II (2)   This is an AAA-1 argument and all such arguments are valid.

(6)   This is an OAA-3 argument. Since the major premiss is negative, Rule 5 requires that the conclusion also be negative. This argument, then, commits the Fallacy of Drawing an Affirmative Conclusion from a Negative Premiss.

III (2)   In standard categorical form this argument is

> All eccentrics are people who see new patterns in familiar things.
> All inventors are people who see new patterns in familiar things.
> Thus, all inventors are eccentrics.

This is an AAA-2 argument. Since the middle term occurs as the predicate term of both premisses and both premisses, being affirmative, have undistributed predicate terms, this argument commits the Fallacy of the Undistributed Middle, violating Rule 2.

(6)   In standard categorical form this argument is

> No writers of lewd and sensational articles are honest and decent citizens.
> Some journalists are not writers of lewd and sensational articles.
> Therefore, some journalists are honest and decent citizens.

This is an EOI-1 argument. This argument commits two fallacies--Exclusive Premisses and Drawing an Affirmative Conclusion from a Negative Premiss--violating both Rule 4 and Rule 5.

IV (2)   The problem is how best to arrive at the valid moods in the first figure that have a particular conclusion.   Although there may be several equally acceptable approaches, one might ought by now to seem natural to you is the one applied in chapter one to the brain teasers: arrive at the satisfactory by eliminating the unsatisfactory.

1. Keep in mind the distribution patterns of categorical propositions:

   a.   Affirmative propositions have undistributed a predicate terms.
   b.   Negative propositions have distributed predicate terms.
   c.   Universal propositions have distributed subject terms.
   d.   Particular propositions have undistributed subject terms.

2. Recall the first figure

> M - P
> S - M
> -----
> S - P

3. Generate the 16 possible patterns for premisses. AA, AI, AE, AO, IA, II, IE, IO, EA, EI, EE, EO, OA, OI, OE, OO

4. Eliminate the unsatisfactory.

   a.   IA, II, OA and OI all have a particular major and an affirmative minor. This means that both occurrences of the middle term are undistributed and that Rule 5 is violated. Thus these forms cannot occur in valid 1st figure syllogisms.

b.   AE, AO, IE and IO all have a negative premiss, so must have a negative conclusion. But all have affirmative major premisses, so the predicate term in those premisses must be undistributed. This would mean that any negative conclusion would violate Rule 3. Thus these forms cannot occur in valid first-figure syllogisms.

c.   EE, EO, OE and OO would all commit the Fallacy of Exclusive Premisses, violating Rule 4. Thus these forms cannot occur in valid first-figure syllogisms.

d.   AA and EA arguments could not have a particular conclusion without violating Rule 6, thus they could not occur in a valid first-figure.

e.   An AII argument would be valid, but AIA would violate Rule 6 and AIE and AIO would both violate Rule 5.

f.   An EIO argument would be valid, but EIE would violate Rule 6 and EIA and EII would violate Rule 5.

Thus the only forms of syllogism which have a particular conclusion, are in the first figure, and are valid are AII and EIO.

(6)   Since Rule 2 requires that the middle term be distributed at least once, the middle term would have to be one of the twice-distributed terms. If the predicate term is distributed, then the subject term cannot be distributed. This means that the conclusion must be an O form. Since both the middle and the predicate terms are distributed, the major premiss must be an E. To avoid violating Rule 6, the minor premiss must be particular; to avoid violating rule 4, the minor premiss must be affirmative. But if the minor premiss is an I, then neither its subject nor its predicate term will be distributed, and that violates the original requirement that the middle term be distributed in both premisses. If the subject term were the other twice-distributed one, then both S and M would be distributed in the minor premiss. That means that the minor would be negative and Rule 5 would demand that the conclusion be negative. However, that would require the predicate term of the conclusion be distributed and that violates the assump tion of only two terms being distributed. Therefore it is not possible to have a valid argument in which two and only two terms are each distributed twice.

CHAPTER SIX SUMMARY

I.   Standard-form categorical arguments are composed of three propositions: a major premiss, a minor premiss and a conclusion.

     A. The major premiss contains the major term (predicate term of the conclusion) and the middle term.

     B. The minor premiss contains the minor term (subject term of the conclusion) and the middle term.

     C. The subject and predicate terms of the conclusion are defined as the minor and major terms, respectively, of the argument.

II.   The mood of a standard-form categorical argument is the three letter sequence naming the major premiss, the minor premiss and the conclusion of the argument in that order.

III.   figure of a standard-form categorical syllogism is determined by the location of the middle term in the premisses.

     A.   First Figure: M-P
                                     S-M

                                     S-P

     B.   Second Figure: P-M
                                       S-M

                                     S-P

     C.   Third Figure: M-P
                                       M-S

                                     S-P

     D.   Fourth Figure: P-M
                                       M-S

                                     S-P

IV.   Syllogistic forms are strictly analogous, that is, if one occurrence of a form is valid (or invalid) then so will all other occurrences be valid (or invalid).

V.   When the two-circle Venn Diagrams of the premisses of an argument are transferred onto a three-circle Venn Diagram, the validity or invalidity of the argument can be seen by whether the two-circle diagram of the conclusion can be read from the three-circle one.

VI.   There are six rules (or conditions) which valid standard-form categorical syllogisms must meet. They must:

A. contain exactly three terms, each of which must be used twice in exactly the same sense.

B. have at least one distributed occurrence of the middle term.

C. have distributed occurrences in the premisses of all terms distributed in the conclusion.

D. not have two negative premisses.

E. have a negative conclusion when and only when there is a negative premiss.

F. have a particular premiss when and only when there is a particular conclusion.

Chapter Seven
Arguments in Ordinary Language

7.1   Reducing the Number of Terms in a Syllogistic Argument

For the most part you have been working with arguments that were stated either in standard categorical form or something very close to it. The difficulty you will encounter in applying the knowledge you have gained about standard-form categorical syllogisms is that most "real-life" arguments do not appear in standard form. If you want to use the tools for evaluating standard-form categorical syllogisms, then you have to be able to translate the non-standard into the standard.

You have already been doing the simplest sort of translation, for example, in the exercises in part III of 6.4 of *ITL*. In those exercises, the propositions were in standard categorical form, but they were not in the "correct" order. The only thing required, then, to translate such arguments into standard form is to follow three simple steps.

1.   Identify the conclusion, its subject and predicate. Place it last.

2.   Identify the major premiss (with the conclusion's predicate term) and place it first.

3.   Check to see that the remaining proposition is the minor (with the conclusion's subject term) and place it second.

The second form of translation is little more complex than the re-ordering required in the first. In the attempt to avoid a childish or boring writing and speaking style, we all learn to use synonyms. But, strictly speaking, in a standard-form argument you couldn't use synonyms without being guilty of having a Four Term Fallacy, a violation of Rule 1. When synonymous terms occur in an argument, all that is required to translate it into standard form is to change one of each pair of synonymous terms to the other. It would thus be possible to translate what looks at first to be a Fallacy of Four Terms (with what seems to be as many as SIX terms) into a standard-form categorical syllogism. Copi and Cohen's example on the second page of the chapter involves three sets of synonymous terms: wealthy people and rich people, vagrants and tramps, lawyers and attorneys. By replacing the second term of each pair by the first, they obtain a standard-form categorical syllogism.

The third way in which you may have to translate elements of an argument to get to standard form seems more complex, but really is pretty straightforward. What you need to do is keep well in mind the valid immediate inferences which you learned in chapter 5. (If you want a quick refresher on them, you might look back at the summary of chapter 5). The use of these inference forms is particularly desirable when you encounter arguments which contain terms representing both a class and its complement.

While translating arguments into the standard form by these methods may not appear terribly complicated, you have to realize that it becomes more complex when you have to apply more than one of them at a time. It would be possible that you might have to translate an argument in all three ways in order to get it into standard form.

For example, three translations are required for the argument:

All canines are animals. Therefore all beagles are animals since no beagles are non-dogs.

1. The position of the clauses of the second sentence must be reversed in order to have the minor premiss and the conclusion in the correct order.
2. One of the synonymous terms "dog" and "canine" must be replaced by the other.
3. The minor premiss must be obverted to replace the term "non-dogs" by its complement "dogs."

Performing all three translations changes the original non-standard- form argument into the standard-form one:

> All dogs are animals.
> All beagles are dogs.
> ---------------
> All beagles are animals.

Of course, the particular translations that were made are not the only ones that could have been used to change the original to a standard form. One alternative set of translations would have yielded:

> All non-animals are non-dogs.
> No beagles are non-dogs.
> -----------------
> No beagles are non-animals.

The first standard-form argument is an AAA-1, the second is an AEE-2, but both are "correct" translations of the original argument and all three are valid arguments.

It is important that you realize that neither of the translations (nor any other legitimate one) is any more correct than any other. What is important is for you to be able to select the methods of translation that work most easily for you. That does mean, however, that the answers given here and in *ITL* to the exercises following 7.1 may not be quite the same as the ones you work out yourself. What you should be able to do, however, is to transform the **form** of your translation into the **form** given here or in *ITL*. For example, the two translations offered were AAA-1 and AEE-2 forms, respectively. Their structures, (using S, M and P as determined from the AAA-1 argument) then, are

| All M's are P's. | All non-P's are non-M's. |
All S's are M's.	No S's are non-M's.
All S's are P's.	No S's are non-P's.

In either of the forms if you contrapose the major premiss and obvert both the minor premiss and the conclusion, then you will obtain the other form.

(2)   Some metals are rare and costly substances.
         All welder's materials are metals.

         Thus, some welder's materials are rare and costly materials.

This "standardization" involved only obverting the minor premiss. In translated form it is now an IAI-1 argument. By the rules of chapter 6 it is an invalid form because its middle term never is distributed: neither term is distributed in the I major and only the minor term is distributed in the A minor.

Had you checked the argument by Venn Diagram, you would have had

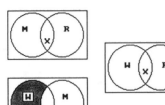
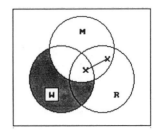

Since the right-hand diagram allows the possibility that the individual that is both M and R might not be W also, the argument can be seen to be invalid.

(6)   All material things are changeable things.
         All worldly goods are material things.

         Thus, all worldly goods are changeable things.

Translating the original into this standard form necessitated changing the order of the propositions and obverting both of the premisses. It resulted in an AAA-1 form. AAA-1 arguments have the middle term distributed in the first premiss and the minor term distributed in both the second premiss and the conclusion. They violate none of chapter 6's rules and are thus valid. Their Venn Diagram check is

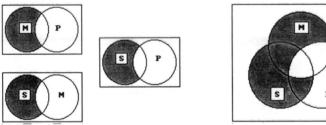

Since the only area left within S (in the three-circle diagram) is also within P, the argument-form is valid.

7.2   Translating Categorical Propositions into Standard Form

It would be too much to hope that the fairly simple and direct translations discussed in section 7.1 would be the only ways in which propositions would need to be altered. The many thousands of years in which language has shifted to meet the changing demands of human life have resulted in our natural languages being very complex and subtle structures. Copi and Cohen offer general ways in which more subtle translations may be made. These, however, ought not be taken so much as rules as they ought be considered rules of thumb. The guiding principle in the more complex transformations that you need to learn to use will be your own common sense applied to the particular context of the argument.

First you need to understand singular propositions. They combine resemblances of both universal and particular propositions. If you say "Charles (son of Elizabeth II and Philip Mountbatten) is the Prince of Wales," then you are asserting that all individuals who are in the (admittedly very small) class of Charleses who also have the appropriate parents are also in the class of Princes of Wales. But you are also asserting that such an individual does exist. Traditionally singular propositions have been handled as if they were universal propositions which happened to have extremely small, that is, one member, subject classes.

Copi and Cohen point out, however, that there is some risk in slavishly following this traditional approach. In the case of an argument which is composed of two singular premisses with the same individual as their subjects, you would be led to evaluate the argument to the conclusion that something shared the predicate properties of the premisses as being invalid. It would, in such a case, actually be valid. They show that a similar difficulty occurs if you try to treat singular propositions as if they were particular, too.

Their solution is quite simple: treat singular propositions as universal propositions with existential import. That approach works quite well when you use Venn Diagrams, but may cause you to feel a bit shaky about the six rules for standard-form categorical syllogisms. Since those rules were not stated for universals with existential import, you may be concerned about difficulties that might arise from the application of these rules to singular propositions. In practice they ought to give you no problems. Arguments which depend upon their resemblance to universals will check out satisfactorily. For example,

> No wrestler is a litterbug.
> Mark is a wrestler.
> -----------------
> Mark is not a litterbug.

when the singular minor premiss and conclusion are treated as universal propositions, becomes an EAE-1 argument. It has three unequivocal terms, a distributed middle term, terms distributed in the premisses which were distributed in the conclusion, only one negative premiss but a negative conclusion following from it, and (as an EAE) no particularity with which to be concerned. Violating none of the rules, it is valid.

Similarly, had the singular propositions in this argument been treated as if they were particular, the argument would have been seen to have been an EIO-1 form. This, too, would check against the rules as being valid.

The challenging cases result from the simultaneous use of two singular propositions as the premisses of an argument. Perhaps a closer look at a problematic argument will suggest a simple solution. Begin with an argument having two singular premisses:

> Morna is a journalist.
> Morna is a soccer player.
> ------------------
> Some soccer players are journalists.

Treating the premisses as universal propositions results in an AAI-3 form which is invalid by violating rule 6 (committing the Existential Fallacy); treating them as particular propositions results in an III-3 argument which is invalid by violating rule 2 and commits the Fallacy of the Undistributed Middle. If you follow Copi and Cohen's advice to "...construe singular propositions as conjunctions of standard-form categorical propositions," then the argument becomes:

> All M is S and some M is S.
> All M is B and some M is B.
> ---------------------
> Some B's are S's.

But this, of course, is *not* a standard-form categorical syllogism. It turns out that what you need to do in such cases to arrive at a standard-form categorical syllogism is to treat one of the premisses as a universal proposition and the other as a particular one. Which you select for each role makes no difference. You will obtain either of the following arguments, both of which are valid:

All M is S.	Some M is S.
Some M is B.	All M is B.
------------	---------
Some B's are S's.	Some B's are S's.

A second form of translation which is a bit simpler to handle occurs when part of the argument is not actually in categorical form. Specifically, statements are frequently made which amount to the same thing as a categorical statement, but which have adjectives describing the subject in place of the categorical predicate. Translation in such cases usually involves nothing more than adding the noun "things" to the predicate. Thus the proposition "no snakes are slimy" translates into the standard-form categorical proposition "no snakes are slimy things."

Similarly, you will sometimes encounter statements which do not use a form of the verb "to be" (which usually functions as the copula of a categorical proposition). In such cases the best technique is to move the concept expressed by the verb into the predicate term. Thus, "some people study hard" would translate into "some people are hard studiers" or "some people are individuals who study hard."

To avoid the sort of subject-verb-object monotony of expression that we frequently associate with first-grade reading texts, a writer sometimes varies the order of the elements within his sentences. This means that the standard-form categorical proposition "all men are mortal" might be expressed as "men are all mortal," as "mortal are all men," as "mortality is a property of all men," or several other ways. When such a non-standardly-formed statement is made, its translation is just the re-arrangement of its elements until you have a standard-form proposition.

Verbal variety also results in synonyms being used for the standard quantity and quality indicators. "Every," "any," "each," and the like are clearly replacements for "all." For clarity, you can always return to *all* as a translation of any of the alternative terms. On some occasions, however, there is no quantity indicator or at least nothing which obviously serves as one. In such cases many people find it helpful to think up a situation in which the quantity-lacking statement might have been used. Once that is done, it usually is a fairly simple matter to decide whether the intention would have been to speak universally or particularly. For example, "the catcher is the most skilled position on a baseball team" and "the catcher was voted Most Valuable Player in the game" are such quantity-less statements. The first statement would likely be said in an argument about the relative merits of the different positions or about the greatest all-time baseball player. It clearly does not mean to address the particular abilities of any one person (who might have been atypical among his peers anyway). It seems evident that it is meant to be an abstract general description of the demands of that position. The second statement would probably be used in describing the performance of a particular individual on a particular occasion. Thus, putting statements into possible contexts seems a useful method of sorting out unstated quantities.

A commonly encountered variant of the universal quantity indicators is the exclusive indicator. "Only" and "none but" are the usually occurring forms. These exclusive usages are universal, but they reverse the order of the terms from the standard universal forms. Thus "all subjects are predicated" would be "only predicates are subjects." One of the most effective ways of insuring that you have the terms in the right order when translating from an exclusive to a categorical form is to test your translation using terms referring to classes whose relationship is perfectly clear. A good example (unless there is a radical alteration of the Pope's position) might be "only women are nuns." Most people raised in a Western culture know that there are large numbers of women who are not nuns, but there are no male nuns. This checks against the translation of the known truth that only women are nuns into "all nuns are women."

Some statements are not categorically formed at all. In some cases they amount to the denial of categorically formed statements. When this occurs, you need to return to the square of opposition and reformulate them as the contradictory of that which they denied. Others require that you figure out what is meant, then express it as categorically as you can. In any event, the primary requirement is that you think carefully and try always to keep in mind what is *meant* by the original statement.

In Copi and Cohen's discussion of numerical or quasi-numerical quantity-indicators, he focuses upon the translation of so-called exceptive propositions. They explain how it is that such propositions actually express two propositions. In the case of the exceptive propositions what you find is a combination of assertion and denial. Thus the exceptive proposition "all students except those on probation are eligible to hold student office" contains the assertion "all non-probationary students **are eligible** to hold student office" and the denial "**No** probationary students **are eligible** to hold student office." Similarly the exceptive proposition "nearly all philosophers enjoy a good joke" contains the assertion "some philosophers **enjoy** a good joke" and the denial "some philosophers **do not enjoy** a good joke." Of course, in this latter case you actually have the additional information that the number who do enjoy a good joke is substantially larger than the number of those who don't, but there is no immediately useful way to express this categorically.

Since standard-form categorical syllogism arguments must have three and only three propositions, arguments in which the two propositions expressed by an exceptive proposition are stated will not be in standard form. To apply the standard-form tests, what you must do is write the argument multiple times, allowing all combinations of the elements of the exceptive propositions in the original premises to appear. If the conclusion of the original argument is an exceptive, then the argument is surely invalid for it would require a violation of the rules for valid syllogisms to allow both elements of the exceptive conclusion to be provable.

You ought now to be fully prepared to work the exercises following 7.2. Your answers should match or be translatable into the answers in *ITL* and here.

(2)   No orchids are fragrant things.

(6)   No non-Havana cigars are Ropo cigars, or, perhaps better, all Ropo cigars are real Havana cigars.

(11)   This one has several possibilities:

All times when she sings are times of inspiration.
All persons who hear her sing are people who are inspired by her singing.
No person who hears her sing is a person who can remain uninspired.

(16)   All party regulars are supporters of any candidate of the Old Guard.

(21)   Some things which glitter are not things made of gold.

7.3   Uniform Translation

In trying to translate from statements which are quite different from standard-form categorical statements, you may find it useful to introduce some additional symbols to ease the translation. In a sense you have already done some of this sort of thing when you did things like add "activities" to "all sports are dangerous" to get the standard form "all sports are dangerous activities." Copi and Cohen want to caution you that the introduction of such an auxiliary symbol may require that you modify the remainder of the argument to insure that you do not commit a Four Term Fallacy. Thus if you introduce time or place, for example, as clarifying parameters in one part of an argument, you may be compelled to make a similar introduction in the other parts. Consider this argument:

> He never had been able to ask a girl of whom he was truly fond for a date, so he never had sought her company for he adored her.

As it appears here it seems a plausible argument, but surely not a categorical syllogism. The occurrence of "never" does suggest a universality of time, so the introduction of the parameter "times" seems reasonable. Doing that yields:

> No times at which he had been truly fond of a specific girl were times at which he was able to ask her for a date.
> All times at which he had known this specific girl were times at which he had been truly fond of her.
> Therefore no times at which he had known this specific girl were times at which he was able to ask her for a date.

This is an EAE-1 argument whose form you can easily show to be valid.

Your answers to the exercises following 7.3 should resemble the ones here and in *ITL* in meaning, if not in specific detail.

I (2)   No times at which she goes to work are times at which she drives.

Of course, being a E proposition this could have appeared in either obverted or converted form:

No times at which she drives are times at which she goes to work, or

All times at which she goes to work are times at which she does not drive.

(6)   All places at which she is are places at which she tries to sell life insurance.

II (2)   All predicables are things that come in contradictory pairs.
No names are things that come in contradictory pairs.

Therefore no names are predicables.

This is an AEE-2 argument. Its Venn Diagram check shows it to be valid.

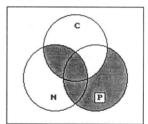

(6)   All acts of fanaticism are acts of vice.
All acts of extremism are acts of fanaticism.

Therefore all acts of extremism are acts of vice.

This is an AAA-1 argument, which is a valid form.

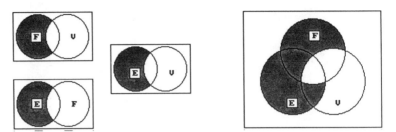

(11)   No inebriated person is a dependable person.
              All alcoholics are inebriated persons.

              Therefore no alcoholic is a dependable person.

    This is an EAE-1 argument and, although Alcoholics Anonymous would surely dispute
the truth of its premisses and conclusion, it is valid.

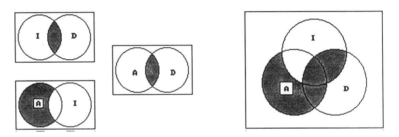

(16)   All people are thinkers.
              All bridge players are people.

              Therefore all bridge players are thinkers.

    This is an AAA-1 argument. Its Venn Diagram will look just like the one for exercise 2
above, so it is valid.

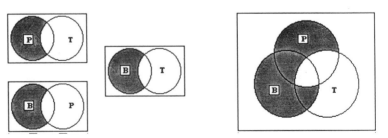

(21)   All acts of medical practice are uses of medical theory.
              All performances of surgery are acts of medical practice.

              Therefore all performances of surgery are uses of medical theory.

This, like exercises 2 and 16, is an AAA-1 argument and has been shown to be valid.

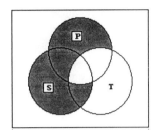

(26)   All conference title games are good games.
         All tomorrow's game is a conference title game.

         Therefore all tomorrow's game is a good game.

This, too, is an AAA-1 valid argument. Note that it required a fairly substantial translation to get it into standard form: the major premiss required use of synonymy and obversion; the minor and conclusion are singular propositions, used here in their quasi-universal form.

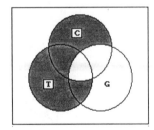

(31)   All cases of disease are occurrences to which the methods of epidemiology can
             usefully be applied.
         All cases of drug abuse are cases of disease.

         Therefore all cases of drug abuse are occurrences to which the methods of
             epidemiology can usefully be applied.

This, too, is an AAA-1 valid argument.

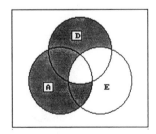

(36)   All express trains are trains that do not stop at this station.
         All trains which, relative to the current time, were the last ones to pass this station
             are trains that do not stop at this station.

         Therefore all trains which, relative to the current time, were the last ones to pass
             this station are express trains.

Note the very awkward circumlocution used to change the singular minor premiss and conclusion into a universal-appearing form. Note also the occurrence of "not" in the middle term; it indicates that the class being used is the complement of the class of trains stopping at the station, but it does not make the premisses negative. This argument is an AAA-2 form and the following Venn Diagrams show that it is invalid.

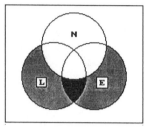

(41)   All times at which a great deal of money is at stake are times at which the competition is stiff.
            The current time is one at which there is a great deal of money at stake.

            Therefore the current time is a time at which competition is stiff.

        This is another AAA-1 valid argument.

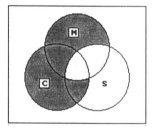

(46)   No sane witness is a person who incriminates himself.
            Some witnesses are persons who incriminate themselves.

            Therefore some witnesses are not sane witnesses.

        This is an EIO-2 argument. The Venn Diagram below proves it is valid.

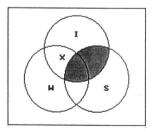

7.4   Enthymemes

If you think back to chapter one, section two (in which the concepts of premiss and conclusion were introduced), you will recall that some arguments were shown to have premisses or a conclusion that were not stated. When the context is clear or when the missing proposition seems obvious, this absence of a part of an argument can occur with categorical syllogisms, too. Such categorical arguments with "understood" elements are called enthymemes. Tradition divided enthymematic categorical syllogisms according to which proposition is unstated: first-order enthymemes are missing their major premiss, second-order ones are missing their minor premiss, and third-order enthymemes have their conclusion unstated.

Of course, if you are trying to evaluate a categorical syllogism which is offered in enthymematic form, you will have to add to what is given what you take to have been assumed. There is a hazard, however, in making such an addition to what an arguer has offered: he may accept no responsibility for what you add to his argument. And, if you can show that the proposition that you have added is necessary in order to make his argument valid, he must accept it or reject his own argument as invalid. Most crushing, obviously, would be showing that *no added proposition* would result in a valid argument. That, however, would require a fairly complex proof, eliminating quite a number of possibilities.

Ultimately, when treating an argument as an enthymeme, you ought to provide the proposition which best serves the purpose of making the argument plausible and valid. In general, deciding what the missing element ought to be is quite simple. Since you already have two of the propositions in the argument, you can determine which proposition is missing: If you have a first-order enthymeme, then you can look to the conclusion to determine the predicate term and the minor premiss to identify the middle term. Once they are identified, there are only eight possible candidates for the missing major premiss: the order M-P as an A, E, I, or O proposition or the order P-M as one of those four-forms. If one of those is not obviously the needed major premiss, you can always resort to an exhaustive check of each of them inserted into the argument. Similarly you can work out one of the third order. An arguer who uses enthymematic arguments must accept the risk of having a proposition other than the one he intended to the argument, but he ought not have to contend with additions which seek to invalidate his argument.

In the exercises following 7.4, you should indicate clearly the proposition which you add to the argument as you present the argument in standard form.

(2)   All things which are ever [*always*] in motion are immortal things.
           [*All souls are things which are ever in motion.*]

           Therefore all souls are immortal things.

The added minor premiss is stated in brackets, indicating that it is not a stated part of the original argument. Since the minor premiss is the one assumed, the argument is a second-order enthymeme. The added premiss is consistent with Platonic philosophy and completes the argument as an AAA-1 valid form argument.

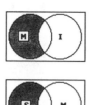

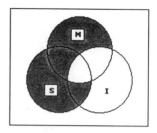

(6)   All successful people are well-groomed.
        Leslie Cole is well-groomed.
        -
        [*Therefore Leslie Cole is a successful person.*]

This is an invalid AAA-2 argument. (See the Venn Diagram below for proof.) You may ask why, when I just argued for why you should make an argument valid if possible, I allowed the added conclusion not to do so. The answer is that there is no standard-form categorical proposition that can be inferred from the union of the two given premises. And how did I know they were premises? The argument as given said "...and we know what that implies..." That is a clear sign that it is the conclusion that is omitted. And none of the eight propositions that could have been formed from the people would follow validly from the given premises. This seems most likely the one intended, violates the second rule for syllogisms and commits the Fallacy of the Undistributed Middle.

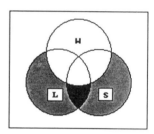

(11)   All physicians are college graduates.
            [*All members of the AMA are physicians.*]
            -
            Therefore all members of the AMA are college graduates.

The added minor converts this second-order enthymeme into a valid AAA-1 argument. Although one would have to check the AMA's membership records to determine the truth of the added minor premiss, it does at least seem plausible.

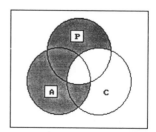

(16)   [*All families with a telephone are families with their name listed in the telephone book.*]

The Adamsons are a family with their name not listed in the telephone book.

Therefore the Adamsons are a family without a telephone.

Treating the given singular minor premiss of this first-order enthymeme as a universal proposition suggests the major premiss which has been added. The form resulting in an AEE-2 which the following Venn Diagram shows is valid.

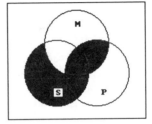

(21)   No sense knowledge is immaterial knowledge.
Some knowledge that we possess is immaterial knowledge.

[Therefore some knowledge that we possess is not sense knowledge.]

The "...therefore, etc." in the quotation from Scotus is a clear indicator that the missing proposition is the conclusion, making this a third-order enthymeme. The EIO argument form is the only one valid in all four figures (due to the convertability of both premisses). You might note that an alternate conclusion, some things that are not sense knowledge are knowledge that we possess, would also have resulted in a valid argument. It, however, would have required translation of the first premiss by obversion to avoid violating rules 1 and 5. This argument, an EIO-2, is shown to be valid by the following Venn Diagram.

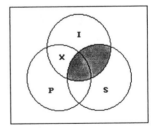

(26)   [All species which tend to increase at a greater rate than their means of subsistence are occasionally subject to a severe struggle for their existence.]

Homo Sapiens is a species which tends to increase at a greater rate than its means of subsistence.

Therefore *Homo Sapiens* is occasionally subject to a severe struggle for its existence.

The needed major premiss for this first-order enthymeme seems both consistent with Darwinian theory and unobjectionable. The resulting AAA-1 argument is, as usual, valid.

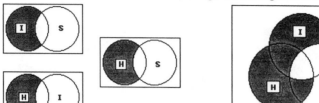

(31)   All times at which the Democrats were successful in politics were times in which they could use the issues of high employment, high interest rates and high inflation against their opponents.
            No current time is one in which they can use those issues against their opponents.

            [Therefore no current time is one in which the Democrats are successful.]

This third-order enthymeme requires the stated conclusion to form an AEE-2 valid syllogism. Since the context was Fraser's summation of Carter's problems, the addition of such a conclusion seems quite reasonable. The Venn Diagram demonstrates the validity of the argument.

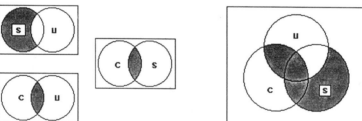

7.5   Sorites

You have seen that arguments may occur with parts missing, with apparently multiple terms, with sentence forms which diverge widely from standard categorical forms, and with more information than is actually used in reaching their conclusions. It ought not, therefore, seem too strange to encounter arguments which appear to be basically syllogistic, but which have too many premisses. In the case of enthymematic arguments it was your responsibility to provide the missing proposition. In a chain argument or sorites, (the term [like "deer"] is both singular and plural), it will not be required that you eliminate excess premisses. If there were spare premisses, ones which were unneeded in the inference, you could, of course, discard them, but a sorites does not have more premisses than strict categorical form allows simply by the addition of irrelevancies. A sorites is, in a sense, an abbreviation for a string of categorical syllogisms. From two premisses you draw a conclusion. That conclusion is then used as a premiss either with another of the given premisses or with another conclusion-used-as-premiss derived from different premises. This using-conclusions-as-premises continues until you arrive at the overall conclusion of the argument.

If you looked at the subject and predicate terms of the conclusion of a sorites as the minor and major terms of the sorites, then all of the other terms in it would be middle terms. Expressed in a skeletal way a sorites might look like:

> All M' is P.
> All M" is M'.
> All M'" is M".
> All S is M'".
> ----------
> All S is P.

Evaluation of a sorites is straightforward: you break the chain into its component standard-form categorical syllogisms and evaluate each of them. If all the component syllogisms of a sorites are valid, then it is valid; if there is at least one of these syllogisms that is invalid, then the sorites is invalid. (Validity and invalidity are in a way like being dead or pregnant: there is no such thing as "a little bit.") When the sorites above is broken into its constituent syllogisms you have

> All M' is P.
> All M" is M'.
> ----------
> All M" is P.
>
> All M" is P.
> All M'" is M".
> ----------
> All M'" is P.
>
> All M'" is P.
> All S is M'".
> ----------
> All S is P.

In this case, since all the arguments are instances of the valid AAA-1 form, this sorites is valid.

In terms of evaluation of arguments, then, sorites add no new difficulties. Since the intermediate conclusions are not stated, sorites constitute a kind of third-order enthymeme. Since they can be broken down into standard-form categorical syllogisms, they need no new evaluation techniques. All they are likely to do is require a bit more patience. You ought now to try your patience in working the exercises following 7.5. The answers here and in *ITL* should serve as a check on your approach.

I (2)   (1')   All experienced persons are competent persons.
          (3')   No competent person is always blundering.
          (2')   Jenkins is always blundering.

          Jenkins is not an experienced person.

This breaks down into two syllogisms:

(a)   No competent person is always blundering.
All experienced persons are competent persons.

No experienced persons are always blundering.

(b)   No experienced persons are always blundering.
Jenkins is always blundering.

Jenkins is not an experienced person.

The first is an EAE-1 form and the second is an EAE-2. The Venn Diagrams below show that both are valid forms.

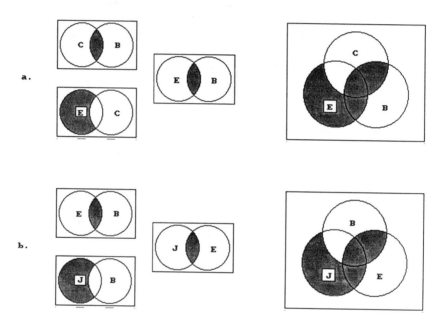

II (2)   The standard-form sorites based upon these premisses is

(3')   No nice things are wholesome things.
(1')   All puddings are nice things.
(2')   This dish is a pudding.

[*This dish is not a wholesome thing.*]

Its component syllogisms are

(a)   No nice things are wholesome things.
All puddings are nice things.

No puddings are wholesome things.

(b)   No puddings are wholesome things.
        This dish is a pudding.

        [*This dish is not a wholesome thing*].

They are both EAE-1 argument-forms and the Venn Diagram below shows that they are both valid.

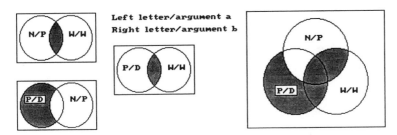

7.6   Disjunctive and Hypothetical Syllogisms

The next level of complexity beyond the categorical syllogism in the study of arguments will be arguments whose component parts are not categories but propositions. More extensive consideration of such arguments will take place in chapter 8, but Copi and Cohen choose to introduce two of the simplest propositional arguments (for so they are called) in this section and a third in 7.7.

One common way you have encountered for compounding propositions is by alternating them, that is, by joining them with the word "or." Such a compound proposition is called a disjunction or an alternation. A very simple form of argument based upon elimination uses such a disjunction. Traditionally an argument with the form called a disjunctive syllogism is

Proposition 1 or Proposition 2.
It is not the case that Proposition 1.

Therefore Proposition 2.

It is a syllogism because it contains exactly two premisses and one conclusion; it is disjunctive because its first premiss is a disjunction. This is the form of argument that Sherlock Holmes usually used when he told Watson he had deduced something. In fact, on numerous occasions Holmes told Watson that if you eliminate all of the possible alternatives except one then that one, no matter how unlikely it seems, is the answer.

It is important to take care to follow the pattern shown above quite faithfully. As Copi and Cohen point out, there do exist arguments which resemble this form but which are invalid. Most common of these is one that argues:

Proposition 1 or Proposition 2.
It is the case that Proposition 1.

Therefore it is not the case that Proposition 2.

Such an argument would only be satisfactory if we had the additional information that the truths expressed by Propositions 1 and 2 were somehow exclusive: that the truth of the one entailed the falsity of the other. Since we do not have such information for disjunctions in general or this one in particular, this second argument-form is not valid.

The second type of propositional argument which Copi and Cohen introduce in this section may actually be broken down into three propositional argument-forms. All three are based upon the compound proposition involving the conditional or hypothetical relationship: if Proposition 1 then Proposition 2. The form, which traditionally is called a hypothetical syllogism, Copi and Cohen call a pure hypothetical syllogism. It is pure because all three compound propositions in it (two premises and a conclusion) assert a conditional relation between their respective elements. If you are familiar with the mathematical concept of transitivity, then you will see that the pure hypothetical syllogism is merely the assertion of the transitive nature of the if-then relationship:

> If Proposition 1 then Proposition 2.
> If Proposition 2 then Proposition 3.
> --------------------------------
> If Proposition 1 then Proposition 3.

On some occasions this sort of argument has been called the "logical domino theory." Just as, with properly aligned dominoes, pushing over the first sets off a chain reaction that does not stop until the last has fallen, evidence for the first proposition in a pure hypothetical carries the inference on until the last is also supported.

Copi and Cohen identify mixed hypothetical syllogisms as mixed because they assert a hypothetical relationship only in one premiss. Their other premiss either asserts the proposition in the if-part of the conditional or denies the proposition in the then-part of it. The mixed hypothetical syllogism, then, has two possible forms:

> If Proposition 1 then Proposition 2.
> Proposition 1 is true.
> ----------------
> Proposition 2 is true.

> If Proposition 1 then Proposition 2.
> Proposition 2 is false.
> ----------------
> Proposition 1 is false.

The upper version traditionally has been called *modus ponens*; the lower one *modus tollens*.

Each of these is often confused with an invalid argument-form which resembles it. These confusions are traditionally identified as the Fallacies of the Denial of the Antecedent and of the Affirmation of the Consequent. Those names make little sense if you do not recall that the if-part of a conditional statement is called the antecedent and the then-part is called the consequent. If you exchange the words "true" and "false" in the *modus ponens* and *modus tollens* argument-forms, then you have these fallacies:

> If Proposition 1 then Proposition 2.
> Proposition 2 is true.
> ----------------
> Proposition 1 is true.

> If Proposition 1 then Proposition 2.
> Proposition 2 is true.
> ---------------
> Proposition 1 is true.

One of the easiest ways to see that these fallacies really are unsatisfactory is to look at actual arguments following their form:

> If you are the result of an Immaculate Conception then you were born.
> You were not the result of an Immaculate Conception.
> ---------------------------------------
> Thus you were not born.

> If you killed him then Abraham Lincoln is dead.
> Abraham Lincoln is dead.
> ---------------------
> Thus you killed him.

The premises of both arguments seem unquestionably satisfactory, but the first conclusion would surely come as a surprise to your mother and the second one as a shock to a lot of American historians.

    In working the exercises following 7.6 all you need to do to determine validity is to remember that disjunctive and hypothetical syllogisms that **exactly** match the stipulated forms are valid, ones that do not are likely invalid.

(2)   This is a mixed hypothetical syllogism of the *modus tollens* type. Re-written in standard form it is

> If I have any more to do with that operation, then I'd have to lie to the Ambassador.
> I can't lie to the Ambassador.
> -----------------------------------
> Thus I can't have any more to do with that operation.

Since it is an exact match for the *modus tollens form, this is a valid argument.*

(6)   This is a disjunctive syllogism in standard form. Since it exactly matches the stipulated form, it is valid.

(11)   This is an exact match for the mixed hypothetical syllogism *modus tollens* pattern. Therefore it is valid.

(16)   This is a mixed hypothetical syllogism, but does not match either of the valid patterns. Instead it follows the form of the Fallacy of the Affirmation of the Consequent and is thus invalid.

(21)   This, too, is a mixed hypothetical syllogism of the *modus tollens* form. Re-written in standard for it is

> If mankind had understood him, then they would surely have built noble temples and
>   altars, and offered solemn sacrifices in his honor.
> Mankind has not done such building and offering.
> -------------------------------------
> Thus mankind did not understand him.

    Following a valid pattern, this is a valid argument.

(26)   This strictly follows the valid disjunctive syllogism form, thus is itself valid.

(31)   Once you have removed the explanatory material about astronomy and why it is not psychology, you are left with the argument:

> If number were an idea, then arithmetic would be psychology.
> Arithmetic is not psychology.
> ----------------------
> Therefore number is not an idea.

Since this matches the mixed hypothetical syllogism *modus tollens* pattern, it is a valid argument.

(36)   This requires somewhat more sophisticated re-writing than any of the other arguments discussed this far. A helpful technique for figuring out how the propositions in the hypothetical clause ("you cannot have a general economic recovery without housing doing reasonably well....") is to substitute propositions of whose relationship you are certain. In this case a useful pair are "you can make an omelet" and "you break eggs." We know that if you make an omelet then you must have broken eggs (or had someone break them for you) and we also know that it is not the case that if you break eggs you will make an omelet (for you may be baking a cake). Look at the two compound propositions obtained by substituting these for the original propositions:

> You cannot make an omelet without breaking an egg.
> You cannot break an egg without an omelet being made.

Clearly the former is plausible while the latter is ridiculous. The correct form for this argument is

> If there is a general economic recovery, then housing will do reasonably well.
> Housing will not do reasonably well.
> --------------------------
> Thus there will not be a general economic recovery.

This is another mixed hypothetical syllogism of the *modus tollens* form, thus it is valid.

7.7   The Dilemma

Copi and Cohen's explanation of the dilemma is both detailed and clear. You probably feel little need for any additional discussion of how a dilemma operates or of how you might grapple with a dilemma whose conclusion you wished to reject. There are, however, a few details that may be of some interest.

The name "dilemma" derives from the Greek prefix "di-" meaning "two" and the Greek word "lemma" which meant in its logical usage "premiss." The "two-premiss-ness" refers not to the two premises of the argument but to the two conditional "premisses" which are conjoined in this form of argument.

A defining characteristic of categorical syllogisms was that they contained exactly three terms. Analogously, a defining characteristic of full-blown dilemmas is that they contain four propositions. For the sake of brevity, I will indicate them as P-1, P-2, P-3, and P-4 in this discussion. The basic, or root, form of the dilemma. Structurally it looks like a sort of alternative *modus ponens* argument:

> If P-1 then P-2, and if P-3 then P-4.
> Either P-1 or P-3.
> -------------------------
> Therefore either P-2 or P-4.

The form is obviously satisfactory because of the *modus ponens* buried within it. Both the conditional statements are asserted, so if P-1 is true then P-2 would follow and if P-3 is true then P-4 would follow. But you also know that either P-1 or P-3 is the case, so P-2 or P-4 (and perhaps both) must be the case.

Since the *complex constructive dilemma* is analogous, loosely, to *modus ponens*, you might suspect that there should be a dilemma form that bears a similar loose analogy to *modus tollens*. Your suspicions are well-grounded. The argument is called a *complex destructive dilemma* and has the form:

> If P-1 then P-2, and if P-3 then P-4.
> Either P-2 is false or P-4 is false.
> -------------------------
> Thus either P-1 is false or P-3 is false.

For reasons like those given with the *complex constructive dilemma*, this is a valid argument-form.

Usually when there is a complex form of something there is also a simple form of it. This is the case with both of these dilemma forms. The simple (or degenerate) dilemma forms involve only three propositions, both conditionals sharing the same consequent in the constructive form or antecedent in the destructive one. The simple constructive dilemma is

> If P-1 then P-2, and if P-3 then P-2.
> Either P-1 or P-3.
> -------------
> Therefore P-2.

The simple destructive dilemma is

> If P-1 then P-2, and if P-1 then P-3.
> Either P-2 is false or P-3 is false.
> -------------------------
> Therefore P-1 is false.

The one thing that a good debater loves to find in a dilemma is that the disjunctive premiss is the alternation of a proposition and its denial. That insures that someone trying to counter his argument has no chance of "slipping between the horns of the dilemma," for there is no third option.

One classic use of a dilemma was offered at the peak of the war in Vietnam by Republican Senator George Aiken of Vermont. He had been a early opponent of that conflict, was convinced that the United states needed to withdraw from it quickly, and argued:

> If we win the conflict in Vietnam then we will lose face because we will appear to be such bullies ("First-rate industrial power smashes tenth-rate agrarian power"), but if we lose the conflict in Vietnam then we will lose face because we will appear ineffectual ("First-rate industrial power smashed by tenth-rate agrarian one"). We must win or lose the conflict in Vietnam. Thus we are doomed to a loss of face.

Of course, he wanted to take the conclusion as a premiss and go one step further: if we are doomed to a loss of face anyway, then we might as well just get out without paying any attention to what anyone else says. His whole argument is subject to the sorts of criticisms and oppositions that Copi and Cohen suggest. You might want to try your hand at arguing against Aiken's dilemma.

Whether you chose to try to refute Aiken or not, you should work the exercises following 7.7, checking your efforts here and in *ITL after* you do the exercises.

(2)   You could probably mount an effective argument for slipping between the horns of this dilemma. It certainly would be plausible to claim that Circuit Courts can be more or less effective both in general and in specific cases. Being useful is subject to a broad spectrum of values, from indispensable to scarcely worth the trouble.

The horns of this dilemma are vulnerable, too. It could prove quite useful to a State to deny all the rights guaranteed in the Bill of Rights. That utility would almost surely not justify abolition of the Bill of Rights. And something's not being useful is surely not justification for its abolition. It would be very difficult to show much practical function in newborn infants, but the human race would find itself in a rather awkward position if newborn infants were banned for a century or so. (That awkward situation is frequently called extinction.)

Lincoln's dilemma, then, certainly is open to refutation, although a counter-dilemma either from the elements of this one or from other sources seems not to be a terribly fruitful approach.

(6)   Convincing arguments could be offered for why you could slip between the horns (starting with the arguments offered by Copi and Cohen against exercise 5). It is also possible to grapple with either horn. An argument can be offered as deductive which turns out to be invalid but which, had it been considered as an *inductive* argument, might have had significant value. The second horn may be rejected because there may be, for example, psychological value in bringing into focus relationships which were already basically known. Refuting counter-dilemmas in this case (having a single-proposition conclusion) might also prove valuable.

(11)   There seems to be rather a significant gap between living extravagantly and living modestly, so these horns ought to be fairly easy to slip between. Each horn has an obvious refuting argument. If you live extravagantly you may well have nothing left to contribute; if you live modestly you may well have had nothing with which to have lived more expansively. Counter-dilemmas would probably result in a conclusion which only appeared to refute this conclusion, actually being compatible with it.

(16)   A good case can be made for claiming that this is not a dilemma in any of the sense of the term that have been discussed either in this *Study Guide* or in *ITL*. This argument's form actually is

If P-1, then either P-2 or P-3.
Both P-2 and P-3 are false.

Thus P-1 must be false.

As an argument, this is valid, but calling it a dilemma is certainly questionable. There are, however, several plausible refutations that one might offer for it. First, it is reasonable to suggest that there is another motion-option: from one place to another. Second, depending upon how broadly you read being "...in the place where it is..." it surely is possible to move there, as when you rock in a rocking chair. And third, given a broad view of interactions (perhaps a sort of radical relativism) there may be no place which really counts as a place "...where it [the moving object] is not..." Since it is doubtful that this ought to be considered a dilemma at all, seeking a counter-dilemma seems pointless.

(21)   Only a devout Muslim would see the alternatives as exhaustive and exclusive. To the rest of the world slipping between the horns by claiming that there are many things which are not in the Koran but which also do not disagree with it (addressing, for example, issues and topics which it does not discuss). But the horns are vulnerable too. Since Islam does not sanction any translation of the Koran from Arabic, there may be necessity of repeating what is in it for all of us who do not read Arabic and who have little facility with languages. To a non-Muslim there probably is nothing at all pernicious about differing with the Koran. A counter-dilemma constructed from the elements of this argument would as in so many of the other exercises, not refute the conclusion of the stated dilemma.

CHAPTER SEVEN SUMMARY

I.   Application of testing techniques for standard-form categorical syllogisms re-
        quires translation of non-standard arguments into standard forms.

        A.   Translation may be by re-ordering propositions.

        B.   Translation may be by using one term for synonyms.

        C.   Translation may be by valid immediate categorical inference.

II.   Some translations into standard form require sophisticated under standing of the
        meaning of the stated propositions.

        A.   Singular propositions combine characteristics of both universal and
                particular propositions.

            1.   They are universal when the individual is treated as a unit-class (class
                        with one member).

            2.   They are particular in that they have existential import.

        B.   Properties delineated by adjectives need to be associated with neutral
                nouns (like "things") when translating to standard form.

        C.   Verbs other than forms of "to be" need to be absorbed into the predi-
                cate when translating to standard form.

        D.   Internal verbal order may have to be rearranged.

        E.   Non-standard quantity-indicators (like "every") must be replaced by
                standard ones.

        F.   Exclusive propositions (indicated by words like "only" and "none but")
                are translated with their terms in the opposite order from the way they
                are given.

        G.   Common sense should rule translation of radically non-categorically-
                formed propositions.

        H.   Exceptive propositions should be treated as the conjunction of their
                assertions.

III.   Time and place parameters may be introduced to maintain a uniformity of cate-
        gorical expression.

IV.   Arguments with unstated premises or conclusion are called enthymemes.

        A.   An enthymeme is first-, second-, or third-order depending upon wheth-
                er the major premiss, the minor premiss or the conclusion is assumed.

        B.   If at all possible, the unstated proposition which is added to the argu-
                ment as given ought to serve to make the argument valid.

V.   A chain argument of categorical propositions is called a sorites.

      A.   Sorites are evaluated by being broken down into a series of categorical syllogisms.

      B.   Sorites are valid if and only if every categorical syllogism in their separate form is valid.

VI. Syllogisms occur in non-categorical forms.

      A.   A disjunctive syllogism argues for one of a pair of alternatives based upon the denial of the other.

      B.   A hypothetical syllogism is based upon one or two conditional (if-then) propositions.

          1.   A pure hypothetical syllogism asserts two conditional premisses linked to show transitivity.

          2.   A mixed hypothetical syllogism relates a conditional proposition with a simple one.

              a.   *Modus Ponens* derives the consequent of the conditional by asserting the conditional and its antecedent.

              b.   *Modus Tollens* derives denying the antecedent of a conditional by asserting the conditional and the denial of its consequent.

VII.   The dilemma mixes conditional and disjunctive propositions to derive a disjunctive (usually) conclusion.

      A.   Dilemmas occur in constructive and destructive forms, both simply and complexly.

      B.   There are multiple ways of attacking a dilemma.

          1.   The alternative premiss may be shown not to be exhaustive. (Slipping between the horns.)

          2.   The conditional propositions may be shown not to be the case. (Grappling with the horn.)

          3.   A counter-dilemma may be offered, supporting the opposite of the conclusion.

Chapter Eight
Symbolic Logic

8.1   The Value of Special Symbols

Most of us have seen the advertisement in magazines that reads: "F U Cn Rd Ths, U Cn B Mkng Bg Mny!" (In case you find it doesn't make sense to you, it reads: "If you can read this, you can be making big money." In general it involves dropping vowels and unsounded letters.) It is, of course, intended to persuade you to enroll in the advertiser's course in rapid writing. This method, or the more famous Gregg and Pitman methods of shorthand, are simply sets of conventional abbreviations. Lots of people find that, in areas where they have to record the same thing frequently, it is very helpful to employ such "shorthand" techniques. Common examples include Rd., Ave., Feb., etc. (Note that even the last is also an abbreviation.) Some abbreviations are ambiguous, such as St., which means "street" in some contexts and "saint" in others. In any event, we all recognize the value of such notations. If it were possible, we would appreciate being able to abbreviate much of what we write. The use of symbolic logic can provide some of that effect.

There is an additional problem that natural languages, that is, ones which men developed through use, seem to share: they all tend to be ambiguous, awkward and inconsistent. English, perhaps as a result of the checkered political history of the British Isles, seems to be particularly blessed (or cursed) with such problems. This is not to say that that is always a problem; in some areas each of the natural languages is quite precise, and sometimes imprecision is desirable. It is, of course, the "mushiness" of the language that allows for its poetry, as was discussed in chapter 2. It has been the drive to "clean up" languages that has led men to the development of such artificial languages as Interlingua and Esperanto. In them the attempt is made to remove the ambiguities, to eliminate the inconsistencies, in short to generate a "logically" appropriate language. Such languages have precise grammars and vocabularies, so that there are no irregular verbs, no homonyms, and no exceptions to the rules. The problem that they encounter, beside the natural resistance of humanity to trade in their old ways for new ones, is that by eliminating the ability of the language to stretch and twist, you also limit the breadth and depth of communication that is possible. When everything is drawn up into compartments, you find that the things that seem to rest on the lines are very discomforting.

The adaptation of a logical set of symbols to be used to represent any major segment of our verbal arguments will have to encounter the same problem, for it all really boils down to one thing--we have to reach some balance between the detailed accuracy of our artificial language (its ability to mirror our natural language) and the usefulness of having it be artificial (its saving our efforts in using it). If the artificial language does a really good job of handling everything that we can handle in English, then it is likely very nearly as complex as the natural language with which we started. If it is that complex then we will probably waste more time shifting back and forth between the artificial language and the natural one than we save by avoiding the natural language. If on the other hand, the artificial one is sufficiently removed from the natural one that we can really operate efficiently in it, it will likely be very difficult to make the translations from one to the other. If we have to spend all of our time figuring out whether or not the artificial language is really expressing meaning enough like the natural one to make the effort worth our while, then the time lost again makes it likely that we are better off with the natural language.

It may be, however, that **if** we go into the use of a very efficient artificial language with our eyes wide open--knowing what its shortcomings are--then we will be willing to accept the discrepancies between the two. If we find that we save more time using the symbols than we spend worrying about how accurately our symbols represent the natural arguments, then we have a net saving. The more efficient the symbolic system is, while still approximating the natural one, the more useful it becomes. It is such a highly useful system that Copi and Cohen present in Chapter 8.

8.2   The Symbols for Conjunction, Negation, and Disjunction

The logic which is introduced in Chapter 8 is called by several names--propositional logic, propositional calculus, sentential logic, the logic of statements, and several others. Those names are a result of the several ways logicians refer to the elements which serve as the building blocks of the logic. No matter what you call those component elements, they are representative of the sort of thing that we express in simple declarative sentences like "it is raining." The reason for the multitude of names is that logicians cannot quite agree about those things "are," if indeed they are anything. "It is raining" and "the rain is falling" are clearly different sentences, but do seem to "say the same thing." It is that property of "saying the same thing" that some logicians refer to as "expressing the same proposition." That also allows the sentence (in English) "it is raining" and the sentence (in German) "es regnet" to be treated identically. The normal clue--whether you opt for calling them sentences, statements or propositions--is that they are the sort of thing that can be said to be true or false.

It is that property of being true of false that makes this sort of statement useful in a system of logic. There are relationships in which statements can occur, be compounded, or be analyzed largely in terms of the relationships between the truth or falsity of the component statements. When the truth or falsity (called the *truth value*) of a component statement can be discovered solely as a product of the truth values of its component statements, that compound is said to be a *truth-functional* compound. The logic of statements (or propositional calculus, etc.), then, is the study of statements, truth-functional connectives, and how to work with them.

The most obvious of the truth-functional connectives really isn't a connective at all, it's an operator. It doesn't hook two statements together; it changes the value of one statement. Most frequently it is called *negation*. Its simplest occurrence in English is the insertion into a statement of the word "not." Thus "it is raining" becomes "it is not raining." The nice thing about negation is its simplicity: a negation precisely denies what it negates. Thus, if any statement is true, its negation is false; if a statement is false, its negation is true. To represent this relationship, two things are necessary: a symbolic representation of the statement and a symbol for negation. In general logicians have agreed to use the lower case letters "p," "q," "r," "s," and so on to serve as *variables* standing for some statement or other. *ITL* uses upper case letters which have some sort of connection to what is said as symbols representing actual statements. The symbol used to represent the operation of negating is the tilde or curl (~). It has been suggested that you arrive at it if you try to write a capital N as a single stroke while trying to do it with ever-increasing speed. Such a series might look like this:

Other systems of logical notation [and there are several] will represent negation as an apostrophe [p'], a dash [-p], a bar [p̄], or a prefixed capital N [Np].) One of the nicest things about the use of such symbols is that they can be fitted into a table that makes all of the relationships quite clear and easy to work with. The table (called a *truth table*) for negation is

P	~P
T	F
F	T

You read across the table. Thus, when p is T (true), ~p is F (false); when p is F, ~p is T. *ITL* says that this table may be regarded as a definition of the negation operation; actually it *must* be regarded as such, at least for logic as it is normally done. (This defining characteristic of the truth tables doesn't seem too important for the curl, but will be quite important later.)

In addition to "not," the curl may be used to stand for any of the many words and phrases that indicate the operation of negation: "It is false that ...," "...is false," "...is not the case," and any of the compounding prefixes such as "il-," "un-," or "dis-." These prefixes are particularly difficult because you have to be very careful to insure that they are really functioning as a "not" would; that is, that they are denying what would be asserted if they were dropped. Thus, the statement "John is immoral" is not the same as "John is not moral" (and cannot be represented as ~J) because there is a third option--John may be amoral, which is neither moral nor immoral. On the other hand "handcuffs were unnecessary," can be read as being the same as "handcuffs were not necessary," and both could be represented as ~H. The key test for the occurrence of negation is to see whether or not the dropping of what you think is a negation causes the truth value of the statement to reverse.

The first connective that Copi and Cohen introduce is *conjunction*. Its most common form is the occurrence of "and." They use a raised, heavy dot to symbolize this connective, and it is a connective that joins two statements. They symbolize "p and q" as p • q. (Other systems of logical notation use an inverted wedge [p ∧ q], a capital K [Kpq], the ampersand [p&q] or, when it is unambiguous, the statements are juxtaposed or written together [pq]. The truth table for conjunction is

p	q	p • q
T	T	T
T	F	F
F	T	F
F	F	F

Again you read across the table. This means that when p and q are both true, then p • q is true, but when either (or both) component(s) is (are) false, the compound statement is also false. This corresponds well with our treatment of "and" statements in English, that the compound assertion "statement 1 and statement 2" is taken to be true if and only if both components are true. In talking of a truth table we frequently read it vertically, top to bottom, as a shorthand way of referring to it. That would make such reference to this standard table for conjunction be TFFF (Tee-Ef-Ef-Ef). If you were to memorize the table, the easiest way would be that when p and q are both true, p • q is true; otherwise it is false.

In addition to "and" Copi and Cohen give you a good list of other words that you could represent by "•". You might, however, find it useful to make a small card on which you record all of the information you collect about each of the connectives. Such a card for conjunction might look like the example below.

p • q

p q	p • q
T T	T
T F	F
F T	F
F F	F

and	nevertheless
but	although
yet	moreover
still	however
also	in addition to

Notice that this sample leaves lots of room for you to add additional words as you encounter them. If you make one such card for each of the symbols, you will find that it is much faster to refer to them as you work problems than it is to look back into the text and the *Study Guide*.

As Copi and Cohen point out, the most problematic thing about conjunction is identifying the cases that look like conjunctions of statements but are not. Thus "John and Jane are married" could appear to be a compact way of writing "John is married and Jane is married" but probably isn't. The former statement seems also to tell us that they are married *to each other* while that does not seem implicit in the latter at all. In fact it seems most likely that we would use the two different statements precisely to distinguish between the cases of persons who are married to each other and persons who each happen to be married. The key point to look for is whether the dropping of one of the supposed conjuncts loses information about the other conjunct too.

The third connective introduced is *disjunction* (or *alternation*). As Copi and Cohen indicate, the English "or" is ambiguous. In Latin, for example, the ambiguity is removed by having two words "vel" and "aut" for the inclusive and exclusive meanings of "or," respectively. It is the "v" from "vel" that is the source of the wedge that is commonly used as the symbolization of alternation. In the absence of solid indication that an "or" is being used exclusively, logicians have accepted the convention of treating "or" inclusively. Thus any use of " v " in the logic means "and/or." This causes no problems, for if one wanted to symbolize "p or q, but not both" it could be done by symbolizing exactly what is there-- $(p • q) • \sim (p • q)$.

The truth table for disjunction is

p q	p v q
T T	T
T F	T
F T	T
F F	F

Note that, if you were memorizing it, the easiest way would be to notice that the only way to falsify a disjunction is to have *BOTH* disjuncts be false; all other cases are true.

The only common expressions symbolized by "v" are "Either ... or ..." "... or ...," and "... unless ...." The occurrence of the "either" has no real effect on the connective; it serves primarily as a sort of punctuation for the sentence. "Either," like "both," however, must be watched with particular care when they are used together with "not." The expression "not either p or q" is equivalent to saying "neither p nor q," while the expression "either not p or q is simply the disjunction; the former pair are symbolized $\sim (p \lor q)$ and the latter expression is $\sim p \lor q$. At first glance these might seem to be the same, but another logical convention applies: the curl applies to as little as it possibly can. This means that the former case has it applying to the *quantity* $(p \lor q)$ while the latter to the "p" alone. Using a few extra symbols, the former is

~[(p) v (q)] and the latter is [~ (p)) v (q)]. One way to indicate "what belongs to what" in a symbolic expression until you get used to operating with these symbols is by the use of underlining. If you start with the simplest elements and progressively underline larger and larger compounds, then you can see at a glance what each operator is doing, then below it is the same expression with the appropriate underlining.

$$\sim([\,p\,v\,(q\,\bullet\,r)\,]\,v\sim[\,\sim(\sim p\,\bullet\,s)\,\bullet\,t\,])$$

$$\sim([\,p\,v\,(q\,\bullet\,r)\,]\,v\sim[\,\sim(\sim p\,\bullet\,s)\,\bullet\,t\,])$$

In this case you can trace, for example, the location of the line which first occurs under the third "~ " (that line is the fourth one down on the right side) and note that it is under exactly the same expression as the previous line *except for the extension under the curl*. That tells you that the third curl negates the quantity (~p • s). If you should try this method and do not get a solid line under the entire expression, then either you have made a mistake in your underlining or the formula is not properly made.

At the end of section 8.2 Copi and Cohen have 100 exercises. The starred ones, of course, are answered at the back of ***ITL***. A few of the others will be discussed below.

To work the problems in part I, you must know a bit of political geography:

London is the capital of England.   Stockholm is the capital of Sweden.
Rome is the capital of Italy.   Paris is the capital of France.

In general, when you know the truth values of the simple statements in a compound one, it is easiest to go through the complex one, substituting T for the true simple statements and F for the false ones. After that you just work inside out until you arrive at a single value for the complex statement. In the first example below you will see each step done separately. In the second you will see that some of them can be done simultaneously.

I (2)   a.   ~(London is the capital of England • Stockholm is the capital of Norway)
      b.   ~(T • F)   [Replacing the true and false statements by T and F]
      c.   ~F   [Replacing (T • F) by F]
      d.   T   [Replacing ~F by T]

   (6)   a.   London is the capital of England v ~London is the capital of England.
      b.   T v ~T   [Replacing the true statement by T]
      c.   T v F   [Replacing ~T by F]
      d.   T   [Replacing (T v F) by T]

Note that in this problem it really did not matter whether London is the capital of England. If it had not been, then step b. would have been F v ~F. This also would have reduced to T.

  (11)   a.   Rome is the capital of Italy • ~(Paris is the capital of France v Rome is the capital of Spain)
      b.   T • ~(T v F)   [With T and F for true and false propositions.]
      c.   T v ~(T)   [T v F replaced by T]
      d.   T • F   [~T replaced by F]
      e.   F   [T • F replaced by F]

(16) a. Rome is the capital of Spain v (~London is the capital of England v London is the capital of England)

      b. F v (~T v T)   [With F and T for false and true respectively]

      c. F v (F v T)   [With F for ~T]

      d. F v T   [With T for F v T]

      e. T   [With T for F v T]

(21) a. ~ [~ (Rome is the capital of Spain • Stockholm is the capital of Norway) v ~ (~Paris is the capital of France v ~Rome is the capital of Spain)]

      b. ~[~ (F~F) v ~ (~T~F)] [With the appropriate F and T]

      c. ~[~F v ~ (F v T)]   [With F for F•~F, F for ~T and T for ~F]

      d. ~[T v ~T]   [With T for ~F and T for F v F]

      e. ~ [T]   [Because (T v (anything) is T]

      f. F   [With F for ~T]

Note that in steps c and d there are two reductions performed at the same time. Since they are separate at this point in the argument, that is, neither depends upon the other, this is acceptable (and space-saving). Of course the " ~T " in step d could have been reduced to "F," but, since the only way a disjunction can be false is to have both of its disjuncts false and since you can see that the first disjunct is "T", it is more efficient to reduce d to e directly.

II   In these solutions, the first step shown will be the substitution of T and F as directed in the instructions. The explanations of what has been done in each step will be abbreviated a bit from the problems in part I. For example, the explanation of step d in exercise 21 (above) would be:

$$[\sim F \Rightarrow T \; // \; F \vee F \Rightarrow F]$$

(2) a.   ~T v F

      b.   F v F   [~T ⇒ F]

      c.   F   [F v F ⇒ F]

(6) a.   (T • T) v (F • F)

      b.   T v F   [T • T ⇒ T//F • F ⇒ F]

      c.   T   [T v F ⇒ T]

(11)a.   (T v F) • (F v T)

      b.   T v T   [T v F ⇒ T//F v T ⇒ T]

      c.   T   [T v T ⇒ T]

(16)a.   ~(T v T) v ~(F • ~F)

      b.   ~T v ~F   [T v T ⇒ T//F • (anything) ⇒ F]

      c.   F v T   [~ T ⇒ F// ~F ⇒ T]

      d.   T   [T v F ⇒ T]

(21)a.   [T v (T v T)] • ~[T v T) v T]

      b.   [T v T] • ~[T v T]   [T v T ⇒ T]

      c.   T • ~T   [T v T ⇒ T]

      d.   T • F   [~T ⇒ F]

      e.   F   [T • F ⇒ F]

In part III of the exercises, generally, if you arrive at a fixed truth value, the statements symbolized by P and Q were not really critical to the compound statement; if you are left with P's and/or Q's, then the compound statement's value is indeterminate until you discover values for P and Q.

III (2)   a. Q • F
          b. F [(anything) • F ⇒ F]

  (6)   a. ~P v (Q v P)
          b. T   [~P v P ⇒ T]

Although there are no determinate truth values in this problem, this form can never be false. In chapter 9 you will learn formal reasons for reordering things joined by a wedge; the rules are called Association and Communication. The point is that because either P or ~P will be true (by the definition of " ~ ") and because the only way for a disjunction to be false, any expression of the form P v ~P is a tautology, that is, can never be false.

(11)   a. (P v Q) • ~(Q v P)
       b. (P v Q) • ~(P v Q)   [(Q v P) ⇒ (P v Q)]
       c. F   [P • ~P ⇒ F]

This resembles exercise 6 (immediately above) in that it, too, has no determinate truth values in it. The transformation in b is called Commutation and will be introduced as a valid rule in chapter 9. Since the two conjuncts in b are contradictory, that is, since ~(P v Q) is the negation of (P v Q), the definition of "~" requires that they have opposite values. That means that, as a conjunction, one of the conjuncts must always be false. But the only way a conjunction can be true is to have both conjuncts be true. Since that can't happen, any time you encounter such a case you will know that you have seen a contradiction and that all contradictions are false at all times.

(16)   a. ~(P • Q) v (Q • P)
       b. ~(P • Q) v (P • Q)   [Q • P ⇒ P • Q]
       c. T   [P v ~P ⇒ T]

Essentially this is the same sort of problem as exercise 6 (above). The only addition is that the disjuncts (which contradict each other) are more complex expressions in this exercise.

(21)   a. [P v (Q • T] • ~[(P v Q) • (P v T]
       b. [P v Q] • ~[(P v Q) • T]   [Q • T ⇒ Q//P v T ⇒ T]
       c. [P v Q] • ~[P v Q]   [P • T ⇒ P]
       d. F   [P • ~P ⇒ F]

The transition from c to d is exactly the same as in exercise 11. The inferences in b and c are based upon the truth table definition of "v" and " • ". Since a conjunction is only true when both conjuncts are true, knowledge that one of them is true leaves the truth or falsity of the whole dependent upon the other conjunct; however, since the only way that a disjunction can be false is to have both disjuncts false, knowledge that one disjunct is true means that the whole expression is true regardless of the truth or falsity of the other. Falsity effects expressions with "•" and "v" in just the opposite manner: if one conjunct is known to be false, then the conjunction as a whole is false; but if one disjunct is known to be false, then the truth value of the whole is dependent upon the other disjunct.

The problems in part IV provide you with your first opportunity to "translate" from your natural (and probably native) language of English into your new (and artificial) language of logic. As with most things, such translation is best undertaken slowly and with short steps. If you do not attempt to deal both with statements and with connectives at the same time, you will find that neither is likely to give you any difficulty; if you do try them together, you are probably going to think that all this is too hard. So, go slow to make it easy. It is often wise to lay out the entire sentence before shifting to symbols.

IV (2) a. Either Iran raises the price of oil or Libya raises the price of oil.
      b. Either I or L.
      c. I v L

Note that a is an expansion of the original. It is done to insure that the "or" really is the truth-functional one and to identify clearly the parts of the statement.

(6)   a. Iran raises the price of oil or Libya raises the price of oil, but it is not the case both that Iran and Libya raises the price of oil.
      b. I or L, but not both I and L.
      c. (I v L) but not (I • L)
      d. (I v L) but ~(I • L)
      e. (I v L) • ~(I • L)

As you become more skilled (practice does it) at symbolizing, you probably will not need to take so many steps as you symbolize. As you learn, however, you will find that it usually is wiser to take more time, to use more steps, to insure that you are correct.

(11)   a. Either it is not the case that E or J.
      b. Either ~E or J
      c. ~E v J

The original exercise did not have to be expanded. It showed the formal detail satisfactorily as given.

(16)   a. Unless both Iran raises the price of oil and Libya raises the price of oil neither Iran raises the price of oil nor Libya raises the price of oil.
      b. Unless both I and L neither I nor L.
      c. Unless (I • L) ~(I v L)
      d. (I • L) v ~(I v L)

There are two equivalent symbolizations for the expression "neither p nor q": ~(p v q) and (~p • ~q). Sometimes you will find one more useful, sometimes the other. In general you should let your own preferences and intuitions choose which one you use.

(21)   a. Either E and S or either J or L.
      b. Either (E • S) or (J v L)
      c. (E • S) v (J v L)

This exercise, like number 11, was stated in satisfactory fashion, so did not need expansion. You should notice that one of the primary values of the "either" part of "either.. or..." is helping identify what the disjuncts were intended to be.

8.3   Conditional Statements and Material Implication

The two remaining connectives are related to each other. They are sometimes called the conditional and the bi-conditional. The conditional relationship, usually expressed by "if... then ...," is discussed at length by Copi and Cohen. The result is the conventional acceptance of the relationship called *material implication* as a useful approximation of at least one important feature of most "if- then" statements. That characteristic that they seem to have in common is the fact that they all seem to be false in the event that the antecedent (the statement that goes between the "if" and the "then") is true and the consequent (the statement that follows the "then") is false. Using the horseshoe as the symbol for this relationship, the truth table is

p q	p ⊃ q
T T	T
T F	F
F T	T
F F	T

Note that if you were memorizing it, the key element is that it is false when the antecedent is true and the consequent false (its defining characteristics) and it is true otherwise. (Other systems of notation use a single or double arrow {[p → q] or [p ⇒ q], a claw [p ─< q], or a capital C [Cpq] for implication). Given the widespread use of the idea of conditionality, there are probably more English expressions that ought to be symbolized by horseshoe than there are for all of the other connectives put together. A few of them (with p and q placed approximately so that they all ought to be represented as (p ⊃ q) are given below:

If p then q	q is entailed by p
p only if q ‡	If p. q
p is a sufficient condition for q	p results in q
q is a necessary condition for p ‡	q if p ‡
q follows from p	p implies q
p entails q	q is implied by p

This dozen is by no means exhaustive, but it does list the commoner expressions. The ones marked with a "‡" are the ones that experience shows tend to be mis-symbolized most frequently, usually by having the p and the q exchanged.

Related to the conditional is the biconditional. Essentially it is just the conjunction of the conditionals p ⊃ q and q ⊃ p. It means that the two statements (or statement-forms) are said to be equivalent, or have the same truth value. It is normally symbolized as a triple bar and its truth table is

p q	p ≡ q
T T	T
T F	F
F T	F
F F	T

Note that if you were memorizing this table you could key on either the fact that the " ≡ " is true when both equivalents have the same truth value or that it is false when their values are different. (Other systems of logical notation use a single or double- headed arrow [p ↔ q] or [p ⇔ q], a double-headed claw [p >─< q] or [p ≡ q], or a capital E [Epq] for equivalence.) There are only three expressions commonly used that are symbolized with a triple bar: "...if and only if...," "...is a necessary and a sufficient condition for...," and "...is equivalent to...." Do not be concerned that you have not seen this symbol yet in *ITL*. It is formally introduced in section 8.5. I have included it here, with the conditional, to emphasize to you the fact that the " ≡ " is simply a *biconditional*, that is, a " ⊃ " going in both directions.

Keeping in mind the truth table for the conditional, you should find the exercises following 8.3 straightforward and fairly simple. Remember, if you arrive at your own solution before looking at the answers here and in *ITL*, you will gain far more from working the exercises. (In the solutions to selected exercises here, the format of the earlier exercises will be followed.)

I (2) a. T ⊃ F
      b. F   [T ⊃ F ⇒ F]

The fact that the assertion that a true statement implies a false one is itself false is something that you should keep well in mind. Perhaps the commonest error made in using the " ⊃ " is getting confused about **order** of truth and falsity that yields a false conditional statement.

(6) a. (F ⊃ F) ⊃ F
     b. T ⊃ F   [F ⊃ F ⇒ T]
     c. F   [T ⇒ F ⇒ F]

(11) a. [(T ⊃ T) ⊃ T] ⊃ F
      b. [T ⊃ T] ⊃ F   [T ⊃ T ⇒ T]
      c. T ⊃ F   [T ⊃ T ⇒ T]
      d. F   [T ⊃ F ⇒ F]

(16) a. [(F ⊃ T) ⊃ F] ⊃ F
      b. [T ⊃ F] ⊃ F   [F ⊃ T ⇒ T]
      c. F ⊃   [T ⊃ F ⇒ F]
      d. T   [F ⊃ F ⇒ F]

(21) a. [(T • F) ∨ (~T • ~F)] ⊃ [(T ⊃ F) • (F ⊃ T)]
      b. [F ∨ (F • T)] ⊃ [F • T]   [T • F ⇒ F//~T ⇒ F//~F ⇒ T
                             T ⊃ F ⇒ F//F ⊃ T ⇒ T]
      c. [F ∨ F] ⊃ F   [F • T ⇒ F (twice)]
      d. F ⊃ F   [F ∨ F ⇒ F]
      e. T   [F ⊃ F ⇒ T]

You should notice that, although the reduction from step *a* to step *b* is quite complicated **looking**, it's just a working out of five quite simple reductions simultaneously.

II (2) a. F ⊃ Q
       b. T   [F ⊃ anything ⇒ T]

The justification here may seem a bit strange to you. However, if you look at the truth table for the " ⊃ ," you can easily see the rationale.

	p q	p ≡ q
(1)	T T	T
(2)	T F	F
(3)	F F	F
(4)	F F	T

Notice the third and fourth rows. In both the antecedent (p) is F and, despite the differences in the consequent (q), the value of the entire expression remains T. For that reason, "F ⊃ anything" is a form that will always be T.

(6)   a. (F ⊃ Q) ⊃ Fr
        b. T ⊃ F   [F ⊃ anything ⇒ T (see 2)]
        c. F   [T ⊃ F ⇒ F]

(11)   a. (P ⊃ F) ⊃ (F ⊃ P)
        b. ~P ⊃ T   [P ⊃ F ⇒ ~P//F ⊃ P ⇒ T]
        c. T   [anything ⊃ T ⇒ T]

This justification series contains two inferences that you may find confusing. The transition from step *b* to step *c* is the other side of the coin to at the discussion in exercise 2. If you look at the table in that problem's analysis, then you will see that in the first and third rows the consequent and the expression as a whole are T despite the fact that the antecedent is T in the first row and F in the third. The stranger inference lies between the antecedents *a* and *b*. If, however, you return to the truth table of the " ⊃ " you will see why the inference "works." In rows 2 and 4 the consequent is F. In row 2 the antecedent is T but the "p ⊃ q" as a whole is F; in row 4 the antecedent is F but "p ⊃ q" is T. Since, in those rows, "p ⊃ q" has the opposite value of the antecedent, it must (when the consequent is F) be in some sense the contradiction or negation of the antecedent.

(16)   a. (P ⊃ F) ⊃ (~F ⊃ ~P)
        b. ~P ⊃ (T ⊃ ~P)   [P ⊃ F ⇒ ~P//~F ⇒ T]
        c. ~P ⊃ ~P   [T ⊃ P ⇒ P]
        d. T   [P ⊃ P ⇒ T]

The transition from "T ⊃ P" to "P" follows a pattern similar to the ones discussed earlier. In this case, however, you must examine the first two rows of the " ⊃ 's" truth table. In those cases, where the antecedent is T, "p ⊃ q" has the same value as q, thus the reduction from *b* to *c*. The inference from *c* to *d* simply recognizes that, if the same term is both antecedent and consequent, then you can never get different values (in particular T then F) for the antecedent and consequent of a statement. That being the case, anything implying itself must always be T.

(21)   a. (~T • P) ⊃ (~T v ~P)
        b. ~P ⊃ (F v ~P)   [T • anything ⇒ anything//~T ⇒ F]
        c. ~P ⊃ ~P   [F v anything ⇒ anything]
        d. T   [P ⊃ P ⇒ T]

Since both conjuncts must be true, the truth of one means the truth of the whole is dependent upon the other. Similarly, since both must be false for the disjunction to be false, knowing one disjunct is false means that the truth of the whole expression is dependent upon the other.

III (2) a. If A then either B or C.
         b. If A then (B v C)
         c. A ⊃ (B v C)

(6)   a. If either A or B, then C.
         b. If (A v B), then C.
         c. (A v B) ⊃ C

(11)   a. If it is not the case that A then not B, and C.
         b. If ~A then ~B, and C
         c. (~A ⊃ ~B) and C
         d. (~A ⊃ ~B) • C

(16)   a. If either B or C, A
       b. If (B v C), A
       c. (B v C) ⊃ A

Notice that in *a*, the word order was reversed to transform a "q if p" structure into an "if p then q" one.

(21)   a. If Argentina mobilizes, then Brazil protests to the U.N.
       b. A ⊃ B

This exercise is intended to remind you that "p is a sufficient condition for q" means the same thing as "if p then q."

One thing that you must always keep in mind is that each of these logical connectives is *defined* by its truth table. That means that, for example, the ' • ' function is always commutative, that is, the two things conjoined by it can always be exchanged. That is **not** true for the English words it is used to symbolize. It is easy to see that the sentences "She became pregnant and got married" and "She got married and became pregnant" convey rather different images of "her" behavior; p • q and q • p are logically interchangeable. There are similar problems for each of the connectives--p ⊃ q and ~q ⊃ ~p are equivalent, but "If you want a piece of cake, it's on the table" and "If there isn't any cake on the table, you don't want any" surely aren't. The questions "Are you coming tomorrow?" and "Aren't you coming tomorrow?" differ by the presence of the contraction "*n't*" (meaning "not") but one responds as if they were identical, while p and ~p are contradictory. There is no obvious way to tell if a natural language is being used in an unusual way; the artificial language of logic cannot be used except according to its definitions. The reason we have settled upon the connectives that are used here is largely one of accommodation to the natural language of English. "And," "or," "if...then," "not," and "if and only if" are commonly used to join or modify statements in English, so we search for the formal connectives that most closely resemble those natural connectives. That search can be seen on the charts below. The first shows all possible one-place operators (using only T and F as possible values); the second shows all possible two-place operators.

p	1	2	3	4
T	T	T	F	F
F	T	F	T	F

p	q	a	b	c	d	e	f	g	h	i	j	k	l	m	n	o	p
T	T	T	T	T	T	T	T	T	T	F	F	F	F	F	F	F	F
T	F	T	T	T	T	F	F	F	F	T	T	T	T	F	F	F	F
F	F	T	T	F	F	T	T	F	F	T	T	F	F	T	T	F	F
F	F	T	F	T	F	T	F	T	F	T	F	T	F	T	F	T	F

Of the one-place operators, three of the four are of no real use to us: (1) and (4) do not really concern themselves with the truth value of the variable upon which they operate; they treat truth and falsity alike; (2) corresponds to an English phrase ("It is true that..."), but it is basically a valueless phrase, one which is usually better omitted. The fourth operator does what we usually want negation to do, that is, it precisely denies that upon which it operates. Thus we adopt it as the nearest symbolic operation to negation in English.

Weeding out the sixteen possible two-place operators is a somewhat more complex task. It may, however, be made much simpler by noting that the second half of the table is the mirror-image of the first half. We can get operator *i* by negating operator *h, j* is ~*g*, *k* is ~*f*, and so on until *p* is *a*. Operators *d* and *f* can be eliminated as being complicated versions of *p* and *q*, respectively. Dropping all of these leaves a considerably shortened table:

p q	b	c	e	g	h
T T	T	T	T	T	T
T F	T	T	F	F	F
F F	T	F	T	F	F
F F	F	T	T	T	F

There is little difficulty recognizing *h* as a reasonable facsimile of "and," and *b* as a fair match for an inclusive "or" (the exclusive one was operator *j*). The problem is with "if... then ...". It seems clear that "if *p* then *q*" is true when both *p* and *q* are true, and is false when *p* is true and *q* is false. It is not so clear what ought to be done when *p* is false. Most of us would prefer responding to the false antecedent by saying "tilt" or "no decision" or the like, but we are bound by the true/false range of the logic and must make a decision. There are only four possible operators which begin T–F, so perhaps it is best to begin by looking at them:

p q	A	B	C	D
T T	T	T	T	T
T F	F	F	F	F
F F	T	T	F	F
F F	T	F	T	F

Notice that each of these proposed operators is true when both *p* and *q* is true and false when *p* is true and *q* is false--that is the part of the conditional that seemed obvious. The cases when *p* is false cover all possible combinations of values. To decide which symbolic definition is most acceptable (or perhaps least unacceptable) it is helpful to look at a conditional statement which could be symbolized p ⊃ and whose components are quite clear: If you fail all of the tests in this course, then you will fail the course. In this statement "you fail all of the tests in this course" is the simple statement located in the "*p*-position" and "you fail this course" is the simple statement located in the "*q*-position." The compound statement *p* ⊃ is a true statement. You can easily see that proposed definition B is just the reassertion of *q*. That would mean that to assert the compound statement *p* ⊃ *q* would be to assert that you will fail the course. That is probably the assertion you would prefer not be made, and you can pretty well see why that definition is unacceptable. Definition D is the one already chosen for conjunction, and it too would entail the truth of *q* following immediately from the truth of the compound. It, obviously, is also unsatisfactory. Proposed definition C will result in the conditional being a commutative function, like conjunction and disjunction. (It is easy to identify commutative operators, because they all have the same values for p = T/q = F and p = F/q = T.) Implication cannot, however, be allowed to be commutative, for, if it were, the following two statements would both be true (when in fact the first is true, but the second is false):

1. If you fed Abraham Lincoln 3 lbs. of arsenic, then he is dead.
2. If Abraham Lincoln is dead, then you fed him 3 lbs. of arsenic.

The non-commutivity of implication eliminates D as an option. (D is, in fact, equivalence.) The only definition left for the conditional, then, is A. The other column that was left (column C) can be identified in short order--it is false when *q* is true and *p* is false and true otherwise. That is a conditional sort of definition, but in reverse order--it is *q* ⊃ *p*.

8.4   Argument Forms and Arguments

A truth table may be constructed for any statement or argument that is given or translated into propositional symbolic form. It is the sort of thing that a computer does very efficiently because it is essentially a purely mechanical task. But first you have to be able to figure out how big the table you will generate will be. Copi and Cohen show guide (or initial or reference) columns of differing lengths. You may wonder what their rationale or their method of generation is. Both are quite simple. The guide columns are intended to be a well-organized listing of all possible combinations of values that the variables involved in the statement (or argument) might have. If they are not well-organized, then it is difficult either to be sure you have listed all combinations or to scan quickly a column to compare tables, If you do not have all possible combinations of values, then you might later find that the one that you omitted was THE crucial one. Below you will find what appear to be three methods for generating guide columns. If you examine them closely you will see that they are actually three alternate ways of describing the same method.

I.   Identify all the distinct variables that occur in the statement or argument you wish to check. A distinct variable is one that is counted on its first occurrence, but not at any later appearance. Thus $p \vee (p \equiv p)$ contains only one distinct variable--p.

II.   Alphabetize them.

III.   Calculate how many rows (horizontal lines--count them vertically).

```
Row 1              C     C . . . .        C
Row 2              o     o . . . .        o
  .                1     1 . . . .        1
  .                u     u . . . .        u
  .                m     m . . . .        m
  .                n     n . . . .        n
  .
Row n              1     2 . . . .        n
```

The calculation is based upon raising 2 (the number of truth values we have--T and F) to the power of the number of distinct variables we will be considering. That is, if n = the number of distinct variables, then 2^n = the number of rows to put in the table. (Raising any number to a power simply means multiplying that number times itself as many times as the "power" says. Thus 2^5 = 2x2x2x2x2.)

IV.   Distribute the T's and F's

   A. (1st method) Under the first variable (alphabetically) put T's in the first half of the rows and F's in the second half. Go on to the second variable and do the same thing, *except* T's go in the first and third quarters and F's go in the second and fourth ones. Continue, shortening the T/F strings, with odd fractions being T and even ones being F. If you have not made a mistake, the last variable will alternate T and F. (If you begin alternating before you get to the last variable, then you have too short a table; if you get to that variable and still are not alternating, then there were more rows than you really needed. If you have to err, the latter is better because it can't omit a critical case.)

   B (2nd method) Under the *last* variable (alphabetically) alternate T's and F's. Go to the next-to-last and alternate pairs of T's and F's. Continue, doubling the length of the T/F strings each time you move back a variable. If you have not made a mistake, when you get to the first variable it will have the first half of the rows T and the second half F. (If it is all T, then you do not have enough rows; if it shifts from T to F and back again, then your table is longer than it needed to be.)

C. (3rd method) Number the alphabetized variables. For any specific variable you will need to alternate groups of $2^{(n-k)}$ T's and F's (where "k" is the number of the variable, "n" is the number of distinct variables, and 2 the number of truth values) until you have reached a string of rows that is 2^n long.

By using any of these methods, you will generate what could be called a set of standard guide columns. Using it as a basis, you are now in a position to generate a truth table for any statement-form.

All of this working with statement-form is fine, but it is not at the heart of logic. Logic is primarily concerned with arguments; its dealing with statements is a preliminary to dealing with arguments. The real value of the truth tables will be found in their use to determine whether an argument is valid or invalid. There are three ways commonly offered to define validity:

A. An argument is valid if and only if whenever all of its premisses are true its conclusion is also true.

B. An argument is valid if and only if whenever its conclusion is false at least one of its premisses is false.

C. An argument is valid if and only if it is never the case that all of its premisses are true but its conclusion is false.

If you look closely at the three you will see that they are actually just three alternative ways of saying the same thing.

The format that Copi and Cohen use to check an argument-form to see if it is a valid one is to write a large truth table on which you simultaneously lay out the truth tables for each of the premisses and the one for the conclusion. Then, using one of the definitions given above, you scan across the table, looking for a case where all of the premisses are true, but the conclusion is false. If there is such a case the argument is invalid; if there is not such a case the argument is valid. The problem with this approach, for some people, is that it is too easy to overlook (or misread) values as you scan.

There is, however, a related method that some find does a good job of avoiding those problems. It is the use of the *associated statement form (ASF)*. The use of the ASF is based upon a similarity between the validity relationship in an argument and the conditional relationship in a statement: the only case where an argument can be proven invalid is when all of its premisses are true and its conclusion is false; the only case where a conditional statement can be shown to be false is when its antecedent is true and its consequent is false. When you add to that the fact that the only way to make a conjunction true is to have all of its conjuncts true, you have the material for the generation of the ASF. First let's look at a "typical" argument, named "A." A has three premisses (P_1, P_2, and P_3) and a conclusion (C). There are two ways which logicians use to write A, depending upon their preferred way of handling arguments. The two ways correspond roughly to the two ways mathematical problems get written. If you wanted to add 7 and 5, you could write the problem/ answer either vertically (V) or horizontally (H).

$$
\begin{array}{r}
7 \\
\text{(V)} + 5 \\
\hline
12
\end{array}
\qquad\qquad
\text{(H)} \ (7 + 5) = 12
$$

Similarly an argument can be written vertically or horizontally. To read them, however, you need to know how to read two symbols with which you may not be familiar. The first is "∴"; the second is "⊢". They are both said to be signs of illation, or conclusion-drawing. The former is usually read "therefore" or "thus" and the latter "yields." The argument from the premises p ⊃ q and q ⊃ r to the conclusion p ⊃ r, then can be written

$$
\text{(V)} \quad
\begin{array}{c}
\text{p} \supset \text{q} \\
\text{q} \supset \text{r} \\
\hline
\therefore \quad \text{p} \supset \text{r}
\end{array}
\qquad\qquad
\text{(H)} \quad \text{p} \supset \text{q, } \text{q} \supset \text{r} \vdash \text{p} \supset \text{r}
$$

Many find that the vertical format is most useful when setting up formal proofs of validity (as you will do in chapter 9) and the horizontal most useful when doing truth tables. Our argument A, then, can be written as

$$
\begin{array}{c}
\text{P}_1 \\
\text{P}_2 \\
\text{P}_3 \\
\hline
\therefore \quad \text{C}
\end{array}
$$

or as $\text{P}_1, \text{P}_2, \text{P}_3 \vdash \text{C}$. We can generate the *ASF* of A simply by joining all of its premises together by conjunction, then using that conjunction as an antecedent and C as a consequent in the statement-form S. S has the form $\{ [\text{P}_1 \cdot (\text{P}_2 \cdot \text{P}_3)] \supset \text{C} \}$. The only way for A to be invalid is for there to be a case where P_1, P_2, and P_3, are all true and C is false. If that is the case, then S will be false at that same set of values. Similarly, the only way for S to be false is for $[\text{P}_1 \cdot (\text{P}_2 \cdot \text{P}_3)]$ to be true and C to be false. But if $[\text{P}_1 \cdot (\text{P}_2 \cdot \text{P}_3)]$ is true, then each element, P_1, P_2, and P_3 must be true, and in that case A would be invalid. This could be summed up by realizing that there is a strict relationship between any argument and its *ASF*.

An argument is valid if and only if its *ASF* is a tautology. (A tautology is a statement-form that is always true.) The *ASF* of the argument p ⊃ q, q ⊃ r ⊢ p ⊃ r is the conditional statement-form $\{ [(\text{p} \supset \text{q}) \cdot (\text{q} \supset \text{r})] \supset (\text{p} \supset \text{r}) \}$.

The reason it is of some use to learn about the *ASF* is that you can check the validity of an argument by setting up a truth table for the *ASF*. If the truth table shows that the *ASF* is a tautology, then the argument is valid; if there is any case where the *ASF* can be false, then the associated argument is invalid. The use of the *ASF* has the advantage of boiling the argument down to the values under a single column--there is no need to scan across a table; you just look at the last column. Using the argument shown just above, the table below shows a validity check through the checking of its *ASF*.

p q r	p ⊃ q	q ⊃ r	(p ⊃ q) • (q ⊃ r)	p ⊃ r	[p ⊃ q]•(q⊃r)] ⊃ (p⊃r)
T T T	T	T	T	T	T
T T F	T	F	F	F	T
T F T	F	T	F	T	T
T F F	F	T	F	F	T
F T T	T	T	T	T	T
F T F	T	F	F	T	T
F F T	T	T	T	T	T
F F F	T	T	T	T	T

Quickly scanning the last column you can see that the *ASF* is a tautology and that, therefore, the argument is valid.

A couple of examples from the exercises after 8.4 will help to solidify the means for checking for validity with truth tables.

II (13)   p ⊃ (q ⊃ r),   p ⊃ q   ⊢   p ⊃ r
                                    [*ASF*: {[p ⊃ (q ⊃ r] • (p ⊃ q)} ⊃ (p ⊃ r)

p q r	q ⊃ r	p ⊃ (q ⊃ r)	p ⊃ q	[p ⊃ (q ⊃ r)] • (p ⊃ q)	p ⊃ r	ASF
T T T	T	T	T	T	T	T
T T F	F	F	T	F	F	T
T F T	T	T	F	F	T	T
T F F	T	T	F	F	F	T
F T T	T	T	T	T	T	T
F T F	F	T	T	T	T	T
F F T	T	T	T	T	T	T
F F F	T	T	T	T	T	T

You can see that the *ASF* is a tautology, so the argument is valid.

III (6)   K v L, K ⊢   ~L   [*ASF*:   {[(K v L) • K] ⊃ ~L}]

K L	K v L	(K v L) • K	~L	[(K v L) • K] ⊃ ~L
T T	T	T	F	F
T F	T	T	T	T
F T	T	F	F	T
F F	F	F	T	T

This *ASF* is not a tautology, since it is false in the first row. That means that the associated argument is invalid. You might also note that, had you been working the problem row-by-row and had you noticed as you finished the first row that the *ASF* was false there, you could have stopped. You would have known at that point that the argument was invalid. Once you know that, further investigation is pointless, except for practice in making truth tables.

Technically the way in which the above problem was worked may not be quite correct. Since "K" and "L" represent actual propositions, they would each have some specific truth value. That means that only one of the four rows in the table actually represents these propositions as they are. The difficulty that you must encounter is that, because you do not even know what "K" and "L" represent, there is no way for you to know which of the rows does represent the actual state of affairs. The basis for claiming that an argument is invalid is that the specific form of that argument is an invalid argument-form. Thus, what you probably should do (to be technically correct in trying to determine the validity or invalidity of an argument) is to check the argument-form that is the specific form of the argument in question. In the case of exercise III.6, that specific form would have been p v q, p ⊢ q. The table which you would have generated to check that argument-form would have looked exactly like the one shown except that it would have had a "p" everywhere the given one has a "K" and a "q" everywhere that one has an "L." It really is pointless to translate the argument to its specific form (where the table beneath them would be unchanged) merely to satisfy a logical technicality. For that reason (and to avoid the simple copying errors that could creep in as you shift from argument to argument-form) in the solutions to exercises as done in this ***Study Guide*** I will use truth tables with both arguments and argument-forms as if there were no difference.

One more example shows an unusual characteristic of some arguments that might give you a bit of trouble. Below is the truth table for exercise III.9.

III (9) (R v S) ⊃ T, T ⊃ (R • S) ⊢ (R • S) ⊃ (R v S)

   [*ASF*: ({[R v S] ⊃ T] • [T ⊃ (R • S)]} ⊃ [(R • S) ⊃ (R v S)])]

RST	R v S	(R v S)⊃ T	R•S	T⊃(R•S)	[(RvS)⊃T] • [T⊃(R•S)]	(R•S⊃(RvS)	ASF
TTT	T	T	T	T	T	T	T
TTF	T	F	T	T	F	T	T
TFT	T	T	F	F	F	T	T
TFF	T	F	F	T	F	F	T
FTT	T	T	F	F	F	T	T
FTF	T	F	F	T	F	T	T
FFT	F	T	F	F	F	T	T
FFF	F	T	F	T	T	T	T

Here again the *ASF* is a tautology, so the argument is valid, but there is a strange feature about the argument. If you look you will see that the conclusion itself is a tautology. Of course, if the conclusion of an argument cannot be false then there will be no way for the premisses to be true **and** the conclusion false. There just doesn't seem to be any need for the premisses; the conclusion stands on its own. Nevertheless it is a valid argument.

Having followed through the several examples here and in *ITL*, you ought to find you have little difficulty with the exercises following 8.4. Remember, an exercise does the most good when you work it **before** looking at anyone else's solution.

I (b)   *6* is the specific form of *b*, so *b* is, of course, a substitution instance of *6*.

  (f)   *16* is the specific form of *f*, so *f* is a substitution instance of *16*.

  (k)   No exercise in part II is the specific form of *k*, but *k* is a substitution instance of *4*:

$$p \qquad\qquad p \lor q$$
$$A \supset B \qquad (A \supset B) \lor C$$

As you can see, if you substitute $(A \supset B)$ for *p* and *c* for *q* in exercise II(4), you get exercise I(k).

p	q	p ⊃ q	~p	~q	~p ⊃ ~q	(p ⊃ q) ⊃ (~p ⊃ ≡)
T	T	T	F	F	T	T
T	F	F	F	T	T	T
F	T	T	T	F	F	F
F	F	T	T	T	T	T

Since the third row shows that the *ASF* is false in the event that *p* is false and *q* true, the argument is invalid.

(6)

p	q	p ⊃ q	p • q	p ⊃ (p • q)	p ⊃ q) ⊃ [p ⊃ (p • q)]
T	T	T	T	T	T
T	F	F	F	F	T
F	T	T	F	T	T
F	F	T	F	T	T

Since the *ASF* of the argument is a tautology, the argument itself is valid.

(11)

pqr	p ⊃ q	q ⊃ r	(p ⊃ q) • (q ⊃ r)	q∨r	{(p⊃q)•(q⊃r)} ⊃ (q∨r)
TTT	T	T	T	T	T
TTF	T	F	F	T	T
TFT	F	T	F	T	T
TFF	F	T	F	F	T
FTT	T	T	T	T	T
FTF	T	F	F	T	T
FFT	T	T	T	T	T
FFF	T	T	T	F	F ⇐

Row 8 clearly shows that the *ASF* is capable of being false and, thus, the argument is invalid.

(16)   One of the difficulties in writing out truth tables is that, when they include lots of premisses and/or variables, they can become very complicated (and long). A shortened approach to validity checks will be introduced in the next chapter, but some relief is available even in working problems in this format. Notice that in the truth table for this exercise some of the early columns are "named" (with Roman numerals) and later columns use the names instead of using the actual formulae. For example, the first premiss is "(p ⊃ q) • (r ⊃ s)." To get the column for that you first had to get columns for "p ⊃ q" and "r ⊃ s." The columns for those expressions are named "I" and "II." The name, then, of the first premiss is "I.II." Subsequent columns can also be given such names, shortening the headings of later columns greatly. The following is the validity check for exercise 16, using the naming device explained above.

pqrs	I p ⊃ q	II r ⊃ s	III I • II	IV p∨r	V III • IV	VI q∨s	V ⊃ VI
TTTT	T	T	T	T	T	T	T
TTTF	T	F	F	T	F	T	T
TTFT	T	T	T	T	T	T	T
TTFF	T	T	T	T	T	T	T
TFTT	F	T	F	T	F	T	T
TFTF	F	F	F	T	F	F	T
TFFT	F	T	F	T	F	T	T
TFFF	F	T	F	T	F	F	T
FTTT	T	T	T	T	T	T	T
FTTF	T	F	F	F	F	T	T
FTFT	T	T	T	T	T	T	T
FTFF	T	T	T	F	F	T	T
FFTT	T	T	T	T	T	T	T
FFTF	T	F	F	F	F	F	T
FFFT	T	T	T	T	T	T	T
FFFF	T	T	T	F	F	T	T

Since the *ASF* is a tautology, the argument-form is a valid one. This table, being 16 rows long, is a hard one to read. It is for that reason that the lines were added crossing the table: the varying density of the lines that separate the rows of the table make it easier to see which values come from which earlier values. Of course, if you were working on regular lines (or even better graph) paper lining up your table will be much simpler.

(21) Notice that the table for exercise 21 uses the same sort of technique that 16 used, but that some columns can be used more than once.

p q	I p∨q	II p • q	III I ⊃ II	IV ~I	V III • IV	VI ~II	V ⊃ VI
T T	T	T	T	F	F	F	T
T F	T	F	F	F	F	T	T
F T	T	F	F	T	F	T	T
F F	F	F	F	T	F	T	T

Since this, too, has a tautologous *ASF*, it is a valid form.

III (2)

C D	I C∨D	II C • D	III I ⊃ II	IV ~I	V III • IV	VI ~II	V ⊃ VI
T T	T	T	T	F	F	F	T
T F	T	F	F	F	F	T	T
F T	T	F	F	T	F	T	T
F F	F	F	F	T	F	T	T

It takes little effort to see that the table under III(2) and the one under II(21) are identical. That happens because III(2) has II(21) as its specific form. Since the specific form of III(2), then, is valid, so is III(2).

K L	K∨L	(K∨L) • K	~L	[(K∨L) • K] ⊃ ~L
T T	T	T	F	F
T F	T	T	T	T
F T	T	F	F	T
F F	F	F	T	T

Had you been working your way across the table, doing one row at a time, you should have seen that you could stop after the first row. Since the *ASF* is false in that row, it is not a tautology. And, when the *ASF* is not a tautology, the argument is invalid. As a matter of fact, most computer programs that construct truth tables generate them a row at a time, allowing the machine to avoid running excess rows.

IV (2)   Despite the apparent obviousness of the appropriate symbols to represent the propositions in this exercise (and the others of this set), it is always wise to specify exactly what you intend each propositional symbol to represent. The symbol "=df" which I used in the beginning of this analysis stand for "equals by definition" with "definition" being used in the stipulative sense (as explained in chapter 4). Thus, exercise IV(2) should have this form:

D =df Denmark drifts further to the left.
E =df Estonia continues to b a puppet of Soviet Russia.
F =dfFinland becomes increasingly subservient to Soviet Russia.

If D then if E then F   [D ⊃ (E ⊃ F)]
E   E
-----------------------------   --------------
So if D then F.   ∴   D ⊃ F)

		I		II	III	
D E F	E ⊃ F	D ⊃ (E ⊃ F	E	I • E	D ⊃ F	II ⊃ III
T T T	T	T	T	T	T	T
T T F	F	F	T	F	F	T
T F T	T	T	F	F	T	T
T F F	T	T	F	F	T	T
F T T	T	T	T	T	T	T
F T F	F	T	T	T	T	T
F F T	T	T	F	F	T	T
F F F	T	T	F	F	T	T

Since the *ASF* is true in all cases (tautologous), the argument is valid.

(6)   E =df Equality of opportunity is to be achieved.
S =df People previously disadvantaged should now be given special opportunities.
P =df Some people receive preferential treatment.

If E then S.	E ⊃ S
If S then P.	S ⊃ P
If P then not E.	P ⊃ ~E
--------------------	---------
Therefore not E.	∴ E

		I	II		III	IV	V	
E P S	E ⊃ S	S ⊃ P	~E	P ⊃ ~E	I • II	III • IV	V ⊃ E
T T T	T	T	F	F	T	F	T
T T F	F	T	F	F	F	F	T
T F T	T	F	F	T	F	F	T
T F F	F	T	F	T	F	F	T
F T T	T	T	T	T	T	T	T
F T F	T	T	T	T	T	T	T
F F T	T	F	T	T	F	F	T
F F F	T	T	T	T	F	T	T

Since the *ASF* is a tautology, the argument is valid. Of course, on any of these problems you could have stopped once you have the table for all of the premises and the conclusion. That would have required you to have figured out whether the argument was valid or not by comparing the values for the premises and conclusion in each row. That seems, to me, to be an approach that is far more likely to produce errors than is the ASF technique. You may, to be sure, use whichever method seems easier to you (unless you have a teacher who specifies method).

8.5   Statement Forms, Material Equivalence, and Logical Equivalence

The relationship between arguments and argument forms which Copi and Cohen explained in 8.4 is essentially the same one as exists between statements and statement forms. In the same way that the substitution of propositions for the propositional variables in an argument form converted the form to an argument, a similar substitution within a statement form yields a statement.

Statement forms themselves can be identified by the sort of logical connectives that they involve: p ⊃ q is a conditional statement form, p v q is a disjunctive one, etc. Just as the specific form of an argument could be easily identified, the specific form of a statement is that form that would yield the desired statement by the consistent substitution of the appropriate simple propositions for the variables in the statement form.

In discussing the truth table generated relative to some given statement, there is another term which you may find makes it easier to identify what is being done. If you recall the complex statement forms that were created when the *ASF* of an argument was laid out, then you remember how the table consisted of a series of columns headed by ever-increasingly complex expressions. The final column was headed by the *ASF*. It is convenient to refer to the column of T's and F's that was under the *ASF* as the ***characteristic column*** or the ***significant column*** of that particular expression. Using these terms allows us, for example, to describe two statement forms which in some sense "mean the same thing" as having the same characteristic column. In the case of the basic connectives you would say that the " ⊃ " has a characteristic column of T–F–T–T, the " v " of T–T–T–F, and so on.

Statements and statement forms may, then, be classified by the sort of characteristic column which they have. Since there are only two truth values in the logic we are currently using, there are only three sorts of characteristic columns possible: ones that are all T's, ones that are all F's and ones that have a mix of T's and F's. Statements and statement forms whose characteristic columns are all T's are called ***tautologies***; ones whose characteristic columns are all F's are called ***contradictions*** or ***self-contradictions***; ones whose characteristics are a mixture of T's and F's are said to be ***contingent***. If you look back to the introduction of the *ASF* IN 8.4, you will see that the use of "tautology" in that context was the same as introduced here.

Any two statements or statement forms which have the same characteristic column are said to be materially equivalent. Although "equivalence" may involve other aspects of similarity when used in everyday language, insofar as the logic we are using is concerned the term simply means that the two expressions that are said to be equivalent have the same characteristic columns is an important reason for standardizing the guide columns that are the reference point for any truth table. If there were variability allowed in the guide column, then equivalence could not be recognized at a glance. For example, look at the two "truth tables" below; the left one has standard guide columns, the left non-standard ones;

p	q	p ⊃ q		p	q	q ⊃ p
T	T	T		T	T	T
T	F	F		F	T	F
F	T	T		T	F	T
F	F	T		F	F	T

If you looked casually at both of these tables you might be inclined to think that the two statement forms were materially equivalent. A bit of careful inspection; however, makes it clear that they are not: the left-hand one is false when p is T and q is F. While the right- hand is false when p is F and q is T. Had the right-hand table had standard guide columns, the characteristic shown would have been T–T–F–T.

You should now be prepared to work the exercises following 8.5. Remember that you ought to do the problems yourself before you look at the solutions here or in *ITL*.

I (2)   Both *a* and *d* could yield *2* with appropriate substitutions: use *C* for p and ~*D* for q in *a*; use *C* for p and *D* for q in *d*. The specific form of *2* is *d*.

(6)   *6* would result from *b* by replacing p with (O v P) and q with (P • Q). There is no specific form of *6* stated.

II (2)   There are two distinct variables here: p and q. That means that there will be 2^2 or *4* rows in the table. Using any of the three methods of generating the guide columns you will get:

p	q
T	T
T	F
F	T
F	F

The elements of the more complex structure are constructed one at a time, always using the standard (or defining) tables for each connective. The table below shows the entire sequence of constructing the truth table.

		1			2				3			4						
p	q	p	⊃	q		(p	⊃	q)	⊃	q	p	⊃	[(p	⊃	q)	⊃	q]
T	T		T						T			T					
T	F		F						T			T					
F	T		T						T			T					
F	F		T						F			T					

Since the characteristic of this statement form (the column headed "*4*") is all T's, the statement is a tautology.

(6)   There are two distinct variable–p and q–so there will be 2^2 rows in the table. Using any of the three methods, the guide columns will be

p	q
T	T
T	F
F	T
F	F

The elements of the more complex structure are constructed one at a time, always using the defining tables for the various connectives as the reference when figuring out the column for any particular expression. The table below shows the sequence in which the entire table is generated.

		1			2	3	4			5					
p	q	p	⊃	p	~q	q	•	~q	(p	⊃	p)	⊃	(q	•	~q)
T	T		T		F		F				F				
T	F		T		T		F				F				
F	T		T		F		F				F				
F	F		T		T		F				F				

First you generate the guide columns.

Second you calculate the values of p ⊃ p given the value in the guide columns and using the definitions of the connectives.

Third you figure that ~q must be the mirror image of q.

Fourth, using the columns of q and ~q, figure the values in the columns under (q • ~q).

Fifth you connect antecedent and consequent, again according to the basic definitions of the connectives.

From the table you can see this is a contradiction.

III (2)	p q	p ⊃ q	~p	~q	~p ⊃ ~q	(p ⊃ q) ≡ (~p ⊃ ~q)	
	T T	T	F	F	T	T	
	T F	F	F	T	T	F	
	F T	T	T	F	F	F	
	F F	T	T	T	T	T	

The characteristic column shows this is contingent, thus is not tautologous.

(6)

p q	p • q	p v (p • q)	p ≡ [p v (p • q)]
T T	T	T	T
T F	F	T	T
F T	F	F	T
F F	F	F	T

The characteristic column is all T's; the statement form is a tautology.

(11)

p q	~q	q • ~q	p v (q • ~q)	p ≡ [p v (q • ~q)]
T T	F	F	T	T
T F	T	F	T	T
F T	F	F	F	T
F F	T	F	F	T

The statement form, of course, is a tautology, but there is a more interesting aspect to the solution. Notice that the conjunction (q • ~q) is a self-contradiction. When it is disjoined with p the resulting column is exactly the same as the original column for p. Obviously, then, when two expressions have the same characteristic column, a truth table of the expression having them connected by the " ≡ " (which is the sign of material implication) will always be a tautology.

(16)   This statement form has three distinct variables, so it must have a table with 2^3 (or 8) rows. The procedure for generating the table, however, is the same as for the earlier exercises.

p q r	q v r	I p•(q v r)	II p • q	III p • r	IV II v III	I ≡ IV
T T T	T	T	T	T	T	T
T T F	T	T	T	T	T	T
T F T	T	T	F	T	T	T
T F F	F	F	F	F	F	T
F T T	T	F	F	F	F	T
F T F	T	F	F	F	F	T
F F T	T	F	F	F	F	T
F F F	F	F	F	F	F	T

The greater number of variables makes the truth table longer, but the key thing to check is still the characteristic column for the statement form. For this statement form the characteristic column is a tautology.

8.6   The Paradoxes of Material Implication

The term "paradox" has several accepted meanings: a statement that appears self-contradictory but is actually true, a statement that appears true but is actually self-contradictory, an unacceptable conclusion that is derivable from seemingly acceptable premises, or a systematically ambiguous situation any resolution of which results in a self-contradiction. The closest of these to what is meant when logicians speak of the paradoxes of material implication is the first. In these particular cases a truth table clearly shows certain expressions to be tautologies but the "plain English" statements based upon these expressions seem at least counter-intuitive.

The logical statement forms which express the paradoxical nature of the " ⊃ " (or material conditional) are "p ⊃ (q ⊃ p)" and "~p ⊃ (p ⊃ q)." Simply stated the first asserts that a statement which we *know to be true* is implied by any statement we might happen to select. That assertion is logically justified by recourse to the truth table for " ⊃ " which, you recall, is a *definition* of that connective. In that defining table it is clear that no statement or statement form whose consequent is true can itself be false. Thus, when the consequent **"p"** of any conditional **"q ⊃ p"** is *known to be true*, the conditional itself is true.

Similarly, when both **"p"** and **"∼p"** are asserted as part of the antecedent of a conditional statement form, whatever you may wish can be claimed to *follow from* the **"p"** and **"∼p,"** and do so truly. By the definition of the **"∼"** we know that one of the pair **"p"** and **"∼p"** must be true and the other false. Both of them, then, cannot reasonably serve as antecedent statements (or forms) within a conditional. The two of them asserted simultaneously would constitute a self-contradiction; that self-contradiction (according to the defining table for **"∼"**) would yield anything whatsoever when it occurred as the antecedent of a conditional statement or form.

All of this paradoxical difficulty is a function of the original definitions relating to the **" ⊃ ."** If you recall the discussion of why the particular table for the **" ⊃ "** that we use *had* to be selected (after the exercises to 8.3, above), then you will see that to mirror ordinary English usage with *if...then....* statements we must also accept these paradoxical qualities. Fortunately, such acceptance rarely causes difficulties.

8.7   The Three "Laws of Thought"

Interestingly, George Boole (a bit of whose work you touched in the Boolean equations of the categorical proposition) titled his most significant work *An Investigation of the Laws of Thought*. It was originally published in 1849 and tried to give a basis for correct reasoning. In fact, he wrote in his opening remarks:

> The design of the following treatise is to investigate the fundamental laws of those operations of the mind by which reasoning is performed; to give expression to them in the symbolical language of a Calculus, and upon this foundation to establish the science of Logic and construct its method....[1]

Copi and Cohen explain, however, that there are three so-called Laws of Thought that have traditionally been treated as if they were the foundation for logic to which Boole refers. There are fairly traditional ways of expressing these Laws of Thought:

> Any true statement must be true. (*Principle of Identity*)
>
> No statement is both true and false. (*Principle of Contradiction*--sometimes called the *Principle of Non-contradiction*).
>
> Any statement is either true or false. (*Principle of the Excluded Middle*)

There probably is no good reason to single out these three tautologies as more fundamental than any others. It is the case, however, that there is a sense in which these principles are "built into" the structure of the truth table (which in many ways is fundamental--at least to logic's efficient operation):

> (1) once a variable is found to be true (or false for that matter) it will have the same truth value throughout the table.
>
> (2) only one value, T or F, can occur at any single location within a problem.
>
> (3) each location within a truth table must have either a T or an F in it.

----

1.   Boole, George *An Investigation of The Laws of Thought* (Reproduction of the 1854 edition). Dover Publications, New York, p. 1.

These can reasonably be taken as the statements of the Principle of Identity, of Contradiction and of the excluded Middle, respectively.

As Copi and Cohen suggest, however, detailed analysis either of the Laws of Thought or of the paradoxes of material implication would require vastly more work and understanding than it is reasonable to demand.

CHAPTER EIGHT SUMMARY

I.   The use of special symbols can be an important aid to reasoning.

   A.   Symbols can significantly decrease the volume of material you are try-ing to handle.

   B.   Symbols can remove emotional content.

   C.   Symbols can increase precision.

II.   Logic can be based upon the proposition as the smallest unit of information. Propositions have two truth values: true and false.

III. There are several connectives which can be defined as ways of combining propositions. The connectives which are important for us are ones which are de-fined in terms of the truth value they derive from set combinations of truth values of the propositions they combine. (Thus these are called truth-functional connec-tives.)

   A.   Specific propositions are represented by capital letters, usually derived from the proposition. (For example, "B" would seem a reasonable symbol for "Betty Brown burnt her banana bread.")

   B.   Lower case letters p, q, r, etc. are used as propositional variables. They represent forms which would become propositions if propositions were substituted for the variables within the forms.

   C.   Negation is represented by a "~" preceding the propositional variable or propositional symbol.

   D.   Although more connectives are identifiable, Copi and Cohen use five:
      1.   "~" represents "*not*" in the sense of contradiction.
      2.   " • " represents "*and*" in the sense of joint assertion.
      3.   " v " represents "*or*" in the sense of inclusive alternatives (p or q or both).
      4.   " ⊃ " represents "*if...then...*" in the sense of material implication (you can't have p but not q).
      5.   " ≡ " represents "*if and only if*" in the sense of either joint occurrence or joint non-occurrence.

IV.   The truth-functional relationships can be defined by tables which show how derived values are obtained from all possible combinations of values of the simple propositions (or propositional variables) in the relationship.

A.   The one useful one-place "*connective*," the "~" is defined:

p	~p
T	F
F	T

B.   Copi and Cohen use four two-place connectives that are defined:

p	q	p • q	p v q	p ⊃ q	p ≡ q
T	T	T	T	T	T
T	F	F	T	F	F
F	T	F	T	T	F
F	F	F	F	T	T

V.   By using the definitions as stated in the tables for each of the connectives, you can derive a truth table for any statement or statement form.

VI.   By using a truth table based upon all of the variables in an argument form, you can determine whether or not that form (or any argument derived from it by substituting statements [or propositions] for the variables) is valid.

VII.   Statements (propositions) and statement forms can be classified by the sort of truth table that is associated with them.

A. If their characteristic column is always true, they are called tautologies.

B. If their characteristic column is always false, they are called contradictions of self-contradictories.

C. If their characteristic column has both trues and falses, they are called contingencies.

VIII. The " ⊃ " has characteristics which do not strictly coincide with our ordinary language uses of "*if...then...*"

A. A false statement "*truly*" implies any statement: any statement with a self-contradictory antecedent is a tautology.

B. A true statement is "*truly*" implied by any statement: any statement with a tautologous consequent is a tautology.

IX.   The three traditional "laws of Thought" are built into truth table structures.

A. "Any true statement must be true" is conveyed by "p ⊃ p" being a tautology. (*The Principle of Identity*)

B. "No statement is both true and false" is conveyed by "p • ~p" being self-contradictory. (*The Principle of Contradiction*.)

C. "Any statement must be either true or false" is conveyed by "p v ~p" being a tautology. (*The Principle of the Excluded Middle*)

Chapter Nine
The Method of Deduction

9.1   Formal Proof of Validity

If a friend was arguing some emotionally loaded issue with you, like abortion, nuclear power, or the sexual revolution, you might, in your own mind, draw upon what you learned in the last lesson in order to make sure that your own arguments were valid. If, however, you tried to "prove" to this friend (whom we shall assume has not had the good fortune to have taken a course in logic) that your argument was valid by the use of a full truth table, you might find this friend less than receptive. As a matter of fact, before you finished laying out your array of variables, connectives and T's and F's, your friend may well have departed to call the little men with the nets to carry you off to an upholstered room. This is because you have to be among the "initiated" for the truth tables to make a great deal of sense to you.

If the problem had been a linguistic one, that is, if your friend had failed to understand you because your vocabulary was too advanced or too specialized, you would have restated your point, so to speak, in "words of one syllable." The problem, then, is to find some way to break a complicated argument into simple components. That is essentially what the use of the propositional rules does. Those rules are a set of relatively simple arguments and equivalences, ones to which, for the most part, no one would object. They are strung together forming what can be called a ***Formal Proof of Validity***. Such a proof is a sequence of steps which start with the premisses of a valid argument, proceed by using the simple, unobjectionable rules of the propositional calculus, and terminate in the conclusion of the argument.

Several of those "simple, unobjectionable rules" are argument forms with which you are already familiar. If you recall the non- categorical argument forms from chapter 7, you already have over half the rules of inference from this section in mind.

One thing which might make the forms of these rules a bit easier for you to use would be a slight change in notation. Since the rules are intended to be patterns of argument, rather than specific argument, or even specific argument forms, you might find the use of "p," "q," and other variables a little confusing. Think for a minute about the relationship between an argument form and an argument. Any argument which could result from the substitution of specific propositions (not necessarily simple ones) for the propositional variables in an argument form is said to be an *instance* of that form. Thus it is easy for you to see that "A ⊃ B, A ⊢ B" is an instance of "p ⊃ q, p ⊢ q." It is also pretty simple to see that "(A ∨ B) ⊃ (C ≡ D), (A ∨ B) ⊢ (C ≡ D)" is also an instance of that same form. The ambiguity which you may feel involves the question of whether "(p ∨ q) ⊃ (r ≡ s), (p ∨ q) ⊢ (r ≡ s)" is an instance too.

A logical expression is sometimes called a ***well-formed formula***, meaning that its components are joined together in a logically appropriate manner. This is usually abbreviated *Wff*. If numbers are associated with the term *Wff* (for example: *Wff 1*, *Wff 2*, etc.), there is then an easy way to rewrite the rules so that their generality is more evident. If *modus ponens* were so rewritten it would appear as

$$(Wff\ 1)\ \supset\ (Wff\ 2)$$
$$Wff\ 1$$
$$\underline{\hspace{5cm}}$$
$$\therefore\qquad Wff\ 2$$

This seems to make it clear that, so long as they appear consistently, any well-formed expression at all may occur in the locations designated as *Wff 1* and and any other (or the same) expression may occur at those locations marked *Wff 2*. If you think of *modus ponens* as a board with a set of windows at the locations marked *Wff 1* and *Wff 2* and a set of mirrors behind (so that whatever appears at any one *Wff 1* or *Wff 2* spot automatically appears at all other corresponding locations), you may have some grasp of how these rules-as- patterns work.

A more graphic mechanism which would have the same purpose would be to represent the *Wffs* of the argument by consistent geometric forms. That would have *modus ponens*, for example, having this form:

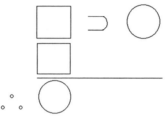

The explanation of use of the rule *modus ponens*, then, is that you can put ANY *Wff* at all on the circle or the square (or the triangle or rectangle in the case of a dilemma) so long as you put the same thing of **every instance** of that shape. Some students have gone as far as to make a card with such geometric representations of the rules and to cut out a supply of circles, squares, etc. When they want to see if an inference fits a form, they fill out the appropriate shapes, lay them on the original card and look to see if the form matches what they wanted to do.

The card for *modus tollens* would have this form:

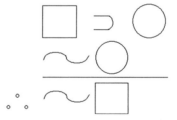

Possible expressions to be written on shapes might be "$(X \vee Y)$" and "$\sim(Z \cdot \sim A)$." Writing them as suggested and laying them on the original *modus tollens* card would yield

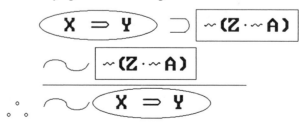

(Incidentally, this particular instance of *modus tollens* is exercise 6 in part I of the exercises discussed below.)

Although this approach may seem awfully elementary to you, I would recommend that if you feel at all uncertain about the use of any of the rules introduced in this chapter you try this sort of technique. All but one of the following argument-forms is an instance of *modus ponens*. Can you recognize which one is not?

A. p ⊃ (q ⊃ r)   B. s ⊃ (r v t)
    p   s
    ─────────   ─────────
∴   r   ∴   r v t

C. (p ⊃ q) ⊃ ~q   D. p v (q • s
    p ⊃ q   p
    ─────────   ─────────
∴   q   ∴   q • s

In these examples, all but D are legitimate instances of *modus ponens*. The D problem cannot be (in fact it is invalid) because the major connective of the first premiss is a " v " instead of a " ⊃ ". This is a common sort of error, but one which is easy to avoid. The internal structure of the expressions filling the locations of *Wff 1* and *Wff 2* (and *Wff 3* and *Wff 4* in the cases of Hypothetical Syllogism and Constructive Dilemma) can be anything at all so long as it is well formed, *but* anything else in the argument-form must remain exactly as it is for the rule-form to apply.

The first two rules of inference are *modus ponens* and *modus tollens*. If you look at their forms, on the inside back cover of *ITL*, you will see how very similar they are. They share a first premiss form: p ⊃ q. That constitutes an assertion that p cannot occur without q also occurring. The second premiss of *modus ponens* asserts that p **does** occur. Given the claim of the first premiss, you see that q must also occur. *modus tollens*'s second premiss, ~q, denies q's occurrence. Given the claim of the first premiss, you surely see that p, then could not occur. You might look at these argument forms as showing alternative outcomes of an initial assertion:

$$p \supset q$$

p   ~q
─────────   ─────────
∴   q   (M.P.)   ∴   ~p   (M.T.)

If you look at problems 11 and 6 in part I of the excercises following this section you will see instances of each of these rules. In exercise 6 the argument given results from the substitution of "X v Y" for "p" and "~(Z • ~A)" for "q" in the basic *modus tollens* form. If you look at the example on the previous page, you will see graphically how that substitution was made. Exercise 11 is a case of substituting "(A ⊃ B)" for "p" and "(C v D)" for "q" in the basic *modus ponens* form. If you used the graphic representation of *modus ponens* you would have this form:

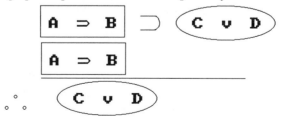

The third and fourth rules of inference are also ones which you encountered in chapter 7: the **hypothetical syllogism** (there called the *pure* hypothetical syllogism) and the **disjunctive syllogism**. Exercise 10, which you could see is an instance of the hypothetical syllogism in *ITL*, is significant for another reason. The form of this rule is

$$p \supset q$$
$$q \supset r$$
$$\therefore \quad p \supset r$$

If you look at $(I \equiv H)$ as the *p-term*, $\sim(H \supset \sim I)$ as the *q-term* and $(H \supset I)$ as the *r-term* of the argument in exercise 10, then it has this form:

$$q \supset r$$
$$p \supset q$$
$$\therefore \quad p \supset r$$

That resembles but is not an exact match for the form given for the hypothetical syllogism: the premisses are in reversed order. For the purposes of the propositional logic proofs, however, that difference is considered to be no difference.

It is also the case that, in longer proofs like those of parts II, III and IV, it is not even necessary that the two premisses of the rule forms appear next to each other. For example, in exericse 2 of part II you obtain step 6 from steps 3 and 5 by the use of the disjunctive syllogism. In this case there is an intervening step *and* the steps are reversed. For all practical purposes, once you have a step accepted in a formal proof of validity (either as a premiss or as a step proven) you may treat it as if it were next to any other step in the proof.

If you find yourself feeling insecure about any of the four rules of inference discussed so far, or the rule of **constructive dilemma**, you should look back at the more extended discussion of them in chapter 7. Incidentally, note that in the exercise just mentioned, number 2 in part II, the fifth step results from the second and fourth by use of the constructive dilemma form (called the complex constructive dilemma in chapter 7).

The sixth rule in Copi and Cohen's list is called **absorption**. It looks more complicated than it is. Consider the case of a conditional statement. There are three ways in which it can be true: a true antecedent and a true consequent, a false antecedent and a false consequent, and a false antecedent and a true consequent. If the antecedent term is false, then the consequent of the "absorbed" form will have at least one false conjunct which means that the consequent and the antecedent are false and the conditional true. If the antecedent is true, then the "absorbed" consequent will be true when the original consequent was true and false when it was false. An alternative way of looking at the relationship expressed in this rule is to consider how the form "$p \supset (p \bullet q)$" could be false. Given the definition of the $\supset$, the antecedent (p) would have to be true and the consequent $(p \supset q)$ would have to be false. But, for $p \supset q$ to be false when p is true (as the assumption above shows) q would have to be false. However, when p is true and q is false, $p \supset q$ is false, not true. Thus absorption cannot lead you astray. You may, by the way, wish to file away in your memory the fact that this rule is often used together with the rule of exportation which will be explained in the next section.

The rules of **simplification** and **conjunction** are really just two sides of the same coin. Simplification occurs as in exercise 2, part I in *ITL*. It is simply the assertion that when you know that a conjunction is the case you may infer that its first conjunct is also true. This ought to seem reasonable since the truth table definition of the " $\bullet$ " is that it is true only when both conjuncts are true. You will need to be very careful using this rule. It is, of course, valid to infer the *second* conjunct rather than the first, but it cannot be done directly. If you examined exercise 2, part II, carefully, you surely noticed that step 5, (G v H), which I asserted came from steps 2 and 4 by D.C., also appears to come from step 1 by simplification. It does not, however, follow so directly. Since it occurs as the *second* conjunct, the rule of simplification will not justify its inference. Do not fear, however, for the means to infer second conjuncts will be offered in the next set of rules.

It is in relation to the rule of simplification that one of the commonest errors is made in generating formal proofs of validity. In the application of the rules of inference, you may only use them upon whole steps that match the forms of the rules. For example, when you encounter an expression like p ⊃ (q • r), it seems quite natural in infer p ⊃ q by Simplification. As a matter of fact the inference to p ⊃ q from p ⊃ (q • r) is valid, but the inference is not a direct one. The reason for forbidding such an inference is that there are cases where what looks like the same sort of move is not a valid argument. Most obvious is the attempted inference of p ⊃ r from (p • q) ⊃ r. The easiest way to see what is wrong here is to replace the variables with three statements: p =df *I throw this lighted newspaper into that tank*, q =df *The tank is filled with 90-octane gasoline*, and r =df *There is an explosion*. The premiss statement, then, becomes:

> If I throw this lighted newspaper into that tank and that tank is filled with 90-octane gasoline, then there is (or will be) an explosion.

That seems a reasonable supposition. If simplification were (incorrectly) applied to the antecedent, the resulting statement would be:

> If I throw this lighted newspaper into that tank, then there is (or will be) an explosion.

That is clearly false. The lesson to be learned from the example is that the logic cannot accept as a rule anything that will not work . ***Thus, even though there are some contexts in which a simplification upon an interior part of a statement-form would seem useful, the rules of inference must be confined to whole steps.***

The rule of conjunction follows an analogous path of reasoning: If two propositions are true apart from each other, then they will remain true as a conjunction.

The final rule of inference is called **addition**. It is a simple, straightforward rule which, at least in my teaching experience, is misunderstood more often than any other. If you know something to be the case, then either that thing or something else (as yet unspecified) is the case. This has to be the case since all that a disjunction needs to be true is to have one of its disjuncts true and you *know* that one of them is true.

The error that frequently is made in applying the rule of addition is the attempt to use it backward. This means that you are trying to infer p from p v q. That, of course, is not addition, but is an invalid inference which, I guess, you might call subtraction or simplification of the wedge. With the rules of inference it is critical that you use them only in the direction that they are given.

The three basic guidelines, then, for using the rules of inference are (1) apply the rules only when you have an exact match of connectives, (2) apply the rules to whole steps only, and (3) apply the rules only in the direction in which they are given.

Copi and Cohen show you many examples of the correct format for formal proofs of validity. You may not be certain about what they are intended to do. The format is set up in such a way that anyone who reads it can re-trace the pattern of reasoning that took place in it. Each step must be justified, in two ways:

(1)   You must be able to identify *how* the person working the problem arrived at that par-
           ticular step.

(2)   You must be able to identify *from where* that particular step came.

In the case of a premiss, saying that it is a premiss is an indication that it came *from* and *by* assumption. In the case of all other steps it is necessary that the justification for a step contain
both a number (or numbers) and a rule name (or abbreviation of a name), the number(s) telling
you *from where* the step came and the name telling you *how* it came. If you double-check to insure that no rule has been used erroneously, then the formal proof is its own verification--when
you are done with it you know that it is right.

        It would be wise for you, now, to work a few of the problems in sections I and II following
9.1. Section 1 problems go from premiss to conclusion in one step; that is, they are really just
examples of the rules where the expressions taking the places referred to as *Wff 1*, etc., are of
varying complexities. The solutions to 1/5 of the problems are in the back of the book. Below
you will find several more solutions to problems which should be helpful to you. Since several
problems have been used as examples in this section, the problems whose solutions appear below may not be the ones you might have expected from previous chapters. The exercises
"solved" below are ones which I judge to be particularly useful in learning tricky techniques.
Work the problems before you look at the answers. Since the answers are a retracing of the reasoning applied to the problem, people who read the answers first tend to think that they understand
how to work the problems better than they actually do. It's like the Exercises in Reasoning in
the first lesson; once you know the answer it's easy.

I (3)   **1, Add.**   *Wff 1* is (H ⊃ I); *Wff 2* is (H ⊃ ~I). Note that you were **not** required
                          to have had *Wff 2* anywhere else in the problem.

   (6)   **1, 2, M.T.** *Wff 1* is (X v Y); *Wff 2* is [~(Z • ~A)]. Note that, since *Wff 2* begins
                          with "~," its negation (in the second premiss) must begin with
                          "~~". Students frequently ask why premiss 2 could not have
                          been (Z • ~A). There are are two basic reasons: (1) there are
                          logic systems in which p and ~~p are not interchangeable, so it's a
                          bad habit treating the dropping (or adding) of a double negation as
                          if it were acceptable, because it's "obvious." And (2) doing so is an
                          intuitive move, and one of the primary motivations for having a
                          formal system was to avoid operation on the intuitive level. The
                          need for avoiding intuition as a justification for reasoning was stat-
                          ed, perhaps most bitterly but eloquently, in 1877 by C.S. Peirce:
                          "Few persons care to study logic, because everybody conceives him-
                          self to be proficient enough in the art of reasoning already. But I
                          observe that this satisfaction is limited to one's own ratiocination
                          [reasoning], and does not extend to that of other men."[1]

   (12)   **1, 2, DS**   *Wff 1* is [E ⊃ (F ≡ ~G)]; *Wff 2* is (C v D). Note that in this case *Wff 1*
                          is quite complex, but can still be handled as if it were simple: you
                          just treat it as a unit.

----

1.   "Illustrations of the Logic of Science--First Paper, The Fixation of Belief," *The Popular Science Monthly*, V. 12 (1877-7;
           p. 1.

(16)   **1, 2, Conj.** *Wff 2* is [N ⊃ (O ∨ P)], *Wff 1* is [Q ⊃ (O ∨ R)]. Note that the premisses occurred in reverse order. That is fine, the order of the premisses is not significant.

(19)   **1, 2, C.D.** *Wff 1* is (H • ~I), *Wff 2* is (C), *Wff 3* is (I • ~H), and *Wff 4* is (D). This is the sort of really simple problem that tends to cause problems because it "looks" so hard.

II. (3)   1. Premiss
          2. Premiss
          3. Premiss
          4. Premiss   Note that the conclusion is stated after the /∴. Be *very* careful not to try to **use** the conclusion as if it too were a premiss.
          5. **1, 2, H.S.** *Wff 1* is I, 2 is J, 3 is K.
          6. **3, 5, Conj.** *Wff 1* is (I ⊃ K), *Wff 2* is (L ⊃ M).
          7. **4, 6, C.D.** *Wff 1* is I, 2 is K, 3 is L, 4 is M

   (7)   1. Premiss
          2. Premiss
          3. Premiss
          4. **3, Simpl.**   *Wff 1* is A, *Wff 2* is D.
          5. **4, Add.**   *Wff 1* is A, *Wff 2* is B.
          6. **1, 5, M.P.** *Wff 1* is (A ∨ B), *Wff 2* is C.
          7. **6, Add.**   *Wff 1* is C, *Wff 2* is B.
          8. **2, 7, M.P.** *Wff 1* is (C ∨ B), *Wff 2* is [A ⊃ (D ≡ E)].
          9. **4, 8, M.P.** *Wff 1* is A, *Wff 2* is (D ≡ ~E). Note that this step uses step 4 for a second time (step 5 had also used it). That is perfectly permissible. Once a step is established, it may be used as often as you like.

The problems in part III are a bit harder, and the ones in parts IV, V and VI a bit harder yet. They are all intended to provide you with a graduated introduction into doing this sort of problem. The difficulty is that the sort in III and IV involve what is sometimes called the "ingenuity" problem. In some subject areas there are absolutely right and wrong answers and/or ways of doing things; in the area of generating formal proofs of validity that is not the case. This does not mean that you cannot make errors--anyone who has tried to learn logic has made a bookful of them--it means that there is seldom one *right* way of doing a problem. The situation may be well compared to the following: Suppose you were told on a Thursday that you were to go from, say, Chicago (where you happened to be) to St. Louis and be there by noon on Tuesday. It is obvious to almost anyone that you could, in that span of time, drive, take a plane, bus, or train, ride a horse, or run (if you were in very good condition). But, if you were particularly perverse (or adventurous) you might catch the Concorde flight to London, take the train from there to the coast, catch the shuttle cruiser (boat) to the continent, rent a car and drive to Paris, fly on the Concorde back to Washington, D.C., and finish out with a non-stop flight to St. Louis. [As of January of 1990 that particular route could get you from Chicago to St. Louis--and would cost you just under $16,000.] That surely would not be an efficient route, but it would get you there. The same is true of some logical proofs--they are roundabout, but they get you there.

It is that very flexibility in doing such problems that makes it difficult to "teach" you how to do them. This is compounded by the fact that different people seldom find that the same sets of rules are comfortable. Copi and Cohen's selection of the rules to use in this text is based upon what they find most useful and upon what they infer, through years of teaching logic, will be easiest for the greatest number of students to use. But the selection is just one of many possible. What you will have to accept is that **this is the set** of rules that you have. It is no more arbitrary than most sets of rules for anything. In baseball, for example, a left-handed batter has a distinct advantage: he stands about six feet closer to first base and, after a swing, his momentum is toward the base to which he has to run while a right-handed batter's is away from it. This could be rectified by letting right-handed hitters run the bases clock-wise (third-second-first-home) while southpaws ran counter-clockwise (first-second-third-home). This would be "fairer" to them, but horrible for the umpires. In any event, there has been no major move for such a system; the rules are just accepted as they are. In logic, too, the rules are the rules. In general, the best that can be done is for you to work enough problems for you to begin to feel comfortable with generating formal proofs of validity. The most helpful thing that anyone teaching this material can do is to warn you about the sorts of errors you are likely to make and to suggest rules of thumb for attacking problems. A *rule of thumb* is a guiding principle which experience has shown to be generally helpful although not universally reliable.

III (2) 1. D ⊃ E   Premiss
         2. D • F   Premiss /∴ E
         3. D   2, Simp
         4. E   1, 3, MP

Note that here premisses 1 and 3 are in the same order as their corresponding forms in the MP rule, but that premiss 2 lies between them. Remember that so long as the internal structure matches the form of the rule, the order of proximity of the premisses is irrelevent.

(6) 1. P • Q   Premiss
     2. R   Premiss /∴ P • R
     3. P   1, Simp
     4. P • R   2, 3, Conj

If you want to be particularly clear about your understanding of the rule forms you might have written the justification of step 4 as 3, 2, Conj. That would indicate that you saw that the elements that you wanted to conjoin appeared in this argument in an order reversed from the conjunction rule form. Although that might be a nice touch, it surely is not necessary.

(11) 1. D ⊃ E   Premiss
      2. (E ⊃ F) • (F ⊃ D)   Premiss /∴ D ⊃ F
      3. E ⊃ F   2, Simp
      4. D ⊃ F   1, 3 HS

This is another of those problems that looks hard but really is quite simple.

(16) 1. (T ⊃ U) • (T ⊃ V)   Premiss
      2. T   Premiss /∴ U v V
      3. T ⊃ U   1, Simp
      4. U   2, 3, MP
      5. U v V   4, Add

The instructions for this section say that you can complete the proof with two added steps. I have included it because I believe that it is the most "natural" way to prove this problem. The two-additional-step proof involves a bit more "cleverness" in its solution:

      1. (T ⊃ U) • (T ⊃ V)   Premiss
      2. T   Premiss /∴ U v V
      3. T v T   2, Add
      4. U v V   1, 3 CD

This is instructive because it shows you a little more of the freedom you have to choose that second disjunct when using addition. In practice, however, few people would quibble about the one additional step in the first proof. If you got the second form on your own, give yourself a gold star.

(21) 1. (K ⊃ L) ⊃ M   Premiss
     2. ~M • ~(L ⊃ K)   Premiss /∴ ~(K ⊃ L)
     3. ~M   2, Simp
     4. ~(K ⊃ L)   1, 3 MT

It is very easy in this exercise to be distracted by the ~(L ⊃ K) in the second premiss. It looks as if you ought to be able to get it out then swap the antecedent and consequent terms. You should see, however, that the simplification rule won't let you get the second conjunct and that you don't yet have (and don't want) a rule allowing the antecedent and the consequent of a conditional to be exchanged.

(27) 1. (E • F) v (G ⊃ H)   Premiss
     2. I ⊃ G   Premiss
     3. ~(E • F)   Premiss /∴ I ⊃ H
     4. G ⊃ H   1, 3, DS
     5. I ⊃ H   2, 4, HS

This may well be the most difficult problem in this set of exercises. It involves treating complex expressions as units (in step 4) and seeing them as separated elements (in step 5). Even with those difficulties, you probably found it a fairly simple exercise.

In working the more complex problems of parts IV-VI, you may find another rule of thumb helpful. The most useful rule of thumb I know (at least for working out formal proofs of validity) is that you should work many problems backward. That sounds strange, but really isn't. Consider this argument:

$$D \supset E, \sim(D • E) \vdash \sim D$$

First instinct says to use simplification of the second premiss, but that is "illicit." (You can't apply an inferential rule within a step.) If you look back over the rules, you will notice that there is only one of the first nine that has a negation in its conclusion-- *modus tollens*. If ~D were taken as the "~*Wff 2*" of the conclusion of a *modus tollens* argument, you would know that there would have had to have been two previous steps of the form:

$$D \supset (Wff\ 2), \sim(Wff\ 2) \quad \vdash \quad \sim D$$

In this problem you are given a premiss with a negation, the second. If this is taken to be ~(*Wff 2*), then the *modus tollens* argument to ~D would have to be

$$D \supset (D • E), \sim(D • E) \vdash \sim D$$

The only difference of this from the original argument is in the first premiss. The problem now is to find an acceptable way to go from D ⊃ E to D ⊃ (D • E). Scanning the list of rules, you will find that there are only two rules with " ⊃ " as their major connective--H.S. and Abs. In the case of the H.S., another premiss containing a " ⊃ " would be needed--that only leaves Abs. It is, of course, the correct answer. You are now in a position to rewrite the formal proof according to the correct format.

     1. D ⊃ E   Premiss
     2. ~(D • E)   Premiss
     3. D ⊃ (D • E)   1, Abs.
     4. ~D   2, 3, M.T.

As a working arrangement, you can even write a proof backward, beginning with step n (the conclusion.) Consider the argument:

$$E \lor {\sim}F, \quad F \supset {\sim}G, \quad {\sim}E \;\vdash\; (F \supset {\sim}G) \bullet {\sim}F$$

| n. | $E \lor {\sim}F$ | m, k, Conjunction |
| | | (This is the only rule thus far that results in a $\bullet$.) |

| m. | $F \supset {\sim}G$ | Premiss |
| | | (This actually is premiss 2.) |

| k. | F | j, i, *modus tollens* |
| | | (This looks like the right approach, patterning after problem 2. As it happens it is not, for you have no way to get ${\sim}{\sim}G$. If you look, however, you will see another choice.)} |

| | | j, i, Disjunctive Syllogism |
| | | (This takes advantage of looking at premiss 1 and 3.) |

The reordered proof, then, is

1.	$E \lor {\sim}F$	Premiss
2.	$F \supset {\sim}G$	Premiss
3.	${\sim}E$	Premiss /∴ $(F \supset {\sim}G) \bullet {\sim}F$
4.	${\sim}F$	1, 3, D.S.
5.	$(F \supset {\sim}G) \bullet {\sim}F$	2, 4, Conj.

As this problem notes (step k), working in reverse order is not always the best approach. A second technique, one that best applies to somewhat more complex problems, is to begin by trying to find where the variables or statements that occur in the conclusion were located in the premisses. Part V, exercise 4 is one in which this approach works well.

Premiss 1	(A)	$(K \lor L) \supset (M \lor N)$
Premiss 2	(B)	$(M \lor N) \supset (O \bullet P)$
Premiss 3	(C)	K
		———————————
Conclusion	(D)	∴ O

The conclusion (D) is the statement O. The only occurrence of O in the premisses is in the consequent of (B). Of the rules you now have, the only one that isolates the consequent of an implication is M.P. To use M.P. you would have to have had the antecedent of (B), that is, $(M \lor N)$. That occurs also as the consequent of (A). Again you would need an antecedent to isolate that consequent by M.P. There the needed antecedent is $(K \lor L)$. Among the rules of inference there are but two that result in a disjunctive statement: C.D. and Add. Since the latter is so much simpler, it is probably best to see if it could be used before going on to check the more complicated rule. And, in this case, addition is the correct route. You wanted to obtain the antecedent of (A), which is $(K \lor L)$; to apply addition you would have to see it as $(Wff\ 1 \lor Wff\ 2)$ with $K = Wff\ 1$ and $L = Wff\ 2$. To arrive at this disjunction by addition you would have to have had its *Wff 1* component, i.e., K, previously, and, of course, you did have it as (C). Using the reasoning that has developed here the problem can be rather straightforwardly written:

1.	$(K \lor L) \supset (M \lor N)$	Premiss
2.	$(M \lor N) \supset (O \bullet P)$	Premiss
3.	K	Premiss /∴ O
4.	$K \lor L$	3, Add.

5.	M v N	1, 4, M.P.
6.	O • P	2, 5, M.P.
7.	O	6, Simpl.

Please notice that there was at least a slight variance of route that would probably occur if the problem had been worked "forward":

1.	Same	
2.	Same	
3.	Same	
4.	(K v L) ⊃ (O • P)	1,2 H.S.
	[with *Wff 1* = (K v L), 2 = (M v N) and 3 = (O • P)]	
5.	K v L	3, Add.
6.	O • P	4, 5 M.P.
7.	O	6, Simpl.

Perhaps one more example of this approach might be useful. It will, however, be offered in a bit briefer terms. In the same set, look at problem 10. Again, you ought to try the problem on your own before looking at the solution.

Expression sought	*Found in*	*Get by*	*Also need*
Conclusion (R)	Conseq. of P-2	M.P.	P v Q
P v Q	Antec. of P-2	Add.	P
P	Conseq. of P-1	M.P.	N v O
N v O	Antec. of P-1	Add.	N
N	Second disj., P-3	D.S.	~Q
~Q	P-4	Premiss	nothing

Thus	1.	(N v O) ⊃ P	Premiss
	2.	(P v Q) ⊃ R	Premiss
	3.	Q v N	Premiss
	4.	~Q	Premiss /∴ R
	5.	N	3, 4, D.S.
	6.	N v O	5, Add.
	7.	P	1, 6, M.P.
	8.	P v Q	7, Add.
	9.	R	2, 8, M.P.

You should now find yourself at the point at which you intellectually understand how to generate formal proofs of validity. However, your situation is much like that of the person who has read all of the how-to books available on tennis: unless that person has "gone onto the court" and practiced, John McEnroe, Martina Navratilova and all of the other leading players have nothing to fear. You should now work as many of the exercises in parts IV, V, and VI as you can find time to attempt. The more "hands-on" time you have with the rules, the easier proofs are to generate. If you choose not to try all of the exercises, be sure to attempt ones from the ends of the sections. The problems sometimes get more difficult, so you do not want to mislead yourself about your preparation by doing only the easier ones. Again, work the exercise on your own before looking at the answers here or in *ITL*: most proofs are easier to follow once done than they are to generate.

IV (3)	1.	(H ⊃ I) • (H ⊃ J)	Premiss
	2.	H • (I v J)	Premiss /∴ I v J
	3.	H	2, Simp
	4.	H v H	3, Add
	5.	I v J	1, 4, CD

This exercise ought to remind you of exercise 16 in section III. It too relies upon the "clever" use of addition. And the problem itself also has another proof involving just one more step:

3.	H ⊃ I	1, Simp
4.	H	2, Simp
5.	I	3, 4, MP
6.	I ∨ J	5, Add

It's also the case that, if you had had a means to infer the second conjunct in premiss 2, you could have arrived at the conclusion directly from that premiss, without any reference to the first premiss at all.

(8)			
	1.	~X ⊃ Y	Premiss
	2.	Z ⊃ X	Premiss
	3.	~X	Premiss /∴ Y • ~Z
	4.	~Z	2, 3, MT
	5.	Y	1, 3, MP
	6.	Y • ~Z	4, 5, Conj

Since, among the rules you presently have, only conjunction results in an expression whose primary connective is a •, chances are very good that you will have had to use that rule. That being the case, your goal was to find the most obvious method of arriving at each of the conclusion's conjuncts. Since "Y" is the consequent of premiss 1 and ~Z is the negation of the antecedent of premiss 2, it should have followed fairly obviously that you were going to use MP and MT. A quick check of premiss 3 showed that ~X is the missing element for both of those inferences, and the proof was complete. Again, the use of premiss 3 twice should have emphasized to you the fact that multiple uses of any step, once assumed or proven, is not only permissible, but sometimes absolutely necessary.

(15)			
	1.	(Z • A) ⊃ B	Premiss
	2.	B ⊃ A	Premiss
	3.	(B • A) ⊃ (A • B)	Premiss /∴ (Z • A) ⊃ (A • B)
	4.	B ⊃ (B • A) 2, Abs	
	5.	B ⊃ (A • B) 3, 4, HS	
	6.	(Z • A) ⊃ (A • B) 1, 5, HS	

It is very likely that you saw quickly that the antecedent of premiss 1 and the consequent of premiss 3 served the same roles in the conclusion. All you needed was to find some sort of HS "Bridge" between the two. Absorption did nicely.

The exercises in section V are of the same sort as those of the earlier sections, just a bit longer. Problems 4 and 10 were solved earlier (pp. 148 & 149), but one more, problem 7, may prove helpful. First, you can see that the conclusion is a disjunction. You have available to you only two rules that result in a disjunction: CD and addition. Since addition is the "simpler" it makes sense to try it first. Addition infers the form "p ∨ q" from "p." In the case of exercise 7's conclusion, A • B would have to be the *p-term* and C • D the *q-term*. The only rule that results in a conjunction is conjunction, so to get the A • B that you need for the premiss of the addition step you must have had A and B previously. But there is the difficulty, for to get B you must use MP (the only rule that gets the consequent of a conditional out by itself) and that would require that you have had an A. The only occurrence of A other than in the first premiss, however, is as the first disjunct of the third premiss. At this point you have no rule that allows you to obtain the first of two disjuncts. Thus, the use of addition is apparently a dead-end.

The other rule that you might have used was CD. It has the form

$$(p \supset q) \cdot (r \supset s)$$
$$p \lor r$$

∴ $q \lor s$

In this problem you know that the *q-term* must be A • B and that the *s-term* must be C • D, since the conclusion sought is (A • B) ∨ (C • D). You can see that you have A ∨ D as the third premiss, so it seems reasonable to assume that the *p-term* is A and the *r-term* is C. Knowing what the *p-, q-, r-,* and *s-term*s are, you also know that the needed first premiss for a CD is [A⊃(A•B)] • [C⊃(C•D)]. As a conjunction it is almost certain that this expression was a result of conjoining its two conjuncts. Seeing the match-up of propositional constants, you surely see that you need to find out how you could have inferred A ⊃ (A • B) from A ⊃ B and C ⊃ (C • D) from C ⊃ D. Of the rules you have available only HS and absorption result in conditionals. Since you don't have premiss expressions with A ⊃ B and C ⊃ D in them, absorption looks like the better choice. In fact the inferences you need are exact instances of that rule.

Tracing back through this mass of discussion, then, you should find buried the elements of the formal proof of ex. 7.

V (7)   1. A ⊃ B   Premiss
         2. C ⊃ D   Premiss
         3. A ∨ C   Premiss /∴ (A • B) ∨ (C • D)
         4. A ⊃ (A • B)   1, Abs
         5. C ⊃ (C • D)   2, Abs
         6. [A ⊃ (A • B)] • [C ⊃ (C • D)]   4, 5, Conj
         7. (A • B) ∨ (C • D)   3, 6, CD

The problems in part VI are simply a combination of the symbolization that you did in Chapter 7 with the formal proofs of validity that you are working now; there is nothing of any added importance in them, except that if you missymbolize, the problem may become unworkable. Most logic teachers have, at one time or another agreed to work in class a problem that the students confidently claim is valid, then have found to the teacher's great embarassment that the problem should have been double-checked, since it was in fact invalid. Some times it has taken as many as 50 or 60 steps before the teacher was willing to recheck validity. Should you hit even the thirty-step level, it would probably be wise to recheck for validity.

VI (2)   If A, then S; and if B, then F.   (A ⊃ S) • (B ⊃ F)
          Either A or B.   A ∨ B
          If S, then B; and if F, then W.   (S ⊃ B) • (F ⊃ W)
          ─────────────────────────   ──────────────────────
          Therefore either B or W.   ∴   B ∨ W

Notice that the symbolization was as close a match for the original English grammatical structure as was possible. The only point that teachers of logic might quibble about was whether or not the semicolon should have been treated as an "and" or as a break between propositions. Had it been split into two premisses, each would have had a simple conditional statement in it. Generally, however, you will find it more useful to treat whole sentences as units, leaving them a single proposition (however complex).

1.	(A ⊃ S) • (B ⊃ F)	Premiss
2.	A v B	Premiss
3.	(S ⊃ B) • (F ⊃ W)	Premiss /∴ B v W
4.	S v F	1, 2, CD
5.	B v W	3, 4, CD

If you are keeping a list of suggested rules of thumb, you might want to include the idea that any time you have a mixture of ⊃'s and v's there is a good chance that you will be using the CD rule.

(6)	If J, then R; but if not J, then E.	(J ⊃ R) • (~J ⊃ E)
	If R, then I.	R ⊃ I
	If J implies R and R implies I,	[(J ⊃ R) • (R ⊃ I)] ⊃
	then either J and I or not J and not I.	[(J • I) v (~J • ~I)]
	If J and I, then T.	(J • I) ⊃ T
	But if not J and not I, then D.	(~J • ~I) ⊃ D
	Therefore either T or D. ∴	T v D

The hardest part of symbolizing (and proving) this problem is psychological: when you have 5 premisses most of which look complex, it is natural to assume that the complexity is a sign of conceptual difficulty. That is not the case.

In this exercise the mixture of ⊃'s and v's should suggest to you that you will, eventually, want to use CD. When you look at the last two premisses you see that their conjunction, with an appropriate disjunction, would yield the conclusion by CD. If you scan the earlier premisses you see that the consequent of the third premiss is that appropriate disjunction. To get the consequent of any conditional, you recall that you must use MP. That means that you also need the antecedent of premiss three. Since it's a conjunction, you probably also need each of its elements separately. You have the second of them in the second premiss and the first as a conjunct in the first premiss. Backtracking this information, you should discover this proof:

1.	(J ⊃ R) • (~J ⊃ E)	Premiss
2.	R ⊃ I	Premiss
3.	[(J ⊃ R) • (R ⊃ I)] ⊃ [(J • I) v (~J • ~I)]	Premiss
4.	(J • I) ⊃ T	Premiss
5.	(~J • ~I) ⊃ D	Premiss /∴ T v D
6.	J ⊃ R	1, Simp
7.	(J ⊃ R) • (R ⊃ I)	2, 6, Conj
8.	(J • I) v (~J • ~I)	3, 7, MP
9.	[(J • I) ⊃ T] • [(~J • ~I) ⊃ D]	4, 5, Conj
10.	T v D	8, 9, CD

9.2   The Rule of Replacement

You may find Copi and Cohen's reference to *the* **rule** of Replacement a little confusing. In a sense they are treating the material as if there were but one replacement rule. In practice they will treat replacement as a general category in which there are 16 subrules. The rule is actually a set of different rules, all of which share the characteristic of allowing intersubstitution of any one member of a pair for the other. It is probably easier to think of replacement as a set of allied rules. In any event, the substitution of one of the given forms for another **anywhere** is acceptable.

From a practical point of view, the reason that you can make such substitutions is that the expressions on both sides of the triple bar will be found to have the same characteristic column when checked on a truth table. If, for example, you worked out a truth table for the first of the DeMorgan's Theorems given you would have the following table:

		I			II	I $\equiv$ II
p q	p • q	~(p • q)	~p	~q	~p v ~q	~(p • q) $\equiv$ (~p v ~q)
T T	T	F	F	F	F	T
T F	F	T	F	T	T	T
F T	F	T	T	F	T	T
F F	F	T	T	T	T	T

When you compare the significant columns below the I and the II you see that they are identical. That means that if you were generating a truth table in which one of the expressions occurred, you could replace the expression with the other without any change in the column and, thus, without any change in the ultimate column generated.

The **DeMorgan's Theorems** were so named for the English logician Augustus DeMorgan who was one of the pioneers of modern formal logic. They make explicit the relationship between "**v**" and "**•**" as logical connectives. Essentially they state that negated conjunctions become disjunctions and vice versa. The second form involves the two alternate ways that you could symbolize "neither...nor...." With either of the Theorems you see that denying the truth of one of these connectives is roughly the same (practically) as asserting that the other relation holds between the negations of the elements of the first.

If you look at exercise 6 in part I on p. 309 of *ITL* then you will see DeMorgan's Theorems in action. The expression "~(R v S)" is replaced by "(~R • ~S)." This follows the second form exactly, so it must be a valid inference. Notice, please, that the consequent of both expressions could be modified by this rule, too. That expression "~R v ~S," matches the *right-hand* side of DeM, form 1. Thus you could have replaced it with "~R • S)" which is the *left-hand* side. It is important to recognize this possibility because, all too frequently, students forget that the rules of replacement differ from the rules of inference in allowing the inference to run either direction.

The second form of replacement rule is the sort that should seem very familiar to you. **Commutation**, or exchanging the order of the expressions, is done all the time in arithmetic. (1 + 2) = (2 + 1) , (2 x 3) = (3 x 2) , and, generally, any additions or multiplications may be commuted. As it happens, equivalences, too, could have been included in the commutation rule, but they were not. The inference from step 1 to step 3 in exercise 2 of part II (p. 309 of *ITL*) is made by commutation. Within the antecedent of (D • E) ⊃ F the D and E are exchanged to yield (E • D) ⊃ F. This inference should also remind you that the rule of replacement, unlike the rules of inference, can be made a step.

Association, like commutation, ought to seem familiar: it shows that among three expressions all connected by either conjunction or disjunction you are free to group them left or right. There is a strong temptation to write a compound statement like "*Gene or Hubie or Dick was elected*" without internal differentiation: G v H v D. According to the agreed-upon conventions of our logic, however, that expression is not well-formed. The wedge connects two well-formed formulae, so the elements must be grouped in pairs: (G v H) v D or G v (H v D). The association rule allows you to transfer back and forth between these two expressions, so, since there is no clear reason for preferring one over the other, you are free to use the one that seems to you more appropriate. The inference of step 7 from step 1 in problem 5 in part II on page 310 of *ITL* is this sort of reasoning.

Association, like commutation also, could have been admitted for equivalence, since p ≡ (q ≡ r) does generate the same truth table as (p ≡ q) ≡ r. Arguments involving the " ≡ " are so rare that it really isn't worth the effort required to learn added rules involving that connective. There is, however, one thing that you need to be very careful to avoid: you must never try to apply either the rule of commutation or that of association to the " ⊃ ." In fact, you can always check to see if a connective is commutative and associative by checking the second and third rows of its truth table. If it has the same value when you have p = T/q = F and when you have p = F/q = T, then it is a communitative/associative function; if its values are different in those cases (as is the case with the " ⊃ ") then you can't commute or associate it.

Distribution looks a lot more complicated, but really is pretty simple. Essentially it confirms that you can carry a conjunction through a disjunction or vice versa. Thus if, for example, you knew that someone had had orange juice and toast or cereal for breakfast, then you would feel sure that she had had either orange juice and toast or orange juice and cereal. The inference "in that direction" seems clear, but many of us tend to forget that you could also have taken the second information ([O • T] v [O • C]) and inferred the former (O • [T v C]). The inference done this way is particularly useful because it results in a form upon which you can use simplification (from the last set of rules).

The other form of distribution, with which you distribute alternation through conjunction, is particularly valuable also for its "setting up" simplifications. If you look again at problem 5 in part II (page 310 in *ITL*) you will see that the inference from step 2 to step 4 is a distribution of this sort. Note that the following step (6) is a simplification of the distributed form.

Inference form 14 will probably look too simple to dignify with a rule of its own. We have all been taught since early childhood about double negations. One of the important values of a formal logic is that it takes us away from relying upon our intuitions. Since there is little we can do to discuss differences in intuition when they occur, except to state the differences, such disagreements tend to become hostile quickly. Thus, it is necessary to include **double negation** as a rule. You should be careful to note that it allows you to insert two negations as well as delete them. One of the common cases in which inserting a double negation is needed is together with DeMorgan's theorems. If you have "A v B" and want to uses DeM, you will see that there is no match for the form you have. There are, however, two ways in which you can use DN to get a form upon which you can apply DeM:

1.	A v B	Given		1.	A v B	Given
2.	~~(A v B)	1, DN		2.	~~A v ~~B	1, DN
3.	~(~A • ~B)	2, DeM		3.	~(~A • ~B)	2, DeM

In the lefthand case you applied the second DeM form within the outer negation; in the righthand case you applied the first form (going right to left) treating A and B as the *p-* and *q-terms*, respectively. Incidentally, you may wonder at the use of "Given" instead of "Premiss." In this case I am not meaning to assert the given expression, as a premiss would do, I am just demonstrating how one relationship could be derived *if you were given* another.

The equivalence called **transposition** is one with which you should feel comfortable because of your work with the categorical propositions. Roughly, it asserts that if q results from p then q's non-occurrence means that p also must not have occurred and vice versa. The inference in exercise 12 of part I on page 309 is a transposition run right to left.

One of the best ways to understand the rule of **material implication** is by looking at the truth table for implication:

$$
\begin{array}{cc|c}
p & q & p \supset q \\
\hline
T & T & T \\
T & F & F \\
F & T & T \\
F & F & T \\
\end{array}
$$

When you check for rows in which the implication itself is true you see that, regardless of the value of the *q-term*, whenever the *p-term* is false the implication is true. You should also see that whenever the *q-term* is true, regardless of the value of the *p-term*, the implication is true. Written together that means that asserting "if p then q" is the same as asserting that "either p is false or q is true." Since so many of our real-life inferences involve conditional relationships, it is very important that you feel at ease with the rule of material implication. Note that exercise 11 of part of I on page 309 is an instance of material implication going from right to left.

It is interesting to observe that another way that you could have asserted the conditional relationship, given the truth table for the horseshoe, would be to deny the occurrence of the second row: $\sim(p \bullet \sim q)$. If it were important for you to derive that expression from p $\supset$ q, you would have to use not only material implication, but also DeM and DN:

1.	p $\supset$ q	Given
2.	$\sim$p v q	1, Impl
3.	$\sim$p v $\sim\sim$q	2, DN
4.	$\sim$(p $\bullet$ $\sim$q)	3, DeM

As you can see, the whole trick to mastering formal proofs of validity while in figuring out just which combination of inferences will carry you from the premises of an argument to its conclusion.

Material equivalence takes two forms. One you should recall: the " $\equiv$ " which is called a *biconditional* is simply the " $\supset$ " read as going in both directions. Its occurrence can be seen in *ITL* in exercise 5 of part I (page 309); the other form of material equivalence is seen in exercise 17 on that same page. That form is easily read from the truth table for " $\equiv$ ":

$$
\begin{array}{cc|c}
p & q & p \equiv q \\
\hline
T & T & T \\
T & F & F \\
F & T & F \\
F & F & T \\
\end{array}
$$

There are two cases where the expression is true: p and q are both true and p and q are both false. Expressed symbolically that would be (p $\bullet$ q) v ($\sim$p $\bullet$ $\sim$q). The "or" used in the expression is, of course, the inclusive one, but you need have no worry about the joint-occurrence case happening, for it would demand p and $\sim$p to occur simultaneously.

The rule of **exportation** will prove a quite useful tool for arrangement of conditions within conditional statements. Take, for example, the statement "*if you have a combustible material, an oxidizing element, and the heat of combustion of that material, then you will have a fire of some sort.*" Although it may be valuable to have the three fire-conditions lumped together, it may also be important to "string them out" in such a way as to be able to handle each of them separately. If that is done to this statement you get the statement: "*if you have a combustible material, then if you have an oxidizing element, then if you have the heat of combustion of that material, then you will have some sort of fire.*" Essentially that sort of transformation is what exportation is all about: you either string out or bunch up the conditions in a conditional. Note that in exercise 3 of part I (page 309) you use exportation to move from the right to the left in the rules form.

The last rule of replacement (or instance of the rule of replacement) is called **tautology**. Since there was an earlier discussion of tautologies, that name may be unfortunate. However, the other likely name would be "identity" which may result in greater confusion in more advanced logic. All of the equivalences under the heading of "The Rule of Replacement" are, of course, tautologies. This rule, however, identifies two quite simple relationships. If you were offered two alternatives and were to discover that they were actually the same thing, you would not hesitate to claim that you have really been offered only one choice. Similarly, if you were told that you were to meet, say, the author of *Tarzan* and the author of the *John Carter of Mars series*, you would expect to meet two individuals only as long as you did not realize that Edgar Rice Burroughs wrote both (among many other works). The conjunctive form of this rule is used in *ITL* in exercise 16 of part I (page 309); the disjunctive one is used between steps 5 and 6 of exercise 5 of part II (page 310).

You should notice that there are some constant principles among the replacements, just as there were among the rules of inference. Your inference may follow the pattern of any of these equivalences, going left to right or right to left. Again the pattern must match exactly. (If the matching is not clear, you might want to consider using the method suggested with the rules of inference.) You might also note that since the replacements are based upon equivalences, if you had a proof in which *only* rules of replacement were used, then you could reverse the order of the steps and prove the premiss from the conclusion. (Note that I said "premiss" not "premisses"--there are no cases of the rule of replacement that use more than one premiss.)

As you did after 9.1, you should work a substantial number of the exercises following 9.2. Recall that Copi and Cohen have about 1/5 of the solutions in the back of the book, that a number of the answers were mentioned above in the explanation of the rules and that several more will be given below. Also recall that it is wise to *work the problems yourself before you look at the solutions*.

I (3)   1, Exp.   This takes place solely within the lefthand conjunct. In it *Wff 1* = I, *2* = J and *3* = K. Note that, relative to the way the form is given in *ITL*, you are are moving right-to-left.

  (8)   1, Distr.   *Wff 1* = (X ∨ Y) =, *2* = X, *3* = Y. One of the hardest things for beginning students of logic to recognize is the use of a compound expression like (X ∨ Y) where *ITL*'s rule-form had had **p**.

  (12)   1, Trans.   This takes place solely within the consequent. *Wff 1* = J, *2* = I. As in problem 3, this inference takes place right-to-left relative to Copi and Cohen's form of the rule.

  (17)   1, Equiv.   *Wff 1* = (∼A • B), *2* = (C ∨ D). The **only** rule that goes from or arrives at a " ≡ " is this rule.

II (3)   1. Premiss
          2. Premiss
          3. 2, Add.
          4. 3, Com.
          5. 1,4, M.P.
          6. 5, Assoc.
          7. 6, Simp.

There are, of course, other routes from these premisses to that conclusion. The proof marked 3A below is an alternative proof that is less direct, but nevertheless quite acceptable. Note how few similarities the two proofs have, except premisses and conclusion.

(3A)   1. (H∨I) ⊃ [J • (K • L)]   Premiss
       2. I   Premiss /∴ J • K
       3. ~(H∨I) ∨ [J • (K • L)]   1, Impl.
       4. [J • (K • L)] ∨ ~(H∨I)   3, Com.
       5. [J • (K • L)] ∨ (~H • ~I)   4, DeM.
       6. {[J • (K • L)] ∨ ~H} • {[J • (K • L)] ∨ ~I}   5, Dist.
       7. {[J • (K • L)] ∨ ~I} • {[J • (K • L)] ∨ ~H}   6, Com.
       8. [J • (K • L)] ∨ ~I   7, Simp.
       9. ~I ∨ [J • (K • L)]   8, Com.
      10. ~~I   2, DN
      11. J • (K • L)   9, 10, D.S.
      12. J   11, Simp.
      13. (K • L) • J   11, Com.
      14. K • L   13, Simp.
      15. K   14, Simp.
      16. J • K   12, 15, Conj.

Note that this alternate proof avoids the use of both modus ponens and addition, but at the cost of nine extra steps.

(7)   1. Premiss
       2. Premiss
       3. Premiss
       4. Premiss
       5. 3, Equiv
       6. 4, 5, DS
       7. 6, DeM
       8. 1, 2, HS
       9. 8, Exp
      10. 9, Taut
      11. 7, 10, MT

III (3) 1. E   Premiss /∴ (E∨F) • (E∨G)
         2. E∨F   1, Add
         3. E∨G   1, Add
         4. (E∨ F) • (E∨G) 2,   3, Conj

It is important here to remember that once a step is justified in a proof it may be used as many times and in as many contexts as you find desirable.

(7)   1. Q ⊃ [R ⊃ (S ⊃ T)]   Premiss
       2. Q ⊃ (Q • R)   Premiss /∴ Q ⊃ (S ⊃ T)
       3. (Q • R) ⊃ (S ⊃ T)   1, Exp
       4. Q ⊃ (S ⊃ T)   2, 3, HS

The pairing of the use of exportation and absorption (for, in a longer proof, step 2 might well have been the result of absorption upon a simpler premiss "Q ⊃ R") is one that merits remembering.

(12)   1. F ≡ G   Premiss
       2. ~(F • G)   Premiss /∴ ~F • ~G
       3. (F • G) ∨ (~F • ~G)   1, Equiv
       4. ~F • ~G   2, 3, DS

Since there are only two forms of the single rule which involve the " ≡ " figuring out what to do with a step containing a " ≡ " is seldom difficult.

(17)	1. (W • X) ⊃ Y	Premiss
	2. (X ⊃ Y) ⊃ Z	Premiss /∴ W ⊃ Z
	3. W ⊃ (X ⊃ Y)	1, Exp
	4. W ⊃ Z	2, 3, HS

The greatest difficulty here is treating X ⊃ Y as a unit rather than as a relationship.

(23)	1. ∼[(U ⊃ V) • (V ⊃ U)]	Premiss
	2. (W ≡ X) ⊃ (U ≡ V)	Premiss /∴ ∼(W ≡ X)
	3. ∼(U ≡ V)	1, Equiv
	4. ∼(W ≡ X)	2, 3, MT

Here the key is not to get excited or overwhelmed quickly. Since the conclusion has occurred between the same proposition-place-holders as it did in the premiss, it is unlikely that you will tamper with that part of the expression. On the other hand, since the first premiss and the second one each contain the same statement symbols, but one has a " ≡ " and the other does not, you must surely use equivalence rule to transform one into the other. That could, however, have taken place in the second rather than the first step. That would have yielded a different, but equally correct, proof:

	1. ∼[(U ⊃ V) • (V ⊃ U)]	Premiss
	2. (W ≡ X) ⊃ (U ≡ V)	Premiss /∴ ∼(W ≡ X)
	3. (W ≡ X) ⊃ [(U ⊃ V) • (V ⊃ U)]	2, Equiv
	4. ∼(W ≡ X)	2, 3, MT

(27)	1. (J • K) ⊃ [(L • M) v (N • O)]	Premiss
	2. ∼(L • M) • ∼(N • O)	Premiss /∴ ∼(J • K)
	3. ∼[(L • M) v (N • O)]	2, DeM
	4. ∼(J • K)	1, 3, MT

The DeM step is the hardest one to see here. If you look at (L • M) as *Wff 1* and (N • O) as *Wff 2*, then the inference from step 2 to step 3 is an instance of the second form of DeM, reasoning right to left. Once that is done all you have to do is is stand far enough back to see that step 3 is the negation of the consequent of step 1. That should suggest the use of MT.

The exercises in part IV are one more step more difficult. The greatest value in your working such progressively harder problems is in the recognition you have come to have of your own skill in constructing formal proofs of validity.

IV (2)	1 ∼B v (C • D)	Premiss /∴ B ⊃ C
	2. (∼ B v C) • (∼ B v D)	1, Dist
	3. ∼B v C	2, Simp
	4. B ⊃ C	3, Impl

You will encounter this sort of inference often. The premiss might have been (B ⊃ (C•D)). If you want to simplify the consequent of conditional statement, change it to a disjunction and follow this pattern.

(6)	1. O ⊃ P	Premiss
	2. P ⊃ ∼P	Premiss /∴ ∼O
	3. ∼P v ∼P	2, Impl
	4. ∼P	3, Taut
	5. ∼O	1, 4, MT

This second premiss is a very curious-looking one. Many people are inclined to think that, somehow, it is a self-contradiction, but it is not. Any time that you encounter the assertion that some statement implies its own negation, you can use the inference pattern in steps 2, 3, and 4 to show that the statement in question is merely false. Similarly, be aware of the pattern derived from statements like "~P ⊃ P." Their reduction can be shown in an inference like this one:

	1. ~P ⊃ P	Given
	2. ~~P v P	1, Impl
	3. P v P	2, DN
	4. P	3, Taut
(14)	1 (N • O) ⊃ P	Premiss
	2. (~P ⊃ ~O) ⊃ Q	Premiss /∴ N ⊃ Q
	3. N ⊃ (O ⊃ P)	1, Exp
	4. (O ⊃ P) ⊃ Q	2, Trans
	5. N ⊃ Q	3, 4, HS

If you have been working exercises faithfully, then this proof should have almost leapt from the page at you: such is the reward of practice. The uses of transposition and HS should also have seemed straightforward, since there are only 4 rules which begin and end with conditional statements.

The problems in part V (page 312 in *ITL*) are of particular importance. As Copi and Cohen indicate these patterns are recurrent ones in formal proofs. In at least half the problems you work either one of these inference patterns or something quite like one of them will occur. It is worth your while, therefore, to work all of them. In addition to the two answers in *ITL*, three more are given below:

V (4)	1. H ⊃ (I • J)	Premiss /∴ H ⊃ I
	2.~H v (I • J)	1, Impl
	3.(~H v I) • (~H v J)	2, Dist
	4.~H v I	3, Simp
	5.H ⊃ I	4, Impl

Notice that this gives you a way to arrive at that "simplification" of the consequent that you couldn't get by the rule of simplification. It is particularly important to remember the "interchangability" of implication and alternation. That gives you a way to use the sorts of rules that you find easiest to understand. For example, if *modus ponens* seems more obvious to you than the disjunctive syllogism, you may change the disjunction (p v q) to (~p ⊃ q) [by way of DN] and then use the ~p with the implication as an instance of *modus ponens*.

(7)	1. (Q v R) ⊃ S	Premiss /∴ q ⊃ s
	2. ~(Q v R) v S	1, Impl
	3. (~Q • ~R) v S	2, DeM
	4. S v ~Q • ~R)	3, Com
	5. (S v ~Q) • (S v ~R)	4, Dist
	6. S v ~Q	5, Simp
	7. ~Q v S	6, Com
	8. Q ⊃ S	7, Impl

If you were given the problem (A v B) ⊃ (C • D) ⊢ A ⊃ C you could, for example, follow the patterns of 4 and 7; then you'd have the solution.

(10)	1. Z ⊃ A	Premiss
	2. Z v A	Premiss /∴ A

3. A v Z	2, Com
4. ~~A v Z	3, D N
5. ~A ⊃ Z	4, Impl
6. ~A ⊃ A	1, 5, HS [Recall the proof on the last page.]
7. ~~A v A	6, Impl
8. A v A	7, DN
9. A	8, Taut

The problems from part VI are picked so that they do **not** utilize the proofs that you worked out in part V. That should show you a few more approaches to formal proofs. And doing them is a lot like any other skill area--the more you do it the better you get at it.

VI (2)
	1 (D • ~E) ⊃ F	Premiss
	2. ~(E v F)	Premiss /∴ ~D
	3. D ⊃ (~E ⊃ F)	1, Exp
	4. D ⊃ (~~E v F)	3, Impl
	5. D ⊃ (E v F)	4, DN
	6. ~D	2, 5, MT

The approach used here is to recognize that, because E and F are together in the second premiss, it is necessary to get them together from the first premiss, too. Once that is done, the conclusion follows quickly.

(8)   Look at this one backward. You want to get A v C and there are only nine of the rules that wind up with a "v." You have no other statements involving A v C, so you probably didn't use Com, Dist, or Assoc, at least directly. There were no " ≡ " or " ⊃ " signs involving them either, so Impl and Equiv are out. The two disjuncts are different, so it isn't a tautology. There are no denied conjunctions, so DeM is an unlikely candidate. All that leaves are Add and CD. To get (A v C) as a result of a CD you had to have had as premisses (or prior references) (*Wff 1* v *Wff 2*) and [*Wff 1* ⊃ A] • [*Wff 2* ⊃ C]. If *Wff 1* = (Y • Z) and *Wff 2* = (Y • B), then premiss 1 fits. You then need (Y • Z) v (Y • B). That would come if you had [Y • (Z v B)], which you can see will tease out of premiss 2. The proof, then is

1. [(Y • Z) ⊃ A] • [(Y • B) ⊃ C]	Premiss
2. (B v Z) • Y	Premiss /∴ A v C
3. Y • (B v Z)	2, Com
4. (Y • B) v (Y • Z)	3, Dist
5. (Y • Z) v (Y • B)	4, Com
6. A v C	1, 5, CD

The sort of elimination of options that was done above is frequently a worthwhile approach to solving such a problem. It can be, however, very time-consuming to try to keep going back through all of the rules to see which ones involve the connective that you happen to be seeking at the time. To try to simplify that task, the following chart has been developed. On it you can look up the connective you have in a premiss (or inferred step)--you do this by looking across the top. And, by reading the headings on the left side as you go down the column under that connective, you will see what other connectives (if any) you can get to. Thus, for example, when you start with a " ⊃ ," you see that you can arrive at a simple statement from the " ⊃ " by MP, a negated one by MT, a "v" by Impl, and another " ⊃ " by HS, Exp, Abs, or Trans. Or, you can begin on the left, selecting the connective at which you wish to arrive, and read across to see from what you could have obtained it. For example, if you have "~(α • β)" you can see that the only rule that results in a denied conjunction is DeM. The chart is, of course, not foolproof: you could, for example, have arrived at that "~(α • β)" by MT if you had had

"$(\alpha \cdot \beta) \supset$ ┼" and "$\sim$┼." You could also have arrived at it by Simp if you had had "$\sim(\alpha \cdot \beta) \cdot$ ┼" as a previous step. The point is, the chart is only intended as a reference tool, suggesting at least reasonable things for which to look.

Premiss / Conclusion	α	~α	α • β	α v β	α ⊃ β	α ≡ β	~(α • β)	~(α v β)
α	MP	DS DN	Simp Taut	DS Taut	MP	none	none	none
~α	DN	MT	none	none	MT	none	none	none
α • β	Conj Taut	none none	Com Assoc	Dist	none	Equiv	none	none
α v β	Add Taut	none	Dist CD	Assoc Com CD	Impl	Equiv	none	none
α ⊃ β	none	none	none	Impl	HS Exp Abs Trans	none	none	none
α ≡ β	none	none	Equiv	Equiv	none	none	none	none
~(α • β)	none	none	none	DeM	none	none	none	none
~(α v β)	none	none	DeM	none	none	none	none	none

IV (17) This problem looks far more difficult than it is because its premisses are so long. A sketchy run backward looks like:

n. F ⊃ (F • I)	m, Abs
m. F ⊃ I	k, l, HS
l. ? ⊃ I	
k. F ⊃ ?	Now there is a "⊃ I" in the second premiss and a "~F v" which can yield a "F ⊃ " (by Impl.) in the first, so that's the way to approach this one. This problem then becomes:

1. ~ F v ~[~(G • H) • (G v H)]   Premiss
2. (G ⊃ H) ⊃ [H ⊃ G) ⊃ I]   Premiss /∴ F ⊃ (F • I)

At least the stuff in the second half of the first premiss and in the first half of the second premiss--supposedly the material from which the "?" of steps k and l (above) will come--is all made up of G's and H's.

3. F ⊃ ~[~(G • H) • (G v H)]   1, Impl
4. F ⊃ [~~(G • H) v ~(G v H)]   3, DeM (a reasonable move, since the chart says that this is the only thing you can do with a denied conjunction.)
5. F ⊃ [(G • H) v ~(G v H)]   4, DN
6. F ⊃ [(G • H) v (~G • ~H)]   5, DeM (same move as step # 4)

7. F ⊃ (G ≡ H)	6, Equiv (because this a sufficiently odd formula, you will come to see it quickly.) Since you now have G ≡ H as a candidate for the role of *?* in j, try to get it as the same for k from step 2.
8. [(G ⊃ H) • (H ⊃ G)] ⊃ I	2, Exp
9. (G ≡ H) ⊃ I	8, Equiv
10. F ⊃ I	7, 9, HS
11. F ⊃ (F • I)	10, Abs

(19)   Backward you'll get

n. Q	3, m, MP
m. ~(M • O)	k, DeM (the route the other chart suggests)
k. ~M v ~O	Several options are available. One of the most promising would appear to be CD, since the first two premisses look so much like a dilemma. The inference from them to k is sometimes called a ***destructive dilemma***. But you don't have it as a rule; you have its cousin the constructive dilemma. What you need is a way to convert one into the other. The way is to transpose the conditional statements in the first premiss. The proof then is:
1. (M ⊃ N) • (O ⊃ P)	Premiss
2. ~N v ~P	Premiss
3. ~(M • O) ⊃ Q	Premiss /∴ Q
4. (~N ⊃ ~M) • (~P ⊃ ~O)	1, Trans (Since you are doing the same thing to both conjuncts, there is no good reason not to do them together.)
5. ~M v ~O	2, 4, CD (Notice that by transposing, what had been the disjunction of the negations of the consequents has become the disjunction of the antecedents.)
6. ~(M • O)	5, DeM
7. Q	3, 6, MP

Here you see that what had appeared to be a very complex proof is actually rather simple.

Some people find that, since, as the chart shows, the greatest number of rules going from a connective to itself is found with the " ⊃ ," it is sometimes helpful to convert anything that you can into " ⊃'s" and then proceed. If that is coupled with another rule of thumb--whenever you can, break things down as far as possible--the proof of this same problem could become:

1. (M ⊃ N) • (O ⊃ P)	Premiss
2. ~N v ~P	Premiss
3. ~(M • O) ⊃ Q	Premiss /∴ Q
4. M ⊃ N	1, Simp
5. (O ⊃ P) • (M ⊃ N)	1, Com
6. O ⊃ P	5, Simp
7. N ⊃ ~P	2, Impl
8. M ⊃ ~P	4, 7, H S
9. ~P ⊃ ~O	6, Trans
10. M ⊃ ~O	9, 8, H S

12. ~(M • O)   11, DeM
13. Q   12, 13, MP

The exercises in part VII are just a combination of the symbolization techniques you learned in chapter 8 and the proof techniques you have been working on in this chapter. One thing that should seem quite noticeable in these exercises is the frequency with which conditional statements are made. You should see that there are more conditional statements than all other sorts combined. One possible explanation of this phenomenon is that human fondness for identifying causal patterns leads us to see as many things as possible in such terms. Since the closest thing that our logic has to expressing causality is the material conditional, that means that we will often find ourselves compelled to symbolize conditional and causal statements in the same way.

VII (3)   A =df   A political leader who sees her former opinions to be wrong alters her course.
           D =df   She is guilty of deceit.
           I =df   She is open to a charge of inconsistency.

If not A, D; and if A, I	$(\sim\!A \supset D)$ • $(A \supset I)$
A or not A	A v ~A

Therefore either D or else I   ∴   D v I

1. $(\sim\!A \supset D)$ • $(A \supset I)$ Premiss
2. A v ~A   Premiss /∴ D v I
3. ~A v A   2, Com
4. D v I   1, 3, CD

There is a real temptation here to overlook the Com step, but without it the proof does not **exactly** follow the rule forms and would then be incorrect.

(9)   C =df   We extend credit on the Wilkins account.
           M =df   They will have a moral obligation to accept our bid on their next project.
           P =df   We figure a more generous margin of profit in preparing our estimates.
           I =df   Our general financial condition will improve considerably.

If C, M.	C ⊃ M
P if M.	M ⊃ P
P causes I.	P ⊃ I

Hence I follows from C.   ∴   C ⊃ I

1. C ⊃ M   Premiss
2. M ⊃ P   Premiss
3. P ⊃ I   Premiss /∴ C ⊃ I
4. C ⊃ P   1, 2, HS
5. C ⊃ I   3, 4, HS

There is surely no problem in generating the proof of this problem. The only thing that might have caused you difficulties is the symbolization. Be sure you know which is antecedent and which is consequent when you symbolize a conditional. In this argument, for example, the first and third premises have their symbols occur in the formal structure, while the second premise and the conclusion have them occur in opposite orders.

(13) C =df   The new courthouse is conveniently located.
     H =df   It is located in the heart of the city.
     A =df   It is to be adequate to its function.
     L =df   It will have to be built large enough to house all the city offices.
     O =df   Its cost will run to over a million dollars.

If C, H; and if A, L.	(C ⊃ H) • (A ⊃ L)
If H and L, then O.	(H • L) ⊃ O
Not O.	~O

Therefore either not C or not A   ∴   ~C v ~A

1. (C ⊃ H) • (A ⊃ L)	Premiss
2. (H • L) ⊃ O	Premiss
3. ~O	Premiss /∴ ~C v ~A
4. ~(H • L)	2, 3, MT
5. ~H v ~L	4, DeM
6. (~H ⊃ ~C) • (~L ⊃ ~A)	1, Trans (twice)
7. ~C v ~A	5, 6, CD

This uses the destructive dilemma form that was used in the solution of problem 19 on page 163 (above).

(18) W =df   World population is increasing.
     A =df   Agricultural production is declining.
     M =df   Manufacturing remains constant.
     N =df   New food sources will become available.
     R =df   There will be a radical redistribution of food resources in the world.
     H =df   Human nutritional requirements diminish.
     P =df   Family planning will be encouraged.

Although W, A and M.	W • (A • M)
If A and W then either N or R unless H.	(A • W) ⊃ [(N v R) v H]
Not N, yet neither P nor H.	~N • ~(P v H)

Therefore R   ∴ R

Important here are the various ways in which you can express the " • ." You should be cautious when symbolizing, lest you accidentally misrepresent knowledge that you have.

1. W • (A • M)	Premiss
2. (A • W) ⊃ [(N v R) v H]r	Premiss
3. ~N • ~(P v H)	Premiss /∴ R
4. ~N	3, Simp
5. (W • A) • M	1, Assoc
6. W • A	5, Simp
7. A • W	6, Com
8. (N v R) v H	2,7, MP
9. N v (R v H)	8, Assoc
10. R v H	9,4, DS
11. H v R	10, Com
12. ~(P v H) • ~N	3, Com
13. ~(P v H)	12, Simp
14. ~P • ~H	13, DeM

15. ~H • ~P	14, Com
16. ~H	15, Simp
17. R	11,16, DS

(25)   G =df   Socrates was a great philosopher.
       H =df   Socrates was happily married.

If either H or not H, then G   (H v ~H) ⊃ G
_____   _____

Therefore G   ∴   G

1. (H v ~H) ⊃ G	Premiss
2. ~(H v ~H) v G	1, Impl
3. (~H • ~~H) v G	2, DeM
4. G v (~H • ~~H)	3, Com
5. (G v ~H) • (G v ~~H)	4, Dist
6. (G v ~H)	5, Simp
7. ~H v G	6, Com
8. H ⊃ G	7, Impl
9. (G v ~~H) • (G v ~H)	5, Com
10. G v ~~H	9, Simp
11. ~~H v G	10, Com
12. ~H ⊃ G	11, Impl
13. ~G ⊃ ~H	8, Trans
14. ~G ⊃ G	12, 13, H S
15. ~~G v G	14, Impl
16. G v G	15, DN
17. G	16, Taut

It is interesting to notice that an argument that is so obviously valid takes so many steps to prove. Since the antecedent of the premiss is a tautology, it would have been nice if there had been a rule that allowed us just to add it to the proof. Had such a move been allowable, the proof would have been

1. (H v ~H) ⊃ G	Premiss
2. H v ~H	Added Tautology
3. G	1,2, MP

There is, however, no rule in the system that allows the addition of selected tautologies to any premisses, so you have to settle for the earlier proof.

9.3   Proof of Invalidity
9.4   Inconsistency

When you were doing truth tables, you may have thought that they were fine for arguments with two or three variables but wondered what happened when the arguments became more complex. That is a wise concern, because the length of a truth table doubles every time a new and distinct variable (or constant) is added. That means that while an argument with three distinct variables has an eight-row table, one with four has a sixteen-row one, one with five has a thirty-two row table and an argument with six distinct variables requires a sixty-four row table. An argument that involves the interrelationships among ten distinct statements (complex but certainly not uncommon in real life) would require that to check it for validity you use a table with one-thousand-and-twenty-four rows!

You may have also thought that there ought to be some way of sorting out the rows of the table that can easily be seen to be unproductive for proving invalidity. For example, you can see that only two of the eight rows of the truth table for problem II (13) (the table is in chapter 8. page 127, above) are even potentially useful for proving invalidity. They are the second and fourth rows. The reason for this assertion is that they are the only rows of the table in which the conclusion, "p ⊃ r", is false. The other six rows, although interesting, are ones where the conclusion is true as a result of the assumed values for the variables, and an argument cannot be shown to be invalid by a case where the conclusion is true. The only demonstration of invalidity is when the *premisses are all true* and the *conclusion is false*. Thus, about three-fourths of the work done on the truth table for III.13 was pointless. Argument III (6) (also shown on p. 127 above) is an invalid one; it required a table with four rows to demonstrate it, but you got lucky and could have stopped at the end of the first row. You would not always be so fortunate. The argument "[~p ⊃ ~q,   qv~r,   s ⊃ r,   s ≡ t,   ~(~t • u) ⊢ ~p ⊃ u]" is also an invalid one, but it requires a table with sixty-four rows and (unfortunately) you will not find that it is invalid until the sixty-fourth row. Fortunately, however, there does exist a method by which you can considerably reduce your efforts at checking for validity. Copi and Cohen discuss it in section 9.3 and call it the *method of assigning truth values*. Essentially it involves a recognition that finding **any** case where all of the premises of an argument are true and its conclusion is false is sufficient to prove that that argument is invalid. The fact that there may be several cases which would do the same is of no consequence. (A truth table would find them all, but why would you want to know them all? Doesn't that seem like some of the "consecutive executions?" A really foul criminal *could* be hanged, then beheaded, then drawn and quartered, then boiled in oil, then burned at the stake. After the first capital punishment, the criminal very likely didn't care about any of the later ones.) Using the 6-variable argument suggested above, the initial assignments of values would look like this:

$$\text{~p} \supset \text{~q,} \quad \text{qv~r,} \quad \text{s} \supset \text{r,} \quad \text{s} \equiv \text{t,} \quad \text{~(~t • u)} \quad \vdash \quad \text{~p} \supset \text{u}$$
$$\underline{\textbf{T}} \qquad\qquad \underline{\textbf{T}} \qquad\quad \underline{\textbf{T}} \qquad\quad \underline{\textbf{T}} \quad\ \underline{\textbf{T}} \qquad\qquad\qquad\qquad \underline{\textbf{F}}$$

This amounts to the assumption that the argument is invalid, since the *only* way it could be shown to be invalid would be precisely this case--where each of the premises is true but the conclusion is false. These values "force" some other values--if ~(~t • u) is true, then (by the definition of "~") (~t • u) is false. Also if ~p ⊃ u is false, then (by the definitions both of " ⊃ " and "~") p must be true and u must be false. The initial assumption of invalidity does not force values immediately for the first four premises, since there are three ways for the " ⊃ " and " v " to be true and two ways for the " ≡ " to be either true or false. A second stage of assigning values, then might look like the following (note that each new set of assigned values is located directly under the element having the assignment and that the order of assignment can be recognized by the distance down from the argument-form):

$$\text{~p} \supset \text{~q,} \quad \text{qv~r,} \quad \text{s} \supset \text{r,} \quad \text{s} \equiv \text{t,} \quad \text{~(~t • u)} \quad \vdash \quad \text{~p} \supset \text{u}$$
$$\text{T} \qquad\qquad \text{T} \qquad\quad \text{T} \qquad\quad \text{T} \qquad \text{T} \quad \underline{\textbf{F}} \qquad\qquad \underline{\textbf{T}} \quad \text{F}\underline{\textbf{F}}$$

If ~p is true, then p is false, and if p is false and u is false in the conclusion, then those same elements must have the same values wherever they occur in the argument--in this case in the first and last premises respectively. Such assignments become:

$$\text{~p} \supset \text{~q,} \quad \text{qv~r,} \quad \text{s} \supset \text{r,} \quad \text{s} \equiv \text{t,} \quad \text{~(~t • u)} \quad \vdash \quad \text{~p} \supset \text{u}$$
$$\underline{\textbf{TF}}\ \text{T} \qquad\quad \text{T} \qquad\quad \text{T} \qquad\quad \text{T} \qquad \text{T} \quad \text{F}\ \underline{\textbf{F}} \qquad \text{T}\underline{\textbf{F}}\ \text{F}\ \text{F}$$

If ~p (as the antecedent of the first premise) is true, then ~ q (as the consequent) must also be true (or the premiss would be false--and to check for invalidity it has to be true).

~p ⊃ ~q,   q v ~r,   s ⊃ r,   s ≡ t,   ~(~t • u)   ⊢   ~p ⊃ u

TF T **T**   T   T   T   T   F F   TF F F

If -q is true, then q must be false in both the first and second premiss.

~p ⊃ ~q,   q v ~r,   s ⊃ r,   s ≡ t,   ~(~t • u)   ⊢   ~p ⊃ u

TF T T **F**   **F**T   T   T   T   F F   TF F F

If q is false in the second premiss, the ~r must be true (or the alternation q v ~r would be F v F and the second premiss would be false--and, of course, to check validity it must be true).

~p ⊃ ~q,   q v ~r,   s ⊃ r,   s ≡ t,   ~(~t • u)   ⊢   ~p ⊃ u

TF T T F   FT**T**   T   T   T   F F   TF F F

If ~r in the second premiss is true, then r must be false in both the second and third premisses.

~p ⊃ ~q,   q v ~r,   s ⊃ r,   s ≡ t,   ~(~t • u)   ⊢   ~p ⊃ u

TF T T F   FTT**F**   T **F**   T   T   F F   TF F F

If r is false in the third premiss, then s must also be false (or that premiss--which has to be true--would be false).

~p ⊃ ~q,   q v ~r,   s ⊃ r,   s ≡ t,   ~(~t • u)   ⊢   ~p ⊃ u

TF T T F   FTTF   **F** T F   **F** T   T   F F   TF F F

If s is false in premiss three, then it must also be so in the fourth premiss. And if s is false then t must also be false for s ≡ t to be true, as it must be.

~p ⊃ ~q,   q v ~r,   s ⊃ r,   s ≡ t,   ~(~t • u)   ⊢   ~p ⊃ u

TF T T F   FTTF   F T F   F T **F**   T   **F** F F   TF F F

If t is false in the fourth premiss, it must also be false in the last one, and ~t there must be true.

~p ⊃ ~q,   q v ~r,   s ⊃ r,   s ≡ t,   ~(~t • u)   ⊢   ~p ⊃ u

TF T T F   FTTF   F T F   F T F   T **TF** F F   TF F F

The problem thus far, is that all of the T's and F's are so crowded that it is a bit hard to read. You might find that using 1/8 to 1/4 inch graph paper would line everything up nicely.

Notice that the order in which values were determined in each premiss is shown by the underlining, but not the order in which values were forced from premiss to premiss (which you saw in the sequence preceeding this last version). You can see that, in the last premiss, when ~t is true and u is false, then (~t • u) is false, which was what the original assignment was. This means that you now have a set of assignments of truth values for all of the variables in the argument and that those values make each of the premisses true and the conclusion false. It might all be summarized by saying that this shows that, when p, q, r, s, t, and u are all false, this argument is shown to be invalid.

Such an extended discussion looks far more complicated than it really is. The problems following 9.3 provide good practice in assigning values to show invalidity. The example below (number 6) is done, with a notation in the margin showing forcings of values.

	A ≡ (B v C)	B ≡ (C v A)	C ≡ (A v B)	~A ⊢ B v C
Assume Invalid	T	T	T	T F
If "v" = F				F F
From conclusion	FFF F	F F	F F	
If ~α=T, α=F				F
From last premiss	F	F	F	
Summary of values	F F FF	F F F	F F F	F F F
Summary of "~"				T
Summary of "v"	F	F	F	F
Summary of "≡"	T	T	T	

You can see that, when all of the elements (A, B, and C) are false, all of the premisses are true and the conclusion is false. The consistent assignment of values shows the argument to be invalid. You may wonder how this method proves something valid. That proof is based upon a time-honored method that is called an indirect proof of a *reducio ad absurdum* (reduction to absurdity). The basic operation of this sort of proof is to assume one thing, to show how that assumption forces you to hold an absurd position. In a formal logic, like the sort that you are now studying, an absurdity is a contradiction. If you find that there is a contradiction (the assertion of something and its negation, or the assertion that something is true and false at the same time), then the assumption with which the method of assigning truth values began, that is, that the argument is invalid, must be wrong. This means that getting a contradiction while using the method of assigning truth values is the way in which you find that an argument form is valid.

A return to the problems following 8.4, in fact to problem II (13) which was earlier shown to be valid by a full truth table, yields an example which shows the use of the method of assigning truth values to prove validity. Notice that there is really nothing to be gained by using the *ASF* when applying this method.

	p ⊃ (q ⊃ r),	p ⊃ q	⊢	p ⊃ r
Assume argument invalid	T	T		F
Forced by definition of ⊃				T F
Forced by assignment above	T	F T		
Forced by definition of ⊃	T	T		
Forced by assignment above	T ⇕			
Forced by definition of ⊃	F			

The two values beneath the second horseshoe of the first premiss, of course, contradict each other -- if p is true, then for p ⊃ (q ⊃ r) to be true q ⊃ r must be true, but q and r are forced elsewhere to be T and F respectively, so q ⊃ r must also be false. Since it cannot be the case that any expression is simultaneously true and false, the original assumption of invalidity must have been wrong -- the argument is valid.

The following problem I (6) from the sets after 9.4 (page 321), is a bit longer, but is worked on in a similar fashion:

	[(D v E) • F] ⊃ G,	(F ⊃ G) ⊃ (H ⊃ I),	H	⊢	D ⊃ I
Assume invalid:	T	T	T		F
Forced by ⊃ :					T F
Duplicated values:	T	T F			
Forced by v & ⊃ :	T	F			
Forced by ⊃ :		F			
Forced by ⊃ :		T F			
Duplicated values:	T F				
Forced by • :	Υ	⇕			
Forced by ⊃ :		Z			

Here you can see that, since G cannot be both T and F, the argument is valid.

It would be nice if problems always worked themselves out as neatly as these have. Unfortunately they don't. Sometimes, when assigning values, you will encounter a case where you become stalled, because there are values yet to be asssigned, but none of them are forced by whatever you already have. A simple example is $p \equiv q$, $q \equiv r \vdash p \equiv r$. Intuitively you probably have no doubt that it is valid, but intuitions are not adequate proof, so you might begin to assign values:

	p	≡	q,	q	≡	r	⊦	p	≡	r
Assume invalid:		T			T				F	

At this point you will find yourself stopped because there are no more forced values--there are two ways for " ≡ " to be true and two ways for it to be false, and there is no way to tell which ones to use. With such a short problem you might decide to generate a full truth table, but that is evading the difficulty. What if it occurs on a problem with a dozen variables? The answer is to make a *secondary assumption*, that is, to assume something more than the original assumption of invalidity. In this case a helpful assumption would be that $p = T$. The problem then goes quickly.

	p	≡	q,	q	≡	r	⊦	p	≡	r
Assume invalid:		T			T				F	
Assumption:	T							T		
Forced:			T							F
Carried:				T		F				
Forced:					F					

The second premiss is now forced to be both T and F. That contradiction proves the argument valid, right? *Wrong!* At this point you have no way to tell whether the contradiction was a result of the initial assumption (that the argument is invalid) or the secondary assumption (that $p = T$). To eliminate the possibility that the contradiciton is due to the secondary assumption, you must go back and recheck *using the opposite secondary assumption*.

	p	≡	q,	q	≡	r	⊦	p	≡	r
Assume invalid:		T			T				F	
Assumption:	F							F		
Forced:			F							T
Carried:				F		T				
Forced:					F					

Even with the opposite secondary assumption there is a contradiction in the second premiss. Since the value of the secondary assumption did not affect the occurrence of a later contradiction--the contradiction occurred no matter what value the secondary assumption had-- the contradiction must have been due to the original assumption, that the argument was invalid. Thus the argument is valid. When you make a secondary assumption it is *always* necessary (if you find a contradiction) to go back and check the opposite assumption. The need for this can be seen in following problem.

	p	⊃	(	q	•	r	),	q	⊃	s,	r	⊃	t	⊦	s	•	t
Assume invalid:		T							T			T				F	
There are no forced values, so assume:	T																
Forced :					T												
Forced:				T		T											
Carried:								T			T						
Forced:										T			T				
Carried:															T		T

The unwary might infer that the contradiction (The first line assumes the conclusion is false but the last one has both s and t true) means the argument is valid, but you should remember to check the opposite secondary assumption.

	p ⊃ (q • r)	q ⊃ s	r ⊃ t	s • t
Assume invalid:	T	T	T	F
There are no forced values, so assume:	F			
Forced:	T (confirms first assumption)			
There are no forced values, so assume:	T			
Carried:		T		
Forced:		T		
Carried:				T
Forced:				F
Carried:			F	
Forced:			F	
Carried:	F			
Forced:	F			

Here all variables have a value, each of the premises is true, and the conclusion is false--there are no contradictions--so the argument is shown to be invalid. Had there been a contradiction, you still would not have known that the argument was valid because there was a tertiary assumption (that q = T) made. If there had been a contradiction, you would have had to go back to the point that q was assumed to be true and check it when q was false. Cases requiring secondary assumptions occur less frequently than ones that have all forced values; ones needing tertiary assumptions are rare; ones requiring four or more could occur, but are so scarce that you need not worry about them.

Once you understand how the method of assigning truth values can show an argument to be valid or invalid, the exercises following 9.3 and 9.4 should be pretty simple. These problems, like the formal proofs of validity, should be worked before you look at the answers. Start after 9.3.

	I v ~J	~(~K • L)	~(~I • ~L)	~J ⊃ K	
(3)					
Assume invalid:	T	T	T	F	(a)
Forced:		F	F	T F	(b)
Carried:	T	F			(c)
Forced:	F	T		F	(d)
Forced:		F			(e)
Carried:			F		(f)
Forced:			T		(g)
Forced:			F		(h)
Forced:			T		(i)
Carried:	T				(j)

(a)   Begin by assuming the argument is invalid. That means assume each of the premises is true and that the conclusion is false. Then work out values that are forced by this assumption.

(b)   The only way that a negation can be false is for what it negates to be true. This means that (~K • L) and (~I • ~L) must both be false. Also the only way for a conditional statement to be false is for its antecedent to be true and its consequent false. This means that ~J must be true and K false wherever in the exercise they occur.

(c)   Carry the values for ~J and K.

(d)   These follow by the definition of negation.

(e)   Since (~K • L) must be false (from b) and ~K must be true (from d) the other
        conjunct, L, must be false.
(f)   The value is carried from e.
(g)   This follows the definition of negation.
(h)   This uses the same reasoning as e.
(i)   This follows the definition of negation.
(j)   Carry the I value. You should now see that all of the premises of the argument can
        be true while the conclusion is false. That means that the argument is shown to be
        invalid.

(6)   Worked earlier.

The problems after 9.4 of *ITL* should give you more realistic challenges: you don't know
in advance which are valid and which are invalid.

I (4)   Always begin by checking the argument to see if it is valid. If it is not, of course, you
        cannot construct a formal proof of validity.

$$M \supset (N \bullet O), \quad (N \lor O) \supset P \quad \vdash \quad M \supset P$$

As always begin by assuming the argument to be invalid, that is, that all the premises are
true and the conclusion is false. Given the single way for the conditional conclusion to be false,
you know that, for the argument to be invalid, M must be true and P false throughout this argument. For the first premise to be true when M is true, you should see that both of the conclusion's conjuncts will also have to be true. But if N and O are both true, then N ∨ O will be true and
P will have to be true to make the second premise true. That, however, forces you to claim that
the P in the second premise is true but that the P in the conclusion is false. That, obviously, cannot be the case. The only thing that could have led you to argue that a statement was both true
and false would have been a bad assumption. But the only assumption that you made was that
the exercise was invalid. Thus that asssumption must be bad, or, what amounts to the same
thing, the argument is valid.

Since it is valid, you need to construct a formal proof of validity. This one is a snap *IF*
you did as I suggested and worked all of the problems in Part V in 9.3 of *ITL*. If you look at exercises 4 and 7 on page 312, then you should see that this exercise is little more than the combination of those two exercises.

To show you how you can use problems which you have already proven to make new
ones easier, I will prove first exercise 4 then exercise 7 from that group, then I will suggest a
proof of exercise 4 of this set to show the two earlier proofs blended.

9.3 *V* (4) 1. H ⊃ (I • J)   Premiss /∴ H ⊃ I
             2. ~H ∨ (I • J)   1, Impl
             3. (~H ∨ I) • (~H ∨ J)   2, Dist
             4. ~H ∨ I   3, Simp
             5. H ⊃ I   4, Impl

V(7) 1. $(Q \lor R) \supset S$ Premiss /∴ $Q \supset S$
       2. $\sim(Q \lor R) \lor S$ 1, Impl
       3. $S \lor \sim(Q \lor R)$ 2, Com
       4. $S \lor (\sim Q \bullet \sim R)$ 3, DeM
       5. $(S \lor \sim Q) \bullet (S \lor \sim R)$ 4, Dist
       6. $S \lor \sim Q$ 5, Simp
       7. $\sim Q \lor S$ 6, Com
       8. $Q \supset S$ 7, Impl

9.4 I(4) 1. $M \supset (N \bullet O)$ Premiss
           2. $(N \lor O) \supset P$ Premiss /∴ $M \supset P$
           3. $\sim M \lor (N \bullet O)$ 1, Impl
           4. $(\sim M \lor N) \bullet (\sim M \lor O)$ 3, Dist
           5. $\sim M \lor N$ 4, Simp
           6. $M \supset N$ 5, Impl
           7. $\sim(N \lor O) \sim P$ 2, Impl
           8. $P \lor \sim(N \lor O)$ 7, Com
           9. $P \lor (\sim N \bullet \sim O)$ 8, DeM
          10. $(P \lor \sim N) \bullet (P \lor \sim O)$ 9, Dist
          11. $P \lor \sim N$ 10, Simp
          12. $\sim N \lor P$ 11, Com
          13. $N \supset P$ 12, Impl
          14. $M \supset P$ 6, 13, HS

   If you look at steps 1 and 3 through 6 you will see that they are formal duplicates of the proof of V(4); if you look at steps 2 and 7 through 13, then you will see that formally they match the proof of V(7). All you added was the hypothetical syllogism at the end.

(7) $(J \bullet K) \supset (L \supset M)$, $N \supset \sim M$, $\sim(K \supset \sim N)$, $\sim(J \supset \sim L) \vdash \sim J$

		T			T		T		T		F	(a)

(Rows of the truth-value analysis:)

```
(7) (J • K) ⊃ (L ⊃ M),  N ⊃ ~M,  ~(K ⊃ ~N),  ~(J ⊃ ~L) ⊢  ~J
              T              T        T               T             F     (a)
                                     F               F             T     (b)
                                 T   F    T   F                    (c)
     T   T    T        T              T               T            (d)
       T          T                                                (e)
            T           T                                          (f)
              F                                                    (g)
```

(a) Assume the argument is invalid, that is, that all the premisses are true and the conclusion false.
(b) Work out forced values based upon negation.
(c) Work out forced values from denied conditionals.
(d) Work out forced values based upon negation and carry determined values to all instances.
(e) The conjunction of true statements is true; the consequent of true when the antecedent is true.
(f) Work out forced values based upon negation or true conditionals with true antecedents.
(g) Work out values as in e and f; note that the argument is valid because, for the premisses to be true while the conclusion is false. M would have to be both true and false. That, obviously, cannot be the case.

Since you know that the argument is valid, you need to generate a formal proof of validity.

1.	(J • K) ⊃ (L ⊃ M)	Premiss
2.	N ⊃ ~M	Premiss
3.	~(K ⊃ ~N)	Premiss
4.	~(J ⊃ ~L)	Premiss /∴ ~J
5.	~(~J v ~L)	4, Impl
6.	~~(J • L)	5, DeM
7.	J • L	6, DN
8.	J	7, Simp
9.	L • J	7, Com
10.	L	9, Simp
11.	~(~K v ~N)	3, Impl
12.	~~K • ~~N	11, DeM
13.	K • N	12, DN (twice)
14.	K	13, Simp
15.	N • K	13, Com
16.	N	15, Simp
17.	~M	16, 2, MP
18.	J • K	8, 14, Conj
19.	L ⊃ M	1, 18, MP
20.	M	10, 19, MP
21.	M v ~J	20, Add
22.	~J	21, 17, DS

As you surely noticed, steps 17 and 20 contradict each other. That means that the premisses are self-contradictory and that any conclusion at all could be derived from them. When you encounter such a contradiction, you can follow the pattern shown by steps 17, 20, 21, and 22 to derive any conclusion at all.

You may have felt a little insecure because the comments about the truth value assignments and about the proofs have not followed a set pattern. That is deliberate. It seems to me that it is important that you see that there are are multiple acceptable approaches. In the above exercise, for example, steps 5 and 11 have the same specific form, but the DeM steps from them (6 and 12) used different approaches.

The exercises in Part II are really no more difficult than the ones done earlier; there are just more operations to be performed. Like anything else, working problems is subject to the rule of thumb that the more times you handle something, the more likely you are to drop it. In these, since you have to symbolize, then check for validity, then (if valid) construct a formal proof of validity, you must be particularly careful not to make careless errors.

II (3) W =df   God is willing to prevent evil.
        A =df   God is able to prevent evil.
        I =df   God is impotent.
        M =df   God is malevolent.
        E =df   Evil exists.
        G =df   God exists.
            If W, but not A; if A, but not W, M.
            E only if either not W or not A
            E
            If G, neither I nor M.

            Therefore not G

[W • ~A) ⊃ I] • [(A • ~W) ⊃ M]
E ⊃ (~W v ~A)
E
G ⊃ ~(I v M)
────────────────────────────

∴ ~G

```
[(W•~A) ⊃ I]•[(A•~W) ⊃ M], E ⊃ (~Wv~A), E, G ⊃ ~(IvM) ⊢ ~G
               T                    T              T   T        F  (a)
        T                     T     T                  T           T(b)
                                          T                 T      (c)
                                                              F    (d)
              F                   F                        F  F    (e)
     F                  F                                          (f)
```

(a)   Assume the argument invalid, i.e., all premisses to be true and the conclusion false.
(b)   Work out the values forced by the definitions of conjunction and negation and carry all determined values to all the instances where they apply.
(c)   When the antecedent of a true conditional is true, the consequent must also be true.
(d)   If a negation is true, what it negates must be false.
(e)   Work out the values of a false disjunction and carry them to other instances.
(f)   When the consequent of a true conditional is false, the antecedent must also be false.

But this leaves no more forced values and as-yet-unvalued statements. You have only two choices available: go back and work a full truth table (in this case one 64 rows long) or make an added assumption. The former seems so undesirable that the latter should be tried.

```
[(W•~A) ⊃ I]•[A•~W) ⊃ M], E ⊃ (~Wv~A), E, G ⊃ ~(IvM) ⊢ ~G
    F              F                                        (f')
  T                        T              T                 (g')
   F               F               F                        (h')
   T        T                              T                (i')
                                     F                      (j')
```

(f')   This is the place where the earlier sequence ended.
(g')   Assume W is T and carry that to all instances of W.
(h')   Work out negations, and note that ~A must be F to make W • ~A be F when W is T.
(i')   Work out from the definition of negation and carry value to other instances.
(j')   Work out from the definition of negation. Since an inconsistency occurs in the consequent of the second premiss, you might think that you have now proven the argument to be valid, but, unfortunately, that is not the cases. To this point you have made two assumptions: the argument is invalid and W is T. One of those assumptions led to the inconsistency in the values for premiss two, but you don't know which is the bad assumption. For that reason, you must go back to step g' and assume the opposite value for W.

```
[(W•~A) ⊃ I]•[A•~W) ⊃ M], E ⊃ (~Wv~A), E, G ⊃ ~(IvM) ⊢ ~G
    F              F                                        (f")
  F                        F              F                 (g")
                    T              T                        (h")
      F       F                              F              (i")
   T                               T                        (j")
```

(f")   This, like (f') is where the original sequence stopped.

(g")   Assume W is F and carry out values (opposite of g').
(h")   Work out the values from the definition of negation.
(i")   If A • ~W is F and ~W is T then A is F and will be so in all its instances.
(j")   Work out from the definition of negation. Since no inconsistency occurs and since
        you have arrived at values for each statement symbol, the argument must be invalid.
        This shows you why it is necessary to check both sides of the assumption, not having
        done so would have led you to believe an invalid argument was valid.

(7)   P =df The butler was present.   R =df The butler replied.
        S =df The butler was seen.   H =df The butler was heard.
        Q =df The butler was questioned.   D =df The butler was on duty.

        If P, S; and if S, Q.   (P ⊃ S) • (S ⊃ Q)
        If Q, R; and if R, H.   (Q ⊃ R) • (R ⊃ H)
        Not H.   ~H
        If neither S nor H, D; and if D, P.   [~(S v H) ⊃ D] • (D ⊃ P)
        ─────────────────────────────────   ───────────────
        Therefore Q   ∴   Q

(P ⊃ S)•(S ⊃ Q),   (Q ⊃ R)•(R ⊃ H),   ~H,   [~(S v H) ⊃ D]•(D ⊃ P) ⊢ Q
         T   T   T   T   F   (a)
    T   T   T   T F   F   F   T   **T**   (b)
                              F   F   (c)
              F   F   (d)
         F   F   FF   (e)
   F   T   T   T   T   (f)
                                                            F   (g)

(a)   Assume the argument invalid.
(b)   Work out forced values of the conjunction and negation, and carry values to other
        instances.
(c)   When the consequent of a true conditional is false, so is the antecedent; so infer and
        carry on.
(d)   Infer as in c.
(e)   Work out as in c, infer the disjunction false, and carry inferred values.
(f)   Work the forced value of the ~ and then, since the antecedent of the implication is T
        the consequent must also be T. Also apply the inference as in c.
(e)   When the antecedent is T and the consequent F, the conditional is F.

You can see here that in the second conjunct of the last premiss the antecedent is true and the
consequent is false. However, earlier inference had shown that that conditional had to be true
(they are marked above). That inconsistency proves the argument is valid and requires proof.

        1. (P ⊃ S) • (S ⊃ Q)   Premiss
        2. (Q ⊃ R) • (R ⊃ H)   Premiss
        3. ~H   Premiss
        4. [~(S v H) ⊃ D] • (D ⊃ P)   Premiss /∴ Q
        5. P ⊃ S   1, Simp
        6. (S ⊃ Q) • (P ⊃ S)   1, Com
        7. S ⊃ Q   6, Simp
        8. Q ⊃ R   2, Simp
        9. (R ⊃ H) • (Q ⊃ R)   2, Com
        10. R ⊃ H   9, Simp
        11. ~(S v H) ⊃ D   4, Simp

12. (D ⊃ P) • [~(S ∨ H) ⊃ D]	4, Com
13. D ⊃ P	12, Simp
14. P ⊃ Q	5, 7, HS
15. P ⊃ R	14, 8, HS
16. P ⊃ H	15, 10, HS
17. D ⊃ H	16, 13, HS
18. ~D	3, 17, MT
19. ~~(S ∨ H)	18, 11, MT
20. S ∨ H	19, DN
21. H ∨ S	20, Com
22. S	3, 21, DS
23. Q	7, 22, MP

But notice that two additional steps would yield an interesting result:

24. R	22, 8, MP
25. H	10, 24, MP

The third premiss was ~H. What these results tell you is that the premisses of this argument are self-contradictory. Nevertheless, having self-contradictory premisses does mean that you have a valid argument and the conclusion *is* provable from such premisses.

(19)   W =df   Weather predicting is an exact science.
        R =df   It will rain tomorrow.

W.   W
___   ___

Therefore R or not R.   ∴   R ∨ ~R

W	⊢	R ∨ ~R	
T		F	(a)
		F̲ F	(b)
		T̲	(c)

(a)   Assume the argument invalid.
(b)   Work out the values for a false disjunction.
(c)   Work out the value for a false negation. Since the forced values would require that R be T and F at the same time, there is an inconsistency and the argument is valid.

1.	W	Premiss /∴. R ∨ ~ R
2.	W ∨ ~R	1, Add
3.	~R ∨ W	2, Com
4.	R ⊃ W	3, Impl
5.	R ⊃ (R • W)	4, Abs
6.	~R ∨ (R • W)	5, Impl
7.	(~R ∨ R) • (~R ∨ W)	6, Dist
8.	~R ∨ R	7, Simp
9.	R ∨ ~R	8, Com

Since R doesn't appear in the premiss, the rule of thumb suggested for using addition ought to tell you to add something to W. In the proof above ~R was added, but R could just as well have been the addition (but would have required a couple of DN steps). Ultimately, however, this is a sort of gimmick proof. The conclusion is a tautology, and it follows validly from any premiss or premiss-set. As a matter of fact, no matter what premiss you had had, you could follow this pattern to prove R ∨ ~R.

CHAPTER NINE SUMMARY

I.   Validity can be proven not only by truth tables but also by identifying a sequence of inferences, each of which is taken to be obviously acceptable.

II.   One group of acceptable inferences is identified as the rules of inference.

     A.   They are listed in 9.1 of *ITL*

     B.   Their application is restricted.

          1.   The beginning (premiss) and ending (conclusion) forms must match the structure of the rules **exactly**.

          2.   The inference must be made in the same direction (premiss to conclusion) as the one in which the rule is stated.

          3.   The inference must be made using whole steps only--it cannot be made within a step.

III.   The other group of acceptable inferences is identified as the rule (or rules) of replacement.

     A.   They are listed in 9.2 of *ITL*.

     B.   Their application is less restricted than that of the rules in inference.

          1.   The beginning and ending forms must match the structure of the rule **exactly**.

          2.   The inference may be drawn left-to-right or right-to-left relative to the original statement of the rule.

          3.   The inference may be drawn upon whole steps or within a single step.

IV.   Validity or invalidity can be proven by assigning truth values to the elements of an argument.

    A.   You begin by assuming the argument is invalid, i.e., that all the premisses are true and the conclusion is false.

    B.   You work out forced values for increasingly smaller elements of the argument.

        1.   If all elements have consistently assigned values, then the argument is invalid.

        2.   If some inconsistency is discovered in trying to assign values, then the argument is valid.

        3.   If there are elements left without values being forced for them, then you must assume some added value.

            a.   If all elements then have consistently assigned values, then the argument is invalid.

            b.   If some inconsistency is discovered, go back and assume the opposite of the added value.

                (1)   If all elements then have consistently assigned values, then the argument is invalid.

                (2)   If some inconsistency is discovered in trying to assign values, then the argument is valid.

                (3)   If there are elements left without values being forced, proceed as in 3.

            c.   If there are elements without forced values left, make another assumption and proceed as in 3.

Chapter Ten
Quantification Theory

10.1 Singular Propositions

You may recall that in chapter 7 (pages 87-89, above) there was an extended discussion of how to handle statements which resemble categorical propositions but refer only to one individual (*ITL*, pp. 218-220). Singular propositions, as they are called, assert that some individual has some property. In the categorical logic part of their book, Copi and Cohen treated the individual as it it were a class with a single member. You read of some of the difficulties with that approach both in *ITL* and in this *Study Guide*. It would be nice to use the techniques of symbolic logic that you have learned in the last two chapters to handle the singular propositions. You can't, however, because the **internal structure** is important in such a proposition but is ignored by propositional logic. What is needed, then, is some means of symbolizing the individual/property relationship.

If, for example, you were to encounter the singular proposition "*Abraham Lincoln wore a beard*," one possibility would be to represent Lincoln by the lower case letter "a" and the property of wearing a beard by the upper case letter "B." That means that the proposition "*Abraham Lincoln wore a beard*" could be represented as "Ba." (Notice that--unless there is some special reason for paying attention to time in a statement--past, present and future are all treated as if they were the same. It is also important to notice that the techniques for "translating" statements into a categorical [or category-like] form that were detailed in chapter 7 will be used here, too.)

The conventions, then, to be used in this refinement of the symbolic logic of the last two chapters are three:

(1) Capital letters symbolize attributes or properties; they are called *predicate variables*.

(2) Lower case letters from *a* through *w* designate specific individuals; they are called *individual constants*.

(3) Lower case letters *w*, *y*, and *z* serve as place holders for individual constants; they are called *individual variables*.

The use of these conventions means that, for example, "Fa" is a representation of some specific singular proposition and is either true or false. "Fx" in contrast does not designate any specific proposition, but would if you were to replace the "x" by some individual constant.

10.2 Quantification
10.3 Traditional Subject-Predicate Propositions

You may wonder why all this emphasis is put on a new way of dealing with concepts and is being introduced when you already knew how to use categorical logic. One reason, obviously, is to avoid the difficulties mentioned in 10.1. Another is the need to have a logical tool that is more sensitive to the internal structure of propositions than is the categorical approach.

An easy way to see the sort of superiority that quantificational logic has over categorical logic is to look at a statement that is sort-of-categorical-but-not-quite: Everyone who smokes runs the risk of cancer or heart disease. It is universal and afirrmative, but to claim that it is an orthodox A proposition is to put it on a Procrustean bed. (This refers to the mythological giant Procrustus who measured his guests according to his bed and altered them to fit--lopped off their legs if they were too long for it, stretched them to fit if they were too short.) If this statement were treated as an A proposition, then the subject term would be "*people who smoke*" and that is unobjectionable, but the predicate would have to be "people who run a great risk of lung cancer or heart disease." But what really seems called for is the use of two predicates-- "*People who run a great risk of lung cancer*" and "*People who run a great risk of heart disease*"--joined together by our old friend the wedge, **v**. Its inclusive character allows the risks to be separate or shared. A start, then, would be to rewrite the statement in a way that emphasizes connectives like the wedge rather than in a way that resembles a standard categorical form. For this statement it might be: "*Pick anyone you choose; if that individual is a person who smokes, then either that individual runs a great risk of lung cancer or that individual runs a great risk of heart disease.*" That is certainly a longer, less comfortable sentence, but it does make the connectives more apparent. However, more can be done. If you follow the lead of mathematics you could replace the phrase "*that individual*" with x and lose little (if any) clarity. That would yield: "*No matter which x you choose, if x is a person who smokes, then x either runs a great risk of lung cancer or x runs a great risk of heart disease.*"

But further reduction is possible, for each of the three proper ties mentioned in the statement couldd be replaced by symbols defined to mean exactly what those property-references mean. In this case we could define as follows:

> Sx=df x is a smoker.
> Lx=df x runs a great risk of lung cancer.
> Hx=df x runs a great risk of heart disease.

The statement would then be written:

"No matter which x you choose, if Sx, then either Lx or Hx."

That clearly is a vast improvement, but more is possible--the connectives can be replaced by their symbols yielding:

"No matter which x you choose, [Sx ⊃ (Lx v Hx)]."

All that seems wanting is a symbol for the phrase "*No matter which x you choose*" to convert the entire statement. Since it might be replaced by (and more traditionally was stated as) "*for all x*," the choice seems to be Ax for a symbol. That, however, will not work, for how could we distinguish between "*for all x*" written as Ax and "*x is an artichoke*" written as Ax? Historically the decision was to invert the A, yielding (∀). For a lot of reasons (which need not be detailed here), it was decided to simplify that symbol further so that (x) as opposed to (∀) was to be used for "*all*." The variable can, of course, vary, but the meaning is constant. This symbol, (x), is called the **universal quantifier** because it indicates that the number (or quantity) of individuals to which it applies is universal--it refers to all of them. By introducing the universal quantifier into the statement-form above, you complete the symbolization of the original statement:

(x)[Sx ⊃ (Lx v Hx)]

If the additional property--Fx=df x is foolish--is introduced, then the statement "*all smokers are foolish*," which is a clear-cut instance of an A proposition, could be cycled into quantificational symbolism:

All smokers are foolish.

No matter whom you choose, if they smoke then they are foolish.
No matter which x you choose, if x smokes then x is foolish.
No matter which x you choose, (Sx ⊃ Fx).

(x)(Sx ⊃ Fx)

Here the basic structure of the categorical A statement is made clear, and the relationship between the earlier, more complex example and the basic form for an A proposition be comes more evident.

If an additional property is introduced--Tx=df x is thoughtful --then the other universal statement-form (that is, the E-form) can be examined. Consider the proposition "*No smokers are thoughtful.*" Its symbolization might go:

No smokers are thoughtful.

No matter whom you choose, if they are smokers, then it is not the case that they are thoughtful.
No matter which x you choose, if x is a smoker, then it is not the case that x is thoughtful.
No matter which x you choose, if Sx then it is not the case that Tx.
No matter which x you choose, (Sx ⊃ ~Tx).

(x)(Sx ⊃ ~Tx)

This shows that, symbolically, the A and the E propositions are in reality quite close to each other.

All that is left to complete symbolization is a way to handle particular propositions. Perhaps the easiest way to approach them is through the universal propositions and the use of the relationships shown on the square of opposition. Since the A and the O are contradictory, the A and the negation of the O (~O) must mean the same thing. Consider the following proof:

1. ~(x)(Fx ⊃ Gx)   Premiss
2. ~(x)(~Fx ∨ Gx)   1, Impl
3. ~(x)(~Fx ∨ ~~Gx)   2, DN
4. ~(x)~(Fx • ~Gx)   3, DeM

But also look at the O statement that would amount to the denial of the A statement "*all smokers are thoughtful*": "*Some smokers ae not thoughtful.*" Try that as a reduction similar to those done upon the universal affirmative statements:

Some smokers are not thoughtful.

There is at least one individual such that he or she is both a smoker and a thoughtless person.
There is at least one x such that both Sx and ~Tx.
There is at least one x such that (Sx • ~Tx).

If the model of the universal is followed, a new symbol needs to be introduced-- (∃x) =df: "*There is at least one x such that,*" and the statement becomes

(∃x)(Sx • ~Tx).

Now, if the last symbolization is compared with the last line of the proof (above), an interesting correspondence can be noted.

~(x)(Fx ⊃ ~Gx)
(∃x)(Sx • ~Tx)

This shows graphically how the universal and particular quantifiers are related to one another. That relationship is detailed more fully in 10.2 of *ITL* (page 329).

The symbolizations of the categorical forms can be of great help when trying to translate statements from English into the quantificational format. The list below gives them all:

A.	All S are P	(x)(Sx ⊃ Px)
I.	Some S are P	(∃x)(Sx • Px)
E.	No S are P	(x)(Sx ⊃ ~Px)
O.	Some S are not P	(∃x)(Sx • ~Px)

*Notice that the universal **almost always** uses the " ⊃ " as the major connective and that the particular **almost always** uses the " • ."*

There is a very practical reason for insisting upon the use of the " ⊃ " for universal propositions and the " • " for existential ones: if you exchange their uses, you wind up with trivialities.

If you didn't have the quantifiers and wanted to represent universal and existential propositions, you would find it difficult but not impossible. If you think about what it takes to prove a universal proposition false or true, you get a clue about how you can represent universality without a quantifier. If you find any one exception to the universal statement, then the universal is false; for the universal statement to be true, it must be true of each and every individual in the universe (or at least in the universe about which you are conversing). When you think about it, those characteristics are roughly the same as the ones that were identified as belonging to the propositional function of conjunction. That means that, if the individuals in the universe were listed as *a, b, c,....* and *n*, then the universal proposition "(x)(Fx ⊃ Gx)" could be represented as "(Fa ⊃ Ga) • (Fb ⊃ Gb) • (Fc ⊃ Gc) • ... • (Fn ⊃ Gn)." [Please notice that this "symbolization" is not strictly correct, for the conjunctions are not grouped in pairs. However, since you know that conjunction is both associative and commutative, there is little likelihood that the shorthand form used here, and in the next paragraph for the particular and alternation, will confuse you.]

Similarly, if you consider what is required to prove or disprove an existential proposition, you see how to handle particularity without quantifiers. All that is needed for a particular to be true is one individual for which it is true; to prove a particular false, you'd have to show that it held for no individual. Using individuals as above, the existential proposition "(∃x)(Fx•Gx)" could be represented as "(Fa•Ga)∨(Fb•Gb)∨(Fc•Gc)∨...∨(Fn•Gn)."

An added benefit of seeing these non-quantified representations of quantificiational relationships is that it makes the equivalences that Copi and Cohen introduce at the end of section 10.2 page 329) more clearly resemble the DeMorgan Theorem relationships with which you are already familiar. Now, if you look at the short proof on the previous page of this book, you see how, if you replace the "~ (x)" in step 4 with "(∃x)" in accordance with the second "DeMorgan-like" equivalence in *ITL*, the denied A proposition becomes the asserted O proposition. If you carry that sort of inference a little further using the non-quantificational representations, then you see how the DeMorgan's theorems allow you to make the same transformation (using the DeM rules a bit loosely):

1. ~[(Fa ⊃ Ga) • (Fb ⊃ Gb) • ... • (Fn ⊃ Gn)]   Given

2. ~(Fa ⊃ Ga) ∨ ~(Fb ⊃ Gb) ∨ ... ∨ ~(Fn ⊃ Gn)   1, DeM

3. ~(~Fa ∨ Ga) ∨ ~(~Fb ∨ Gb) ∨ ... ∨ ~(~Fn ∨ Gn)   2, Impl

4. (~~Fa • ~Ga) ∨ (~~Fb • ~Gb) ∨ ... ∨ (~~Fn • ~Gn)   3, DeM

5. (Fa • ~Ga) ∨ (Fb • ~Gb) ∨ ... ∨ (Fn • ~ Gn)   4, DN

You now have most of the tools necessary for symbolizing quantificational statements (and arguments). You will find that making the transition from English to symbols in the manner that has been shown here (by successively replacing elements by their symbolic counterparts) may take slightly longer than trying to leap from full English to full symbol. However, you will almost surely find that the greater the leap you make the more likely you are to make a mistake. By making the "translation" gradually, you avoid the sort of confusion that usually results when you are trying to do more than one new thing at once. To check out the symbolization technique, look at a few of the problems from 10.3 (pages 335-336).

I (3)   This is affirmative, but does not assert that all reporters are present, thus is particular affirmative (I).

Some reporters are present.

There are some individuals that are reporters and are present.

There are some x such that x are reporters and x are present.

There are some x that (Rx and Px).

There are some x such that (Rx • Px).

($\exists$x)(Rx • Px)

(7)   No boy scout ever cheats.

No matter whom you choose, if that person is a boy scout, then that person does not cheat.

No matter which x you choose, if x is a boy scout, then x does not cheat.

No matter which x, if Bx then not Cx.

No matter which x, (Bx $\supset$ ~Cx).

(x)(Bx $\supset$ ~Cx)

(12)   Not all children pointed their fingers at the emperor. (You can attack this statement in two ways.)

a.   It is not the case that you can pick anyone you choose such that, if that individual is a child, then that individual pointed a finger at the emperor.

It is not the case that you can pick any x such that, if x is a child, then x pointed a finger at the emperor.

It is not the case that you can pick any x such that if Cx then Px.

~[you can pick any x such that (Cx $\supset$ Px)].

~(x)(Cx $\supset$ Px)

b.   There is someone who is a child but did not point a finger at the emperor.

There is an x such that x is a child and x did not point a finger at the emperor.

There is an x such that Cx and not Px.

There is an x such that (Cx / ~Px).

($\exists$x)(Cx • ~Px)

(Notice that the *a*-case is the denial of an A proposition, while the *b*-case is the assertion of the contradictory O proposition.)

(14)   None but the brave deserves the fair.

This particular phrase *none but*, like *only*, tends to be confusing. Probably the best way to clarify them is by using them with classes the relations of which are certain to you. The statement is clearly true, at least for the present, that all nuns are women. Its converse that all women are nuns is clearly false. If you consider the statement *none but women are nuns* and *none but nuns are women* (or the same expressions with *only* replacing *none but*), the first statement is the true one, the second false. All that is necessary is to reconize that the two true statements must be roughly equivalent.

Thus *All nuns are women* and *Only women are nuns* can be treated as if they were the same. This technique (of clarifying awkward cases through the use of known class-relationships) may prove helpful to you anytime you encounter a new expression.

No matter whom you choose, if that individual deserves the fair, then that individual is brave.
No matter which x you choose, if x deserves the fair, then x is brave.
No matter which x you choose, if Dx then Bx.
No matter which x you choose, (Dx ⊃ Bx).
(x)(Dx ⊃ Bx)

II (2)   (∃x)(Cx • Dx)

One of the easiest ways to find the appropriate normal form formula (one where negations apply to simple predicates only) is to use the relationships on the traditional square of opposition. In this case the original expression was ∼(x)(Cx ⊃ ∼Dx) which is the denial of the universal negative (E) proposition "No C's are D." Since, on the square of opposition, the contradictory of an E is an I with the same subject and predicate terms, you could infer that the desired expression would be the symbolization of the I proposition "Some C's are D's." This, you should see, ought to be symbolized as (∃x)(Cx • Dx), which is the answer above. A proof-like tracing of the inferential sequence from the original in *ITL* to the answer might look like this:

1. ∼(x)(Cx ⊃ ∼Dx)   Given
2. It is false that no C's are D's   1, symbolic definitions of E and neg.
3. Some C's are D's   2, square of opposition
4. (∃x)(Cx • Dx)   3, symbolic definition of I proposition.

(8)   (x)(Px ⊃ Ox) or (x)(Ox v ∼Px)

This is an expression that looks far more complex than it really is. As you can see, the normal form formulas are rather simple and easy to understand. You could arrive at them by a relatively straightforward proof if you use the equivalences in 10.2 of *ITL* as if they were rules of replacement. (Given their resemblance to DeMorgan's Theorems, perhaps they should be called the DeMorgan's Quantificational Theorems [DeMQ].)

1. ∼(∃x)[∼(Ox v ∼Px)]   Given
2. (x)∼[∼(Ox v ∼Px)   1, DeMQ
3. (x)(Ox v ∼Px)   2, DN
4. (x)(∼Px v Ox)   3, Com
5. (x)(Px ⊃ Ox)   4, Impl

As you can see, the proof works just like the ones you did in propositional logic, with the addition of the DeMQ step as if it were a replacement rule. You can tell that the DN step (from 2 to 3) is one that follows the form, despite the brackets that appear to intervene between the negations, because there is *nothing else but the brackets between the two negations*.

10.4 Proving Validity

Once you have mastered the transformations called DeMQ above, you will have no difficulty positioning your quantifiers so that they are initially placed and apply to the whole following formula. The only other thing you will then need to generate quantificational proofs is a set of rules that account for the removal and addition of quantifiers. If you begin with the simplest of valid arguments, you will find that the needed rules quickly make themselves evident. The argument that Copi and Cohen introduce to discuss the **UI** rule in 10.4 (pages 336-337) with Greeks, Humans, and Mortals, is fine for our purposes. A proof of the argument, indicating the rules that "cry out to be introduced" might look like:

1.	(x)(Hx ⊃ Mx)	Premiss
2.	(x)(Gx ⊃ Hx)	Premiss /∴ (x)(Gx ⊃ Mx)
3.	Hy ⊃ My	1, a needed (x)-take-off rule
4.	Gy ⊃ Hy	2, the same rule
5.	Gy ⊃ My	3, 4, HS (the same old rule)
6.	(x)(Gx ⊃ Mx)	5, a needed (x)-put-on rule

Similarly, the argument with the same first premiss, but "Some vegetarians are human" (∃x)(Vx • Mx) as a second premiss and "Some vegetarians are mortal" (∃x)(Vx • Mx) as the conclusion suggests more needed rules:

1.	(x)(Hx ⊃ Mx)	Premiss
2.	(∃x)(Vx • Hx)	Premiss /∴ (∃x)(Vx • Mx)
3.	Vy • Hy	2, a needed (∃x)-take-off rule
4.	Hy ⊃ My	3, the needed (x)-take-off rule
5.	Vy	3, Simp
6.	Hy • Vy	3, Com
7.	Hy	6, Simp
8.	My	4, 7, MP
9.	Vy • My	5, 8, Conj
10.	(∃x)(Vx • Mx)	9, a needed (∃x)-put-on rule

There would appear, then, to be four rules that need to be added so that quantified logic can be worked: two universal rules and two existential ones--one of each that takes off the quantifier (called *instantiation* because it is taking an instance of the quantified statement), and one of each that put quantifiers on (called *generalization*). There is a problem, however, with these rules: not all of them are valid as they stand. This is most easily seen in cases where using the rules in the fashion suggested above would lead you into trouble. Simplest would be to exchange the following tenth step for the one that occurs in the second example above:

10.	(x)(Vx • Mx)	9, the (x)-put-on rule

There seems to be little doubt that you would not want to be able to reason from the fact that all humans are mortal and some humans are vegetarians to the conclusion that *everything*, no matter what else it might be, is both a vegetarian and mortal. That would have you asserting such nonsense as that your immortal soul (if you believe you have one) is mortal since everything is, or that man-eating tigers are vegetarians (which might lead you to rather foolish actions in the presence of one).

A second problematic inference might be generated from the premisses "Some animals are dogs" and "Some animals are cats." It could go:

1.	(∃x)(Ax • Cx)	Premiss
2.	(∃x)(Ax • Dx)	Premiss
3.	Ay • Cy	1, the (∃x)-take-off rule
4.	Ay • Dy	2, the (∃x)-take-off rule
5.	(Ay • Cy) • (Ay • Dy)	3, 4, Conj
6.	[(Ay • Cy) • Ay] • Dy	5, Assoc
7.	[Ay • (Ay • Cy)] • Dy	6, Com
8.	[(Ay • Ay) • Cy] • Dy	7, Assoc
9.	(Ay • Cy) • Dy	8, Taut

10. Ay • (Cy • Dy)   9, Assoc
11. (∃x)[Ax • (Cx • Dx)]   10, the (∃x)-put-on rule

But this has you asserting that some animals are both cats and dogs.

Informally it is not hard to see that the first problem is due to taking particular information (in the form of an existential premiss) and arriving at a universal conclusion. The second
problem results from having information about two, at least potentially, different individuals
and treating it as if it were definitely about a single individual. (Had the properties A, C, and D
in the above example stood for actors, charming persons, and debonair, the inference would not
have seemed so ridiculous, for that conclusion is at least reasonable.) There are a number of
ways that these problems can be resolved, but it must be done in such a way that the rules are
still reasonable. The best approach is to apply restrictions to the use of the rules in such a way
as to prevent them from leading an inference astray.

If you know that some statement is true of all individuals, then there ought to be no problem with choosing to apply it to any specific individual. That is what the rule of *universal instantiation* does: it permits the removal of the universal quantifier and, if desired, the replacement of
every occurrence in the expression of the variable contained in that quantifier by any individual
symbol. This rule, called *UI* for brevity, is essentially unrestricted insofar as it will be used in this
book. Similarly, if you have a property (or properties) asserted of some individual symbol (no
matter what that symbol might be), then you ought to feel free to assert that that property (or
those properties) is true of something. That is what the rule of *existential generalization* does: it
permits that addition of the existential quantifier and, if desired, the replacement of every occurrence in the expression of any individual symbol which is not affected by an already posi-
tioned quantifier by the variable found in that existential quantifier. This rule, called *EG* for
brevity, is essentially unrestricted, too, insofar as it will be used in this book.

The other two rules are the ones that require restriction. The only time you want to
avoid the use of the rule of *UG* (*universal generalization*) is when the information upon which
you are generalizing is about specific individuals. Thus Copi and Cohen add the restriction that
this rule can be used only upon "arbitrarily selected variables," meaning that you can't use it in
most problems that, in their premises, contain either individual symbols that are not governed
by a quantifier or that in their proofs contain uses of *EI* (the fourth rule). Given this restriction,
the rule is fine. So long as you do not inadvertently identify distinct individuals, there is no problem with *existential instantiation*. The simplest of the possible restrictions that might be applied
to ensure that is not to ever use EI in such a way that the individual constant at which it arrives
had appeared earlier in the proof. If you look back at the dog-and-cat example, you will see
that the use of EI would have been no problem had the steps involved instantiated to different
individual constants instead of to the "arbitrarily selelcted individual" y.

The best way to get the rules firmly seated in your mind is to use them in the generating
of some proofs. You will notice that all of the problems in part I after 10.4 (pages 341-342) are
basically variations upon two proofs, the one with all universal premises and the one with a
universal and an existential one. Problems 3 and 7 can be taken as representing the two types.

I (3)   1. (x)(Gx ⊃ Hx)   Premiss
         2. (x)(Ix ⊃ ~Hx)   Premiss /∴ (x)(Ix ⊃ ~Gx)
         3. Gy ⊃ Hy   1, UI
         4. Iy ⊃ ~Hy   2, UI
         5. ~Hy ⊃ ~Gy   3, Trans
         6. Iy ⊃ ~Gy   4, 5, HS
         7. (x)(Ix ⊃ ~Gx)   6, UG [Acceptable because y is an ar-
                                            bitrarily chosen variable.]

(7) 1. (x)(Sx ⊃ ~Tx)   Premiss
     2. (∃x)(Sx • Ux)   Premiss /∴ (∃x)(Ux • ~Tx)
     3. Sa • Ua   2, EI [Acceptable since a is an individ-
                               ual constant that has not appeared
                               previously in the proof. If you always
                               do your EI steps first, this restriction
                               should never bother you.]
     4. Sa ⊃ ~Ta   1, UI [which can go to *any* individual
                               symbol]
     5. Sa   3, Simp
     6. Ua • Sa   3, Com
     7. Ua   6, Simp
     8. ~Ta   4, 5, MP
     9. Ua • ~Ta   7, 8, Conj
    10. (∃x)(Ux • ~Tx)   9, EG

If you look closely at the remaining eight problems in part I and at the nine problems (after the first) in part II, you will see that, with the use of an occasional commutation or MT-for-MP-substitution, all of the proofs are variants of these two.

II (3)   Dx=df x is a dancer.
          Ex=df x is exuberant.
          Fx=df x is a fencer.

There are two approaches to the sort of step-wise transition from natural language to complete symbolism. You can try to make the language sound as categorical as possible or you can try to approximate the quantificational structure. Take, for example, the first premiss of this exercise. The English version is "*all dancers are exuberant.*" The categorical one is "*all D's are E.*" The quantificational one is "*for all x's, if x is a D, then x is an E.*" So long as the statement is fairly simple, you are probably better off approaching symbolism from the categorical form. Since you know how to translate each of the categorical forms into quantificational form, symbolizing by means of a categorical step probably requires less effort than any other way. For exercise 3, then the transition to symbols is straightforward.

All D are E.	(x)(Dx ⊃ Ex)
Some F are not E.	(∃x)(Fx • ~Ex)
————————————	————————————
Therefore some F are not D.	∴ (∃x)(Fx • ~Dx)

     1. (x)(Dx ⊃ Ex)   Premiss
     2. (∃x)(Fx • ~Ex)   Premiss /∴ (∃x)(Fx • ~Dx)
     3. Fa • ~Ea   2, EI
     4. Fa   3, Simp
     5. ~Ea • Fa   3, Com
     6. ~Ea   5, Simp
     7. Da ⊃ Ea   1, UI
     8. ~Da   6, 7, MT
     9. Fa • ~Da   4, 8, Conj
    10. (∃x)(Fx • ~Dx)   9, EG

When you compare this proof with that of exercise 7 from Part I you can see that there is very little difference in the two proofs. As was suggested there, as long as the argument is categorical, the proof must be one of those two proofs discussed earlier.

(7)   Sx=df x is a swindler.
        Tx=df x is a is a thief.
        Ux=df x is a is underprivileged.

All s's are T's.	(x)(Sx ⊃ Tx)
All T's are U's.	(x)(Tx ⊃ Ux)
─────────────────	───────────
Therefore all s's are U's.	∴ (x)(Sx ⊃ Ux)

1. (x)(Sx ⊃ Tx)   Premiss
2. (x)(Tx ⊃ Ux)   Premiss /∴ (x)(Sx ⊃ Ux)
3. Sy ⊃ Ty   1, UI
4. Ty ⊃ Uy   2, UI
5. Sy ⊃ Uy   3, 4, HS
6. (x)(Sx ⊃ Ux)   5, UG

The most difficult thing in working this exercise is translating it from English to symbols. If you do not already have notes to yourself indicating some of the unusual wordings possible and how to symbolize them, you might want to start one. One way to identify how to symbolize is to decide what was meant by using analogous statements in which the relationships are clear, For example, in the case of the first premiss you might offer this analogy:

> To make an omelet you must break eggs.

There is little doubt that the statement means that if you want to make an omelet then you must break eggs. It seems equally clear that the converse, if you break eggs then you must make an omelet, is false. The order of the elements of premiss one is therefore as indicated. The approach to symbolizing statements like premiss two was explained in some detail in the solution of problem 14 of section 10.3 of this *Study Guide* (pages 183-184). Symbolizing the conclusion is uncomplicated.

This exercise requires the "other" categorical proof. The point is that a categorical argument (at least a valid one) either has two universal premises--in which case you will have to combine them by using a hypothetical syllogism--or it has one universal and one particular one--in which case you will use conjunction, simplification and either *MP* or *MT*. Given the very few categorical forms, there can be little variety in the corresponding quantificational proofs.

10.5 Proving Invalidity

In his description of how you prove a quantificational argument invalid (or valid), Copi and Cohen introduce the rough equivalences of quantifiers and propositional statements. However, they are quite clear that the quantifiers are *not* truth functions like the connectives of the propositional calculus, and you therefore need some way to convert from expressions with quantifiers to expressions with only truth functions.

Obviously, one method which he suggests is easier than using those equivalences. If you can come up with an argument which has **exactly** the same form as the argument undere consideration, but your "other" argument is clearly invalid, then the argument under consideration must be valid. The difficulty with this method of showing invalidity is that it really has no negative force. That is, if you are unable to think of such an invalidating analogy, you have no guarantee that your argument is valid. The difficulty is that you have no way to tell whether the inability to come up with the appropriate analogy is because no such analogy exists or because you are just not a very talented analogy-maker. The issue resembles the problem of determining whether or not a man can run a sub-four-minute mile: the fact that I cannot even come close to doing this is merely an autobiographical datum about me; it says nothing about general human capacity for running speed.

The use of the equivalences to convert quantification to truth functions is more reliable, but a good deal more complex. The key difficulty that you will encounter in trying to apply it is the determination of how many individuals you need to take into account when setting up your truth table. Intuitively, the number of individuals to be considered should be sufficient to allow any references to individuals in the argument to refer to separate individuals. For example, consider this argument:

> Some people reading this book are male.
> Some people reading this book are female.
>
> _____
>
> Therefore some females are males.

Symbolically this would be

$$(\exists x) (Rx \cdot Mx)$$
$$(\exists x) (Rx \cdot Fx)$$
_____
$$\therefore (\exists x) (Fx \cdot Mx)$$

If you checked this argument for a single individual, you would have this assigned truth value check:

```
(Ra • Ma),   (Ra • Fa)  ⊦   (Fa • Ma)
      T            T              F    (a)
   T     T      T    T        T     T  (b)
                                T      (c)
```

(a)   Assume the argument invalid.
(b)   Work out the values forced by the definition of conjunction.
(c)   Carry the forced values and recognize the contradiction in the conclusion. This means that, relative to a single individual, this argument is valid.

If, however, you were to expand your check to apply to **TWO** individuals, you would find this check:

```
(Ra • Ma) v (Rb • Mb),   (Ra • Fa) v (Rb • Fb)  ⊦  (Fa • Ma) v (Fb • Mb)
         T                        T                       F              (a)
                                                       F        F        (b)
    T                                                                    (c)
 T     T                      T                          T               (d)
                                  F                   F                   (e)
                            F                                            (f)
                                          T                              (g)
       T                          T    T                 T               (h)
          F                                                     F        (i)
          F                                                              (j)
```

(a)   Assume the argument invalid.
(b)   Work out values based upon disjunction.
(c)   Since there are no more forced values, make an assumption.
(d)   Work out values based upon conjunctions and carry over forced values.

(e)   When one of a false conjunction is true, the other one must be false then carry
        forced values.
(f)   Work out values based upon conjunction.
(g)   If one disjunct of a true disjunction is false, the other must be true.
(h)   Work out values based upon conjunctions and carry out the forced values.
(i)   If one of a false conjunction is true, then the other one must be false and carry over
        forced value.
(j)   Work out value based upon conjunction.

When you arrive at (j) with a value for each of the elements of the argument and have not encountered an inconsistency, then you know that the argument is invalid.

The fact that the argument was invalid when considered to apply to a pair of individuals
but was valid when applied to a single one suggests that you must tread softly when claiming a
quantificational argument is valid. The intuitive solution is that you will be safe if you use
enough individuals to let all the particular information elements apply to separate individuals.

For the most part you would be secure in your selection of individuals for such validity
checks if you were to count the number of existential quantifiers and add that to the number of
distinct individual constants. That number of individuals (or 1 if that sum happened to be zero)
would usually suffice for your validity check. Exceptions could occur, but they would be a result
of kinds of expressions that you will not encounter in *ITL* or in this *Study Guide*.

Roughly, once an argument is proven valid for some set number of individuals, you know
that it is also valid for any smaller number of individuals. In contrast, once an argument is prov-
en invalid for some set number of individuals, you know that it is also invalid for any greater
number of individuals.

You ought now to feel ready to work the exercises following 10.4 (pages 341-342). The
often-repeated suggestion that you do your own work before looking at the solution still applies.

I (2)   Consider for one individual.

$$Da \supset {\sim}Ea, \quad Ea \supset Fa \quad \vdash \quad Fa \supset {\sim}Da$$

T		T			F	(a)
			T	T	F	(b)
T					T	(c)
	T					(d)
	F	F				(e)

(a)   Assume the argument invalid.
(b)   Work out values based upon the conditional and carry them.
(c)   Work out value based upon negation and carry it.
(d)   Work out value based upon the conditional.
(e)   Work out value based upon negation, carry the value and note the absence of contra-
        diction. That proves the argument invalid.

(8)   Consider for one individual.

$$Va \bullet {\sim}Wa, \quad Wa \bullet {\sim}Xa \quad \vdash \quad Xa \bullet {\sim}Va$$

T		T		F		(a)
T	T	**T**	T	T	T	(b)
	F	**F**		F		(c)

(a)   Assume the argument invalid.
(b)   Work out forced values based upon conjunction.
(c)   Work out values based upon negation and carry earlier values.

Since there is a contradiction in the value of Wa in the second premiss, clearly a one-individual check is not adequate. You may wonder why, when there were three existential statements between the premises and conclusion, I tried to check for only one individual. The reason is economy. As an operating principle, it's not a bad idea to check out any quantificational argument in the single individual case before going on to consider more complex cases. The time lost in checking cases where the single individual case is indecisive is usually more than offset by the time saved in cases that will prove invalid in that single individual case. In this case, however, a "bigger" check must be done.

Consider for two individuals.

(Va• ~Wa)**v**(Vb• ~Wb),(Wa• ~Xa)v(Wb• ~Xb) ⊢(Xa• ~Va)v(Xb• ~Vb)

	T					T				F		(a)
								F			F	(b)
				T			*T*					(c)
				F				F				(d)
T				F				T				(e)
						T						(f)
		T			T	T						(g)
		F				F			F		(h)
	F											(i)
T												(j)
T												(k)
F			F									(l)

(a) Assume the argument invalid.
(b) False disjunctions have both disjuncts false.
(c) Since there were no forced values, make an assumption and work out values.
(d) Work negation and conjunction values.
(e) Work conjunction and negation values.
(f) When one of a true disjunction is false, the other is true.
(g) Work conjunction values and carry.
(h) Work negations and carry.
(i) Work conjunction.
(j) When one of a true disjunction is false, the other is true.
(k) Work conjunction.
(l) Work negation and carry.

Since there is no contradiction in the assignment of these values, you should see that this argument is invalid. You might wonder why, after the check for a single individual failed, I didn't go directly to three. If the argument had been valid you would have had to check it out with three individuals, you can feel secure in proving it invalid in the simplest case you can find.

The exercises in Part II are really pretty much the same as the ones following 10.3 and 10.4 with regard to symbolism and are like the ones in Part I in the way that you show them invalid.

II (2)   Dx=df x is a diplomat.
Ex=df x is an extremist.
Fx=df x is a fanatic.

No D are E.	(x) (Dx ⊃ ~Ex)
Some F are E.	(∃x) (Fx • Ex)
Therefore some D are not F.	(∃x) (Dx • ~Fx)

$$\text{Da} \supset \sim\text{Ea}, \quad \text{Fa} \cdot \text{Ea} \quad \vdash \quad \text{Da} \cdot \sim\text{Fa}$$

T		T		F		(a)
	T	T	T		T	(b)
F		F				(c)
F				F		(d)

(a)   Assume the argument invalid.
(b)   Work out forced values based upon conjunction and carry those forced values.
(c)   Work out forced values based upon negation.
(d)   When the consequent of a true conditional is false, then the antecedent must also be false. When you carry that forced value to the conclusion, you will see there are no contradictions and that the argument is invalid.

(8)   The trick here is to remember the discussion of problem 14, discussed earlier in this chapter. Keeping the fact that "*none but*" and "*only*" statements are universal and affirmative but that they state their subject and predicate in reversed order, neither the first premiss nor the conclusion will give you any difficulty.

All D are B.	$(x)(Dx \supset Bx)$
All S are B.	$(x)(Sx \supset Bx)$

Therefore all S are D.	$\therefore \quad (x)(Sx \supset Dx)$

$$\text{Da} \supset \text{Ba}, \quad \text{Sa} \supset \text{Ba} \quad \vdash \quad \text{Sa} \supset \text{Da}$$

T		T		F		(a)
F		T		T	F	(b)
T		T				(c)

(a)   Assume the argument invalid.
(b)   Work out values based upon the conditional and carry forced values.
(c)   When the antecedent of a true conditional is true, then the consequent must also be true. Carry the forced value and note that there is no contradiction. Therefore the argument is invalid.

10.6 Asyllogistic Inference

All of the quantificational arguments that have been considered thus far have been roughly syllogistic. It was, however, the claim at the beginning of this chapter that the syllogism was not adequate to handle the sort of arguments you will encounter in everyday discourse. Copi and Cohen use section 10.6 to introduce this kind of argument, the kind that he calls *asyllogistic* (meaning not-of-syllogistic-form) arguments.

Many of the asyllogistic arguments depend upon propositions which still resemble categorical forms but are somewhat more complex. The argument which was introduced here (on page 180.) to show the inadequacy of the categorical form is such a case. The statement "*everyone who smokes runs a grat risk of lung cancer or heart disease*" could have been treated as an A proposition with the subject class being "*people who smoke*" and the predicate being "*people who run a great risk of lung cancer or heart disease*." If these were represented, respectively, by "Sx" and "Rx," then that statement would be symbolized as "$(x)(Sx \supset Rx)$." But to assert "Rx" would really be to assert "*either* Lx *(people who run a great risk of lung cancer) or* Hx *(people who run a great risk of heart disease)*." Since you learned how to represent "either...or...." while working propositional exercises, the transformation of "$(x)(Sx \supset Rx)$" into $(x)[Sx \supset (Lx \lor Hx)]$ should not seem particularly unusual.

In symbolizing asyllogistic arguments you must be careful not to allow the ambiguity of the language mislead you. Copi and Cohen particularly note three forms that tend to be mis-symbolized.

A teacher might look up the files for a class and find out a fact which he could express as *"all members of this class are either 18 or 19 years old."* It would be important to realize that in saying this, he would not mean to assert the disjunction of the two categorical statements "all members of this class are 18 years old" and "all members of this class are 19 years old." With, for example, a lower-division college course, it would not be particularly unusual for the original statement to be true, but for either of the latter ones to be true would certainly seem surprising. Using the obvious symbols, then, the correct symbolization should be "(x)[Mx ⊃ (Ex v Nx)]."

A second misleading locution would be a form like *"Oysters and clams are delicious."* Copi and Cohen discuss it near the end of 10.6 (pages 348-349). Their explanation makes it quite clear in terms of what is *meant* by the statement why it must be symbolized with a " v " where the English clearly has an "and." You may, however, still feel a bit insecure in making such a change in symbol from the English. The following proof may make the formal reason for the symbolization a little clearer:

1.	(x)[(Ox v Cx) ⊃ Dx]	Given symbolization.
2.	(x)[~Dx ⊃ ~(Ox v Cx)]	1,Trans
3.	(x)[~Dx ⊃ (~Ox • ~Cx)]	2,DeM
4.	(x)[~~Dx v (~Ox • ~Cx)]	3,Impl
5.	(x)[(~~Dx v ~Ox) • (~~Dx • ~Cx)]	4,Dist
6.	(x)[(~Dx ⊃ ~Ox) • (~Dx ⊃ ~Cx)]	5,Impl(on each conjunct)
7.	(x)[(Ox ⊃ Dx) • (Cx ⊃ Dx)]	6,Trans (on each conjunct)

First, you should particularly notice that all of the steps were justified by rules of replacement. That means that you could write the proof in reverse order: step 6 could come from step 7 by transposition, step 5 from step 6 by implication, and so on. The proof shows you that, from a logical point of view, when you assert (x)[(Ox v Cx) ⊃ Dx] you are really asserting that, no matter what you happened to pick, if it is an oyster then it is delicious **and** if it is a clam then it is delicious.

The third kind of expression that may cause some kind of difficulty is the exceptive. Copi and Cohen discuss the sort of exceptive that can be handled as a biconditional at the end of 10.6. There is a second kind of exceptive that occurs in a statement like "all members of the team except those who joined the team after the cut-off date are eligible to play in post-season competition." In this case there is a greater difficulty in figuring out exactly what is meant by the given statement. If the exceptive part of the sentence ("except those who joined the team after the cut-off date") had not been there, the remaining statement would have been "all members of the team are eligible to play in post-season competition." Using the natural symbolism, this would be (x)(Mx ⊃ Ex). If the "members of the team" part of the statement had not been there, you would have had an exceptive of the sort that Copi and Cohen discussed, one that would be symbolized as (x)(~Jx ≡ Ex). The most reasonable way, it seems, to symbolize the statement in its entirety is by combining the two simpler forms to get (x)[Mx ⊃ (~Jx ≡ Ex)].

In general it is easiest to approach asyllogistic statements by first relating them as best you can to one of the four categorical forms. Thus, among the problems in part I following 10.6 in *ITL* (pages 350-353), you would approach number 3 in the following sort of way:

I (3)   No car is safe unless it has good brakes.

This is a "sort-of-E-Form"--had it been "no car is safe" it would have been an E. Fortunately "safe" is a word that can easily have a negation attached directly to it ("unsafe"), so the statement can be rewritten as

> All cars are unsafe unless they have good brakes.

Following the symbolization-technique-model introduced for categorical statements the statement can be treated in a relatively straightforward manner:

> No matter what you choose, if it is a car, then it is unsafe unless it has good brakes.
> No matter what x you choose, if x is a car, then it is unsafe unless x has good brakes.
> No matter what x you choose, if Cx, then not Sx unless Bx.
> No matter what x you choose, [Cx ⊃ (~Sx v Bx)].
> (x)[Cx ⊃ (~Sx v Bx)]

(7)   Not all people who are wealthy are both educated and cultured.

It is easiest to approach this sort of problem as if the initial "*Not*" were not there, then tack on a "~" at the beginning when you are otherwise done. Categorically, the subject class is people-who-are-wealthy and the predicate class is they-who-are-both-educated-and-cultured. If you deal with these expressions first (sort of "pre-symbolize," so to speak), the overall problem becomes fairly simple. Using the property symbols that Copi and Cohen suggest, the subject becomes (Px • Wx), and the predicate becomes (Ex • Cx). With the initial negation set up outside, the original statement becomes:

> ~[All (Px • Wx) are (Ex • Cx)]

This is just the negation of an A-form, which you can easily symbolize as

> ~{(x)[(Px • Wx) ⊃ (Ex ⊃ Cx)]}

Of course, you could have first restated the original so as to shift from the denied-A-form to the O-form:

> Some people-who-are-wealthy are not educated-and-cultured.

This would have become:

> (∃x)[Px • Wx) • ~(Ex • Cx)]

Either symbolization is acceptable, but the first seems to require less thinking effort.

A couple of the problems from Part II show how the rules are uused with more complex formalisms.

	II (3)		
	1.	(x){[Ix ⊃ (Jx • ~Kx)] • [Jx ⊃ (Ix ⊃ Kx)]}	Premiss
	2.	(∃x)[(Ix • Jx) • ~Lx)]	Premiss /∴ (∃x)(Kx • Lx)
	3.	(Ia • Ja) • ~La	2, EI
	4.	[Ia ⊃ (Ja • ~Ka)] • [Ja ⊃ (Ia ⊃ La)]	1, UI
	5.	[Ja ⊃ (Ia ⊃ Ka)] • [Ia ⊃ (Ja • ~Ka)]	4, Com
	6.	Ja ⊃ (Ia ⊃ Ka)	5, Simp
	7.	(Ja • Ia) ⊃ Ka	6, Exp
	8.	Ia • Ja	3, Simp
	9.	Ja • Ia	8, Com
	10.	Ka	7,9, MP
	11.	Ia	8, Simp
	12.	Ia ⊃ (Ja • ~Ka)	4, Simp
	13.	Ja • ~Ka	11,12,MP

| 14. | ~Ka • Ja | 13, Com |
| 15. | ~Ka | 14, Simp |

[Notice that at this point steps 10 and 15 contradict each other. Once you find such a contradiction in a problem, any conclusion at all follows in the way shown by steps 16 and 17.]

| 16. | Ka v (∃x)(Kx • Lx) | 10, Add |
| 17. | (∃x)(Kx • Lx) | 15,16,DS |

(8)   This appears to be quite complicated, but it's really straight-forward--you remove each of its quantifiers by UI, work the heart of the problem, then add on the quantifier by UG. Thus the first eight steps and the last one are already determined by "premiss" and UI and UG.

1.	(x)(Hx ⊃ Ix)	Premiss
2.	(x)[(Hx • Ix) ⊃ Jx]	Premiss
3.	(x)[~Kx ⊃ (Ix v Hx)]	Premiss
4.	(x)[(Jx v ~Jx) ⊃ (Ix ⊃ Hx)]	Premiss/∴ (x)(Jx v Kx)
5.	Hy ⊃ Iy	1, UI
6.	(Hy • Iy) ⊃ Jy	2, UI
7.	~Ky ⊃ (Iy v Hy)	3, UI
8.	(Jy v ~Jy) ⊃ (Iy ⊃ Hy)	4, UI
9.	~(Iy v Hy) ⊃ ~~Ky	7, Trans
10.	(~Iy • ~Hy) ⊃ ~~Ky	8, DeM
11.	(~Iy • ~Hy) ⊃ Ky	10, DN

[Steps 9-11 are, in a sense, the key ones for the problem. The conclusion is an alternation, in particular the alternation of the consequents of steps 6 and 11. The alternation of the antecedents of those steps is one of the equivalence forms. In steps 5 and 8 you will have the seeds of the needed equivalence.]

| 12. | (~Hy • ~Iy) ⊃ Ky | 11, Com |
| 13. | [(Hy • Iy) ⊃ Jy] • [(~Hy • ~Hy) ⊃ Ky] | 6,12,Conj |

[The difficulty facing you now is that you need to get the Iy ⊃ Hy from the consequent of step 8. The antecedent Jy v ~Jy is a tautology, so Iy ⊃ Hy must follow, but there is no rule allowing any tautology to be "stuck into" a proof. Clever manipulation, however, will do the job.]

14.	~(Jy v ~Jy) v (Iy ⊃ Hy)	8, Impl
15.	(Iy ⊃ Hy) v ~(Jy v ~Jy)	14, Com
16.	(Iy ⊃ Hy) v (~Jy • ~~Jy)	15, DeM
17.	[(Iy ⊃ Hy) v ~Jy] • [(Iy ⊃ Hy) v ~~Jy]	16, Dist
18.	[~Jy v (Iy ⊃ Hy)] • [~~Jy v (Iy ⊃ Hy)]	17, Com(twice)
19.	[~~Jy v (Iy ⊃ Hy)] • [~Jy v (Iy ⊃ Hy)]	18, Com
20.	~~Jy v (Iy ⊃ Hy)	19, Simp
21.	~Jy v (Iy ⊃ Hy)	18, Simp
22.	Jy ⊃ (Iy ⊃ Hy)	21, Impl
23.	~Jy ⊃ (Iy ⊃ Hy)	20, Impl

[To this point the steps 14-23 ought to look a bit familiar--it is essentially the same sort of problem as 9.2, III(7) which was discussed earlier in this **Study Guide** (page 157).]

24.	~(Iy ⊃ Hy) ⊃ ~Jy	22, Trans
25.	~(Iy ⊃ Hy) ⊃ (Iy ⊃ Hy)	24,23, HS
26.	~~(Iy ⊃ Hy) v (Iy ⊃ Hy)	25, HS
27.	(Iy ⊃ Hy) v (Iy ⊃ Hy)	26, DN

28.	Iy ⊃ Hy	27, Taut
29.	(Hy ⊃ Iy) • (Iy ⊃ Hy)	5,28, Conj
30.	Hy ≡ Iy	29, Equiv
31.	(Hy • Iy) v (~Hy • ~Iy)	30, Equiv

[You now have the conjunction of conditionals [step 13] and the alternation of their antecedents [step 31] to perform the CD implied by the discussion after step 11.]

32.	Jy v Ky	13,31, CD
33.	(x)(Jx v Kx)	32, UG

The important thing to see here is that the difficulties that are encountered in this problem have nothing to do with the quantification; they are proof subleties of the sort studied in Chapter 9.

The exercises in parts III and IV add the complication of symbolization. Care in translating from English to symbols becomes even more important when you do not know whether the argument in question is valid or not. A misplaced parenthesis, an extra negation, exchanged quantifiers and the like can convert a valid argument into an invalid one, or vice versa.

III (3)   Ax=df x is an argon compound.
         Sx=df x is a sodium compound.
         Ox=df x is oily.
         Vx=df x is volatile.

> A's and S's are either O or V.
> Not all S's are O.
> _____
> Therefore some A's are V.

Before symbolizing the first premiss, you should think a moment about what it *means*. Although it would not deny the possibility of a sodium-argon compound, the premiss surely does not mean to claim that such are the only sort that it asserts are oily or volatile. This statement, then, must be like the example of oysters and clams discussed in *ITL* (pages 348-349) and here in section 10.6 (page 193. Thus the argument is symbolized as follows:

> (x)[(Ax v Sx) ⊃ (Ox v Vx)]
> ~(x)(Sx ⊃ Ox) OR (∃x)(Sx • ~Ox)
> _____
> ∴   (∃x)(Ax • Vx)

```
(Aa v Sa) ⊃ (Oa v Va),   Sa • ~Oa  ⊢   Aa • Va
           T                  T              F      (a)
      T                    T    T                   (b)
      T            F                   F            (c)
              T                                     (d)
              T                             T      (e)
      F                              F             (f)
```

(a)   Assume the argument invalid.
(b)   Work out values based upon conjunction and carry across.
(c)   Work out value based upon negation and disjunction.
(d)   If the antecedent of a true conditional is true, then the consequent must be true, too.
(e)   If one disjunct of a true disjunction is false, the other disjunct must be true, then carry value.
(f)   If one conjunct of a false conjunction is true, then the other conjunct must be false, then carry value.

Since there are no contradictions and all statements have values assigned to them, the argument is invalid.

(7)   Tx=df x is made of tin.
Cx=df x is cheap.
Rx=df x is a ring.
Lx=df x is made of lead.

For all x not both T and not C. (x) ~ (Tx • ~Cx)
No R are L.   (x) (Rx ⊃ ~Lx)
Not all things are T or L. ~ (x) (Tx v Lx)

_____   _____

Therefore not all R are C.   ∴ ~ (x) (Rx ⊃ Cx)

When you assign values you will find that applying the DeMQ equivalence to the last premiss and the conclusion will significantly simplify your work. Thus they become (∃x) ~ (Tx v Lx) and (∃x) ~ (Rx ⊃ Cx).

~(Ta • ~Ca),	Ra ⊃ ~La,	~(Ta v La)	⊢	~(Ra ⊃ Ca)	
T	T	T		F	(a)
F			F		T	(b)
F		F	F F			(c)
		T			(d)

(a)   Assume the argument invalid.
(b)   Work out values based upon negation.
(c)   Work out values based upon disjunction and carry.
(d)   Work out value based upon negation.
(e)   Since no more values are forced, make an assumption. In this case, if you assume that **"Ca"** is true then no further values are needed to determine that each of the premisses is true and the conclusion false under the assignments already made. Thus the argument is invalid.

Notice that the "~Ca," which could have been worked out as F after the assumption was made, was unnecessary, as was any value at all for **"Ra."** The point is, once enough information is gathered to demonstrate that an argument is invalid, there is no value in further exploration of values for its elements.

IV (3)   Lx=df x is a lawyer.
Px=df x is a politician.
Mx=df x is a member.
Cx=df x is a college graduate

Only L's and P's are M's.
Some M's are not C's.

_____

Therefore some L's are not C's.

You should recall that "*only F's are G's*" is properly understood as "*all G's are F's*." That would seem to mean that the first premiss should become "*all M's are L's and P's*." But, again, this is an expression that means to assert a disjunction despite the use of the word "and" as its connective. Surely there is no intention to claim that those who are not both lawyers and politicians are barred from membership. Thus, the following is the correct symbolization.

f

$$(x)[Mx \supset (Lx \lor Px)]$$
$$(\exists x)(Mx \bullet \sim Cx)$$

∴ $(\exists x)(Lx \bullet \sim Cx)$

```
Ma ⊃ (La v Pa),   Ma • ~Ca    ⊢    La • ~Ca
         T              T                 F        (a)
   T                T     T             T          (b)
         F T                 F        F     F      (c)
            T                                      (d)
```

(a) Assume the argument invalid.

(b) Work out values based upon conjunction and carry across.

(c) Work out value based upon negation and implication and carry across.

(d) A false disjunct to a true disjunction means the other disjunct is true. This also means that all elements have had values assigned to them without contradiction. Therefore the argument is invalid.

(8) Predicates are given with the exercise.

All C who K are V if F.	$(x)[(Cx \bullet Kx) \supset (Fx \supset Vx)]$
All C are F except I or P.	$(x)[Cx \supset (Fx \equiv \sim(Ix \lor Px))]$
All C are K.	$(x)(Cx \supset Kx)$
No K is P.	$(x)(Kx \supset \sim Px)$
Not all C are V.	$\sim(x)(Cx \supset Vx)$

Therefore there are I'.　　∴ $(\exists x)Ix$

The complex-appearing first premiss is quite straight-forward. The second, with its exceptive, is not difficult if you keep in mind the discussion of exceptives both by Copi and Cohen and here. Otherwise the exercise is fairly simple.

If you try to prove this argument invalid, no matter for how many individuals you expanded the statements, you will find your check indicating validity. Since there were no individual constants in this argument and there were only two existential quantifiers (one, in effect, in the last premiss and one in the conclusion), a check that allows 2 or perhaps 3 distinct individuals should have been adequate to find a case where the argument was proveably invalid if there were such a case possible. The fact that invalidity wasn't so proven suggests that you ought to try to prove it.

1.	$(x)[(Cx \bullet Kx) \supset (Fx \supset Vx)]$	Premiss
2.	$(x)[(Cx \supset (Fx \equiv \sim (Ix \lor Px))]$	Premiss
3.	$(x)(Cx \supset Kx)$	Premiss
4.	$(x)(Kx \supset \sim Px)$	Premiss
5.	$\sim(x)(Cx \supset Vx)$	Premiss /∴ $(\exists x)Ix$
6.	$(\exists x)\sim(Cx \supset Vx)$	5, DeMQ
7.	$\sim(Ca \bullet \sim Va)$	6, EI
8.	$Ka \supset \sim Pa$	4, UI
9.	$Ca \supset Ka$	3, UI
10.	$Ca \supset (Fa \equiv \sim(Ia \lor Pa))$	2, UI
11.	$(Ca \bullet Ka) \supset (Fa \supset Va)$	1, UI
12.	$\sim(\sim Ca \lor Va)$	7, Impl
13.	$\sim\sim Ca \bullet \sim Va$	12, DeM
14.	$\sim\sim Ca$	13, Simp
15.	$\sim Va \bullet \sim\sim Ca$	13, Com

16.	~Va	15, Simp
17.	Ca	14, DN
18.	Ka	9, 17, MP
19.	~Pa	8, 18, MP
20.	Fa ≡ ~(Ia v Pa)	17, 10, MP
21.	Ca • Ka	20, Conj
22.	Fa ⊃ Va	21, 11, MP
23.	~Fa	16, 22, MP
24.	[Fa ⊃ ~(Ia v Pa)] • [~(Ia v Pa) ⊃ Fa]	20, EQ
25.	[~(Iv Pa) ⊃ Fa] • [Fa ⊃ ~(Ia v Pa)	24, Com
26.	[~(Ia v Pa) ⊃ Fa]	25, Simp
27.	~~(Ia v Pa)	23, 26, MT
28.	Ia v Pa	27, DN
29.	Pa v Ia	28, Com
30.	Ia	19, 29, DS
31.	(∃x) Ix	30, EG

The fact that this proof is so long might discourage you from trying to prove similar exercises. However, if you look closely at it, you will see that any complexities in it are not due to its being a quantified argument but to the number and complexity of its premisses. And, if you review the steps of this proof, you will see tht it is actually quite simple and straightforward. Of its thirty-one steps, five are premisses, five are quantifier-removal steps (1–EI, 4–UI), four are *modus ponens*, three each are simplification and commutation, two each are double negation and *modus tollens,* and the remainder are single uses of rules like conjunction, implication and the disjunctive syllogism. Probably the most difficult step in the entire proofs is the transformatiton of the last premiss by the DeMorgan Quantification theorems. And the only reason that that might seem a bit obscure is that those equivalences are not explicitly described as rules by Copi and Cohen. It turns out that formal proofs of validity, like the longest journey mentioned in the proverb, begins with (and is made up of) the smallest step.

If any of these exercises is likely to intimidate you, it is exercise 10. Nine premisses would seem too much for a mere mortal to attempt. But, if that is your reaction to this argument, then you are almost surely underestimating your skill with quantificational arguments. The predicates are defined with the argument.

(10)	Some C are R.	(∃x) (Cx • Rx)
	Whoever is R is either S or B.	(x) [Rx ⊃ (Sx v Bx)]
	To be B one must D or P.	(x) [Bx ⊃ (Dx v Px)]
	Only L are P.	(x) (Px ⊃ Lx)
	Had one been D one would be H.	(x) (Dx ⊃ Hx)
	Nobody was H.	(x) ~Hx
	If C who R'ed was F, then A.	(x) { [(Cx • Rx) • Fx] ⊃ Ax}
	No R unless F.	(x) (~Rx v Fx)
	No C is both L and A.	(x) [Cx ⊃ ~(Lx • Ax]
	Therefore some C was S.	∴ (∃x) (Cx • Sx)

As was the case with exercise 8, there is no proof of invalidity for this argument. Thus it must be proven.

1.	(∃x) (Cx • Rx)	Premiss
2.	(x) [Rx ⊃ (Sx v Bx)]	Premiss
3.	(x) [Bx ⊃ (Dx v Px)]	Premiss
4.	(x) (Px ⊃ Lx)	Premiss

5.	(x) (Dx ⊃ Hx)	Premiss
6.	(x) ~Hx	Premiss
7.	(x) { [(Cx • Rx) • Fx] ⊃ Ax}	Premiss
8.	(x) (~Rx v Fx)	Premiss
9.	[Cx ⊃ ~(Lx • Ax)]	Premiss/∴ (∃x) (Cx • Sx)
10.	Ca • Ra	1, EI
11.	Ra ⊃ (Sa v Ba)	2, UI
12.	Ba ⊃ (Da v Pa)	3, UI
13.	Pa ⊃ La	4, UI
14.	Da ⊃ Ha	5, UI
15.	~Ha	6, UI
16.	[(Ca • Ra) • Fa] ⊃ Aa	7, UI
17.	~Ra v Fa	8, UI
18.	Ca ⊃ ~(La • Aa)	9, UI

Notice here that the proof is already 18 steps long and all you have done is state the premisses and remove their quantifiers.

19.	Ca	10, Simp
20.	Ra • Ca	10, Com
21.	Ra	20, Simp
22	Sa v Ba	21,11, MP
23.	(Ca • Ra) ⊃ (Fa ⊃ Aa)	16, Exp
24.	Fa ⊃ Aa	10, 23, MP
25.	~Da	15, 14, MT
26.	Ra ⊃ Fa	17, Impl
27.	Fa	21, 26, MP
28.	Aa	24, 27, MP
29.	~(La • Aa)	18, 19, MP
30.	~La v ~Aa	29, DeM
31.	~Aa v ~La	30, Com
32.	Aa ⊃ ~La	31, Impl
33.	~La	28, 32, MP
34.	~Pa	33, 13, MT
35.	~Da • ~Pa	25, 34, Conj
36.	~(Da v Pa)	35, DeM
37.	~Ba	12, 36, MT
38.	Ba v Sa	22, Com
39.	Sa	37, 38, DS
40.	Ca • Sa	19, 39, Conj
41.	(∃x) (Cx • Sx)	40, EG

At first glance this exercise would have looked more difficult than the previous one because its proof is longer. However, that greater length was, in part, due to the fact that this one had four more premisses and, thus, four more required quantifier-removal steps. Add to that the fact that this argument used nine steps justified by either *modus ponens* or *modus tollens* and you will have seen just how simple its proof really is.

The only thing that is likely to give you any problem in such proofs is your own memory: with more than three dozen steps it is easy to forget what you have already proven and what you were trying to do in proving any individual step. So long as you are careful in your symbolizations and can keep in mind the strategy that you map out for proving multi-premiss arguments, quantificational arguments should give you little difficulty.

CHAPTER TEN SUMMARY

I.   Arguments in which internal structure is as important as the relationship between propositions cannot be satisfactorily represented in propositional logic.

II.   Arguments in which the internal structure is more complex than the subject/predicate relationship cannot be satisfactorily represented in categorical logic.

III.   Quantificational logic allows the representation of both propositional and categorical relationships with only slight modifications to the propositional calculus.

   A.   Properties are symbolized by upper case letters together with an indication of some individual.

   B.   Specific individuals are symbolized by lower case letters "*a*" through "*w.*"

   C.   A place for an individual may be marked by an individual variable: "*x*," "*y*," or "*z*."

   D.   The acceptability of any individual as a substitution for an individual variable "x" is indicated by prefixing the universal quantifier "(x)" to an expression.

   E.   The acceptability of at least one specific substitution for an individual variable "x" is indicated by prefixing the existential quantifier, "$(\exists x)$," to an expression.

IV.   Quantified expressions can be approximated by truth-functional expressions based upon substitutions of individuals for variables in the original expressions.

   A.   Universally quantified expressions are treated as conjunctions of the assertation for all individuals: $(x) \Phi x$ becomes [$\Phi a \bullet \Phi b \bullet \Phi c \bullet \ldots \bullet \Phi n$ (where *a-n* are all the individuals that are)].

   B.   Existentially quantified expressions are treated as disjunctions of the assertation for all individuals: $\exists x) \Phi x$ becomes [$\Phi a \vee \Phi b \vee \Phi c \vee \ldots \vee \Phi n$ (where *a-n* are all the individuals that are)].

V.   The universal and existential quantifiers are related to each other by equivalences here called the DeMorgan Quantification Theorems.

VI.   Formal proofs of validity in quantificational logic are basically the same as they were in propositional logic, with the addition of rules for the addition of and elimination of the quantifiers. Those rules are found in section 10.4.

VII.   Invalidity is proven through the use of the method of assigning values, as in chapter 9.

    A.   Since the quantifiers are not truth functions, the premisses and conclusion must first be converted to truth-functional form as explained in IV (above).

    B.   In general, the conversion (mentioned in VII-A) must include enough individuals to allow one for each distinct individual constant and for each existential quantifier in the argument to insure that a validity check that indicates "valid" is correct.

Part Three:
Induction

11.1 Argument by Analogy

If you were able to find a copy of the short story "Love is a Fallacy" that was mentioned in chapter 3, you will recall that it mentioned a fallacy called *False Analogy*. In the story Dobie Gillis was accused by Polly Espey of committing this fallacy when he claimed that they were well-matched, based upon five dates and that their compatibility was proven by the fact that you didn't have to eat a whole cake to know that it was good. Her rejoiner was that, being a girl, she was too dissimilar to a cake for the reasoning to be useful. She was correctly inferring that he was using the analogy between their relationship and the cake as an argument. Whether the analogy was a bad one, however, will be a question for you to decide later in this chapter, after you have had a chance to see what makes a **good** analogy.

Although Copi and Cohen indicate the analogical argument is among the commonest forms of nondeductive argument, not all analogies are intended to be argumentative. Drawing parallels between things that might otherwise seem quite different can serve to explain ideas or make them more vivid. Such vivacity was achieved by one observer of American foreign policy. He wished to point out how ill-trained he considered many of our high-ranking diplomats to be, especially concerning the beliefs and customs of the lands to which they are posted. He told of a state banquet in India, where our ambassador served roast prime rib of beef to his guests. He was unaware that Hinduism, the major religion of India, is vegetarian, believing that animals, especially cattle, possess the souls of people. His descriptive analogy was to suggest that the serving of a beef roast to Hindu dignitaries would have had about the same effect upon them that Americans would have felt had they been invited to dinner and been served broiled six-month-old human babies. This analogy does exactly what he wants it to do; no one who hears it is likely to forget about Hindu restrictions, ever.

By contrast, an analogy may be used to relate the unfamiliar with the familiar. Most people are not terribly well informed about the details of the biological theories of spontaneous generation of life and evolution to contemporary forms of life. In particular most of us cannot well evaluate the work by Miller, Urey, Nakashima, Ponnamperuma, and others in the synthesis of pre-living organic compounds. Thus, when someone wants to explain what he takes to be the probabilistic assumptions involved in a theory of the spontaneous generation of life, he offers analogies like "the probability of life originating from accident is comparable to the probability of an unabridged dictionary resulting from an explosion in a print shop." We may not know what would go into creating life, but the type in a print shop and the ordered character of an unabridged dictionary are things to which we can relate.

The key in each use of analogy is to discern the intent of the writer/speaker. If the purpose of an analogy is to explain, describe or clarify, then any evaluation should be of its effectiveness in doing so. If, on the other hand, the analogy is used to lay out evidence and show how that evidence serves as support for some conclusion, then clearly it is argumentative and can be evaluated by how well the stated evidence supports the stated conclusion. A few examples of the exercises following 11.1 in *ITL* may help clarify how such distinctions are made.

(3)   Conclusion: Marriage as an institution is not dead as it might seem.
         Evidence: The Church is accused of becoming defunct, so is marriage.

God has been pronounced dead, so has marriage.
Preachers of the Church claim a revival is coming, so do advocates of marriage.
Churches **are** being revived.

(7)   Nonargumentative--This is an attempt to clarify what goes on mentally by laying out a physical model that it is supposed to mimic.

(12)   Conclusion: Having his tooth extracted without anaesthetic hurt him.
Evidence: His physiology and nervous system are roughly like the writer's.

The writer's tooth hurt when it was worked upon.

(By the way, Ayer's reference to having a tooth "stopped" is a British colloquialism meaning having a tooth filled, that is, having a filling put in a tooth.)

(20)   Nonargumentative--This is an attempt to describe a business cycle in physical terms to which most readers can relate.

11.2 Appraising Analogical Arguments

Some nondeductive arguments are clearly better than others, but none of them can ever be valid. This means that we need some means other than a validity check, truth table, or formal proof of validity for determining the satisfactoriness of arguments which are not deductive. Copi and Cohen offer half a dozen criteria for evaluating analogies which are used as arguments:

(1)   The greater the number of individuals (or the like) about which the evidence is known, the more sure the conclusion becomes. This is simply because, as we all know, things do happen in atypical ways sometimes. Recently the Social Security Administration found that they had issued the same number to two women. Both women lived in the same state, had the same name, were born in the same year, and applied for their cards in the same month of the same year. Apparently their applications hit the computer at the same time, and it treated them as if they were one individual. That sort of thing happening is a fluke. If instead the SSA had found that everyone with the same name, or with the same birthdate, or something similar, had been assigned the same number, then it would be reasonable to infer that there was some sort of flaw in the program and that anyone else who shared that characteristic would wind up with that same number. The larger the group from which the analogy is drawn, the less likely that they will all be similarly atypical for the sort of thing they are. This group is sometimes called a reference class. The individual or case pointed to in the conclusion is sometimes called the target individual and the characteristic claimed in the conclusion to be shared by the reference class and the target individual is sometimes called the target characteristic.

(2)   The greater the number of characteristics that the members of the reference class share, the greater the chance that they will share other characteristics, too. Two people who come from the same socio-economic background might be claimed (weakly) to be more likely to behave in a certain manner than two persons of widely different antecedents. The greater the number of other things they have in common, like education, employment, religion, hobbies, family size and composition, ethnic background, the more reasonable it would seem to expect them to behave in a similar fashion when placed in similar surroundings. These characteristics that they share are sometimes called the reference characteristics.

(3)   The wider the range that the conclusion accepts as a "match" for the evidence, the more likely the conclusion is to be true. Recent Amtrak publicity has emphasized that the trains are running on schedule more frequently now than they did a year ago (90+% on time now as opposed to less than 60% a year ago). What they have not said is that they revised their definition of "on time" to become "within an hour" where it had been "within fifteen minutes." By accepting a wider range of times as "on time," they made it more likely that a train would be so.

(4)   If the case identified in the conclusion is too different from those used as evidence, then the argument is significantly weakened. If you were hiring someone to replace your best worker, you might initially be drawn to someone from a similar background and with similar education to that worker. The more things that you found out that they did not have in common, however, the less sure you would be that getting the new person really was like getting a younger version of the person whom you were replacing.

(5)   The fourth criterion spoke about the dissimilarlity of the case in the conclusion from the reference class. The greater the disparity among the cases used as the reference class, however, the more secure the conclusion becomes. What happens in this situation is that great range among the cases in the reference class serves as a sort of insurance against the conclusion being dissimilar to all of them. That is, if the individuals in the reference class are sufficiently disanalogous, then criterion 4 ought not to be a problem.

(6)   Relevance is, of course, the most important of the criteria, for if the characteristics held in common by the reference class and the conclusion case are not characteristics relevant to the one about which the conclusion is drawn, then the argument is worth nothing. Caligula, Attila the Hun, Adolph Hitler, and Idi Amin have (or had) two arms, two legs, two eyes, weighed less than 20 pounds at birth, and were more than four feet tall at maturity. You (probably) share all of those characteristics. There is good evidence that all of them were/are mass-murderers. Thus, by analogy, you are probably a mass-murderer. Hopefully, this conclusion is false, despite the analogous "fit" shown in the reference class and you. The reason is that those properties are not relevant to the characteristic of being a mass murderer. Virtually every human being ever born shares those properties. Such a list doesn't sort out the mass murderers from the rest of humanity.

The problems in part I after ll.2 (pages 367-368) provide practice in applying the criteria in limited contexts. You can identify what sort of change each new piece of information brings about and, from that, identify which, if any, criterion is being evoked. Problem 4 seems typical:

a.   This shows disanalogy among the reference cases, and criterion 5 applies. It strengthens the argument.
b.   This adds another characteristic which the conclusion case has in common with the reference class and evokes criterion 2. It strengthens the conclusion.
c.   This shows the conclusion case to be disanalogous with the reference class. Criterion 4, which this suggests, says that the conclusion thereby becomes less certain.
d.   Here the conclusion is substantially less emphatic than the evidence, pointing to criterion 3 and strengthening the conclusion.
e.   Copi and Cohen suggest that this might fail criterion 6 and thereby have no impact, but they also indicate that, given some personal preference of Bill's for morning classes, it might be another case of additional characteristics in common, thereby recalling criterion 2, which asserts a strengthened conclusion.

f.   If you are willing to accept the common ground of the social sciences, then, since these other courses are such, this evidence strengthens the conclusion.

In part II, Copi and Cohen have a substantial number of analogical arguments for analysis. If you look at the examples of the starred problems at the back of the book, you will see very extensive analysis. It may even be more detailed than necessary in most cases. A somewhat briefer approach to, say, problem 3, would be:

The argument concludes that children, like vines, need direction and support so that they can grow. Information is listed below according to the criteria:

1.   Although there are only two groups--children and vines--there are large numbers of each of them. Moderate plus.

2.   That they are living organisms and that they seem to go off in all directions when left to themselves seem to be the only things they have in common. Moderate minus.

3.   Since there are vast differences in positions which would all be seen as direction and support, the conclusion is not very specific with regard to the evidence. Strong plus.

4.   The differences between children and plants are tremendous. The sort of direction and support meant for the vines is physical; for the children it is psychological, emotional, etc. You could probably list several dozen differences in a few mintues. Very strong minus.

5.   There are undoubtedly great numbers of different types of vines all of which benefit by support, but what is really needed is a wider range of types of things that benefit from support. Essentially neutral.

6.   That we even use the word "support" in the two cases is due to metaphor. It is very difficult to identify the connection between a vine's climbing up a pole and a child's accepting guidance from teachers. Neutral to negative.

All of these criteria, taken together, add up to an argument by analogy which is not terribly persuasive. It provides an interesting image, but little more.

II (7)   The argument concludes that a single cell could, given enough time, evolve into the human race.

1.   Although the argument makes reference to "a single cell" becoming "a person," it is likely that Spencer intends to include not only the billions of people who do or have inhabited the Earth but also all other multicelled beings as data. **All** of them began as a single cell and became whatever complex being they now are. Moderate plus.

2.   People (and other organisms) share some degree of complexity and a process of development, but little else. Moderate minus.

3.   The claim that "there can be *no* difficulty" [my emphasis], is an awfully strong assertion to be grounded on such vague evidence as is offered. Significant minus.

4.   There are modest differences between human individuals and significant ones between humans and other organisms (if we read them into Spencer's hypothesis). Nevertheless all develop into what they have become from a one-celled origin. Plus.

5.   There is a significant difference between the mechanisms of development within a single individual and within either a species or a group of them. For example, at least in the case of higher organisms, "development" (i.e., reproduction) involves exchange of gene plasm, while individual development does not. Significant minus.

6. The straightforward development of a mature being from its one-celled origin, although an element in species evolution, is probably only modestly relevant to that evolution. All the mutations, adaptations, mofications or whatever required for one species to be transformed into another, seem to be largely different than simple growth. Significant minus.

Overall Spencer's analogical argument, although clever, is not a very good way to support a claim for evolution.

(11) One would certainly be inclined to think that this is an argument. After all, the last line begins "the would, therefore, I infer, is an animal...." If Hume is inferring *and* the conclusion-indicator "therefore" is there, then an argument seems to be present. (One might, however, claim that the argument-signs were incidental.) Assuming that Hume is arguing here, the conclusion seems to be that the universe is a soul-bearing animal.

1. The reference class of animals is quite large, but in many theological circles the question of whether or not all those animals bear sould is not rhetorical. (A rhetorical question is one to which you do not expect an answer, believing the answer is obvious. For example, a very angry parent might ask a child who has done something very foolish, "What kind of idiot are you?" In such a case the parent expects no reply because what looked like a question was really a statement, or at least an expression of anger.) Thus, the large reference class may be a plus for the argument *if* the analogs are held to be related in any significant way.

2. Hume states four ways in which he claims the universe is like an animal: circulation of matter without disorder, self-repair, internal "sympathy" (which, historically, was a medical term meaning physiological interdependence), and the "fitting" of each part into its proper place in the whole. This is not an extensive list of similarities and, in all probability, many observers would question the truth of the list, too. Probable minus.

3. The conclusion is actually rather strong, in the sense of being rather specific in the role of the Deity as analogous to that of the soul. Additionally, there had been no mention of the soul or the Deity in the analogy prior to the conclusion. Strong minus.

4. Although they are not stated in the exercise, there are many differences between the universe and animals (beginning with the organic/inorganic chemistry of the two). Very strong minus.

5. If, as you did in point 1, you ignore the question of whether all animals do have souls, then the incredible variety of animals even on our realtively insignificant planet would seem to suggest about as much dissimilarity as you could ask for. Plus.

6. As had been hinted at in the earlier points, the real issue here must be the question of relevance. There are so many dissimilarities between animals and the universe and there is so little offered by Hume to show that they are alike in any important ways, that this argument surely fails the relevance test. Strong minus.

Overall, if this passage is read as an argument, it cannot be considered to be a very good one.

1⅔.3 Refutation by Logical Analogy

Very commonly we use analogies, not to establish a point, but to show how it is that an idea that had sounded plausible reallly was not. What you are doing in such cases, in a fairly loose sense, is appealing to a sort of "semi-formal" criterion. Roughly the refuting argument you are offering is a *Modus Tollens*:

> If an argument *like this* of this form is valid then another argument *like that* of the same form must also be valid.
> That argument is clearly invalid.
> Therefore this one must be invalid, too.

The refuting argument, then, serves to show that the argument it refutes is an invalid one.

But there are invalid arguments that we all want to use as good- but-not-valid. The entire range of inductive, analogical and hypothetical arguments is one of arguments we know not to be valid but which we can use effectively within restricted circumstances. Despite the nondeductive character of such arguments, we frequently choose to refute them by analogy. The key, then, to a refuting analogy in which the pivotal term is not "valid" but "good," where "good" is relative to the criteria for goodness *for that sort of argument*. The *Modus Tollens* argument becomes

> If an argument *like this* of this form is good then another argument *like that* of the same form must also be good.
> That argument is clearly bad.
> Therefore this one must be bad, too.

The greatest difficulty you will encounter with refutation by logical analogy is coming up with them. Just as a given individual's inability to generate a formal proof of validity does not constitute any proof of the argument's invalidity, a given individual's inability to think of a refuting analogy is no significant proof of that argument's reliability. Again, however, practice helps, so you should try to work as many of the problems after 12.3 (pages 373-376) in *ITL* as you can.

(3)   The analogy claims that the original argument is roughly

> All individuals who are allowed to fight are individuals who should be allowed to vote.
> 18-year-olds are allowed to fight.
> Therefore, 18-year-olds should be allowed to vote.

But this is easily represented by a valid quantificational argument.

> Fx=df x is allowed to fight.
> Vx=df x should be allowed to vote.
> Ex=df x is an 18-year-old.

$$(x)(Fx \supset Vx), \quad (x)Ex \supset Fx) \vdash (x)(Ex \supset Vx)$$

The refuting analogy is the also-valid quantificational argument

> Fx=df x is allowed to fight.
> Vx=df x should be allowed to vote.
> Tx=df x is a trained fighting animal (mule or dog).

$$(x)(Fx \supset Vx), \quad (x)(Tx \supset Fx) \vdash (x)(Tx \supset Vx)$$

The refutation *in this case* goes, the arguments are both formally valid; the first premisses of the two arguments are identical; the formal structure of the arguments is also identical; and the second premisses of both arguments are indisputably true; therefore the first premiss must be false *in both arguments*.

(9)   The argument to be refuted can be represented "semi-formally" as

> If non-violent protest is effective then it would work in any political situation.
> Non-violent protest would surely not have worked against the Hitler Nazis.
> Therefore non-violent protest is ineffective.

The refutation takes the form of two refuting arguments

> If a car is an effective mode of transportation then it would work in any driving situation.
> Virtually any car you pick would not win the Indy 500.
> Therefore virtually any car you pick is ineffective.

and

> If a Cuisinart chops things effectively then it ought to be able to chop any material.
> A Cuisinart will not chop firewood.
> Therefore a Cuisinart cannot chop things effectively.

The refutation here might be seen as semi-formally showing that the first premisses in each argument must be false (since the arguments are all cases of *Modus Tollens* and have true second premisses) or as simply suggesting that there is a misinterpretation involved in understanding the first premisses, that each demands too much. The sought conclusion of the refutation might be that a "tool" does not have to be effective in *all* situations to be useful.

(14)   The letter-writer's argument can be represented semi-formally as

> If a material is a gift from God then no one ought to complain about it in any way.
> Tobacco is a gift from God.
> Therefore no one ought to complain in any way about tobacco.

The refutation takes the form of a refuting argument.

> If a material is a gift from God then no one ought to complain about it in any way.
> Poison ivy is a gift from God.
> Therefore no one ought to complain in any way about poison ivy.

The refutation here might be seen as semi-formally showing that the first premisses in each argument must be false (since the arguments are both cases of *Modus Ponens* and have true second premisses) or as simply suggesting that there is a misinterpretation involved in understanding the first premisses, that each demands too much. The sought-after conclusion of the refutation might be that a "gift from God" does not have to be desireable.

CHAPTER ELEVEN SUMMARY

I.   Analogies can be used to explain, describe, make a point vivid or to argue.

    A.   Explanations, descriptions and sharpening images are evaluated by how effective they are.

    B.   Arguments are evaluated by how much support their premisses provide for their conclusions.

II.   Analogical arguments are judged to be reliable or not according to six criteria:

    A.   If the reference class contains a large number of individuals, then the argument is likely to be more reliable.

    B.   If the reference class and the claimed analog share a large number of characteristics, then the argument is likely to be more reliable.

    C.   If the conclusion is not too broad, if it allows a fairly wide range of events to count as acceptable, then the argument is more likely to be reliable.

    D.   If there are very many ways in which the claimed analog differs from its reference class, then the argument is less likely to be reliable.

    E.   If the memmbers of the reference class are fairly dissimilar to each other, except of course in the critical analogical ways, then the argument is more likely to be reliable.

    F.   If the ways in which the claimed analogy is like the reference class are significantly realted to the additional way in which we claim it resembles the others, then the argument is more likely to be reliable.

III.   Analogies are effective ways of refuting arguments.

    A.   If you can offer an argument which strictly parallels the formal structure of the one you wish to refute but which has a premiss (or premisses) whose truth value matches the analogous premiss (or premisses) of the original argument and whose conclusion is obviously false, then the original is clearly bad.

    B.   If you can offer an argument whose "feel" parallels the original and whose premisses seem to match the analogous ones in the original, then the original is likely to be bad.

Chapter Twelve
Causal Connections:
Mill's Methods of Experimental Inquiry

12.1 The Meaning of "Cause"

You may find the title of this section a bit misleading, for, as Copi and Cohen explain the word "cause" has several rather different meanings. Frequently what you mean by "cause" is a function of *why* you want to know what the cause is. A student who finds that she "clutches" on examinations, finding herself unable to fully demonstrate what she had learned, will surely wonder what the *cause* of her behavior is. In all likelihood, her reason for wanting to know the cause is her desire to avoid the problem in the future. She seeks a necessary condition for her clutching, a condition which if eliminated would result in her no longer being unable to utilize her full knowledge. Necessary conditions are frequently symbolized (in a symbolic logic) as the consequents of conditions. In the implication "$p \supset q$" "q" is said to be the necessary condition for "p." The student's curiosity about that necessary condition is coupled with a desire to apply a *Modus Tollens*-type effort to the situation. For example, our clutching student might find out that the "cause" of her freezing up on exams was her fear of being ridiculed by the teacher if she made a mistake. (Perhaps this fear was remotely caused by a teacher who *had* behaved in such an irresponsible manner.) In conditional terms the causal relationship would be expressed like this: if she clutches on the exam then she fears the teacher's scorn if she errs. Understanding this she reasons that if she can overcome the fear of ridicule then she won't clutch (a simple transposition). She comes to not harbor such a fear. Therefore, she will not clutch. In such a way one demonstrates the view of causality-as-necessary-condition is based upon a desire to avoid certain undesirable occurrences.

A second view of causality, the sufficient condition one, is usually based upon a desire, not to avoid some consequence, but to achieve some end. For example, in Shulman's "Love is a Fallacy" Dobie Gillis claims that successful lawyers are, almost without exception, married to beautiful, gracious, intelligent women. With that in mind he seeks to make the beautiful and gracious Polly Espy intelligent in order that she be a "fit wife" for him. Although Shulman is writing humor, Dobie is seeing such a wife as a cause of a lawyer's success, Obtaining such a wife, he seems to reason, will cause him to become a successful lawyer himself. The sufficient-condition causality that Dobie seems to use follows a pattern like the following: if Dobie marries a beautiful, gracious, intelligent woman then he will become a successful lawyer. Assume that his efforts with Polly are not, as they are in the story, wasted and that he subsequently marries her. In that event he ought to feel secure in his future. Thus this view of causality seems to be based upon the desire to attain some predetermined goal.

The third approach to causality would be to combine the two, treating causal explanation as requiring both a necessary and a sufficient condition in order to be satisfactory. The necessary and sufficient condition model of causation demands that there be one unique cause for a given event. For example, assume that a group of colonists landed on a distant planet and that their genetic makeup was accurately known. Further assume that there are two unique individuals among the colonists, fortunately a man and a woman, who respectively possess the genetic complexes for telepathy and telekinesis and that no combination of the genes of any other colonists could result in those powers. An appropriately timed union of the correct gametes from those two individuals would then be both a necessary and a sufficient condition for the production of a telepathic, telekinetic offspring. This approach satisfies some objections that could be raised relative to either the necessary or the sufficient views of causation and also raises significant questions about the appropriateness of trying to approach a causal situation from more than one perspective at a time.

The greatest difficulties, however, with any attempt to clarify the concept of "cause" are that both our philosophical and our scientific conceptions of causation are vague and also that there is no consensus upon the meaning of "cause." In fact, the argument has been advanced that there is no such thing as causation, just regularly occurring conjunction of events. If, for example, you put a very powerful magnification device over the edge of a billiard ball and observed as the cue ball hit it, you would see both balls and the table, but you would not see a cause. At no time would a small figure wearing a jersey marked "Green Bay Causes" go leaping across from one ball to the other. If you think for a minute about the skills of the Hollywood special effects crews, then you would have little doubt that they could build a billiard table on which the **appearance** of a brilliant shot would occur without the cue or balls ever having made contact with each other. If their budget were sufficient, there is no question that they could do the whole sequence skillfully enough to have even close observers believe that they had seen a skillfully executed shot when in fact they had not. The claim, then, is that the only evidence that we have for the existence of causality is the sequential occurrence of the supposed causally-related events. For our purposes, however, it makes little difference whether causality is a "real" property of events or an "impressed" quality which we read into our experience: our practical use of the idea and the term will be the same.

Inductive generalization by simple enumeration occurs when you observe that several instances of some event share some property or characteristic and infer that ALL such events will share it, too. It is a very short step from a simple enumeration to a generalization to a causual generalization. If you begin with such an enumeration, you will see how such steps occur:

> John got married while in college and his grades improved.
> Jeff got married while in college and his grades improved.
> Gail got married while in college and her grades improved.
> _____
> Thus all those who get married while in college will find that their grades improve.
> _____
> Thus getting married while in college *causes* one's grades to improve.

If you recall the fallacy of converse accident (hasty generalization) in chapter 3, then you will see that such inferences are not as reliable as you might hope. Obviously, some more sophisticated means of arriving at causal relationships is desirable. The next section will provide five such approaches.

12.2 Mill's Methods

John Stuart Mill was one of the finest minds of his century (the nineteenth) and, perhaps, of any century. His philosophic career spanned the middle forty years of the century, and his impact reaches until today. In the social-political sphere he defended Irish rights against England, radical freedom of speech, participatory religion, and the equality of women (among other unpopular positions). His *Autobiography* may be second only to Benjamin Franklin's in its candor and clarity. If you can find a copy in your local library, you should certainly take the opportunity to read it, if for no other reason than to see how the life of a full-blown genius develops.

In his massive (and influential) work *A System of Logic*, he laid out what he referred to as canons of inductive reason. What he wanted to do was find a way, based upon the work he had done in formal logic, to apply an at least partially-formed technique for handling inductive reasoning. In particular he wanted some method for generating hypotheses about what, among a set of events, could be identified as the cause of some subsequent event. The methods at which he arrived are simple and straightforward. That simplicity makes them relatively easy to learn and apply, but it also leads to some rather problematic conclusions. Ultimately, however, their ease of use and accuracy of hypothesis far outweighs any difficulties encountered in applying them to actual data. In any event, the fact that you know that they are sometimes problematic can forewarn you against such problems.

First indicated, and probably simplest, is the ***Method of Agreement***. Copi and Cohen's example of the students' becoming ill after a meal shows the format for examining a supposed candidate for application of Mill's Methods. In general, the key to such use is that the conclusion claims to have uncovered a *causal* relationship. For this method, like all the others, you begin by identifying the things that happened immediately prior to the event whose cause you are seeking. This collection of prior occurrences Copi and Cohen call the "antecedent circumstances." The event whose cause you are seeking they call the "phenomenon."

To identify a use of the Method of Agreement, you first check to see that all of the antecedent circumstances/phenomenon cases do have the same phenomenon; you then examine the antecedent circumstances to see if there is some one circumstance which is the only one to have occurred each and every time that the phenomenon occurred. If there is such an event, it is hypothesized to be the "cause" of the phenomenon. The simplest occurrence would be the following two cases and their conclusion:

CASE	ANTECEDENT CIRCUMSTANCES	PHENOMENON
1	John Doe, injection of drug "a"	End of headache.
2	Jane Doe, injection of drug "a"	End of headache.

Therefore, the injection of drug "a" cures headaches.

This has minimal structure:

CASE	ANTECEDENT CIRCUMSTANCES	PHENOMENON
1	J_1 "a"	h
2	J_2 "a"	h

Thus "a" causes h

This is, of course, an argument based upon inadequate information: What else did they have in common? How long had they had the headaches? What was the dosage of the drug each took? How quickly did the headache subside for each? The list could be extended without difficulty. Nevertheless, it does show in its simplest form how the Method of Agreement works.

Look at exercise 3 of the problems following the presentation of this method (page 385). It provides a real-life example to which this method can be applied. Jenner's cases are only listed in part, so the "formal" representation of the argument will have ellipses in it. (Ellipses are marks of omission. The are usually represented by three periods--four if at the end of a sentence. They may occur horizontally, as in the discussion that follows, or vertically, to indicate the existence of additional cases that are not specified.) It is also the case that there is no detailing in the analysis of characteristics unique to each of the individuals involved: such individual properties are assumed and listed here in parentheses. Those characteristics could include age, health, height, weight, normal activity level, diet, etc. The pivotal occurrences are the infection with and recovery from cowpox (symbolized C), the infection with smallpox (S) and the failure to contract smallpox (F). Symbolically, then, the data looks like:

PERSON	ANTECEDENT CIRCUMSTANCES		PHENOMENON
Portlock	(A,B,D . . .E)	C,S	F
Barge	(G,H,I . . .J)	C,S	F
Wynne	(K,L,M . . .N)	C,S	F
Nichols	(O,P,Q . . .R)	C,S	F
Merret	(T,U,V . . .W)	C,S	F
Rodway	(X,Y,A . . .AA)	C,S	F
Phipps	(BB,CC,DD . . .EE)	C,S	F

Therefore C is the cause of F.

There is an obvious problem with this formal representation of the situation--there are *two* antecedent circumstances which occur every time the effect occurs. Intuitively we might reject S as a cause of F, for infection with a disease would seldom be seen as a reason not to have the disease--quite the opposite. Mill's Method of Agreement does not, by itself, give us any reason for such a rejection of the data. Given the formal logic that you learned in Chapters 8-10, you may see that a better way to deal with the S-circumstance is to move it over to the phenomenon, but as an antecedent. This "conditional phenomenon" would then be "S ⊃ F" and would indicate that the occurrence of which you are seeking the cause is "failure to contract smallpox *when* infected by it."

This sort of difficulty is relatively esily handled, but there are other cases that are more problematic. One sort is that where the antecedent circumstances are not well enough differentiated, as shown in the following:

A young man entered college and was away from parental supervision for the first time in his life. In order to appear more sophisticated than he was, he went out drinking every weekend. On the first Saturday evening he went to Barney;s and drank rum and cola. The next morning he had a terrible hangover. The second Saturday he went to The Golden Apple and drank bourbon and cola. He awoke the following morning with a terrible hangover. On the third Saturday he went to a private party and drank vodka and cola. Subsequently he spent Sunday morning terribly hungover. In the attempt to uncover the cause of his hangovers he applied Mill's Method of Agreement. It looked like the following:

CASE	ANTECEDENT CIRCUMSTANCES	PHENOMENON
1	Barney's, Rum, Cola	Hangover
2	G. Apple, Bourbon, Cola	Hangover
3	Private party, Vodka, Cola	Hangover

Therefore Cola is the cause of his hangovers.

While it may be that the sugar and caffeine could have some negative effect, no one would doubt that the real cause of the hangovers was the alcohol in the various liquors he drank with the colas. The antecedent circumstances needed more detailing. Notice that, even had alcohol been separated out as another of the antecedents, Mill's Method of Agreement would not have provided a means for determining whether alcohol, cola, or the combination of the two was the cause of the hangover. That is the same sort of problem that was suggested in the analysis of problem 3, but it is not so easily resolved. Fear not, for a means of resolving it will be shown shortly.

The second sort of difficulty results when there is no *one* antecedent circumstance which causes some phenomenon. This would be shown in the case of several radio broadcasts which all suffered from a phenomenon known as feedback, a high-pitched whistle or squeal heard over the radio. If you laid out, say, half a dozen cases it would be very likely that you would find great variety in the antecedents; in fact there might be NO occurrence common to all the cases of feedback. Some of the cases would involve call-in broadcasts where the caller has his or her radio tuned into the show being broadcast and has the volume too high; the remaining cases would probably involve the broadcaster having the headset earphones too close to the microphone. Here, again, if you knew enough about the electronic principles involved, you might be able to sort out the detail that both types of case involved the broadcast somehow being looped back and being re-broadcast **almost** simultaneously. But if you couldn't find such a technical commonality, what you ought to be able to conclude is that there are **two** antecedent circumstances **either of which** can cause the phenomenon. This sort of complexity increases if there are two antecedents which cause the phenomenon when they occur together but neither of which is sufficient alone. Pregnancy is a great example of this sort of situation: ovulation and intercourse cause pregnancy (usually) when they occur together (without any intervening agents), but either alone is inadequate. The advent of computer-assisted searches of antecedent phenomena does much to eliminate this sort of problem.

The second sort of approach to causal hypotheses is the ***Method of Difference***. When it is used, you lay out the antecedent circumstances of an initial case as you did with the method of agreement, but you seek as a second case circumstances which are almost identical to the first case. The sought-after difference is to be the absence of the phenomenon to which you seek a cause coupled with the absence of some one single antecedent. The inference runs that if the missing circumstance is the only difference in the antecedents, then it must be the reason the expected phenomenon did or did not occur.

The fourth problem among the exercises following the introduction of this method (page 389) provides a good example of how to analyze an occurrence of the method of difference. As a matter of fact, this is an example of the method's having been used twice. The first case is based upon the germ-free laboratory work. The types of laboratory rats, the diet, etc., are all assumed to have been held constant. The difference is simply that one group of rats had normal oral bacteria while the others were kept germ-free. The latter had no cavities while the former averaged four apiece. Symbolically, using R, D . . . E for the common elements of being rats, having a standard diet, etc., and using G for the circumstance of having oral bacteria, and using c for having cavities, the argument looks like:

1. R, D, . . ., E, G $\Rightarrow$ c

2. R, D, . . ., E, $\overline{G}$ $\Rightarrow$ c
                        G $\Rightarrow$ c (G causes c).

The second argument in the passage is absed on the feeding-technique research. The difference here is the method of feeding--oral or stomach. Using about the same symbols as above, with the addition of F for normal oral feeding (F being the symbol for the case of any other mode of feeding, including the direct stomach feeding suggested), the argument looks like:

1.   R, E, . . ., G, F $\Rightarrow$ c

2.   R, E, . . ., G, $\overline{F}$ $\Rightarrow$ c
                        F $\Rightarrow$ c (F causes c)

This case even includes the spectacular sub-case where the mutuality is extended to provide a case where the two rats share a circulatory system.

The greatest weakness of this method, like the previous one, comes when the "cause" is really some combination of circumstances. In the case, for example, of a fire, one could have the antecedents H =df heat of combustion of some material, C =df that combustible matter, and O =df an oxydizing element, with f =df the fire. Date supporting each of the three following arguments could be easily obtained.

	1'	H,	O,	C	⇒	f
	2'	H,	O,	$\bar{C}$	⇒	f
				C	⇒	f
But	1"	O,	C,	H	⇒	f
	2"	O,	C,	$\bar{H}$	⇒	f
				H	⇒	f
And	1"'	C,	H,	O	⇒	f
	2"'	C,	H,	$\bar{O}$	⇒	f
				O	⇒	f

Here, by what seem to be proper uses of this method, there are three different things each claimed to be the "cause" of the fire. The truth, of course, is that all three are required for the fire.

One way to resolve the sort of difficulties mentioned with respect to the methods of agreement and difference is Mill's third method, the ***Joint Method of Agreement and Difference***. It is exactly what the title suggests, the simultaneous use of both of the first two methods. In the case of the inference derived by the method of agreement (that cola drinks led to a hangover) all one would have to have done was tried drinking the rum , bourbon or vodka but *not* the cola. If the hangover had also absented itself (an unlikely occurrence) then you would have had the joint method at work. The fact that, probably, he would still have been hungover despite avoiding the cola would in itself provide incentive for him to have more carefully examined the antecedent conditions. Perhaps then he would have realized that all of the liquors contained alcohol. In the case of the requisite conditions for a fire, if you took cases 1', 1", and 1"' together as the agreement part of the inference, you would see that it is the triad of O,C and H that seem to yield fire.

Problem 5 in the exercises following the exposition of this method (page 393) is a simple and clear demonstration of the method at work. Pasteur's experiment begins by using the method of agreement upon the several chickens whose body temperatures were lowered and which proved susceptible to anthrax. Notice that the representation below utilizes a conditional effect like the one discussed above on page 214 above. The B,C and D characteristics are the assumed individual characteristics of the various hens; T is the use of the waterbath to lower the body temperature; A is the infection by the anthrax bacillus; f is the eventual death due to anthrax.

1	B',	C',	D',	T	⇒	A ⊃ f
2	B",	C",	D",	T	⇒	A ⊃ f
		.				
		.				
		.				
n	B^n,	C^n,	D^n,	T	⇒	A ⊃ f
∴			T		⇒	(T ⊃ f)

Pasteur then picks another hen, which the experiment assumes is a reasonably good match for some one (or more) of the hens that died, and sets up the same conditions. The only variances are the return of the hen to normal temperature (basically the omission of T) and the subsequent return to health of the hen. This can be represented as:

$$1 \quad B_i, \quad C_i, \quad D_i, \quad T \quad \Rightarrow \quad A \supset f$$

$$2 \quad B_{ii}, \quad C_{ii}, \quad D_{ii}, \quad \overline{T} \quad \Rightarrow \quad A \ \& \ \overline{f}$$

These two instances, taken together, follow closely the pattern for the joint method.

A residue is a leftover, and that is the sort of material upon which the *Method of Residues* is based. In contrast to the methods discussed earlier, this method involves the occurrence of several phenomena together with their several antecedents. Once you have laid out the antecedent circumstances and the consequent phenoma, the approach of this method is to match them with each other, insofar as that is possible. If the example fits the method well, you will then be left with one antecedent and one phenomenon which you infer are causally related. Archimedes' famous example of using water displacement to determine the genuineness of the gold in a crown is a case of this method in about its simplest form. He had been ordered to determine whether the crown was truly gold, or just gilded lead, but with the added proviso that the crown was in no way damaged. He is said to have come upon the solution while bathing, whereupon Archimedes lept from his tub and nude (or clad only in a towel--depending upon the modesty required by the storyteller) ran through the streets shouting "Eureka" (which is Greek for "I have found it"). What he had realized in the tub was that any material has a fixed weight/volume ratio. If you fill a spouted pitcher just to overflowing with water, then slowly lower the crown into it, catching the overflow water, then the volume of the water that overflows will be the volume of the crown. If you then remove the crown and weigh it you can calculate the weight/volume ratio. If you take known gold and measure out the same volume as was in the crown, then weigh it, you have both the weight/volume ratio for gold and the weight that the crown ought to weigh. Any variance between the weight of the crown and the weight of the same volume of pure gold (a left-over) or rsidue) must be accounted for by the presence of some non-gold material in the crown (another residue). This example is valuable not only because it is so simple, but because it shows a slight variance from the "form" of the method. The "normal" way of showing the method of residues would be (for an adulterated crown):

$$G, \quad L \quad \Rightarrow \quad g, l$$
G (the gold in the crown) is known to have weight g

Therefore L (the lead in the crown) is known to have weight l.

But that is not really quite the way this inference (or many such method of residues inferences) took place. It really would have been more like this:

V (volume of the crown) has W (weight of the crown)
V (same) has G (weight of that volume of gold) *if* the crown is pure gold.
W - G = x (some figure greater than 1)

Therefore there must be something heavier than gold accounting for part of W.

Since the only two elements commonly occurring in the third century B.C. (when Archimedes lived) that were heavier than gold were lead and mercury, it stood to reason that one of them had to be added to the crown to account for the excess weight. Given known weight/volume ratios for lead and mercury it would not be difficult to calculate what gold/mercury and gold/lead mixes would be required to produce a crown with that specific weight/volume ratio. Note that when Copi and Cohen discuss the discovery of Neptune they refer to "the (hypothesized) planet Neptune" as a causal antecedent. This is done in order to be able to add it to the list of antecedents in accord with the "normal" pattern for residues. In actuality, that inference, like the Archimedes one, follows the second pattern more closely than the first.

Example 4 after the discussion of this method provides a historical example of the use of the method. In a semi-formal fashion, the inference runs:

   a. When body temperature rises, the hemoglobin count increases dramatically to
        level z.
   b. The normal hemoglobin count is x.
   c. The hemoglobin production rate for bone-marrow is y.
   d. $(x + y) < z$ [or $\{z - (x + y)\} = k$]
   e. Therefore k (the excess red blood cells) must be accounted for elsewhere.

Now--given this pattern--the whole can be transformed into the "normal" method of residues:

   C,B,S   ⇒   x,y,k
   C (the circulatory system--a known red blood cell repository) accounts for x cells.
   B (the bone marrow--a known red blood cell producer) accounts for y cells.
   _____

   Therefore S (the spleen--a known red blood cell repository) must account for the k
   cells which appear when body temperature rises.

The last of the methods listed is the only one that takes into account the fact that most information that we encounter is not of the yes/no, off/on, necessary/impossible sort--most of it comes in many increments. It tends to be found in greater and lesser quantities. It is the pattern of variability that Mill identified as the ***Method of Concomitant Variation.*** ("Concomitant" is a six-bit word meaning "associated with.") Since many of the things that will be studied in science are quantified, this method utilizes the quantities, as they vary, as a means of recognizing causal relationships. The simplest sort of example is the conclusion one might draw after reading a chart of recommended calorie intake for adult males. The chart would normally say that for a 30-year-old, 150 lb. man, it takes 2700 calories/day to maintain health and body weight if he is normally active, 2300 if he is sedentary and 3000 if he is active. In a symbolic form with A =df average activity level, B =df 30-year-old male, C =df 150 lbs., a =df calorie intake needed, b=df weight maintenance, and c=df health maintenance, this inference looks like:

   A,   B,   C   ⇒   a,   b,   c
   A^-,   B,   C   ⇒ a^-,   b,   c
   A^+,   B,   C   ⇒ a^+,   b,   c
   _____

   Therefore A is the "direct" cause of a. (Or the more active you are, the more calories
   you require.)

Note that reading another aspect of the same sort of chart, the age level, with O =df 35, O^-= df age thirty, O^+ =df age forty, the inference would be:

   O,   B,   C   ⇒   a,   b,   c
   O^-,   B,   C   ⇒ a^-,   b,   c
   O^+,   B,   C   ⇒ a^+,   b,   c
   _____

   Therefore O is the "inverse" cause of a. (Or the older you get the fewer calories you
   require.)

The sixth problem following the discussion of this method shows its use in a case that is interesting, in part, because it does not quite conform to the structures shown above. Although the passage does not spell out the individual cases in any detail, what it surely intends to show is something like:

A,	B,	C	$\Rightarrow$	c (where A is the rate of alcoholism, B and C are other constant factors, and c is rate of cirrhosis)
A^+,	B,	C	$\Rightarrow$	c^+
A^-,	B,	C	$\Rightarrow$	c^-

Therefore A is the causes of c (Or the increase in the rate of alcoholism causes an increase in the incidence of cirrhosis of the liver.)

In each of the uses of Mill's Methods shown above there is a common element that is obvious: they are keyed to developing an hypothesis about the causal relationships between sets of antecedent circumstances and subsequent phenomena. But there is another, more subtle common element: being non-necessary inferences which could have false conclusions, there is always additional information which you would like to have before drawing the conclusion. In the Jenner/smallpox use of agreement, it would be nice to have more details about the backgrounds of the individuals to see if there are other common elements that might account for the smallpox immunity. In the rat/tooth-decay application of difference, there had to be added assumptions about the diets of the various rats; it would have been well to have had them stated. In the Pasteur/anthrax use of the joint method, there surely were not enough cases tested, and it would be informative to try to RAISE the body temperature of an anthrax-susceptible animal to see if that would destroy the bacillus. When the spleen was inferred to be the locus of the additional hemoglobin, it would have proven helpful had there been some attempt made to "flag" the red blood cells in the spleen (radiologically, perhaps) to see if they are the ones that flood into the system when body temperature rises. And finally, in the alcoholism/cirrhosis application of concomitant variation, there surely is evidence from other countries or of cases where the rate of alcoholism declined.

A significant part of the analysis of applications of Mill's Methods is such indication of areas in which the argument is weak, where the details are unclear (or even lacking), where additional research is necessary (or would be helpful), or where the same material might lead to different conclusions. This same material might lead to different conclusions. This last sort could often occur in applications of the concomitant variation method. Why, for example, was it concluded that rise in alcoholism led to rise in cirrhosis? Why not the reverse, that rise in cirrhosis led to increased alcoholism? Couldn't we hypothesize that the disease leads to an uncontrollable desire for alcohol? The "secret" (if there is any) to the application of Mill's Methods is to apply them cautiously and with an eye to further experimentation should the application yield a positive result.

12.3 Criticisms of Mill's Methods
12.4 Vindication of Mill's Methods

Copi and Cohen indicate that there are two sorts of criticism that are leveled against Mill's Methods: They do not do what Mill claimed they do, and they do not supply a complete account of the scientific method. His discussion in 12.3 (pages 401-407), however, focuses only upon the first of these.

Mill's claims, stated simply, are that the methods (1) show how to make causal discoveries and (2) serve as a means of proving that causal connections exist. The Scientific Drinker example, either in Copi and Cohen's version or mine shows how use of the Method of Agreement can result in an incorrect conclusion. However, a bad conclusion could be reached using any inductive method, and, in this case, the difficulty is not with the method itself but with the application of it. It is, of course, a legitimate criticism to point out that a method is likely to be misapplied, but that seems not to be the point here.

Similarly, the criticism of the Method of Difference in showing that the description of the antecedent circumstances omitted a major, significant piece of evidence (the unfairness of the test) is not really a criticism of the method. Had the arguer done a respectable job of laying out the antecedent circumstances, there would have been no such erroneous argument. Thus neither of these criticisms is at all significant as a critiques of Mill's claims.

More importantly, such examples of weakness in the use of Mill's Methods ought to incline us to be more sensitive to their use and less reliant upon the "rule of the law" in applying Mill's Methods. In any event, the bulk of such criticisms ought to be directed toward Mill (or, since he is dead, anyone who uncritically applies the Methods) rather than at the Methods themselves. It certainly would be nice if we had handed to us a set of techniques that would guarantee us the ability to uncover causal relationships whenever we wanted to find them. The inability to find such a set of techniques, however, does not by itself suffice as a reason for scrapping the techniques. The fact that your Phillips head screwdriver is used seldom and, when erroneously used, causes damage is no reason for throwing it away. You may use it infrequently, but on those occasions when it does work it is irreplaceable. This would suggest that, if there are any circumstances at all in which Mill's Methods are useful, then they are justified.

Mill's Methods, then, are not applied within a vacuum. To be in a position to draw any sort of causal hypothesis, you must already know (or suspect or intuit) what is relevant. That is a preapplication necessity.

The second claimed failure to meet the claims for the Methods lies in the area of proof rather than discovery. As Copi and Cohen suggest, the mere fact that you could lay out the factual evidence in such a way as to match one of Mill's Methods does not constitute proof that there is a causal relationship present. For example, if you were to look at women's hemlines since the First World War you would find that whenever hemlines go up or down the stock market goes up or down. Hemline highs in that period would include the "Flapper" period of the late 20's, the knee-top skirts of World War II and the micro-miniskirts of the late 60's; corresponding market highs would be found, with the Dow-Jones averages finally breaking 1000 during the micro-mini era. Low hemlines would be found in the 30's, the 50's and the early 70's (with the ankle-length maxi being worn); of course, the Great Depression, the "rolling recession" of the Eisenhower years and the post-Vietnam economic woes correspond to the hemline lows with similar economic ones. If you actually bought into this inference, then you would be likely to claim that women who were truly patriotic would go back to the mini (or perhaps even resort to nudity) to heal the world's economic ills. While there are those who might wish to see such a move in the fashion industry, I have serious doubt about the economic nature of that preference. As a matter of fact, you could probably make a better case for the causality going the other way, claiming that economic security would lead to more openness or exhibitionism in dress. In any event, it seems clear that Mill's Methods do not provide the sort of certainty either in discovery or proof that Mill claimed.

You may feel that you have missed Copi and Cohen's discussion of the second charge against Mill's Methods, that they do not constitute a complete account of the scientific method. I do not believe that you will find that discussion as an issue separated from the discussion of Mill's claims for this Methods. It is a fairly straightforward inference from the inability of the Methods to discover all causal relationships or even prove their causal nature to the position that the Methods do not provide a complete explication of the scientific method (if, in fact, there is one). Thus, if there is any way to show how causal laws are discovered or proven, then, since Mill's Methods are inadequate to do either, Mill's Methods must also be an inadequate account of scientific method.

All of these criticisms, however, should seem to you to be a bit off-target. Their focus is not so much Mill's Methods themselves as it is the claims made for them. An analogy might be useful here. (Perhaps you should try to decide whether it is explanatory or argumentative.) In the last several years many brands of a kitchen device called a food processor have been widely advertised. The machine is essentially a motor which drives an assortment of blades which cut up (process) food in several ways, depending upon the design of the blade and of the housing. If you listen to the proponents of the machine and watch demonstrations done by the sales force of the manufacturers, you can be convinced that the device can do virtually anything you would ever want to do in a kitchen, that it can replace almost any other appliance. As a matter of fact, however, it falls short of specialized appliances in many of its functions. For example, a machine designed only to grind meat, say, to make hamburger turns out uniform, evenly-textured meat; the "ground" meat from many of the processors tends to be irregularly textured and more mashed than ground. Similarly, vegetables sliced by the machine tend to be tapered form one edge to the other while hand-sliced ones (if the slicer knows what he or she is doing) will be of uniform thickness. In fact, the products of the food processor tend generally to be inferior to the products of hand work or specialized devices. On the other hand, the food processor does better work at doing all these things than does any other device. The point is, if you were evaluating the food processor, you would concentrate on what *it can do*, not upon what someone may have claimed for it. By analogy it seems reasonable to claim that criticisms of Mill's Methods ought to be centered upon how well they do what they do and upon how useful they are, not upon what Mill may have hoped they would do. (Incidentally, the analogy *was* an argument.)

It turns out that Mill's Methods are quite useful when they are used in the context of hypotheses which have already eliminated most of the extraneous material from the antecedent circumstances. The Methods, then, become devices for organizing evidence, for helping show relationships in clear relief. If you were to find, as actually happened, that some of the sensor readings in a laboratory devoted to radiation research, occasionally but irregularly, were radically different than you expected, then you would seek a cause for the anomalous effects. It is almost certain that, among the hypotheses you might consider, you would be quite unlikely to suspect the material of the shoes of the lab workers. In the actual case it turned out that the artificial leather (plastic) of one person's shoes was a sort that, when exposed to low level radiation, released a gas that caused the sensors to malfunction. Without the hypothesis that the material being carried into the laboratory was apparel of the workers, it is doubtful that Mill's Methods could do anything to suggest that causal element. In the presence of that hypothesis, the Methods will do a quite respectable job of *confirming* it. Mill's Methods, then, can be seen as another tool to be maintained for the benefit of the rest of society.

Examination of two more of the problems relating to Mill's Methods (at the end of chapter 12) may help clarify their use in practice. Again it is far more valuable to you if you attempt the problem on your own before looking at the answers either in *ITL* or here.

(4)   This seems clearly to be a use of the method of difference. There are two groups of men, they are all patients at the veterans' hospital in Los Angeles, and the only supposed difference in the groups is in the amount of saturated fat in their diets. The argument in quasi-symbolic form has this form:

| (424 members) vets, men, unsaturated fats | 31.3% c-v disease |
| (422 members) vets, men, saturated fats | 47.7% c-v disease |

Therefore the saturated fats cause the additional 16.4% cardiovascular disease.

There is an assumption that the subjects are men--not certain but likely. In this case there is a built in assumption that the elements common to the two cases cause the 31.3% cardiovascular disease.

The fact that there are changes in percentages of c-v disease sufferers might have led you to suspect that the method of concomitant variation was being used, but you really don't have enough information for that method, you would really need at least one more group with some significantly different balance of saturated to unsaturated fats which led to some equally different result in rate of c-v disease. For example, if the third group consumed more saturated fats than the first group but less than the second and if that group had a c-v disease rate somewhere around 39 or 40%, then a variation would be apparent and concomitant variation could be claimed. Without the third case, however, it seems more accurate to describe this argument as a case of the method of difference.

Copi and Cohen have not asked you to evaluate the argument, but it may be worth a little effort to think about problems that this argument has. The biggest difficulty that can be ascribed to this argument is the inadequacy of the information presented. To properly evaluate this, you would need a good deal of information about the two groups, how similar the individuals in them are, how closely matched the other elements in their lives and diets are, how closely their genetic makeups resembled each other, and so on. Even then, the preferred conclusion about the effect of saturated fats upon c-v disease rate would be on shakey ground. The groups selected for testing are certainly not representative of humanity in general, omitting (probably) women. It is also a reasonable suspicion that there might have been something in the service experience that might have made these subjects more sensitive to the saturated fats (perhaps a by-product of eating military food over an extended period of time). Thus, it seems reasonable to claim that this is not a terribly good argument, even though you might believe (on other grounds) that the conclusion is correct. This ought to reinforce the idea that the quality of the argument may not have anything to do with the truth of the conclusion.

(15)   It seems particularly appropriate that Copi and Cohen end the chapter on Mill's Methods with an example drawn from Mill's *A System of Logic*. It should not require much effort to see the clue in the fourth line from the bottom of the example: "...a *residual* phenomenon appeared..." [emphasis mine]. Clearly Mill sees this as a use of the method of residues. The dangling needle stops in a fixed length of time when it is not held over the plate, but when it is held over the copper plate it stops more rapidly. The analysis as a use of the method of residues would look like this:

Needle, thread, vibration, plate ⇒	needle at rest in a fixed time period
Air resistance to the needle ⇒	needle stopping in a given time
Incomplete elasticity of the thread ⇒	needle stopping in a given time

Therefore the copper plate causes the difference between the expected stopping time of the needle and its actual stopping time.

The interesting thing is that you could make a plausible case for claiming that this, like several of the previous arguments, was a case of the methods of differences: the plate is the antecedent phenomenon that occurs or not and the speeded stopping time is the effect that occurs with the plate.

Whichever approach is taken to this argument, you ought to see that there is a series of further experiments that would make the inference much more reliable (if they yielded the same conclusion). If you set up the experiment where you were sure that there were no outside influences and where you could vary the distance from the needle to the copper plate, then you should arrive at a reliable use of the method of concomitant variation. If your work were careful and if modern physics is correct, then you would find that the closer you got, the faster the needle would come to rest. As a matter of fact, the difference in stopping time should be inversely proportional to the square of the distance between the needle and the plate.

To avoid working too many of the problems from this set, I'll include a couple of problems from the 7th edition of *ITL* that were not included in the 8th edition.

In the Spring of 1922, while the downy green of spring masked the discouragement of those Terra Ceia lands, Howell laid out his test plats: some with no tons of limestone; some with two tone to the acre; others with four; yet others with six--exactly as Hoffer had said. But he did more, did this Farmer Howell. Other little plats he laid out, with all the different amounts of limestone--from no tons to six tons per acre. But to each of *these* plats he added phosphate.

And to another set of little oblongs of ground, exactly like the first two, with more and more limestone, Howell added potash, crude sulphate of potash. . . .

Into all of them he sowed good seed of maize.

"I am testing the relative value of different fertilizer elements, both individually and collectively, in connection with lime and no lime," wrote Howell to Hoffer. Both individually and collectively--there he was at the very guts of science. . . .

Carefully Howell plowed each of these dozens of little plats of corn, the right number of times he cultivated them like the efficient farmer that he was; then he laid them by, and waited.

By late July he had the answer to his needs, the cure of the troubles of the tired Terra Ceia land. On the phosphate plats, and on the plats that had got phosphate and limestone, and on the land that had got limestone alone--even six tons to the acre of it!--there was sadness, there were broken-stalked, droop shanked plants of maize with ears hanging down, chaffy, dejected.

But on every little plat where he'd put potash, the corn trees shot up straight and strong. It was wonderful. Nearly as good these plants grew as if they were on the best black Iowa loam. It was potash that turned the trick--oh, no doubt of it. That stuck out like a sore thumb. "It has increased our yield from two hundred to three hundred percent," wrote Howell to Hoffer, in jubilation.[1]

It might help to draw a diagram of what Howell's plats might have looked like:

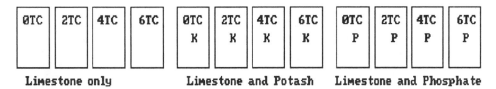

On any plat, "K" means potassium was added, "P" means phosphorus was added and "C" (with a number and "T") means that some given number tons of limestone (calcium carbonate) was added.

It seems clear that Howell had intended his research to yield results under a concomitant variation type model, else why would he have varied the concentrations of limestone? They seem clearly to be the joint method of agreement and difference.

----

1.   Copi, Irving M. *Introduction to Logic, 7th edition*. Macmillan Publishing Co.: New York, 1986, page 467. Quoting Paul de Kruif, *Hunger Fighters*, Harcourt Brace Jovanovich, 1928.

On the plats that contained potash, (the bottom row) regardless of the additional factors (like limestone, location, etc.), the common antecedent condition is the occurrence of potash and the common effect is the strong, healthy corn. This fits the pattern of the method of agreement:

First plat:	No added C,K, no added P,(A,B,...,M)	Good corn
Second plat:	2T added C,K, no added P,(D,E,...,M)	Good corn
Third plat:	4T added C,K, no added P,(F,G,...,H)	Good corn
Fourth plat:	6T added C,K, no added P,(I,J,...,L)	Good corn

Therefore K causes good corn.

This seems a reasonable version of the method of agreement. There is, however, also the possibility of setting up several instances of the method of difference, too: there is such an instance corresxx ponding to each of the plats in the agreement argument above. At least on the assumption that Howell kept other variables reasonably well under control, the plat shown being in the left group should be a good match for the corresponding plat in the middle group. That would yield four instances of the method of difference:

| First plat (l): | 0 added C,(A,B,...,N) | Bad corn |
| First plat (m): | 0 added C,K,(A,B,...,N) | Good corn |

Therefore K causes good corn.

| Second plat (l): | 2T added C, (D,E,...,M) | Bad corn |
| Second plat (m): | 2T added C,K, (D,E,...,M) | Good corn |

Therefore K causes good corn.

| Third plat (l): | 4T added C,(F,G,...,H) | Bad corn |
| Third plat (m): | 4T added C,K,(F,G,...,H) | Good corn |

Therefore K causes good corn.

| Fourth plat (l): | 6T added C,(I,J,...,L) | Bad corn |
| Fourth plat (m): | 6T added C,K, (I,J,...,L) | Good corn |

Therefore K causes good corn.

Each of these is a reasonable use of the method of difference. Using all the arguments together, there is a substantial use of the joint method.

It would be possible, also, to perform a few tests on the Terra Ceia soil, based upon the inferences already drawn, and check to see that it is deficient in potassium. That might lead you to set up a series of agreement arguments for all of the non-potash-added plats which would conclude that potassium deficiency causes bad corn. Doing this, however, seems a bit foolish, for it really is only the complement (of sorts) of the original agreement argument.

If you were to evaluate this argument in general, you would probably conclude that it is a pretty good one but not without defect. One would hope that Howell would repeat the experiment, this time varying the amount of potash added to the plats. It also would have been nice to have had him lay out the details of the location, soil and care of the plats in general. The differences in the quality of the corn *could*, of course, have been due to other variations not mentioned in the passage. All in all, however, the inference seems reliable enough to warrant significant further experimentation, and that actually is about all one ought to hope from the results of using one of Mill's Methods.

A second problem from the last edition of *ITL* focuses on the California parole system:

> The commissioners are convinced that many more inmates should be paroled. For prison experience unquestionably boosts the chance that an offender will break the law again. In one experiment, conducted by The California Youth Authority, a group of convicted juvenile delinquents were given immediate parole and returned to their homes or foster homes, where they got intensive care from community parole offers. After five years, only 28% of this experimental group have had their parole revoked, compared to 52% of a comparable group that was locked up after conviction.[1]

This argument, like the sixth one (discussed earlier), compares two groups: the juveniles who were given immediate parole and those locked up. The former group has a lower parole-revocation rate than the latter. As in exercise six, you might be tempted to argue that this is a concomitant variation, but the same arguments against that apply. Described as a use of the method of difference, this argument would have this form:

| Juveniles, Criminals, Paroled,... | 28% parole-revoked |
| Juveniles, Criminals, Imprisoned,... | 52% parole-revoked |

Therefore imprisonment causes higher parole-revocation rates.

The argument fairly cries out to be criticized. The question of what counts as "comparable" in the two groups is certainly relevant. More violent, less remorseful criminals would be less promising candidates for parole. Were members of the paroled group picked at random for parole or were they selected very carefully? Were those in the "comparable" group who were initially imprisoned given the same sort of follow-up observation and aid once they were paroled, that is, the "intensive" care from parole officers, or were they simply cast into the mill with dozens of other ex-offenders? Were members of the experimental group put into better living environments than those they had left? Were the imprisoned people returned to the same problematic circumstances? All these questions suggest that the argument is quite inadequate.

----

1.   Copi, *Ibid.*, p. 472. Quoting "Crime & The Great Society" *Time*, March 24, 1967.

CHAPTER TWELVE SUMMARY

I.   The meaning of "cause" is subject to significant dispute.

    A.   The **necessary-condition** view of "cause" identified "cause" with those things which, if eliminated, would also eliminate the event they are claimed to cause.

    B.   The **sufficient-condition** view of "cause" identifies "cause" with those events which, if they occur, will insure that the event they are claimed to cause will also occur.

    C.   The **necessary and sufficient condition** view of "cause" identifies "cause" with those things whose presence insures their effect and whose absence insures the nonoccurrence of their effect.

II.   Mill's method of agreement has the following form:

$$
\begin{array}{llll}
A, & B, & C, & D & \Rightarrow & e \\
A, & E, & F, & G & \Rightarrow & e \\
A, & H, & I, & J & \Rightarrow & e \\
\hline
\therefore \quad A & & & & \Rightarrow & e
\end{array}
$$

III.   Mill's method of difference has the following form:

$$
\begin{array}{llll}
A, & B, & C, & D & \Rightarrow & e \\
A, & B, & C, & \overline{D} & \Rightarrow & \overline{e} \\
\hline
\therefore \quad D & & & & \Rightarrow & e
\end{array}
$$

IV.   Mill's joint method of agreement and difference has the following form:

$$
\begin{array}{llll}
A, & B, & C, & D & \Rightarrow & e \\
A, & B, & C, & \overline{D} & \Rightarrow & \overline{e} \\
E, & F, & G, & D & \Rightarrow & e \\
H, & I, & J, & D & \Rightarrow & e \\
\hline
\therefore \quad D & & & & \Rightarrow & e
\end{array}
$$

V.   Mill's method of residues has the following form:

$$
\begin{array}{ll}
A, B, C, D & \Rightarrow & a, b, c, d \\
A & \Rightarrow & a \\
B & \Rightarrow & b \\
C & \Rightarrow & c \\
\hline
\therefore \quad D & \Rightarrow & d
\end{array}
$$

VI. Mill's method of concomitant variation has the following forms:

A. Direct:
$$A^+, \; B, \; C, \; D \qquad \Rightarrow \qquad e^+$$
$$A, \quad B, \; E, \; F \qquad \Rightarrow \qquad e$$
$$A^-, \; C, \; D, \; F \qquad \Rightarrow \qquad e^-$$

$$\therefore \quad A \qquad \Rightarrow \qquad e$$

B. Inverse:
$$A^+, \; B, \; C, \; D \qquad \Rightarrow \qquad e^-$$
$$A, \; B, \; E, \; F \qquad \Rightarrow \qquad e$$
$$A^-, \; C, \; D, \; F \qquad \Rightarrow \qquad e^+$$

$$\therefore \quad A \qquad \Rightarrow \qquad e$$

VII.   Mill's Methods are subjected to two basic criticisms.

A.   They do not do what Mill claimed they did.

   1.   They seem unable to guarantee discovery of a casual relation-ship of which you do not already have suspicion.

   2.   They seem unable to prove that a claimed case of causality is not just a set of coincidences.

B.   They are not a complete account of scientific method.

VIII.   The criticisms of Mill's Methods can be answered on grounds apart from the claims made for the methods.

A.   Mill's claims are independent from the functioning of the methods.

B.   They show great value as a means to organize information.

C.   They can be used to suggest routes for further investigation.

Chapter Thirteen
Science and Hypothesis

13.1 The Values of Science

Philosophers frequently describe values as being either instrumental or intrinsic. An object or action is said to be instrumentally good if its value is derived from its utility relative to some goal apart from it. For example, under normal circumstances if you saw one person holding another down on a restaurant table and cutting at the "victim's" throat with a steak knife, you would probably suspect that that action was "bad." However, if you later found out that the victim had a blockage in his throat and that the "attacker" was actually a skilled surgeon who was performing an emergency tracheotomy to save the supposed victim's life, then you would surely believe the action had been "good." The point is that the action of cutting a person's throat cannot be judged apart from the context in which it is done. And the value it has, whether it is good or bad, is a function of whether or not it leads to or contributes to the achievement of some desired goal. The cutting of another's throat by someone who knows what he or she is doing in order to prevent strangulation is instrumentally good. Any action or thing, then, that aids us in achieving some sought-after goal will be called an instrumental good.

Those things that we claim are good (or bad) in and of themselves, without reference to any other occurrence or set of circumstances, are said to be intrinsically good (or bad). for example, we frequently justify an action by saying, "I felt good when I did it" or "I was happy when I did it." The action would be characterized as being an instrumental good, but the feeling good or happy was unjustified. In fact, to most of us, asking someone why they wanted to feel good or be happy would seem a pretty strange inquiry. Being happy seems to be "obviously" desirable. Try for a minute to think of how you would respond to someone who asked you why you wanted to be happy. Chances are that the only reply you can offer is that you like the way being happy feels. If the question were then shifted to ask why you should do what results in a way of feeling that you like, you would probably either shrug your shoulders and walk away or else suggest that the questioner might be best off in a well-padded room where he couldn't hurt himself. In either event, what you are doing is, in effect, asserting that being happy or feeling good is intrinsically good, that no justification is needed for claiming either is good.

The reason for this discussion of sorts of "goods" is its application to science. One of the common ways in which science is claimed to have value is the benefits it has brought to humanity. The lists of diseases conquered, consumer goods manufactured, living and farming space reclaimed, all are instrumental justifications of science. Any discussion of the practical applications of science is such a justification of the business of science as an instrumental good. The sorts of such arguments that you encounter are common, for example, in the defense of the government's spending large amounts of money on the space program. Defenders of the thrust into space will point as justification to the nonstick pans you use in your kitchen, to the digital watch that you wear and consult continually, to the Space-Invaders-type game into which Americans stuffed over **4 billion** quarters during 1980, and to the paperback-book-sized computer that you can buy for about three thousand dollars but which can do more than the biggest computer on earth could have done twenty years ago. They can show that the extremely effective long-range telemetry needed for the outer planet fly-by's of the Voyager series is what led to the communications satellites that allow you to watch from fifty to one hundred television channels on your backyard "earth station." None of these defenses makes any claim for intrinsic merit for science, merely for its instrumental worth in bringing about the society that we think we want.

Alternative defenses of the scientific enterprise focus upon what is claimed to be humanity's native desire for knowledge. On those accounts wanting to know what is currently unknown is a natural human drive and its satisfaction is seen to be good without any further justification. An example of this sort of drive in people is the so-called Rubik's Cube fad. (If you have been in a Tibetan monastery for the last few years, or are too young to recall The Cube and don't know what it is, the description follows: the cube is composed of 26 small cubes and an internal spring-and-pivot arrangement. When new [or solved] each face displays nine small squares or a single color. Entire faces--top, bottom, front, back, left or right side--may be rotated as a unit. Once the colors have been scrambled, the object is to manipulate the cube in such a way as to restablish the original one-color-per-side arrangement.) With the occasional exception of persons driven to solve the cube as a means of bolstering their egos, there is no good reason for seeking to solve the cube except that it is there. The use of such an ability to solve the cube, except for the person who wrote and sold the solution book, is virtually impossible to justify on instrumental grounds. Nevertheless, millions of the cubes have been sold and probably hundreds of millions of hours of person-effort have been expended. Why? The challenge of trying to learn something that you did not previously know or of trying to accomplish a difficult goal.

Opponents of the intrisic value view of science have a persuasive attack: if there is an inborn human drive toward knowing, then the knowing itself is still good only instrumentally, as a release of the tension generated by unfulfilled desire. Knowing, they would claim, like eating, sleeping and keeping warm, derives its "goodness" from relieving you from an unpleasant state of want. Few people would offer scratching as an intrinsic good, preferring to identify it as instrumentally good in relieving an itch; similarly, couldn't you claim that knowledge is good because it "scratches" the "itch" of ignorance? If you'd like to explore this sort of position a bit further, you might look for "The Fixation of Belief" by Charles S. Peirce. It first appeared in the *Popular Science Monthly* in 1878 but is commonly reprinted in introductory philosophy texts.[1]

No matter which view of the value of science that you take, you will surely see that one of the most critical characteristics of science is its systematizatioan of the facts that it encompasses. The attempt by the scientist to place facts, usually derived from observation, into some order is directed at arriving at more than a mere record of data. In general the scientist hopes to understand what is happening and why it is happening. When Charles Darwin took his now-famous tour of duty on the H.M.S. Beagle, he gathered a great deal of information about the plants and animals that he observed. The science, however, in his efforts was his attempt to put all of the data together in some sort of coherent whole, so that he could *understand* how and why these organisms had come to be as they were. The theory of evolution at which he arrived was his attempt to *explain* both the living organisms which he had encountered and hte fossil record that was just coming to light at mid-nineteenth century. Whether or not you choose to accept his work as accurate, it is important to understand that he was trying to organize the data with which he was confronted in such a way as to explain both the similarities and the differences of living and fossilized organisms. The key was an attempt to arrive at a systematic prsentation of data in such a way as to explain the existent phenomena.

13.2 Explanations: Scientific and Unscientific

It is far beyond the scope of an introductory logic book to try to work out all the possible issues and problems that might be uncovered in trying to clarify the concept of "explanation." In

----

1.   Peirce, Charles S., "The Fixation of Belief" in *Popular Science Monthly*, XII (1877), p. 1.

everyday life you will encounter everything from a child's "explaining" a broken cookie jar by appeal to a mischievous imaginary friend to a cable-television operator "explaining" a bad picture in terms of sunspots, lines of magnetic force and ionospheric variation. The difficulty with trying to understand what explanation is comes from seeking common ground to account for both of these cases.

One school of philosophic thought suggests that a good way to identify and evaluate explanations is by thinking of them as resembling predictions. This means that the same thing that is acceptable as an explanation after the fact would have served well as a predictor before the fact. This parallel is not itself without difficulty, for the explanation always has the datum of the event's actually occurring while the prediction never has it. That is, you never explain the occurrence of an event which has not occurred (except in strange cases like the "explanations" that were printed before the votes were counted of Truman's defeat by Dewey in 1948) and you could scarcely claim to predict an event that you know has already occurred. Nevertheless, the sort of things that would seem acceptable as explaining one event would seem relevant as predictors, when they occurred, of another event of the same sort.

In general an explanation, whether scientific or not, has two kinds of elements: a description of the circumstances (like the antecendent phenomena of Mill's Methods) and the rules, laws or principles by which those circumstances are governed. When I try to explain why one child exposed to chicken pox caught the disease and another similarly exposed did not, I try to be sufficiently detailed in my investigation of the circumstances to show why, under the laws of contagion in our current medical science, circumstances were sufficient for the one child but not for the other. One obvious, and simple, explanation might have been to point out that the unaffected child had already had the disease, so was immune. Another explanation might refer to the basic health of both children. A third might appeal to probability laws and the Brownian motion of air molecules. The point is that, in any given set of circumstances, there are likely to be several possible explanations.

A critical issue will be to sort out the good explanations from the bad ones. A first step in doing this usually is to separate the scientific and the unscientific explanations from each other. This is important because the unscientific ones, at least insofar as they are so identified by Copi and Cohen, are not likely to be productive. They are almost always dogmatic. The attitude that they express is like the one which was such an unfortunate political slogan for Senator Barry Goldwater in his 1964 bid for the Presidency. His followers rallied to the cry "*IN YOUR HEART YOU KNOW HE'S RIGHT!*" Some of the more extreme of them were heard to say things that amounted to saying, "I don't want to be bothered with the facts because I already am sure that I know the Truth" (and you could almost **hear** the capital T in "Truth"). A scientist acting as a scientist (or "*qua* scientist" as a philosopher might say), as opposed, say, to acting as a believer in a religious doctrine, has a different attitude toward facts. The scientist actually welcomes any new data, whether it supports a previously established explanation or calls it into question. All scientific explanations, then, are taken to be provisional, subject to revision or rejection in the light of new information. This is never the attitude with dogma. Be aware, however, that something arrived at as science can degenerate into dogma. Ptolemy was doing the best science he knew how to do when he explained the positions and motions of the celestial bodies in terms of a geocentric (or Earth-centered) universe. His followers, many generations removed, who opposed Galileo, Kepler, and Copernicus, however, were operating dogmatically. They were so convinced of the truth of the geocentric theory that they wouldn't give supporters of the heliocentric (or Sun-centered) theory a fair hearing.

This dogmatic attitude of nonscientific explanation is most clearly indicated by the attitude toward evidence held by the unscientific explainer. To such a person the best evidence is a reference to some authoritative source. The possibility of looking to the world for evidence is largely unthinkable. In Isaac Asimov's book *Foundation* the Encyclopedia Foundation is visited by Lord Dorwin, a self-professed archeologist and representatiive of what Asimov takes to be degenerate science. The following passage shows the authoritarian approach to science at its worst (or at least at its most humorous). Note that for clarity I have altered spellings away from the lisping accents that Asimov gives to Dorwin.

"...I have done an awful amount of work in the science. Extremely well-read in fact. I've gone through all of Jordan, Obijasi, Kromwill...oh, all of them, y'know.

"I've heard of them, of course," said Hardin, "but I've never read them."

"You should some day, my dear fellow. It would amply repay you. Why, I certainly consider it well worth the trip here to the Periphery to see this copy of Lameth ... Lameth, you must know...presents a new and most interesting addition to my knowl-edge of the 'Origin Question.' ...Surely you must know that it is thought that originally the human race occupied only one planetary system."

"Well Lameth goes off on a new trail completely. He tries to show tht archeo-logical remains on the third planet of the Arcturian system show that humanity existed there before there were any indications of space-travel."

"And that means it was humanity's birth planet?"

"Perhaps. I must read it closely and weigh the evidence before I can say for certain. One must see just how reliable his observations are."

Hardin remained silent for a short while. Then he said, "When did Lameth write his book?"

"Oh--I should say about eight hundred years ago. Of course, he has based it largely on the previous work of Gleen."

"Then why rely on him? Why not go to Arcturus and study the remains for yourself?"

Lord Dorwin raised his eyebrow and took a pinch of snuff hurriedly. "Why, whatever for, my dear fellow?"

"To get the information firsthand, of course."

"But where's the necessity? It seems an uncommonly round-about and hope-lessly rigmarolish method of getting anywhere. Look here, now, I've got the works of all the old masters--the greatest archeologists of the past. I weigh them against each other--balance the dis agreements--analyze the conflicting statements--decide which is probably correct--and come to a conclusion. That is the scientific method. At least"--patronizingly--" as I see it. How insufferably crude it would be to to to Arctu-rus, or to Sol, for instance, and blunder about, when the old masters have covered the ground so much more effectually than we could possibly hope to do."[1]

In contrast, the scientist takes any explanation as being hypothetical. This means that the scientist looks for proof in the world that we all share, the world of our senses.

In his paper, "The Fixation of Belief," the American philosopher and logician Charles S. Peirce lays out what he takes to be the four possible ways of arriving at a belief. Simplest, he says, is the method of tenacity. It involves "grabbing" the nearest (or most available) belief and

----

1.   Asimov, Isaac, *Foundation*. New York: Doubleday, 1951, pp. 58-60.

holding it regardless of the evidence that may appear. That seems quite close to the unscientific dogmatism that Copi and Cohen describe. Second, Peirce explains the method of authority. Its followers let some outside agency state what will and will not be believed, again without regard for experimental confirmation. This, too, seems to resemble what Copi and Cohen have called unscientific explanation. The third means "from the former" method. It claims that one arrives at beliefs by seeing if they are consistent with reason". Essentially this amounts to a reliance upon intuition as opposed to fact. This, too, seems closer to the position of dogmatism than that of science. The fourth method is, of course, the scientific method. Its value is tht it allows continual testing of your beliefs, permitting (or perhaps demanding) that beliefs be changed to keep them in line with the most current data available.

The key concept in the acceptance or rejection of a scientific explanation is *testing*. Those explanations which are not subject to test are, for the most part, to be rejected out of hand. Those that are testable are accepted or rejected in accordance with the outcomes of the tests. The most obvious, but least common, sort of testing in the sciences is direct testing. Most sciences, once they pass beyond a very primitive statge, are concerned with ideas, concepts and explanations which can only be verified indirectly. Direct verification, like putting a drop of *aqua regia* on a mineral suspected of being gold to verify (or falsify) the hypothesis that it *is* gold, is seldom of crucial importance in modern theory-laden sciences. Direct verification is not terribly common, but at least has the benefit of being quite secure.

Indirect verification is never as secure an inference as direct but is used quite frequently in the sciences. An indirect test usually involves the use of both deductive and inductive reasoning. You begin by working out, deductively, some directly observable result of that which you wish to verify; then you perform the non-deductive testing of those results. A classic case of indirect verification occurred in Sir Arthur Conan Doyle's *A Study in Scarlet*. Sherlock Holmes hypothesizes that Irene Adler has secreted in her house the evidence of her former relationship with Holmes's client. Holmes cannot directly search the house. He infers that if the house were imperilled that evidence would be among the first things she would wish to rescue. (The "deductiveness" of this inference depends upon several premises about the behavior of people toward endangered possessions which are held to be of value.) Holmes then conspires to be in her home when a fire appears to break out. By observing her actions, that is, where she looks, he locates what he takes to be the hiding place and later checks it for verification of that implicant of his original hypothesis. The confirmation that he receives is not quite what he had expected (to find out what it was, read the book), but he does receive such confirmation. This serves as indirect proof that his original hypothesis about her having the evidence hidden in her house was correct.

The question that this discussion should raise in your mind involves proper evaluation of these explanations, tests and verification procedures. That is the subject of the next section.

13.3 Evaluating Scientific Explanations

If the scientific enterprise were so structed as to provide only a single explanation for any given set of data, then the job of evaluation would seem pretty straightforward. Unfortunately the job is somewaht more complicated than the single-explanation situation would yield. In the same way that infinitely many lines may be drawn through a single point, very many (if not infinitely many) explanations may be offered to account for the same set of facts. One of the most dramatic instances of htis sort of multiple-explanation situation can be found in the study of UFOs. The pivotal fact is that there is no reliabel evidence, that is, e vidence that we can put out on a table for us all to examine, of there being "stuff" from, for example, a flying saucer. Persons who deny the existence of flying saucers will claim that this lack of a crashed saucer, of their equivalent of beer cans strewn about, or of a smashed-up alien corpse all serve to prove the non-existence of flying saucers. On the other hand, persons who assert the existence of such vehicles take exactly that same data and use it as evidence that such things *do* exist. Their argument is that any beings sophisticated enough to get here and not get caught yet will be beings who will have accepted their moral responsibility to clean up after themselves. Thus the very lack of such alien refuse serves indirectly, to confirm the existence of such aliens. It is these sorts of conflicting hypotheses that tell us that some set of evaluative criteria are necessary to get the job of evaluating scientific explanations done. Copi and Cohen identify and discuss five such criteria.

First is the criterion of *relevance*. If the proposed hypothesis does not account for the facts the explanation of which was the reason for developing said hypothesis, then we might as well forget the explanation. Explanations which do not relate to the issue at hand may be interesting, but they have no functional value unless they somehow tie into what you wish to explain. For example, a discussion of the sorts of ways in which the Egyptian pyramids were built may be interesting, true, and verifiable, but, barring a great deal of currently unavailable information, is not relevant enough to serve as a reasonable explanation of how (an author believes) the Mayas of Yucatan are descendants of the original inhabitants of Atlantis.

As was indicated earlier, *testability* is crucial to scientific hypothesis. If you and I have different hypothesis, for example, about why the Roman Empire fell, then we are going to have to agree at the beginning about what will "count" in our tests. If my hypothesis is that the Empire fell becuase its leadership suffered from lead poisoning due to the drinking of water which had passed through the lead pipes of Roman plumbing, then there are several elements of that hypothesis which could be indirectly tested. The tests which would have to be done would need to be such that both you and I would see their relevance to the hypothesis and that both of us would agree about the meaning of certain types of results. I might suggest that a test of lead pipe to see if the lead were soluable in sufficient quantities to affect human functioning would be appropriate. If you deny that this test is of any great significance, pointing to a supposed lack of a general show if impaired function in those Romans as relevant, then we have little area for communication. It is only after such differences about relevance, reliability, and the conclusiveness are ironed out that the process of testing, which is a great part of the business of science, can take place.

The third criterion for the evaluation of a scientific explanation which Copi and Cohen suggest is *how well it "fits in" with other hypotheses* which have themselves received previous favorable evaluation. This is a rather touchy means of evaluation, for it is evident that a new explanation which is intended to *replace* an old one that had been thought to be fairly satisfactory will be incompatible with that earlier explanation. On the other hand, a new explanation which is intended to *supplement* established explanations should be compatible with them.

The question of the nature of scientific progress is one that has been of particular interest to philosophers of science, especially in the last couple of decades. In the early 1960's attention was drawn to this question by the book *The Structure of Scientific Revolutions* by Thomas Kuhn. In it Kuhn suggests that there are two quite different sorts of change in science. The first is the type to which this compatibility criterion applies, for this kind of change focuses upon the extension and clarification of existing ways of looking at the world. Kuhn calls this kind of science "normal science." The second type of change in science occurs when there is growing difficulty with getting observations and inferences to fit into normal science. When normal science finds itself patching itself up frequently, the time is right for a scientific revolution. Events that have been suggested as such revolutions include the Copernican revolution from geocentricity to heliocentricity, the Lavoissierian revolution from Phlogiston to oxygen, and the quantum revolution from classical to quantum mechanics. This criticism, then, is applicable only to normal scientific explanations, not revolutionary ones.

The fourth criterion for scientific explanations is *predictive* or *explanatory* power. If an explanation is used predictively, then the accuracy of such predictions can serve as a means of evaluating the original explanation. For example, in the last several years the statistically higher incidence of leukemia among those men who, as a part of their military service, were present at the testing of nuclear weapons in the early 1950s has been explained as being a long-term reaction to exposure to significantly higher than normal rates of radiation. Using that explanation predictively, one would expect to find similarly elevated leukemia rates among miners of radioactive ore, researchers into radioactive effects, medical personnel using radioactive substances, persons who painted "radium" dials on watches (to make their faces glow in the dark) and others similarly exposed. If, as a matter of fact, we were to find that these people **did** have significantly elevated rates of suffering leukemia (or even other radiation-related diseases), then we could consider the original explanation to have been confirmed.

Another application of this criterion involves what has traditionally been called the crucial experiment. You will frequently encounter two competing explanations; sometimes (but not as often as you would wish) these can constitute a crucial experiment. In such an event the two explanations, used predictively, imply strictly incompatible, that is, contradictory, results. Since one of a pair of contradictories must always be true and the other false, the crucial experiment set-up provides a mechanism for rejecting one of the alternate explanations. The inference in such a case looks like the inference form referred to in chapter nine as a destructive dilemma:

$$(H_1 \supset P) \cdot (H_2 \supset P)$$
$$\sim P \vee P$$
$$\therefore \quad \sim H_1 \vee \sim H_2$$

The results of such crucial experiments is to provide **deductive** evidence against one of the hypotheses and **inductive** evidence for the other. Of course it is important that you remember that a crucial experiment does provide only inductive evidence for that second hypothesis, for the assertion of $\sim H_1 \vee \sim H_2$ does admit of the possibility that *both* $\sim H_1$ and $\sim H_2$ are false.

The fifth criterion which Copi and Cohen suggest is *simplicity*. In the sciences this is frequently referred to as the "Principle of Parsimony"; in philosophy as "Occam's Razor." (The "Occam" to whose "razor" this refers was William of Occam, the fourteenth century philosopher who made one of the clearest early formulations of the idea.) Basically the assertion is that, given a choice, it is most reasonable to assume that the simpler of two (or more) possible explanations is likely to be the correct one. For example, a child might explain to his teacher that the reason that he was late to school was because a minor earthquake caused a the to fall, blocking the door to his home, in falling the tree tore out the telephone lines, and he had had to crawl out a window, go to the neighbor's home to call for help, and then wait until that help arrived to get back into the house to dress for school. The teacher might hypothesize that, given the child's previous tendency to daydream on the way to school, the boy had simply dawdled and had made up the story to avoid punishment. If the school's principal were to choose between the explanations, she might accept the teacher's explanation simply because the teacher had offered it. On the other hand, she might believe the teacher because his explanation was simpler. For the child's account to be true, there would have to have been a very long chain of coincidental occurrences. It seems unlikely that such a chain would have happened. There is, of course, no guarantee that such complex sequences don't occur, but they aren't very common.

The problem with trying to use the criterion of simplicity is that it frequently is hard to tell which of competing hypotheses, explanations or systems is really the simpler. And this criterion alone is not sufficient as a decision procedure. It is not terribly difficult to devise *ad hoc* explanations (ones designed to account only for a single present situation) which satisfy the simplicity criterion but fail all the others.

13.4 The Detective as Scientist
13.5 Scientists in Action: The Pattern of Scientific Investigation

These two sections are interesting parallels of each other. That is not terribly surprising, for Conan Doyle described Holmes as a **scientific detective**. Thus one would expect Holmes to use the tools of proper scientific investigation. It is particularly significant that you realize that science is a **process**, a series of occurrences which lead from some initial point to some identifiable conclusion.

Whether in seeking the solution to a scientific or a criminal problem, the point of departure must always be the **problem**. Until you recognize the necessity of explaining or understanding some event, thing, or idea, there is nothing to do. If you did read Peirce's "The Fixation of Belief," you will recognize this as being in the situation which he calls doubt. When the situation is such that you are not comfortable, where you do not know how to act, when there is some difficulty felt, then there is motivation for investigating to try to become comfortable, to know how to act, to eliminate the difficulty. The point is that, although a detective could stumble upon the solution to a crime while investigating another, he couldn't try to solve a crime that he did not know had happened. Similarly, a scientist couldn't set out to investigate a phenomenon that he didn't realize was in need of investigation.

Once a problem is identified, the scientist and detective must begin by formulating some sort of **preliminary hypothesis**. This is necessary in order that the investigation may begin. This does not mean that you are going into the investigation with some preconceived conclusion at hand, but it does mean that, to do any research at all, you must have some idea of what sort of information is and what sort is not relevant. When the H.M.S. Beagle, with Charles Darwin aboard, visited the Galapagos Islands, the crew encountered an interesting varitey of finches. The several types of finches seemed to share a basic coloartion but not to share body, beak, foot and feather forms. The similarity and differences could be seen as a problem: why are these birds (later to be knows as "Darwin's finches") as they are? A little pondering suggests that there are two fairly straightforward preliminary hypotheses that Darwin, or others of the Beagle's crew, might have offered: the birds constitiute several typs of finch that share the same coloration for some reason that is likely to be environmental; or they are of a single type, but there is some environmental factor that has led them to have varying body forms. Although I can find no evidence to indicate that Darwin ever considered the former hypothesis and rejected it, there would be good reson for such rejection: the most plausible reason for shared coloration would be if it were of a protective nature (like a fawn's spotted coat), and that would presuppose similar environments, which Darwin did not find. The second suggested hypothesis, with which he did start, could be explained by a common origin and subsequent differentiation. The key thing, however, was that the preliminary hypothesis that the finches were of a single type that had somehow differentiated into the several forms gave him a starting point. There was no commitment to it's ultimated truth, just a belief that it was the best possible hypothesis about the phenomenon as it was then understood.

Given a starting point for an investigation, the first step is to **gather additional information**. It is, of course, always possible that what you had thought was the case was merely the by-product of chance circumstances. It is not hard to imagine a supposed psychic claiming a means

of seeing the future after he had made such a prediction which had come ⌐
case that such a person would gain believers as the number of correct predictⁱ⌐ ⸍ⁱₛ also the
of us, however, would remain skeptical unless the supposed mystic powers were p⌐ Most
severe tests.

One leading psychic, for instance, claiming wondrous powers, said she had predicted the assassinations of John and Robert Kennedy, Martin Luther King, and George Lincoln Rockwell and the shootings of George Wallace, Ronald Reagen and Pope John Paul II. Initial checks with persons who had heard her predictions confirmed her claims. At that point it was a reasonable hypothesis that she **did** possess some sort of occult power, but additonal information was needed. In this particular case the facts that were first sought were the times, places and exact formulations of the claimed predictions. It turned out, upon close examination, that the predictions had been made anywhere from a couple of weeks before the shooting to more than eleven years in advance. It was also the case that the predictions had been made in varying circumstances ranging from the psychic's newspaper column to informal chats with single individuals. But worst of all was what had actually been said in the so-called prediction. Most detailed was her statement concerning Rockwell (he was leader of the American Nazi party) that anyone who so strongly advocated violence as a political tool should fear its being turned back on him. Least detailed was her statement (made in 1969 supposedly predicting the Pope's shooting in 1980) that the Roman Catholic Church could expect to be under fire in the last quarter of the 20th century. Her claims, then, that she had predicted specific events were certainly open to question.

More problematic with regard to her predictions was the record found to indicate that the predictions which she had made that were, more or less, correct were overshadowed by there really damning facts. First it was found that she was in the habit of making predictions which sounded very like the ones which she claimed to have come to pass. When people say in January of each year that the President of the United States will find himself in peril and are willing to accept political, social, economic or physical peril as "satisfying" the prediction, they don't find it hard to make correct predictions. Second, it was easy to see that her predictions, for most part, were so vague as to be practically meaningless. And, third, when people are willing to ignore (and perhaps conceal) all of the occasions on which predictions have not been fulfilled, then her record tends to look better than it ought.

As you can see, then, the gathering of additional information which is relevant to thee preliminary hypothesis can be quite useful in disproving the hypothesis. If the added evidence does not seem to show the preliminary hypothesis to be wrong, then you are in a position to refine your original hypothesis (which may well have been little more than a hunch). The step of **formulating the hypothesis** in somewhat more detail is pivotal in the scientific enterprise. Unfortunately it also is the least understood element in the process of "doing" science. The developing of hypotheses is an act of creation no less mysterious (and womderful) than the painting of a picture or the composition of a symphony. Like paintings and symphonies, however, hypotheses may be amateurish, ill-conceived or sloppy. A well-done hypothesis takes into account all of the information available, ties it into a coherent package and suggests avenues for further investigation. (Of course such an ideal may not immediately present itself, and you may have to settle for a time for a "near miss," but you always hope for the best.)

Once you have a reasonably clearly formulated hypothesis is hand, you need to prepare for its evaluation. If you recall my discussion of indirect testing you remember that indirect tests usually involve checking to see if some expected result of that which you wish to test does, in fact, occur. To perform this sort of test, it is necessary that you decide what those expected results are. This is the point at which, if you are very careful, you can put your skills in deductive logic (the ones you learned while studying part II of this book and *ITL*) to work. You **deduce** quences of the hypothesis which you have formulated. That there be such is very furth not only for their value as testing devices but also for you to be confident to know that im·hypothesis is something more than a collection of previously known facts. If there aren't eas which you can come to understand by means of your hypothesis, what good has it done you? In Moliere's play *The Doctor In Spite Of Himself*, the character Geronte, trying to tell whether the supposed doctor Sganarelle is medically knowledgeable, asks if he can explain morphine's ability to put people to sleep. Sganarelle's response, that it possesses a dormative property, is the sort of explanation that, as a hypothesis, would have no significantly different further consequences deducible from it. Hence, it would not be a terribly desirable explanation.

If you have generated a fruitful hypothesis based upon the facts available to you, then you will be able to deduce from it results which you would otherwise not have expected. Those results are the material for the sixth step for either a detective (at least of the Holmesean sort) or a scientist. Once you have deduced those consequences from your hypothesis, you need to **check to see if they actually occur**. If they do not occur, then you have a refutation of your hypothesis by means of *Modus Tollens*:

$$\text{Hypothesis} \supset \text{Expected Results}$$
$$\sim(\text{Expected results})$$
$$\therefore \quad \sim(\text{Hypothesis})$$

If the results **do** happen, unfortunately you do not have a deductive proof that your hypothesis was true. What you have is support, confirmation, or corroboration for your hypothesis. The formal argument which you have is a case of what was called in chapter seven the fallacy of the affirmation of the consequent:

$$\text{Hypothesis} \supset \text{Expected Results}$$
$$\text{Expected Results}$$
$$\therefore \quad \text{Hypothesis}$$

The argument is invalid, but if you find sufficient cases of the expected results of the hypothesis actually occurring, then you can consider the hypothesis confirmed. Confirmation, however, does not constitute proof, so you must always be ready to accept new tests, one of which could well disprove the hypothesis no matter how well-confirmed it had previously been.

The seventh step which Copi and Cohen list in the procedure of the scientist and detective is **application**. In many ways it is not somuch an additon to the six earlier steps as it is the reward you derive from having done the earlier ones carefully. Once you have confirmed your hypothesis through testing, you have obtained a tool for your use. It is important, however, to keep in mind the possibility that each of the applications to which the confirmed hypothesis be prepared at any time to find that experience has proven your hypothesis not to be quite as good as you had thought it to be. The longer you go without a disconfirmation, the more secure you may feel, but always remember that Ptolmaic astronomy stood confirmed for 14 centuries, but that didn't stop the Copernican revolution from overthrowing it.

13.6 Crucial Experiments and *Ad Hoc* Hypothesis

The concept of a crucial experiment is a problematic one. As a process, science is not simply identified with a single idea or statement. As Copi and Cohen's example of the competing hypotheses of a flat and a spherical Earth shows, even the most straightforward-looking hypotheses usually turn out to be more complex than they originally appear.

The significance of this complexity for the understanding of the idea of a crucial experiment is most easily understood by looking at a formal representation of a hypothesis being refuted by showing one of the "deduced further consequences" not to occur. Begin by assuming that the hypothesis is composed of three elements; p, q, and r. The consequence that is deduced is s. Formally the following is what happens:

1.	[(p • q) • r] ⊃ s	Given (hypothesis ⊃ result)
2.	~s	Given (result doesn't occur)
3.	~[(p • q) • r]	1,2, MT
4.	~(p • q) v ~r	3, DeM
5.	(~p v ~q) v ~r	4, DeM

As you can see, the conclusion results in a disjunction. A disjunction, however, has many ways of being true. The truth table for the last step of this proof is instructive:

p q r	~p	~q	~p v ~q	~r	(~p v ~q) v ~r
T T T	F	F	F	F	F
T T F	F	F	F	T	T
T F T	F	T	T	F	T
T F F	F	T	T	T	T
F T T	T	F	T	F	T
F T F	T	F	T	T	T
F F T	T	T	T	F	T
F F F	T	T	T	T	T

Here you see that there is only one situation in which the expression could be false: when all three propositions are true. Any situation in which at least one of the three is false will result in the overall expression's being true. In this case there were only three elements in the antecedent; in some of the more sophisticated theories and hypotheses of real-world science there could be dozens.

What Copi and Cohen want you to understand is the difficulty of identifying a situation in which you can isolate the single antecedent hypothesis in order to claim that you have located a crucial experiment. Because science is such a complex interweaving of hypotheses, laws, theories and the like, it would seem that you always have the option of scrapping the bulk of established science rather than giving up some particular pet hypothesis. This possibility has sometimes been likened to the possibilities of rearranging things in a physical sense. Let's try one using magnetic monopoles made into marbles. A magnetic monopole is a body which has only a magnetic north or a magentic south polarity (and, in the real world, cannot exist). Assume that you are in space, away from any significant gravitational field, and that you have your bag of monopoles (all the same pole), a transparent nonmagnetic sphere with a trapdoor, and a set of nonmagnetic tongs with which you can grip a monopole. If you were to dump the monopoles into the sphere, quickly close the door and wait, then you would find, sooner or later, that they would come to rest spaced throughout the sphere. If you suddenly realized that you had neglected to put one or two monopoles into the sphere and were then to inset them, then you wuld upset the established balance a bit. Most of the required adjustment, however, would be minor, involving very slight rearrangements of the previously located monopoles. But, if you decided that there was some one monopole whose position you particularly liked, then you could reach in with the tongs and, essentially, clamp it in place. That would very likely require a much more substantial rearrangement of the other monopoles in order to keep the one in its place. If you think of the original positions of the monopoles as representing the previously established hypotheses (laws, theories, etc.) of a science, the monopoles to be added as new data, and the use of the tongs as representing the decision to hold on to some one particular hypothesis no matter what, then the physical rearrangements would probably mirror the conceptual rearrangements necesary in the addition of the new facts: willingness to make small adjustments in anything yields little major alteration overall while stubbornly clinging to some one pet hypothesis may entail a radical adjustment of all the rest of your conceptual framework.

The other point that Copi and Cohen want you to understand from this section is the nature of *ad hoc* hypotheses. They trace the three possible (according to them) meanings of the term "*ad hoc*." If you trace the history of the meanings of the words, then you find that, roughly, calling a hypothesis *ad hoc* in the etymological sense merely means that it was developed in response to some situation. But, in the two preceding sections you learned that the business of science proceeds by first identifying the problem and then setting forth hypotheses. It is virtually a definition of "hypothesis," then, that it be formulated in response to some occurrence. There would be no reason, however, for anyone to be at all distressed at having a hypothesis called *ad hoc* if this were the term's only meaning.

To account for the negative emotional reactions shown by scientists when their hypotheses are called *ad hoc*, Copi and Cohen suggest two other possible meanings for the term. The first would be to accuse a theory of being rather like Sganarelle's "explanation of morphine's actions: nothing is accounted for except the phenomenon under investigation. But even Sganarelle's explanation has a slight power of generalization attached to it, for it is not restricted to accounting only for the effect of morphine upon any one individual. Thus it seems unlikely that anyone who believed that he was doing something scientific would ever be guilty of an *ad hoc* hypothesis in the sense of accounting **only** for some particular fact. For example, one might want to account for the *Star Wars* phenomenon, including the movies, books, and all the auxilliary merchandise. It is unlikely, however, that the analysis and discussion would be strictly limited to this one set of happenings. Discussion would surely include hypotheses about why *The Black Hole*, *Saturn 3*, *Galaxina*, *Battlestar Galactica*, and even *Star Trek* did not result in the same sort of reaction. One would also expect the analysis to include suggestions about how a repetition of the phenomenon could be achieved, at least approximately.

This sort of consideration leads Copi and Cohen to the third possible meaning for "*ad hoc*". If the generalization involved in a hypothesis were just a simple extension of the known data into very strictly analogous situations, then that hypothesis would not appear to be of very great scientific interest. There is some difficulty in understanding what would count as a "very strictly analogous" situation, but the example that Copi and Cohen use, of Eijkman's experiments with chickens, suggests the sort of criterion that you ought to apply. Eijkman's generalization ran from his evidence that his chickens developed polyneueritis when deprived of rice polish to the generalized statement that any chickens so treated would become polineuritic. (Polyneuritis is a disease in fowl which is closely akin to beriberi in humans.) Generalization from Eijkman's experimental chickens to all chickens is, at best, only slightly different from the second sort of **ad hoc** hypothesizing; after all, it is only vaguely possible that he had chickens with some sort of special that he had chickens with some sort of special susceptibility, that some othere breed would be resistant. Had he, however, generalized that elimination of rice polish in the diet of ducks, turkeys and other fowl would result in their also developing polineuritis, then he clearly has gone beyond the facts that he had discovered.

Copi and Cohen explain that such generalizations of empirical data **without some theoretical basis for the generalization** are the sorts of hypotheses that ought to be called *ad hoc* in the derogatory sense. Although this appears to be a pretty clear cut and reliable criterion, you must be quite cautious in applying it. After all, couldn't a reasonable case be made for the claim that either of the generalizations from Eijkman's research (to all chickens or to all fowl) contains a significant theoretical element: that chickens (or fowls) as a whole can be expected to react in roughly the same manner as some group of them selected as experimental subjects?

Perhaps the point should be made that it will be quite difficult to specify what it takes for a hypothesis to be correctly accused of being *ad hoc*. It is clear that the third sense of the term is the one which Profes sor *ITL* takes to be the accurate one, but the above discussion shows that at least rasonable exception can be taken even to this example. In practice, it seems to me that the term "*ad hoc*" is used most frequently as an indicatiton of the user's dissatisfaction with a hypothesis for any of several reasons: lack of theoretical grounding, lack of generality, lack of simplicity, lack of testability or lack of other desirable properties. All too frequently the statement "this is an *ad hoc* hypothesis which I find flawed in a manner or manners which are difficult to specify" (or, perhaps more briefly, "this is a hypothesis with which I don't agree").

You may recall that Copi and Cohen's reason for invoking the concept of an *ad hoc* hypothesis was to show that the hypothesis that they added in the discussion of the possible crucial experiment between a flat and a curved Earth was not *ad hoc*. Moreover, they wanted to show that there is no need to resort to *ad hoc* hypotheses in order to point out difficulties in obtaining truly crucial experiments. The whole mass of assumed theories that underlie almost any scientific enterprise make it almost certain that the supposedly crucial experiment will in fact be likely to resemble the formal example that I laid out earlier.

The search for crucial experiments, however, is not a useless one. In the attempt to avoid ignoring hypotheses that were unstated as you formulated your own ideas, you are likely to discover assumptions which were necessary for your new hypothesis to be correct, assumptions of which you had not previously been aware. It is obviously a desirable result for such a search to uncover these "hidden" assumptions.

13.7 Classification as Hypothesis

The criticism offered against Eijkman's research with chickens might have been rephrased to accuse Eijkman of "mere" classification instead of theorization. It dos not take much of a scholar, however, to see that classification is a major stage through which all sciences pass. The mass of data that the world sends to us is so great that we could not function if we didn't have some means to classify it. For example, most of us find that there is some "type" of food of which we are particularly fond and another "type" (or "types") for which we do not care at all. If you had a particularly sensitive digestive system, you might find that you had best avoid so-called Mexican foods because they tend to be highly spiced. If you were to move to a new home in a large city with whose restaurants you were unfamiliar, then, without some system of classification, you would probably spend the rest of your life trying one restaurant after another in the attempt to find which cuisine you liked best. With a classification system, however, you could begin by eliminating all Mexican restaurants and all others that featured spicy foods. If you then sorted out the remaining possibilities according to the type of food served, you would be able to try one or two representatives from each group and to identify the general types of food you prefer. The process could then be refined by subclasses, sub-subclasses and so on until you had identified your very favorite place to eat. The critical point was the necessity of having some way of systematically sorting the phenomena with which you were confronted. Without some means of classification, you were left with a welter of sensations and no means to do science.

The example that Copi and Cohen choose to show how descriptive fields are theory-dependent is history. Many people would doubt that history ought even to be considered a science, but there is good evidence to show that history follows the same patterns as the more traditionally recognized sciences. Copi and Cohen suggest two approaches to history that obviously ought to be considered to be scientific: the identification of some overarching unity among the whole of history, and the identificatiton of historical laws from which we could also predict future events. Either of these would require explanations which would mirror the sort of explanations we use in physics, chemistry or any other "hard" science.

The more modest claim of more traditional historians is that they are merely trying to sort out a chronicle of past events. But even this group is dependent upon scientific considerations. It is a very naive view to think that the past is present for us to observe. One of the most fascinating tales of science and history is found in the quest of Troy by Henrich Schliemann. Although untrained in archeology, Schliemann was fanatically de voted to the search for the historical city which was the root of the tales of the *Iliad* and the *Odyssey*. The "professionals" in the field were inclined to ridicule his efforts, claiming that Homer's heroic fiction was just that--fiction. Where the men trained as archeological investigators, using all the tools that the science had in the latter half of the nineteenth century, were inclined to ignore the details in the literary record, Schliemann chose to treat both the *Iliad* and the *Odyssey* as reasonably accurate historical records. Any good library can provide you with the story of Schliemann's discoveries, most of which read like "thrillers," but the most significant thing about his work was that he did discover, on the site described by Homer what he took to have been the ruins of Troy. As a matter of fact what he found was a site on which a dozen cities had been built and rebuilt. But one of them showed evidence of destruction by fire and of the main gate having been pulled down **as if to admit some object too large for the gate** (like a giant horse?). The point of all this account of Schliemann's work is to point out how a piece of theory gets used without anyone having noticed its use. In this case the theory is that literary documents provide details which ought to be treated as significant historical data. But, of course, all such literary allusions cannot be taken to be acccurate accounts of historical occurrences. Thus, for the historian to use the myriad sources of information available to him, it is necesary that there be some theory (or theories) which aid in the identification of the relevant fragments within whole mass of data.

The detective work used by the "field" historian is of very much the same sort as that used by the criminal detective or the practicing scientist. The pattern of steps which the historian follows in working out an explanation of a historical event is the same as those suggested as the scientist's or detective's method in sections 4 and 5 of this chapter. The historian must begin by identifying some problem, some event or sequence of events the occurrence of which needs to be explained. For example, the historian might begin by studying a map of the western United States, one that showed the locations of Indian reservations. One detail might catch his attention: Colorado is the only western state in which there are, for all practical purposes, no reservations. Given the fact that at least seven major tribes--Ute, Lakota, Kiowa, Comanche, Blackfoot, Arapaho and Apache--were known to have ranged across the state, it is strange that no reservations were located there. This would provide the historian with an interesting problem: why, historically, were there no reservations in Colorado?

I won't try to go through all of the seven steps in the scientific process here, but do want you to have some feel for where the investigation of this problem would lead. Relevant data which would be uncovered would include the newspaper accounts of anti-Indian sentiment, the Sand Creek massacre (in which unprotected Indian women and children were killed with the justification that "nits make lice"), and the domination of the state legislature by mining, ranching, and agricultural interests (which wanted no land to be placed out of their reach). Hypotheses would be developed suggesting that the tradition of anti-Indian feeling coupled with powerful economic forces which opposed having any land that might prove valuable set aside for the Indian would have spurred opposition to the formation of any reservations. Refinements would add facts about the impact of the silver-mining industry and its immensely wealthy owners upon national politics and would, thus, add to the earlier hypothesis the suggestion that the "powers-that-were" in Colorado had sufficient influence in Washington to prevent any significant rservation territory from being located within the state. Additional "testing" could be accomplished by examining presonal and Congressional memoirs of the period for corroborating data.

Copi and Cohen indicate that the process of classification in biology is, if anything, more clearly theoretical than it is in history. In particular, classification in biology is done for the purpose of aiding the scientist in the attempt to better understand the organisms which are being classified. The attempt, then, is always made to identify relevant similarities and differences between organisms. There is, however, a difficulty with this goal: the identification of what is relevant may well depend upon the classification which you are attempting to make. For this reason, the classifier will frequently be compelled to make preliminary groupings based upon whatever criteria seem handy at that moment. You see, once there is a hypotheis available for evaluation, you are in a position to perform research, examine further data and evaluate that hypothesis with an eye to refining it. Until you have the hypothesis, you are left just casting about for random data.

One of the strangest-seeming common classifications is that of trees. When you think of plants ranging from the hundred-year-old Bonsai which can be placed on a bookshelf to the California redwoods through which a car may be driven, you may find it difficult to identify what it is that counts as the criterion for being a tree. Bananas, for example, grow on things that look like trees but are classified as herbs; bamboo yields material that seems like wood (the product of trees), but bamboo is actually classed as a grass. The species *juniperus* contains both trees and shrubs, some of which are virtually indistinguishable to the untrained eye. The justification usually offerd for making such counterintuitive classifications is that there are characteristics shared by some sorts of plants--called trees--that not only set them apart from other sorts of plants but also provide models or structures according to which it is easier to understand what the plants are and how they function. But these models or structures which the botanist uses in order better to understand the class of plants which he calls trees constitute a theoretic approach to what it is to be a tree. Thee classification depends upon probably many but at least one theoretical construct, just like almost any other scientific explanation.

In the following exercises Copi and Cohen ask you to identify the data (the problem), the hypothesis, and those elements relevant to an evaluation of the hypothesis you discover. This is exactly the sort of thing you must do for yourself when you encounter supposedly scientific arguments which you cannot reduce to formal logic. Obviously, what you happen to know about the material in the argument will significantly affect your evaluation of that argument. When you encounter an exercise focused upon a subject about which you judge that you know virtually nothing, I would recommend that you make a quick trip to some reference material--an encyclopedia is often a good bet. This should at least put you in a position to understand what the argument is trying to say.

(2)   (a)   The problem that needs to be explained in this passage is the correlation between years of schooling and state of health, in particular why education seems to be the closest correlate to health.

(b)   Grossman's initial hypothesis is "the schooling increases the individual's efficiency in producing health."

(c)   The hypothesis is surely relevant because much of our past experience has shown the profound effect that education can have upon behavior. Who among us has not heard the story of the Pilgrims changing their entire approach to agriculture as a result of some demonstrative education by the Indians?

This hypothesis would seem to be testable both directly and indirectly. Most direct would be to identify two isolated groups which were quite similar in composition and general health, but whose members were ill-educated. One could then select one group for improved education and observe to see whether the general state of health of its members, in comparison with the unaided group, improved, too. If it did you would have a positive result from the test, that is, a confirmation of hypothesis; if there were no significant improvement, then this negative result would count as disconfir-matiton. (Such testing, of course, does not address the moral issues relative to using people for such experiments.) More indirect testing could be done by checking to see whether there were a "washdown" effect in the event, for example, of improved educa-tion of only one member of a family or of a fraction of a population.

This hypothesis would seem to be compatible with previous hypotheses about the usefulness of education in bringing about social change. After all, the pro-grams of forced integration of schools were intended to bring about social acceptance of racial differences by education through acquaintance. (Incidentally, there are con-flicting conclusions about the reliability of this hypothesis). It has also long been the practice of persons of some wealth but little family background to send their children to rather exclusive boarding schools with the intention of changing the social attitudes and behavior patterns of their children so that they can better "fit in" with the so-called upper classes.

This hypothesis would do very well as an explanation of the ill-health of peo-ples of the third world, pointing to their woefully inadequate, and sometimes nonexist-ent, eduations. It would also serve well to predict, for example, increased need for health care among the poor as a result of decreases in public aid to schools. In fact, it might be offered as an argument against such budgetary cuts on the grounds that the savings effected would only result in substantially greater necesary expenditures in the areas of health care.

The explanation is simple. There is no great complexity in the hypothesis, even when given a more detailed exposition pointing out the ways in which more edu-cation could alter behavior relevant to the obtaining or maintaining of good health.

Overall the hypothesis seems a reasonable, useful and probably fruitful one.

(8)   (a)   The problem to be explained is Dr. P's *lapsus linguae* (slip of the tongue).

       (b)   The basic hypothesis is that people tend to say what is really on their minds, to speak truly, in situations in which they are busy concentrating on something other than the thing they wish to conceal.

       (c)   The relevance of the hypothesis is a bit difficult to confirm, but Dr. P's problem surely would be on his mind and in the conversation with Brill there would be little reason for him to be on his guard.

It would be difficult to set up specific tests for this hypothesis. For the most part testing would have to be in the form of checking out anecdotal accounts of such slips. The difficulty with this sort of data is that the correlation between such slips of the tongue and the psychological state that is claimed to cause them is largely a matter of interpretation.

The hypothesis seems compatible with the bulk of Freudian theory. The only difficulty with this is that there are several other competing models for the underlying structure of the human mind. In fact, persons who are unsympathetic with psychiatric theory in general have been known to claim that one could find some psychiatric theo-ry that would be compatible with almost anything.

The hypothesis could explain other *lapsi linguae* and perhaps might be extended also to explain other behavioral quirks, like a dieter opening the refrigerator instead of the cupboard he had intended to open. It might also be used to predict that an individual who seemed troubled might let slip clues as to the source of her or his difficulty.

The hypothesis in itself seems pretty simple, unless you also consider the whole complex of Freudian theory. In the latter case you are dealing with a set of hypotheses that are not at all simple.

Overall the hypothesis seems plausible, but it is not terribly compelling.

(11)   (a)   The phenomenon to be explained is the occurrence of so-called balancing rocks.

(b)   The hypothesis offered is that the pressure of the capstone retards erosion under its center of mass, causing greater erosion on areas not under that point. The result is shifting of the center of mass and subsequent erosion in the area previously retarded. Ultimately it means gentle movement back and forth, but with the capstone staying generally atop the column.

(c)   The hypothesis is relevant to the phenomenon under question. It states a mechanism for symmetric erosion that correlates nicely with the curiosity of the rather common balancing rocks.

Testing this hypothesis could take a **long** time. You could probably construct physical models to simulate the columns that weather into shafts topped by the balancing rocks, but couldn't be sure that you had duplicated the natural conditions. Probably the best test you could apply would be indirect, based upon predictions of likely occurrences of the phenomenon in aeas in which they had not yet been discovered. This would be based upon knowledge of geologic structures where rivers had cut columns and where upper strata were more durable than lower ones, promoting undercut erosion.

The hypothesis fits well with the theories of erosion, of dynamic forces, or pressures, etc. It is, in fact, a nice application of already well-accepted theories.

The hypothesis explains the phenomenon in question very persuasively. A variant of it might also be used to account for balancing rods, long cylindrical rock formations that look like logs balanced on ridges. To see possibilities for prediction, look back at the comments on testing.

Although the hypothesis as stated above appears rather complex, and is not as simple as many of the others that you have seen here, it does not bring into use any ideas outside the realm of accepted theories. It also has the benefit of doing a neat job of explaining. This seems to be as good a hypothesis about what appears to be a puzzling phenomenon as one could hope for.

CHAPTER THIRTEEN SUMMARY

I.   There are two sorts of value which science may be claimed to have.

    A.   When science is justified by pointing to its values in achieving other goals, it is said to be instrumentally justified.

    B.   When science is justified as an end in itself, it is said to be intrinsically justified.

II.   Explanations can take many forms.

    A.   Regardless of form, explanations include a statement of circumstances and the operative laws and/or principles in those circumstances.

    B.   Unscientific explanations tend to be dogmatic.

    C.   Scientific explanations are provisional, subject to revision in the light of changing information.

III.   Scientific explanations are evaluated by five criteria.

    A.   The hypothesis must be relevant to the data it explains.

    B.   The hypothesis must be testable.

    C.   The hypothesis must be compatible with previously established theorries, laws and hypotheses.

    D.   The hypothesis must have some power of explaining things beyond the original data and/or must be usable as predictions.

IV.   Investigation, detective or scientific, generally follows a pattern.

    A.   First you must identify what the problem you wish to explain is.

    B.   To begin investigating you need a provisional hypothesis to order data.

    C.   Given a preliminary hypothesis, you must then begin to gather additional data.

    D.   On the basis of that additional informataion, you then need to formulate a more detailed hypothesis.

    E.   Given a full-blown hypothesis you then deduce further consequences of it.

    F.   Once these consequences have been deduced, you must check to see if they actually occur.

    G.   A confirmed hypothesis is ready to be applied in practice.

V.   A crucial experiment is one the completion of which will definitely confirm one of a set of competing hypotheses and dis confirm all others.

      A.   Crucial experiments are rare.

      B.   Within a context of accepted science, the attempt to identify a crucial experiment may help clarify the context.

VI.   An *ad hoc* hypothesis is one that is created to account only for a single phenomenon, without outside application.

VII.   Classification is more than a recording of events, it is a hypothesizing about events and the records indicating their character and occurrence.

14.1 Alternative Conceptions of Probability

Copi and Cohen indicate several uses of the term "probability" and then focus upon the *a priori* and relative frequency theories as the ones that are the basis of the calculus of probabilities. The *a priori* (called the theory of equally likely chances by its earliest significant devotee--Laplace) assumes that all outcomes of a set of circumstances are **equally likely** unless there is clear evidence to the contrary. The relative frequency theory is the one that you have probably encountered in previous classes that talked about probability. It uses "s" to represent the number of successful occurrences you have found, "p(a)" to represent the probability of event "a," and "f" to represent the number of unsuccessful occurrences you've encountered, yielding a symbolic representation of the probability of event "a":

$$p(a) = \frac{s}{s + f}$$

There is, however, a third approach to probability that is consistent with the *a priori* and relative frequency theories. It is called a propensity theory (sometimes a dispositional-relative-frequency theory). Its claim is that certain types of events or experimental arrangements have **as properties** certain propensities or dispositions. No one questions the disposition of crystal to shatter when severely impacted, or of lead to melt at relatively low temperatures, or of book paper to burn at 451° F. Why not, then, claim that homogeneous cubes with their centers of mass in their exact centers have a propensity when rolled to turn up each fact very, very slightly less than one-sixth of the time? (The other infinitesimal probability will be divided up among the edges and corners upon which-- rarely--the cube will come to rest.) If that seems a reasonable position, then your sympathies may well lie with the propensity theorists. In general, however, the proponents of the various schools of thought about the "real" nature of probability are in substantial agreement about the use of probabilities, once they are known, in calculating other probabilities.

14.2 The Probability Calculus

At the outset, Copi and Cohen introduce the idea of independent events. Two (or more) events are said to be independent if the occurrence or nonoccurrence of one of them has no effect on the occurrence or nonoccurrence of the other(s). This means that drawing one card from a deck and *not* replacing it will mean that any other draw from that deck will not be independent of the first draw, since the first-drawn card is no longer a possible outcome of the second draw. Had you replaced the first card and shuffled the deck well, then the second draw, having all the same possibilities as the first, would be independent of the first. Similarly, rolls of a fair die (*die* is the proper singular form of *dice*) are frequently seen as the most clearly independent events, since a face can't fall off after being rolled. Unless you are given information that indicates otherwise, you should assume that events stated in the exercises in *ITL* are independent.

Joint Occurrences

Calculations of probabilities are based upon two fundamental relationships, conjunction and alternation. Virtually any complex event is the result of joint occurrences of simpler events [the occurrence of (a and b) is the conjunction of event a and event b], alternate occurrences of simpler events [the occurrence of (a or b) is the alternation of event a and event b], or some combination of the two. Joint occurrences are calculated by using the **product theorem** "P(a and b) = P(a) x P(b)." In this formula, the set of symbols "P(...)" is read *"The probability of ...."* And, normally, P(a and b) is written P(ab). As Copi and Cohen indicate, in the absence of contrary evidence, we take all possible events in a situation to be equally probable. Given the flipping of a coin twice, we consider the probability of getting heads (or tails) is 1/2. The following is what happens:

	1/2 of the time we get	H	(a)
1/2 of the time we get	H{		
	1/2 of the time we get	T	(b)
	1/2 of the time we get	H	(c)
1/2 of the time we get	T{		
	1/2 of the time we get	T	(d)

If you read across this structure you will see that

- (a)   1/2 of 1/2 of the time we get H followed by H
- (b)   1/2 of 1/2 of the time we get H followed by T
- (c)   1/2 of 1/2 of the time we get T followed by H
- (d)   1/2 of 1/2 of the time we get T followed by T

The nice thing about looking at the situation in this way is that it does not depend upon the equiprobable assumption. That means that is you should have the (mis)fortune to own a coin that had a probability of 1/3 of falling H and 2/3 or falling T, the diagram would look like this:

	1/3 of the time we get	H	(a)
1/3 of the time we get	H{		
	2/3 of the time we get	T	(b)
	1/3 of the time we get	H	(c)
2/3 of the time we get	T{		
	2/3 of the time we get	T	(d)

Reading across this you will see that

- (a)   1/3 of 1/3 of the time we get H followed by H
- (b)   2/3 of 1/3 of the time we get H followed by T
- (c)   1/3 of 2/3 of the time we get T followed by H
- (d)   2/3 of 2.3 of the time we get T followed by T

In numeric terms, we get HH 1/9 of the time, HT 2/9 of the time, TH 2/9, and TT 4/9 of the time.

This calculation also indicates another very important characteristic of probabilities: the sum of the probability of an event and the probability of its complement (not-a is the complement of a) is always 1. More generally, the sum of the probabilities of any set of exhaustive and exclusive events always adds to 1. *Exclusive events* are events which **cannot** occur together; *exhaustive events* are events at least one of which **must** occur. Thus in a set of events is exhaustive and exclusive, they cannot occur together but one of them must occur (more than one cannot occur since they are exclusive). In the examples above, a, b, c, and d are exclusive (since none of them can occur together) as well as exhaustive (there is no other event that can occur on the flip of two coins). The formal notation for complementarity is made by placing a bar over the event. Thus the complement of a (that is, a not occurring) is $\bar{a}$. Since the sum of the probabilities of an event and its complement add to 1, the formal statement is

$$P(a) + (P(\bar{a}) = 1$$

By subtracting P($\bar{a}$) from both sides we get

$$P(a) = 1 - P(\bar{a})$$

This means that if it is easier to calculate the probability of the complement of an event than that of the event itself, you have a choice of working the easy one and subtracting from 1. This will prove **very** useful later.

A few problems will make all of this easier to see. Look first at number 3 after Copi and Cohen's discussion of joint occurrences (page 466). There are 67 balls: 27 white and 40 black. Thus on the inital draw there is a probability of 40/67 of drawing a black ball, 27/67 of drawing a white one. In the (a) case, since you replace after drawing, that same probability will be the case on all draws. If you figure that the event (complex) that you want is P(BBBB), then you could also figure that the event BBBB could be looked at as [(BB) • (BB)], that is, blacks on the first two and blacks on the last two. Following the pattern for joint occurrence, we get

$$P[(BB) • (BB)]=P(BB) \times P(BB)$$

But since P(BB)=P(B) x P(B), this becomes

$$P(BBBB)=P(B) \text{ of } x P(B) \times P(B) \times P(B)$$

This principle is generalizable so that the probability of the joint occurrence of any number of independent events is the product of the probabilities of those events. In the case of 3(a) all of this translates into

$$P(BBBB) = (\frac{40}{67})^4$$

In the case of 3(b) there is no replacement of the balls, so the probability of each successive black ball is different from the preceding one. The (b) case, of course, takes you into the area of events that are **not** independent. There is no difficulty in using the probabilities of such events in calculating probabilities of joint occurrences of events, at least as long as you know what the probabilities are. Thus, for example, if you were to figure the probability of picking out a pair of black socks in the dark from a drawer containing 6 black socks and 7 non-black ones, you would get 6/13. The probability of picking out a second black sock from the same drawer (still in the dark) after having picked a black one the first time would be the same as the probability of drawing a black sock from a drawer with 5 black ones and 7 non-black ones. That is to say, some probabilities that depend upon the outcome of previous events can be calculated as if they were independent events, but where the circumstances in which they occur include the prior events already having happened. In a case like the one with the socks, if you wanted to know the probability of drawing a pair of black socks, you would figure p(ab) where a is the event of drawing a first black sock and where b is the event of drawing a second black one when one black sock has already been drawn. This p(ab) would be calculated just as any other:

$$p(ab) = p(a) \times p(b)$$

In this particular case the result would be 6/13 x 5/12. The second probability would be 5/12 because there were 5 black socks and 7 non-black socks left in the drawer.

With the balls the initial probability is the same as (a), 40/67. After a black ball has been drawn, there are 39 black and the 27 white remaining, so P(B) = 39/66. The case where a white was drawn first doesn't enter into the figuring, because it would have been a failure and you'd be done already. By similar reasoning, the probability of the third black ball would be 38/65 and the fourth 37/64. Putting them all together, 3(b) becomes

$$P(BBBB) = \left(\frac{40}{67}\right) \times \left(\frac{39}{66}\right) \times \left(\frac{38}{65}\right) \times \left(\frac{37}{64}\right)$$

Problem 7 is straightforward. The probability of their having such a celebration is P(he lives 25 years and she lives 25 years and they are not divorced in 25 years). According to the formula, that means

$$
\begin{aligned}
P(H \text{ and } S \text{ and } D) \quad &= \quad P(H) \times P(S) \times P(D) \\
&= \quad .742 \times .801 \times .902
\end{aligned}
$$

Note that the answer is **not** multiplied out. Since this is not a book on arithmetic, there is no great value in multiplying out the answers. As an matter of fact, there are pretty good reasons for not working out the arithmetic. Very few of us are capable of doing flawless arithmetic, so multiplying out an answer adds another step in which you could make an error. Even more significant is the fact that an answer written out as the answers to problems 3(b) and 7 are, gives an observer of your work, like a teacher, a better view of what you have done. This is important, particularly when you have made a mistake. In decimals, the sock-drawing problem discussed earlier has the correct answer of .193. Had your answer been, for example, (a) .178, (b) .213, or (c) .231, how would an outside observer know you had gone wrong? One possibility, of course, would have been an arithmetic error. If your arithmetic is acceptable, then the observer must try to guess what your error was and then check to see if your math is correct for that error. The three incorrect answers suggested earlier resulted from (a) assuming replacement, that is, 6/13 x 6/13, (b) realizing that you had one less black sock but forgetting that you had one less total socks, too, that is 6/13 x 5/13, and (c) realizing that you had one less total socks but forgetting that you have one less black sock, too, that is, 6/13 x 6/12. There is another possibility, too: you might have calculated from (b) and then transposed the lst two digits, yielding the results appropriate to the error in (c). An instructor might choose to spend a great deal of time "teaching" you to avoid an error that you actually had not made. It seems clear, then, that the wisest course is to leave the answer in its most helpful form, the one in which no more arithmetic is done that necessary.

Problem 8 is another direct problem. What you want is P(right closet and right carton and right can and right fruit and right second fruit). If these events are represented as D(door), B(box), C(can), F1(first fruit), and F2 (second fruit) you have

$$
\begin{aligned}
P(D \, B \, C \, F1 \, F2) \quad &= \quad P(D) \times P(B) \times P(C) \times P(F1) \times P(F2) \\
&= \quad 1/2 \times 1/3 \times 6/24 \times 3/300 \times 2/299
\end{aligned}
$$

Problem 10 is a bit tricky, the most evident answer would seem to be to split the balls between the urns, getting 1/2 x 1/2 as the answer. However, if you want to maximize the probability of getting two white balls, you should insure getting one. To do that, you put one white ball in one urn and the other 99 in the remaining urn. Then,

P(W-1) = 1 and P(W-2) = 49/99, so
P(W-1 and W-2) = 1 x 49/99 = 49/99 (which is almost 1/2)

There are two approaches to solving problem 6. One way is to figure that it makes no difference which door "a" (the first patient) enters. What you want to know is what is the probability that "b" and "c" (the second and third patients) came in the same door. If for each of them all five doors were equally probable, the probability for each of them that he or she entered the same door as "a" is 1/5. Thus

$$P(bc) = P(b) \times P(c) = 1/5 \times 1/5 = 1/25$$

The second approach requires that you be able to calculate alternative occurrences, the next topic for discussion.

Alternative Occurrences

If you were playing roulette on a standard wheel, you would see on the wheel 18 red numbers, 18 black numbers and two green ones (0 and 00). If you could bet in such a way that the only failure was green, you would have bet upon (red or black). In this case, the event (red or black) can be directly calculated as the sum of the probabilities of (red) and (black). Note that in this case you could also have calculated on the basis of $1 - P(\overline{red\ or\ black}) = P(red\ or\ black)$. Since the only way you could fail to get (red or black) would be to get (green), you have

$$
\begin{aligned}
P(\text{red or black}) \quad &= \quad 1 - P(\text{green}) \\
&= \quad 1 - 2/38
\end{aligned}
$$

Calculated directly you had 18/38 + 18/38 = 36/38; calculated indirectly you have 1 - 2/38 = 36/38. The two should always agree.

This is, however, an atypical example of alternative occurrences. In most cases there is a possibility that the two events might both occur, while in the roulette case you cannot get red and black at the same time. If you used the apparent formula that was applied to the roulette case, which would have been

$$P(a \text{ or } b) = P(a) + P(b)$$

to the case of getting a head on the flip of a dime or a head on the flip (made at the same time) of a penny, you would have

$$P(Hd \text{ or } Hp) = 1/2 + 1/2 = 1$$

But it is **not** certain that you would get at least one head; you could get two tails. What has happened? You have accidently counted an event twice. The event "Hd" is actually a composite formed by the above formula: $P(Hd) = P(HdHp) + P(HdTp)$. Now you cannot have those events together, since you can't get both a head and a tail on the penny at the same time. Similarly you used $P(Hp) = P(HdHp) + P(TdHp)$. When you added $P(Hd)$ and $P(Hp)$ you accidentally got the following:

$$P(Hd \text{ or } Hp) = P(HdHp) + P(HdTp) + P(HdHp) + P(TdHp)$$

Notice that you counted the joint occurrence of heads twice. That is what led to the too-large number. What needs to be done is to remove one of them. To do that you must alter the formula to be:

$$P(a \text{ or } b) = P(a) + P(b) - P(ab)$$

This formula will still work for cases like the roulette problem, since the joint probability of exclusive events (such as red and black in roulette) is always a zero.

Returning to that problem of the patients going to the dentist (which was promised above), you now have the tools necessary to try the second appraoch. That approach would say that the probability that all three patients go through any given door is

$$\left(\frac{1}{5}\right)^3$$

This means that P(abcI), i.e., the probability that a, b, and c go in door I is $1/5^3$, as is the probability of all three going in each of the other doors. This means that the second approach would be to calculate on the basis of the five alternatives that would have counted as successes. What it becomes is

$$P[(abcI) \text{ or } (abcII) \text{ or } (abcIII) \text{ or } (abdIV) \text{ or } (abdV)] =$$

$$P(abcI) + P(abcII) + P(abcIII) + P(abcIV) + P(abcV) =$$

$$(1/5)^3 + (1/5)^3 + (1/5)^3 + (1/5)^3 + (1/5)^3 = 5 \times (1/5)^3 = (1/5)^2$$

Note that this is the same solution that was obtained on page 252. The addition of alternatives here did not require any subtraction because the events were exclusive: they couldn't all come through different doors together simultaneously.

Coins provide simple examples for calculation of alternative occurrence probabilities. Problem 3 at the end of 14.2 (page 470 of *ITL*) is representative. What you seek is P(H-1 or H-2 or H-3). Recalling that you must take care to avoid double counting, you can look back to the general formula for alternative occurrences, but you will find that it is for two events, and this problem deals with three. As a first approach to this sort of problem it is wise to begin with a complete array of the events that could occur on three tosses of a coin. Each of the triads is exclusive of each other one, and the eight of them together are exhaustive. Here is the array:

	First Toss	Second Toss	Third Toss
a.	H	H	H
b.	H	H	T
c.	H	T	H
d.	H	T	T
e.	T	H	H
f.	T	H	T
g.	T	T	H
h.	T	T	T

Any of the exclusive events a-g would count as a success in seeking the probability of at least one head; only event h would be a failure. You may start by calculating the probability of each of the events a-g (they each happen to be 1/8) and then add them. That would give you the correct answer of 7/8 but wouldn't give you any insight into how the formula from page 253 is generalized. You could also calculate 1 - failure (1 - 1/8) and get the same 7/8. Or you could take the events H-1, H-2, and H-3 apart. H-1 is a + b + c + d; H-2 is a + b + e + f; H-3 is a + c + e + g. Combined that means that P(H-1) + P(H-2) + P(H-3) = a + a + a + b + b + c + c + d + e + e + f + g. That counts "a" three times and "b," "c," and "e" twice each. Thus you try to apply the general formula, subtracting pairwise occurrences. Among three events there are three pairs: (H-1 H-2), (H-1 H-3), and (H-2 H-3). Taking them apart, as was done for H-1 and the others, you find that (H-1 H-2) is a + b, (H-1 H-3) is a + c, and (H-2 H-3) is a + e. If you subtract them from the earlier combination you will remove "a" three times and "b," "c," and "e" once each. That leaves you with b + c + d + e + f + g. You have taken away one too many of the "a" cases, so it must be added back in. Since "a" is (H-1 H-2 H-3), the generalization of the alternative occurrences formula for three events becomes

$$P(a \text{ or } b \text{ or } c) = P(a) + P(b) + P(c) - P(ab) - P(ac) - P(bc) + P(abc)$$

Applied to the coin toss problem (which was the problem under discussion) it becomes

$$P(\text{H-1 or H-2 or H-3}) \quad = \quad 1/2 + 1/2 + 1/2 - 1/4 - 1/4 - 1/4 + 1/8$$
$$3/2 - 3/4 + 1/8$$
$$7/8$$

It is comforting to see that each of the three approaches arrives at the same numeric solution.

Problem 8 in the same set (page 471) offers a slightly different challenge. Since you cannot choose both cases, each has an *a priori* probability of 1/2 of being selected; one case (A) contains 6 soft drinks and 4 beers; the other case (B) contains 10 soft drinks and 2 beers. By the joint occurrence formula, P(picking A and getting a soft drink) is (1/2 x 6/10) or 3/10, and P(picking B and getting one) = (1/2 x 10/12) or 5/12. Since these are exclusive events, their probabili ties add: either would be a success. Thus P (getting a soft drink from one case or the other) = 3/10 + 5/12. Had you put all the bottles in a single case you would have had 16 soft drinks and 6 beers. The probability of a soft drink then would be 16/22. The difference resolves to: the first way you have a .717 probability of a soft drink, while with all of the bottles in one case you have a .726 probability of getting a soft drink. If you think about it, there is something of problem number 10 (page 252), where organization has an effect, built into this.

Problem 9 offers an opportunity to introduce another way to deal with alternative success patterns. In the problem given, there are 47 cards remaining that you have not seen, so your two will be drawn from them. (Any card you have not seen you should count as if it were still available in the deck--that seems strange, but it's really an averaging of the chances that any specific card is out, and thus unavailable, with the higher chances of its being drawn if it is not out, since the deck is smaller). For ease of reference, let us assume that your original hand was J-J-J-x-y (where x and y are two different small cards). Your possible successes after discarding the x and y will be J-anything, anything-J, and a pair of non-J's. This problem is short enough that you could solve it by generating all the possibilities:

P(J next) = 1/47

P(anything else next, followed by a J) = 46/47 x 1/46

P(a pair of x's) = 3/47 x 2/46 (since you discarded an x, three remain, then two)

P(a pair of y's) = 3/47 x 2/46 (since you discarded an x, three remain, then two)

P(a pair of z's) = 40/47 x 3/46 (once the first z is chosen, three remain)

Since these are exclusive, they add to give

P(J or pair) = 1/47 + (46/47 x 1/47) + (3/47 x 2/46) + (3/47 x 2/46) + (40/47 x 3/46) = 224/2162

The alternative structure, when you know that you are going to have alternate ways of achieving success and where subsequent choices are restricted by present ones, is to use what is called a *probability tree*. In it you can "branch out" your choices, calculating the probability of each branch. One of the handiest characteristics that this approach has is that it tends to be the easiest way to insure yourself against omitting some options. It also has the benefit that each of the branches of the tree is an exclusive path which none of the other paths overlap. In problem 9 you begin with the hand as the trunk, then branch to the successful draws:

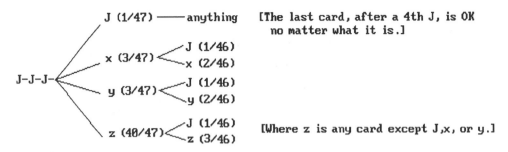

[The last card, after a 4th J, is OK no matter what it is.]

[Where z is any card except J,x, or y.]

To calculate the probability of the tree as a whole, you mulitply out the branches and add them together. In this case you get

$$(1/47 \times 46/46) + (3/47 \times 1/46) + (3/47 \times 2/46) + (3/47 \times 1/46) + (3/47 \times 2/46) + (40/47 \times 1/46) + (40/47 \times 3/46)$$

which is what you reached by the other method. For this case the tree structure was of no particular advantage, but, the longer the problem, the greater the advantage.

If, for example, you were asked to calculate the probability of drawing a full house (three of one card and two of another), the direct method is complicated and confusing while the tree is just a large version of the above. In it, "a" is the first card you draw and "b" is the second unique card you draw. You can't get any others without failing to get a full house. The tree for a full house looks like this:

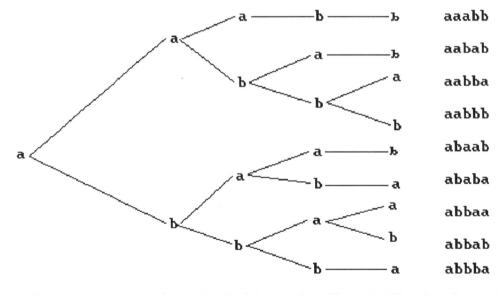

At the right are the written-out forms of each of the branches. The probability of the first card drawn is always 52/52. At the second drawing of any card there are 3 of them left out of however many are left in the deck; at the third there are 2 out of what remains. At the first drawing of the second unique card ("b") there are 48 of them out of the remaining deck (52 - 4 a's). The denominator with the cards will always decrease one at a time--52 x 51 x 50 x 49 x 48. In this problem, then, the first "a" is 52, the first "b" is 48, the second "a" 3, the second "b" 3, and the third of a kind (whether "a" or "b") is 2. Thus the numerator for any branch of this tree will be 52 x 48 x 3 x 3 x 2. Since there are ten exclusive branches on the tree, they are all added, which means the entire fraction is multiplied by 10, yielding as the probability of drawing a full house from a fair poker deck as

$$10 \times \frac{52 \times 48 \times 3 \times 3 \times 2}{52 \times 51 \times 50 \times 49 \times 48}$$

There is one crucial question which all this discussion of card-playing has not answered: *What about the cards in the other players' hands?* If, for example, you hold two aces and two kings (together with some other card) on the original deal of a poker hand, what is the probability of getting a Full House (either 3 aces and 2 kings or 3 kings and 2 aces) if you discard the fifth card and are dealt a replacement? Clearly the specific cards held by the other players makes a significant difference. If there are five players, each has drawn two additional cards, and you are drawing fifth, then they have held a total of 28 cards in addition to the five you have had. Possibilities range from four to no acceptable cards remaining. *IF neither the aces nor the kings is among their 28 cards* then among the 19 cards remaining when you prepare to draw yours there are four satisfactory ones--the other two aces and the other two kings. At the other extreme is the possibility that both aces and both kings have already been dealt to the other players, leaving no chance of your drawing them. How, then, do you calculate the probability of your Full House? Curiously, the answer is that you act as if all the cards you have not seen (that is, all those dealt to the other players) are still in the deck.

This idea is certainly as counter-intuitive as Copi and Cohen's problem 10 (page 471). Why, you might well ask, should you take such a strange position? The answer is fairly simple. If you were to treat this as a problem of alternative probabilities, you would need to consider five possible events: none of the desirable cards has been dealt, exactly one has, exactly two have, exactly three have, or exactly four have. Since these cannot occur simultaneously, you could calculate the probability of each together with the subsequent probability of your getting one of the "good" cards and then add them together.

In a case like the Full House, the calculations are fairly complex, but the same principle can be seen with a simpler problem. Begin with the same small "deck" of cards that Copi and Cohen introduce in problem 10--the four aces and the four kings. Assume you are playing a game with one other person and that each of you is to be dealt two cards, face down. You look at your first card and find it is an ace. What is the probability of your second card also being an ace? The answer, if you treat all unseen cards as if they were still available, is 3/7 (three remaining aces out of seven remaining cards).

If you approach the question as a problem of alternative probabilities, the four possible arrays of cards *prior to your getting your second one* is shown below.

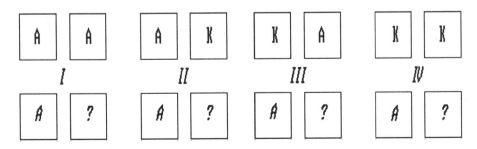

If you calculate the probabilities of each of the possibilities you may then add them together (since they cannot occur simultaneously) to get the probability of your getting the second ace. The probabilities are

Event	Her 1st	Her 2nd	Your 2nd	P(event)
I	3/7	2/6	1/5	1/35
II	3/7	4/6	2/5	4/35
III	4/7	3/6	2/5	4/35
IV	4/7	3/6	3/7	6/35

$$P(I + II + III + IV) = (1 + 4 + 4 + 6)/35 = 15/35 = 3/7$$

The result, obviously, is exactly the same as the one obtained by assuming that all seven cards were still available. Why? The alternative possibilities "average out" to the same answer. This makes calculations for card problems much easier.

14.3 Expectation or Expected Value

Expectation is a tool for deciding how "good" a choice may be. In the context of gambling, it's the way you tell whether or not you have a bet worth making. Essentially, it involves figuring out what results might occur, what the possibility of each is, and what you would win (or lose) on each of the possible outcomes. If you have been careful to insure that the possible results are exclusive, then the sum of the amounts that you could win on each of the given outcomes multiplied times the probabilities of the appropriate results is the expected value.

Copi and Cohen detail the workings of a calculation of expected values as they apply to the game of roulette. The only thing that might be confusing to you is the number of calculations that have to be used. Recently I encountered a carnival game that was a bit less complicated than roulette but which also was an appropriate subject for a calculation of expected values. It involved the use of a regular dodecahedron. The one in the carnival must have been a foot thick at its widest, but you have encountered dice-sized dodecahedrons if you play Dungeons and Dragons: it is the 12-sided die. The carnival die had four red faces, three blue ones, two white ones, and a single face each in green, orange and gold. The wager was a quarter, and a roll of red paid nothing, of blue 10 cents, of white 25 cents, of green or orange 50 cents and of gold $1.00. The cost of playing was a quarter. The expectation for this bet can be seen in the following table:

Color	Probability (P)	Return (R)	Expectation (P x R)
Red	4/12 (1/3)	$ .00	$ .00
Blue	3/12 (1/4)	$ .10	$ .25
White	2/12 (1/6)	$ .25	$ .042
Green	1/12	$ .50	$ .042
Orange	1/12	$ .50	$ .042
Gold	1/12	$1.00	$ .083

Total Expected value			$ .234

This makes the dice roll game at that carnival a worse game on which to bet than Copi and Cohen's game of roulette. Why? Because the expected value in roulette was just under 95 cents on the $1.00 bet while this game has an expected value of 93.6 cents on the same bet.

In a similar manner you could calculate the expected value in any gambling situation for which you knew the probabilities and the payoff. This lets you make an informed judgment on which "game of chance" you wish to put your money. Of course, you should always remember that gambling establishments are seldom in the business of losing money. One way that they try to insure against that possibility is by calculating expected values themselves. Since they set the payoffs, you can be confident that the expected value will be less than the entry cost. A good example of this sort of manipulation being done consciously is in the adjustment of slot machines. The working mechanism of a "one-armed bandit" is three wheels with pictures on their rims. By varying the number of lemons, cherries, bars and the like that are on each of the wheels, the owner can determine (within reasonable limits) what the probability of each possible combination of pictures is when all three wheels are set into independent motion and are separately and independently brought to rest. All the owner would have to do, then, would be to assign such returns to each of the possible outcomes as to insure that the expected value is less than the cost of playing. Barring a really freak distribution of results, this gives the machine owner a way of guaranteeing herself whatever level of profit she wished to have. The only constraint will be having enough return to encourage the player to come to the machine in the first place and to continue to play once there. In fact, on rare occasions when the operator of a gaming establishment sees business dropping, one machine might be adjusted to pay off **above** the expected value. That would be done as a form of advertising, to encourage others to play all of the available machines in the hope that others were also maladjusted. With the advent of electronic hardware, the weighting of the wheels and altering the distribution of pictures became unnecessary. The operator now simply programs payoff patterns into the machine and selects the one that seems most appropriate at any given time. The pattern, however, remains constant: with the exception of those rare times when an unfavorable (to the house) expectation is acceptable as part of the cost of advertising, the expected value of games of chance is always lower than the cost of playing them.

The pattern for solving problems dealing with expected values is actually quite simple. You must determine which of the possible outcomes will bring you a return, what the return of each is, and what the probability of each of these successful outcomes is. The expected value of that situation (game, problem or whatever), then, is the sum of the products of each of the returns and the probability of its occurring. One value of thinking about the calculation of expected values in this way is that it makes it easier to see how to apply such techniques, for example, in the realms of investing and employment. If you had a choice between two jobs, one of which was likely to lead to advancement of a minor sort (say an 85% chance of getting a 10% raise) and the other of which was less likely to lead to advancement but where the advancement was more dramatic (say a 17% chance of a 450% raise), which job should you choose? By calculating the expected value of each option, you will find that the first job has an expected value of .935 while the second has one of .935. Curious, isn't it? Given such a wide disparity of the probability of any increase at all, it seems likely that most of us would choose the more secure option. However, when the expected values are the same, there is no justification **in probability theory** for the choice of one over the other. That choice must come from some other source: your sense of luck, your self-confidence, your willingness to gamble, the desperation of your need, or some other nonprobabilistic reason.

The job decision just discussed has an analog in the history of probability theory. It involves an interesting wager. You pay me $100.00 to start a game, and I agree to pay you on the basis of the flips of a coin known to be reasonably fair. Your repayment, however, can take two different forms: I can agree to pay you $2.00 for every head you flip in 100 flips of the coin, or I can agree to pay you $2.00 if the first flip is heads, $4.00 is the first two are, and so on doubling until you flip your first tail or until you reach 100 flips. The calculations of expected values are more complex than are warranted here, but the result is like the one to the job decision example; in the long run, each method of repayment has an expected value of $100.00. There are significant differences between the two--the first method is unlikely to vary much from a return of $100.00 while the second is very likely to do so and the first cannot yield a major profit while the second can--but the differences do not involve expectation.

One of the things one has to "watch out for" is the trick question. Problem 2 (page 474) might well be thought to be such a question. What you run into a problem that *seem* too hard to work, begin by looking *very carefully* at what you are being asked. This one asks you the probability of having the white pile and the black pile have exactly the same number of chessmen. First ask yourself *where* any given chessman might wind up. The answer is (*i*) in the black pile, (*ii*) in the white pile, or (*iii*) in the box. But, if you think about the ones in the box you'll realize that *the same number of each color must wind up in the box* (since men are put into the box only when one of each goes in). That means that, because you start with 16 of each color, any that aren't in the box must be in one of the piles and because that means the remaining number of pieces of each color must be the same. This means that the black pile and the white pile must, at the end of the drawing, *always* have the same number of pieces in them (and that must always be an even number).

(7)   The calculation done here is very like the example that Copi and Cohen discuss on pages 474-475. You compare expected values for each investment. The expected value figure for the preferred stock is $93.50 (.85 x $110); for the common stock it is $93.80 (.67 x $140). Obviously the common stock is a slightly better investment.

CHAPTER FOURTEEN SUMMARY

I.   There are many uses of the term "probability."

    A.   The commonest nonquantitative use of the term is as an indicator of evidential support, as in a **probable** hypothesis.

    B.   There are three quantitative uses of the term which compete as characterization of "probability."

        1.   The *a priori* theory assumes that all options are equally likely in the absence of evidence to the contrary.

        2.   The relative frequency theory identifies probability as the ratio of events judged to be successes to events judged to be either successes or failures.

        3.   The propensity (or dispositional relative frequency) theory holds that probabilities are properties belonging to events or circumstances and that they are approximated by relative frequencies.

II.   Two (or more) events are independent if the occurrence or non-occurrence of one does not affect the occurrence or non- occurrence of the other(s).

III. If the probabilities of two events are known, then the probability of their joint occurrence can be calculated:

$$p(a + b) = p(a) \times p(b)$$

IV.   If the probabilities of two events are known, then the probability of their alternate occurrences can be calculated:

$$p(a + b) = p(a) + p(b) - p(ab)$$

V.   Probabilities always lie between 0 and 1.

VI.   The probability of an event's occurring or its complement occurring always adds to 1.

VII. The expected value of an event is the sum of the products of the possibilities of its successful occurrences times the returns received for each of those occurrences.

Chapter Fifteen
Logic and the Law

After studying fourteen chapters of logic, you might be tempted to say, "So, what **practical good** is all this logic stuff?" This chapter, covering material new to this 8th edition, introduces you to a use of logic in the *Real World*. The United States has more lawyers *per capita* than any other country in the modern world. We have also been called "the most lawsuit-prone civilization ever." Even our dramatic entertainment is filled with the law, from the venerable *Perry Mason* to *L.A. Law* to daytime soap operas. And, in the past few years, television has expanded from fictional courts to *The People's Court*, *Divorce Court* and *The Judge*. Clearly we are a national not only run by but also fascinated by the law. You should find Copi and Cohen's explanation of the role of logic in legal areas both interesting and eye-opening.

15.1 Laws, Courts, and Arguments

Copi and Cohen begin by explaining several of the various *kinds* of law, classifying them within the two basic areas of criminal law and civil law. They then go on to clarify different sorts of cases that might be considered within each sort of law.

Criminal law in general deals with what sort of behavior the society is willing to accept. In general, criminal actions, although they may be directed to a specific individual or group of individuals, are seen as offenses against society. This means that the victim does not always have to "press charges." The police may arrest, for example, a man who is beating his wife in public and the prosecuting attorney may seek an indictment (that is, have the court accept the case for trial) whether or not the wife wants it done. [Domestic violence, however, is frequently not prosecuted because the only witnesses are the criminal and the victim. When this occurs and the victim is unwilling to testify--and in most areas a wife cannot be **compelled** to testify against her husband--the prosecutor has little choice other than dropping the charges.]

Civil law in general deals with relations between persons, groups of people, institutions, companies, and the like in their **private** dealings with each other. The civil law may be further broken down into *contract law*, which oversees the performance (or non-performance) of agreements, and *tort law*, which oversees compensation for injuries that one party does another.

Unfortunately for us (but fortunately for our lawyers) in law the issues are seldom simple. If you think back to Chapter Two and its discussion of the multiple uses of language you will have a feel for the sorts of blendings that are possible in the law as well as in language. It is certainly possible that a single set of actions may have both criminal and civil elements. And, within its civil area, it may have both contract and tort aspects. For example, before the government stepped in to formalize such businesses, I might have set up a a real estate "scam." As a part of it I would, say, offer you lakefront lots in my new resort village at a "special low introductory price." I might show you photographs of the lake and the other homes near the property I was offering, promise services, utilities and other improvements and maintenance by a specific date, and then sell you a lot, signing a contract containing several "non-performance" clauses with you. If, when you went to inspect your property, you found that there was no lake, that the property that I owned was not improved in any way, that the photographs were of another development with which I had nothing to do, and while trying to see the property your car was damaged by the rotten roads, you would be justifiably distressed.

In such a case, the local prosecutor would probably be very interested in charging me (under *criminal law*) with several things: fraud, theft by deceit, operating a business without a license, and the like. You, however, might well wish to sue me (under *civil **contract** law*) to have me pay the penalties specified in the contract. But you might also want to sue me (under *civil tort law*) for the damages to your car and the subsequent losses you suffered as a result of its being out of service while being repaired. The prosecutor's case would focus on the misrepresentation involved in using the photographs to "sell you." Your contact case would center on the provisions of the contract which were not met and the agreed-upon penalties specified within the document. The tort suit would emphasize the negligence I had shown in not maintaining the road, the injuries you and your car had suffered as a consequence of that negligence, and the appropriate recompense for my behavior. [If I was shifty enough to set up such a scheme, sadly for you, it is likely that my ill-gotten gains will have been safely hidden away so that I appear to have no assets for you to recover from me.]

The entire discussion of law and logic should remind you of chapter 4 (on definition). If there is any one characteristic associated with law it is precision. Because ours is a government of law it has been accepted as crucial that matters pertaining to law be as unambiguous as possible.

Copi and Cohen distinguish among the **nature**, the **sources**, and the **kinds** of laws. The **nature** of law is either to be *positive*, i.e., set through some process by the community, or *moral*, i.e. rules of right conduct supposedly in force in any society. The "law" of this chapter is the former sort. The **kinds** of law are, of course, criminal and civil.

The **sources** of law are quite diverse. The most obvious such laws are the result of the actions of legislative bodies--Congress, a state legislature, a city council or the like. These laws generally define what is to be considered unlawful. [On rare occasions they also specify what is lawful, but usually is is accepted that all those things that are not specifically forbidden are legal.] This sort of law is called a *statutory* law [another name for laws being *statutes*]. When the intent of a statutory law either is or is claimed to be unclear, the appeals courts have to examine the lower courts' decisions. Their responsibility is to rule on how the law is to be applied or interpreted. Such interpretations are called *case law*. Sometimes a legislative body grants to some agency or department the power to set rules about behavior in a specified context. For example, a state legislature may set up a Bureau of Environmental Quality with the express power to determine what may or may not be done in areas that have significant impact on the environment. The Bureau might rule that anyone building a structure with more than 750 square feet of ground coverage has to file both a report analyzing the impact of such construction and a request for permission to build before they can start erecting the structure. This sort of policy/rule is called *administrative* law. And, at the highest levels of law in the United States (or other constitutionally-founded nations), you will find *constitutional* law. This is an amalgam of the specific statements of the land's constitution together with the interpretations set but the nation's highest court.

In most countries there is another source of law that blends into all those described by Copi and Cohen--*common law*. This is the body of customary principles that is a sort of undercurrent to all our specifically-instituted laws. The instance of it that you have most probably heard of is "common-law marriage." In many of the United States it is an accepted custom that a man and a woman who have been living together as husband and wife, especially if they have represented themselves to the community-at-large as being wed, for a period of seven continuous years *are as a matter of law married*. This means that they have the same legal rights and obligations toward each other as couple who went through the more usual ceremonies and legal licensing behaviors. Common law, of course, extends far beyond this one case, but it always has the same sort of application--social principles that are so widely-accepted within a society that its legislature hasn't felt the need to put it into statutory law.

The thing that makes law such an appropriate area to showcase logic is its dependence upon reasoning. No matter what kind, nature or source a law has, no matter whether you see the goal of law as justice, fairness, equity or moral behavior, legal proceedings are always directed toward some conclusion. You may work from fact, conjecture, circumstantial evidence or whatever else seems relevant, but any legal proceedings involve the presentation of premises and conclusions--presumably logically correct arguments. Thus, it should be the case that all of the techniques that you have learned during your introduction to the field of logic ought to be worthwhile tools for the functioning of law.

15.2 Language in the Law

1.   The Functions of Legal Language

As you surely remember from Chapter 2, language generally is used as some combination of conveying information, expressing emotions and directing behavior. Under normal circumstances, legal language is either directive [*Do Not Sound Horn*] or informative [*Trespassers will be prosecuted*], but seldom expressive. Frequently statements are intended to serve both functions, that is, both to inform you about the law and to direct you as to how you ought to behave. When, for example, you see a sign that says "*No Stopping or Standing, Violators Will Be Towed at the Owner's Expense*," it is **telling you** that the law does not permit parking or even waiting in the car without moving for someone *and* **directing you** not to stop or stand there. Both functions are performed simultaneously and no reasonable claim could be made not to understand <u>both</u> of them.

The greatest difficulties in language involved in the law are the complexity inherent in legal terminology and the likelihood of misunderstanding the context in which the statements are made. Handling the first is reasonably straight-forward: go to law school, ask a lawyer or consult Black's (or some other) Law Dictionary. In the latter case you have to do what you do in *any* case of communication--pay careful attention to what the context is and, when in doubt, ask lots of questions. In other words, language problems are no greater in law than in any other field that uses a large and specialized vocabulary.

2.   Fallacies in the Law

One of the greatest difficulties we encounter in ordinary (and other) communication is knowing when the appearance of fallacies is a real one and when it is not. In legal areas this is especially true. For example, the notorious gangster Al Capone was only convicted of Federal income tax evasion, no murder, theft, extortion or any of the many other crimes of which he has been accused. It seems that witnesses against him had a way of either disappearing or losing their memories or lives. Under the Anglo-American principles of jurisprudence that are the basis of our entire legal system (that is, the basis of our statutory, constitutional, case and common laws), an individual is "considered not to be guilty unless **proven** guilty." This means that, under the law, Capone must have been treated as if he were not guilty of the crimes, even though we (and everyone else) are reasonably certain that he was "guilty as sin."

Such a viewpoint certainly appears to be an institutionalization of the fallacy of *ad igno-rantiam*. Although there is such an appearance, if you are thoughtful about what is being claimed there really is no reason for the presumption of innocence. For, you see, we are not claiming that he is *in fact* innocent, we are merely asserting a principle of behavior within our society--persons for whom we do not have enough evidence to convict are to be **treated as if they are not guilty** regardless of whether or not we believe them to be innocent. We are not claiming that they **are** innocent, just that that is how we must behave towards them.

An even more devastating apparent *ad ignorantiam* is the celebrated Dreyfus case. When I discussed the Capone question, I referred to "Anglo-American jurisprudence." By look-ing at the words you could probably tell that that is law as applied in the United States, England, its Commonwealth and those countries that were at one time or another under the influence of the British Empire. In contrast, France and its former dependents operate according to the Napoleonic code. Under this principle the accused is presumed guilty until proven innocent.

In 1894 Alfred Dreyfus, who was then the highest-ranking Jewish officer in the French Army, was convicted of treason, stripped of his rank and sent to Devil's Island. Over the next 14 years many Frenchmen tried to get the case re-opened, claiming that evidence had been sup-pressed by the Army, evidence that would have proven him innocent. Officers who thought Dreyfus had been ill-used were transferred to distant posts; the essayist Emile Zola was impri-soned for a year for accusing the government of bad faith in Dreyfus' appeals. Finally, however, so much proof was amassed proving that another officer named, Esterhazy, was the traitor that Dreyfus was exonerated and restored to his rank. The point was that, even at the point of initial conviction, the thing that condemned Dreyfus to prison was his inability to prove his own inno-cence. Again, here as in the Capone case, there is not an *ad ignorantiam*. No claim needed to be made that Dreyfus was **actually guilty**, just the policy that accused persons who cannot prove their innocence **are to be treated as if they are guilty**.

A second apparent case of fallacious reasoning in the law that Copi and Cohen list con-cerns what is called "the precedential theory of law." Under this doctrine, previously-made court decisions--especially those of higher courts--have a special authority. In the absence of specific information exempting a case from the precedent, the principle it asserts is held to have force of law. But, you might well ask, how can some appellate judge decades ago and leagues distant be considered to be an authority in some specific case here and now? Aren't precedents just *ad verecundiam* arguments?

The answer is that for an argument to be the **fallacy** of appeal to authority, it must be an *inappropriate* appeal. As was noted in Chapter 3, the bulk of what we learn in life is through authority. If we couldn't rely on the learning of others, it is doubtful that we could even advance to the point of re-inventing the wheel. This means that the key issue in the use of precedents is their appropriateness. And what is the justification that Copi and Cohen (and the mass of legal scholars) offer for this position? In this case it is *stability*. If a society is to really have a sense of solid values, the rules of appropriate behavior have to remain reasonably constant. [Think, for a moment, about the "great debates" in baseball that center around the designated hitter and lighting Wrigley Field. Many feel that both these are essentially heretical, because they involve a change in the rules. If changing the rules in a game is so distressing, think of the impact that rapidly-changing social rules would have.]

Copi and Cohen's third-indicated potential legal fallacy is *ad hominem*. Again, here, the issue is one of appropriateness. In the question of testimony in a court, the reliability of a wit-ness **is** very relevant. If you had six witnesses to an armed robbery--three accusing a defendant and three exonerating her--you **should** want to examine the reputability of the six. Assume that the accusers are a cocaine dealer, a lapsed alcoholic and the police's #2 suspect while the sup-porters are a long-term Boy Scout leader, the local Greek Orthodox priest, and the native

American field director for the Save the Children Federation. It would take a very strange set of values and circumstances to justify claiming that the accusers were more reliable witnesses than the defenders. However, if the court forbade the defense attorney from raising the question of witness reliability (on the grounds of preventing *ad hominem* attacks), how could a jury fairly decide **on the evidence?**

Remember, the *ad hominem* was listed by Copi and Cohen as a fallacy of **relevance**. That means that, whether the apparent *ad hominem* is abusive or circumstantial, the key issue is not the attack on the source but the question of whether the reliability of the source is **relevant** to the judgment to be made.

Similarly, it is not uncommon to find appeals to pity occurring within legal contexts. The famous (fictional) case of Jean Valjean in Victor Hugo's *Les Miserables* is one where such an appeal was surely appropriate. Valjean was caught stealing bread to feed his starving children. He was sentenced to 20 years as a galley slave. While the question of his guilt was certainly not in question, the reason he stole certainly should have qualified as an extenuating circumstance. If such a case came before a judge, we would hope that she would show some compassion in determining the correct penalty. It might, for example, be wise to put such a person into a work-training program, where he could prepare himself to care for his family. Again, as in the cases of witness reliability and social stability, what might have been claimed to be fallacious was not because it was relevant.

The final "apparent fallacy" that Copi and Cohen address is that of the use of threats to generate a desired behavior. Almost all postings of potential penalties may well have the character of *ad baculum* arguments. Here, too, you are encountering questions of relevance. If I threaten to beat you to a pulp if you don't leave a house, I am almost certainly committing an *ad baculum*. If, on the other hand, I tell you that the building is on fire and that if you don't leave promptly you will be seriously injured or killed, then I am almost equally certainly **not** committing such a fallacy. In the case of a legal warning you are being **warned**, not threatened. The "Freedom Riders" of the 1960's, who knowingly violated laws that they considered immoral, were making a choice based upon their knowledge of potential penalties. By making a similar sort of choice you might knowingly violate a law, say parking in a "No Parking" zone. If you did it in order not to be late to a final exam, you might well judge that the towing fee and fine were worth it. If you did it in order to carry a friend who had just suffered a heart attack into an emergency room, you might hope that a judge would show clemency, accepting the illness as offsetting the offense. If, however, you parked in such a zone in order to avoid the the inconvenience of walking half a block to return a library book and avoid a 10¢ fine, your behavior was foolish. The sign telling you that you were in a tow-away zone, however, in none of these cases is a threat: it's either a warning, informing you of laws of which you might have been unaware, or it's a statement of information, allowing you to make an informed judgment.

3.   Definitions in the Law

When our basic approach puts high value on precedents, it becomes of great importance that we avoid as much ambiguity as possible in the statement of law. Since this means that precision is quite important, definitions must therefore receive special attention. Of the sorts of definition suggested by Copi and Cohen, the two of greatest value in the law are the *stipulating definition* and the *precising definition*.

It is evident that, in the case where a law is being introduced by a legislature, it is helpful to future jurists if the meanings of the terms are made explicit within the law. The accusation made against those who support the performance of medical abortions is that they are advocating murder. Murder, as Copi and Cohen indicate (page 480), is "the unlawful killing of a human being with malice aforethought."[1] This means that the accusation that medical abortion is murder would seem to involve at least five necessary elements: (*i*) medical abortion must be a violation of already established law, (*ii*) medical abortion must be a killing, (*iii*) the object of a medical abortion must be a human being, (*iv*) the decision to have a medical abortion must be malicious, and (*v*) the decision to have a medical abortion must be premeditated.

Probably you are wondering about the insistent repetition of "medical abortion" instead of just "abortion." My reason for the two-word usage is, like many elements of medical-language and law-language, driven by a need for precision. In medical terminology an abortion is the ending of a pregnancy short of a natural (or caesarean) delivery. Many women who are ardent opponents of the abortion-by-choice movement are shattered when they read their own medical records and see a notation that their doctor has recorded that they have had an abortion. Assuming that they have not, voluntarily or involuntarily, had a medical abortion performed, what has likely happened to them is that they have had what is popularly called a miscarriage. In medical terms they have undergone a "spontaneous abortion." In almost all cases this is a result of serious damage to or defect of the fetus. Gentle doctors sometimes explain a spontaneous abortion as nature's way of correcting its own errors. ***But***, think what would happen if the more vocal of the so-called Pro-Life movement had their stated wishes become law ("***Abortion is Murder***"). That would mean that every woman who suffered a miscarriage would find her pain compounded by an immediate charge of murder. Surely that is not what the so-called Pro-Life advocate wants, but that would be the **legal** thing to do.

In analyzing the U.S. Code definition of murder and its applicability to the medical abortion, let's look at the five criteria. Number*V* is surely the easiest to consider. No one going to a doctor's office, clinic or hospital for a surgical procedure can reasonably claim that what happened was not premeditated (unless they have legitimate ground for a massive malpractice suit). Number*I* is a matter of fact: either there is a statute prohibiting medical abortion or there isn't. Number*II* involves a whole philosophical/scientific debate about what constitutes life. It will also entail the distinction between *Life* and *Living*. The malignant tumor your surgeon removes from your body to save your life surely is living. Few would argue it is a case of life, that it has a right to live. Number*III* depends upon the definition of a human being. The history of humanity has suggested that this definition has not been obvious. Number*IV* would require proof that a person having a medical abortion "had a desire to cause harm or pain to another."

Numbers *III* and *IV* were, for Missouri, neatly solved in the Fall 1989 Supreme Court decision known popularly (for the Missouri attorney general William Webster) as the Webster decision. In the preamble to the Missouri law in question there was a *stipulative definition* that life begins at birth. The Court felt that that part of the law was irrelevant to their decision, but they let it stand. The problem of proving another's intention makes number*IV* extraordinarily difficult to prove. And, unless medical abortion has been outlawed, number*I* would entail that it could **not** be murder.

Stipulative definitions are also are also crucial within contract law. I recall contracting for the building of a house in an extremely foolish way. I agreed to have the builder construct my house "just like the house at" another location. That house was about half done when I signed my contract. Imagine my surprise when, a month later, I walked through the "reference house" and saw one wall of the dining room covered with a very expensive and oddly-colored paneling. In my case the stipulation of being just like the other house was far too vague. Without specific details of what is wanted and not wanted, what is agreed upon and not, there is little way to resolve disputes about whether the contact has been fulfilled.

----

1.   **18 U.S.C. 1111**. See Copi, p. 480 for an explanation of this reference.

By the same token, legal affairs frequently require the use of precising definitions. If you contract to build a deck for a neighbor "in a reasonable time," how long do you have to get it finished? If the weather is good and you have all the materials, you could probably get the deck in in three 12- to 16-hour days: one to prepare the site and pour the footings, one to build the understructure and floor and one to attach railings and steps and do general finish-work. Would it be reasonable to expect you to put in so much time? What if the weather is bad? What if the suppliers of materials can't deliver? Contracts **need to be precise**. As you learned in the first four chapters of this book and *ITL*, language is filled with words that have multiple meanings or shadings of meaning. When such vague words must be used in legal areas, precising definitions can save a lot of cases from going to court.

When you introduce **new** terms into laws, as, for example, when copyright law had to start dealing with so-called electronic publishing, there is great need for stipulative definitions. This makes clear what the terms mean. When you use **common** terms in special or specific ways, then there is a need to make precise *which* meaning is intended in this context.

All these definitions make legal discourse seem very cumbersome and jargon-laden. That probably is true, but necessary. In a sense laws are the rules by which society "plays its game." Just as in an athletic competition you couldn't reasonable participate without understanding the rules, so too you can't "play the social game" without knowing its rules, i.e., its laws.

15.3 Inductive Reasoning in Law

Law, like almost any other area of human activity, involves both inductive and deductive reasoning. [Unfortunately, for all of us, it also contains its share of invalid, fallacious and otherwise sloppy reasoning; fortunately, due to the intense scrutiny to which legal arguments are subjected, the proportion of bad inference to good in the law tends to fairly low.] It seems to be the case that deductive reasoning is dominant in appellate decisions, where judges are attempting to justify either upholding or overturning the decisions of lower courts. In general these rulings are based upon either matters of law or matters of evidence. The appellate judge is not in as good a position to evaluate the evidence of the earlier trial as was the trial court itself. It is his (or their in the case of higher courts) responsibility to examine the transcripts of the earlier proceedings, together with briefs from both sides involved, as a kind of quality control supervisor. This helps insure that the trial court did not violate accepted rules of evidence, exhibit prejudice toward a defendant or misinterpret, misapply or ignore the statutes relevant to its decision. Commonly, then, the decisions of an appellate court are framed in deductive format.

Arguments in trial law, in contrast to case law, tend to be more commonly inductive. This is because trials center largely around matters of fact, about questions of what did or did not occur, about the reliability of witnesses and their observations.

1. The Method of inquiry in Law

At the original trial level the primary reasoning is inductive. Juries (or sometimes judges) are given the responsibility of evaluating the testimony and the exhibits presented, then to weigh them with factors like the behavior and believability of witnesses, and arrive at some conclusion about the claims made by the parties to the case. It would be more comfortable if such conclusions could be arrived by deductive means, but that seldom is possible. Although "courtroom drama" is usually far more sensational than "real-life" cases, it does give you a feel for the sorts of things that are presented as relevant evidence.

Commonly the "facts" will include testimony of witnesses, documents, and the like, many of which appear to contradict each other. Attorneys frequently claim inconsistent implications from the same data. Occasionally so-called *hearsay* evidence, where one person reports what she claims she heard another say, will be offered. Sometimes hearsay is acceptable, sometimes not. Hearsay usually is disallowed because it is not "best evidence;" it usually is better to have a witness testify directly (with the possibility of cross-examination) than to have someone else report what they believe they heard. Remember when, as a child, you played "Gossip" or some similar game. It is easy either to mis-hear what was said or to misunderstand what was intended. [As a test of this, I frequently have college classes "play" this sort of game. In passing through 30 to 35 people, it is not uncommon for a statement with a lot of "mushy" sounds, like *He was only an aspirin-maker's son, but you should see him Bayer*, seldom survives close to intact. My most recent trial of it resulted in *He was born in the ashes of the Sun, but used to be a bear.*] The likelihood of misunderstanding is particularly great when the witness has an interest in the situation, that is either has strong feelings in favor of or opposed to one side or the other of a dispute.

When you serve on a jury it is your responsibility to sort out all the conflicting elements of the trial and come to a conclusion about the matters of fact involved in the case. To do this successfully you will probably have to use the tools suggested in Chapter 13. Your job as a juror is not far from that of a detective, comparing what is presented as evidence, evaluating reliability, sifting the important from the peripheral. And, of course, the ultimate objective of any legal proceedings is *fairness*. This is of such over-riding importance that Supreme Court Justice Louis Brandeis wrote, more than half a century ago, of the **principle of jury nullification**. According to this doctrine the jury not only has the *right* to ignore **both** the facts and the law, if it serves the interests of fairness and justice they have the **obligation to do so**. The basis for making such judgments of justice and fair play is almost invariably inductive.

2.   Causation in Legal Reasoning

In many legal disputes the key issue to be decided involves a question of causation. Fortunately for most of us, the judgments don't require teasing out causal relations, as described in Chapter 12. Generally the judge and jury are asked to confirm (or disconfirm) the claim of that a cause/effect relationship either did or did not occur.

Normally the courtroom action has three stages of judgment: (*i*) the disputed events did actually occur in the claimed sequence, (*ii*) the claimed cause can reasonably be inferred to have resulted in the claimed effect, and (*iii*) a reasonable person should have been able to see that this cause would lead to this effect. This means that, *if* I have property containing a public sidewalk (for whose maintenance I agree to be responsible),the walk extends from one attached to a retirement apartment building to a shopping area, a snowfall occurs that heavily covers my sidewalk, **and** over several days I make no attempt to clear my walk, *then*, when one of the elderly apartment residents falls and is serious injured thereby, I am almost always going to be held liable for the injury. All three criteria were met: (*i*) the walk was not cleared, (*ii*) the treacherous walk surely cause the fall and injury, and (*iii*) only the extremely gullible would believe that I didn't realize that the folk in the apartment would try to go across my walk, despite its condition, and that for the elderly such conditions were quite likely to result in an accident like the one that occurred. In other words the person who fell could probably sue my tail off.

3.   Analogical Reasoning in Logical Arguments

The arguments to resolve many legal disputes are analogical. Since precisely the same circumstances seldom recur, we are forced to draw conclusions based upon *similarity*. The same half-dozen criteria that were introduced in Chapter 11 (pages 363-365) can be applied in legal contexts. This is especially true in the law of torts, where determination of responsibility frequently makes reference to "common standards of behavior." When the engineers responsible for the design and construction of the infamous Skywalk and the Kansas City Hyatt Regency claimed that they were not responsible for its collapse, the crucial part of the expert testimony centered upon how an engineer calculated overload capability. Virtually no other location had contained a block-long concrete pedestrian "bridge" suspended inside a building. There were, therefore, no other identical cases of such structures with which to compare. Civil engineers (and their predecessors) have, however, been building bridges for decades. Despite its fanciful name, the Skywalk was, in fact, just a suspension bridge. Pragmatically similar structures, from the world's most famous one --the Golden Gate Bridge--to the world's highest one--over the Black Canyon of the Gunnison--and the standards to which they should be built are quite well-known.

The engineers' claim that they could not have anticipated people dancing on it, thus creating harmonic impact on its structural members, was at best foolish and at worst criminal negligence. Armies have known for centuries that they must break step crossing bridges to avoid collapse. Surely professional builders should have known that rhythmic impact was at least a possibility. The analogy was obvious and reasonable.

4.   Probability in Legal Argument

Probability enters into legal reasoning both in its informal, intuitive form--preponderance of the evidence--and in its specific--calculus of probability--form. Anyone who listens to Judge Joseph A. Wapner of *The People's Court*, hears him explain, on an almost daily basis, that civil decisions are made on this principle of "preponderance of evidence." He decides for a plaintiff because she gives him three estimates of the cost of repairs on her car, has photographs of the damage and offers affidavits from several witnesses while the defendant has his buddy testify that the damage wasn't too great, that he could fix it for half the estimates and that the plaintiff is just "out to get" the defendant anyway. In such a case the objectivity of the plaintiff's evidence, its volume and mode of presentation outweighs the limited and possibly biased information provided by the defendant. What he has done is informally assigned probabilities to the elements of evidence, calculated the likelihood of each block of evidence being false, and compared the resulting probabilities. The litigant (party to a legal action) with the more probable case has achieved the preponderance of evidence.

Specific calculations of probabilities, however, also have an important place in the courtroom. The American philosopher/logician Charles S. Peirce was once called as an expert witness in a claimed case of forgery. He measured the angle of the strokes of the pen through a significant volume of writing both of the person whose signature was claimed to have been forged and of others. From that he calculated the probability of letters having identical slopes in multiple occurrences of a word. Using this as a base he calculated the probability of several signatures on a will matching as well as the ones did in the case at hand. His expert testimony was that the signatures matched so well that, on the basis of probability, it was almost certain that they had all been traced from some one original. The court verdict upheld his conclusion.

Similarly we could expect expert testimony by statisticians in other cases where significant deviation from statistically (i.e., probabilistically) expected results to be an important kind of testimony. For example, current lawsuits, as yet unresolved, filed by U.S. Army veterans against the Army as a result of their exposure to radiation during the nuclear weapons tests of the early 1950's are largely based upon statistical comparisons of the rates of occurrence of certain diseases (leukemia, for example) among the veterans of these tests and among men in the general population. The claim is that if there is a statistically significant difference in the two rates then it is reasonable to infer that there is some causal link between the tests and the diseases. The same sort of inference has led the Food and Drug Administration to, applying administrative law, ban the use of several of the artificial sweeteners, on the ground that there is a higher incidence of cancers among test animals who have eaten such sweeteners than among those who have not. In any such cases the calculus of probability is a crucial element in the legal argument.

In contrast, however, a slight probability balance is generally considered inadequate in criminal proceedings. The standard there is *beyond a reasonable doubt*. The principle by which we make such decisions affirms that, like the case of *innocent until **proven** guilty*, we would usually prefer letting a guilty person go free than imprison (or otherwise punish) someone who is innocent. This approach to enforcement and punishment, however, is not universally accepted, even in our relatively tolerant society. As the incidence of serious crime accelerates, as more people find violence and anti-social behaviors having a more direct impact upon them, calls for "toughening up" enforcement increase. Accusations lodged toward the judiciary, claiming that these increased social difficulties are the direct result of their leniency, probably reflect fear.

15.4 Deductive Reasoning in the Law

Deductive reasoning is more central to case law than to trial law. Since the facts themselves are seldom in question after the trial, the function of appellate courts is to rule on the reasoning (usually deductive) that held the case together. The grounds of appeal might be that evidence was improperly obtained or admitted, that the precedents cited were not appropriate, or that some other impropriety occurred during the trial. In such arguments there are sets of rules that can be identified, actions in the trial that can be specified and deductive arguments that can show that the trial judgments were or were not correct. Characteristic of deductions, if the premises (rules of law and facts about how the trial proceeded) are true and the arguments offered are valid, then the conclusions about the correctness or error of the trial must necessarily follow.

1.   Determining the Correct Rule of Law

It may well be that the most famous appellate ruling in modern history is the so-called **Miranda Decision**. In this case an offender confessed to committing the crime for which he was arrested. During the trial his attorneys argued that, although he had made the admission of guilt to the police, he had done so out of fear of abuse. They contended that he had not **known** that he had the right to counsel and, especially, that he had not been told that the state would arrange for a public defender if he couldn't afford his own attorney. The trial judge ruled that all this was irrelevant, that Miranda had not been beaten or even threatened and that, therefore, he had confessed of his own free will. In overturning his conviction, the Supreme Court argued that Miranda's ignorance of his rights together with the police's not informing him of them amounted to denying him his constitutional rights under the fifth amendment (freedom from self-incrimination). Put in deductive terms (and greatly simplified) the Court's argument was

> If people's convictions are legal then they were granted their constitutional rights in their trials.
> Miranda was not granted his constitutional rights in his trial.
> Therefore his conviction was illegal.

This is a simple case of *modus tollens*, one of the commonest of the deductive forms.

Frequently appellate courts, in accepting the decision of lower courts, say nothing at all, merely allowing the decision made to stand. However when they decide to overturn a lower court ruling (whether trial court or lower appellate court) there is need to justify the rejection of the earlier decision. The argument may focus on matters of procedure, as in the Miranda case, or it may emphasize matters of substance. In the latter case the argument offered must show that the earlier decision was wrong because it somehow either applied the wrong law or misinterpreted the intent of the appropriate law. In either case the **correct law to be applied** must be decided, the **nature and intent of that law** must be stated precisely, and the **correct application of the law** must be described. When these three things are done fully then the argument should deductively show why the lower court decision was overturned. When you take into account the hundreds of thousands of court decisions in the many jurisdictions within both the United States and so-called British Common Law, then you understand why law schools, courthouses (and even major law firms have libraries that run to tens of thousands of volumes.

2.   Identifying, Formulating and Applying Rules of Law: The Law of Libel

Copi and Cohen include this section to try to give you a sense of the operation of legal appeal and decision in actual practice. The choice of libel is particularly appropriate because almost all of us has, at one time or another, felt that we were the victim of maliciously-intended falsehoods. This ought to give each of us a "feel" for the position of plaintiff in a libel case. On the other hand, one of the most crucial of our democratic freedoms is the freedom of the press. If wrong-doers can silence the investigative press with the threat of lawsuits for libel, then we are all made poorer. Since the statutes surrounding libel are not crystal-clear, it falls first to the trial court, then (if necessary) to a series of appeals courts and finally to the U.S. Supreme Court to decide when and how libel has occurred.

In each of the cases that Copi and Cohen discuss all three elements for decision appear: identification, formulation and application. What they show you is a progression in the Court's interpretation of the actual statutes, widening the range of persons for who the standards of malice are more severe. The laws in question, as identified, remain fairly constant. The formulation, however, shifts "in line with the greater public interest" until, in effect, the court has written new law. And, of course, with each new formulation a new application results. In each case the deduction involved is reasonably straight-forward, the tangles come in the formulation, in the judgments about where and how the law should be adapted to meet shifting social circumstances.

15.5 Logic as Right Reasoning

In the law as in all life, Copi and Cohen conclude, there are no guarantees. You are free to discover evidence then draw both inductive and deductive conclusions from it. You are never sure, however, that your conclusions are true. The continuing furor over the assassination of John Kennedy and media focus on sightings of unexplained flying objects and apparently alien beings (as happened during the summer of 1989 in the U.S.S.R.) are proof of that. The conclusion of any argument is no more reliable that the evidence offered in it premises. So long as we do not possess divine omniscience (the power of knowing everything), the best we can hope for is security based upon the reliability of the inferences you have studied in *ITL* and in this book.

CHAPTER FIFTEEN SUMMARY

I.   Law has many subdivisions all of which operate according to logical principles.

    A.   There are laws of two different kinds:

        1.   Criminal law focuses on offenses against public order, thus including the state as a party to the legal proceeding.

        2.   Civil law focuses on the obligations of one party to another.

            a.   Contract law focuses on agreements between parties and their fulfillment or failure to be fulfilled.

            b.   Tort law focuses on injuries done one party by another, whether by intent or negligence.

    B.   There are five different sources of laws:

        1.   Laws may result from specific decisions by legislatures (that is, law-making bodies).

        2.   Laws may result from specific decisions made by appellate courts.

        3.   Laws may result from specific decisions made by administrative bodies to whom legislatures have granted such powers.

        4.   Laws may result from specific statement in or interpretations of the constitution.

        5.   Laws may result from long-term social practices rooted in general cultural attitudes and values.

    C.   There are laws of two difference natures:

        1.   Laws of any of the sorts mentioned above are called positive laws and reflect choices of the society.

        2.   Laws governing "right behavior" abstractly, religiously or cross-culturally are called moral laws and are not the subject of this chapter.

II.   Language is a critical component of any legal function.

     A.   Legal language in generally restricted to informative and directive functions.

     B.   Some legal arguments appear to be fallacies, but are not.

         1.   The doctrine that persons are innocent until proven guilty is not an *ad ignorantiam* argument. Rather it is a stipulation that we treasure freedom so much that we are willing to treat the guilty as innocent rather than risk punishing the innocent.

         2.   Reliance upon authorities, especially at the appeals levels, is not an *ad verecundiam* appeal, for these authorities really are authorities.

         3.   Attacks upon the credibility of witnesses is not an *ad hominem* appeal, since the testimony of unreliable witnesses should be discounted.

         4.   Appeals for leniency or claims of mitigating circumstances are not *ad misericordiam* appeals because it is appropriate that "the punishment fit the crime."

         5.   The apparent threat in posting penalties for violations is not an *ad baculum* appeal, but a combination of warning and explanation.

     C.   Stipulative and precising definitions make clear the intent and scope of specific laws.

III.   Inductive Reasoning is the focus of trial law.

     A.   Most inference about facts, that is evidence and testimony, is evaluated and structured in the same way scientific investigations are handled.

     B.   Most responsibility is assigned in law on the basis of claims of causal relationships between behaviors and results.

     C.   Many factual questions are decided by analogical inferences that can be appraised just as any other analogical argument.

     D.   Judgments about the reliability of evidence are almost always based upon either intuitive senses of likelihood or formal calculations of probability.

IV.   Deductive Reasoning is the focus of case law.

     A.   Appellate courts must decide on the correctness of trial procedures.

     B.   Appellate courts must decide on the correctness of the laws applied.

     C.   Appellate courts must decide on how the laws will be applied in the future.